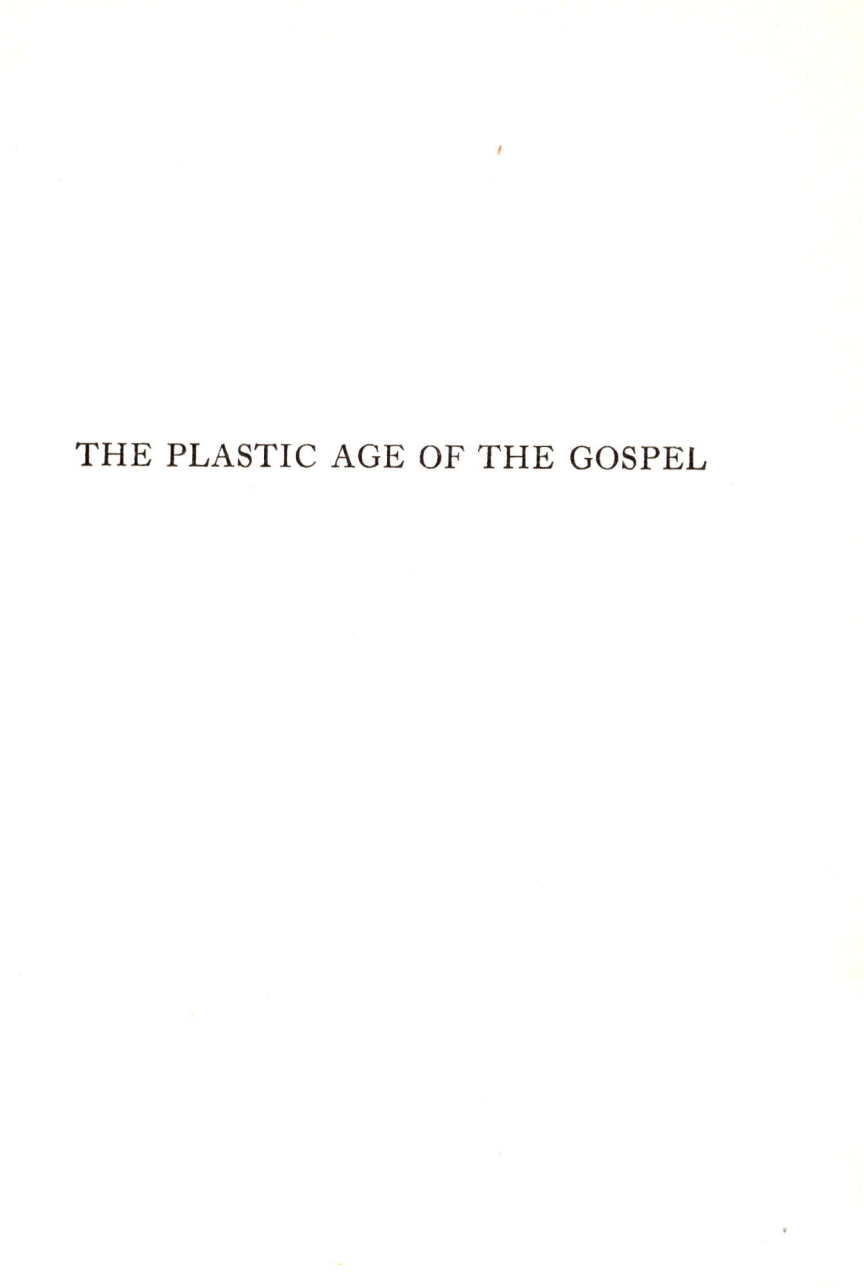

THE PLASTIC AGE OF THE GOSPEL

THE MACMILLAN COMPANY
NEW YORK · BOSTON · CHICAGO · DALLAS
ATLANTA · SAN FRANCISCO

MACMILLAN & CO., Limited
LONDON · BOMBAY · CALCUTTA
MELBOURNE

THE MACMILLAN CO. OF CANADA, Ltd.
TORONTO

THE PLASTIC AGE OF THE GOSPEL

A MANUAL OF NEW TESTAMENT THEOLOGY

BY

ANDREW C. ZENOS, D.D., LL.D.

DEAN AND PROFESSOR OF HISTORICAL THEOLOGY
MCCORMICK THEOLOGICAL SEMINARY

New York
THE MACMILLAN COMPANY
1927

Copyright, 1927,
By THE MACMILLAN COMPANY.

Set up and printed.
Published October, 1927.

PRINTED IN THE UNITED STATES OF AMERICA
BY THE CORNWALL PRESS

TO THE AFFECTIONATE COMPANY OF THE ALUMNI OF MCCORMICK THEOLOGICAL SEMINARY, WHOSE SYMPATHETIC INTEREST MADE THE DISCUSSION OF THE SUBJECT OF THIS WORK A JOY FOR MANY YEARS.

PREFACE

The justification for a fresh treatment of the progress of thought in the New Testament lies in the fact that recent research and discussion have thrown much light on the subject. In this light several aspects of the Christian faith loom out into clearer visibility. A full century of research in the history of its beginnings has not only made the world acquainted with a vast mass of facts totally lost sight of during the ages, but it has also led to the realization of the specific character of history itself. Just what is historic? What may the historic method be expected to do? What must it not be looked for to accomplish? Answers to these questions bring into view the potentialities as well as the limitations of the purely historic point of view.

The labors of many scholars during the last forty years have concerned themselves with the principles involved in historic study. This book is an effort to reflect in a compendious picture the outline and the color of the reality, as it is now seen, of the flow of spiritual life in the age of Jesus and his first disciples.

From another point of view the work is the expression of a rather long experience in teaching theological students. Many times during this experience the author has been requested to reduce his teaching into book form for use by a wider public. He has hitherto resisted the impulse to accede to the request partly because he has been conscious that the value of any teaching may be due either to the way in which the teacher deals with his subject or to the substance of the teaching itself, or again to a certain happy mixture of both. In the circumstances he could not be sure that the values he may have unearthed out of the mine of reality did not carry in them some disvalues intermingled with them in the very process of their production. The work of construction in the realm of the intellect and spirit is unlike that in the mechanical and physical sphere. In the latter the builder can always see the difference between his tools and the product of his labor. In the former this is not, usually, at least, the case. And the worker in this field may very well remain unconvinced of the worth-whileness of putting into cold print what has been found useful only in relations of personal contact.

If he ventures now to lay aside the distrust, it is only because he has become convinced in other ways that his readers (such and as many as he may have) will judge his work with generosity and fairness.

CONTENTS

	PAGE
PREFACE	vii

PART I. THE MIND OF JESUS

CHAPTER
I. INTRODUCTION 3
    1. The Bible and Theology. 2. The Rise of Biblical Theology. 3. What Is Biblical Theology? 4. Is a New Testament Theology Possible?

II. ANTECEDENTS AND BACKGROUND 10
    1. The Old and the New. 2. The Contemporary Background. (1) Tradition. (2) Apocalyptism. (3) Hellenism.

III. JOHN THE BAPTIST 18
    1. The Life and Personality of John. 2. John's Message.

IV. THE SOURCES 27
    1. The Gospels. 2. The Synoptic Problem.

V. JESUS 35
    1. The Historicity of Jesus. 2. Jesus as Teacher. 3. The Forms of His Teaching.

VI. THE KINGDOM OF GOD 44
    1. Jesus' Conception of the Kingdom. 2. The Development of the Conception.

VII. THE FATHERHOOD OF GOD 49
    1. The Idea of Divine Fatherhood Before Jesus. 2. Jesus' New Revelation of It.

VIII. THE CHILDREN OF GOD 55
    1. What Is Man? 2. Sin. 3. Salvation. (1) Repentance. (2) Faith. (3) Forgiveness. 4. The Filial Relation. (1) Confidence in the Father's Care. (2) Prayer.

IX. THE MESSIAHSHIP 65
    1. The Son of Man. (1) The Older Usage of the Phrase. (2) The Usage of Jesus. (3) The Messianic Consciousness of Jesus. 2. The Son of God. 3. The Messiah's Work.

X. THE MESSIANIC COMMUNITY 74
    1. Jesus and the Church. 2. Membership of the Messianic Community. 3. The Task of the Church.

CONTENTS

CHAPTER		PAGE
XI.	THE NEW RIGHTEOUSNESS	86

1. The Old Righteousness and the New. 2. The Ethical Ideal of Jesus. 3. The Social Teaching of Jesus.

XII. THE KINGDOM IN THE FUTURE 99

1. The Kingdom in Prospect. 2. The Place of Jesus in the Future of the Kingdom.

PART II. THE EARLIEST APOSTOLIC MESSAGE

XIII. GENERAL VIEW 111

The Sources of Information. (1) The Book of Acts. (2) The Epistle of James. (3) First Peter. (4) Second Peter. (5) The Epistle of Jude.

XIV. THE PRIMITIVE CHRISTIAN CONVICTION 119

1. The First Preaching of Jesus as Christ. 2. The First Interpretation of Jesus' Messianic Work.

XV. THE SPIRIT AND THE CHURCH 125

1. The Holy Spirit. 2. The Church.

XVI. THE CHRISTIANITY OF JAMES 132

1. Religious Texture. 2. The Person of Christ. 3. The Royal Law of Love. 4. Sin. 5. Christian Salvation. 6. The Gospel in Life.

XVII. THE PETRINE TEACHING 139

1. Who Is Christ? 2. How Does Christ Save? 3. How Men May Benefit by What Christ Did. 4. Development and Manifestation of the Redeemed Life. 5. Issues of the Christian Life.

PART III. THE GOSPEL OF PAUL

XVIII. PAUL THE WRITER AND THE MAN 149

1. The Writings of Paul. 2. Paul and His Background. (1) Paul's Parentage. (2) Paul's Education. (3) Paul's Conversion. (4) Paul's Missionary Experience.

XIX. PAUL'S RELIGIOUS PHILOSOPHY 159

1. Ills of Religion. 2. Idea of Righteousness. 3. Idea of Sin. (1) Nature of Sin. (2) Origin of Sin. (3) Universality of Sin. (4) The Results of Sin. 4. Idea of Law. 5. Idea of the Promise. 6. Idea of Scripture.

XX. THE GRACE OF GOD IN CHRIST 170

1. The Grace of God. 2. Righteousness through Christ. (1) The Person of Christ. (2) The Work of Christ. 3. Justification.

CONTENTS

CHAPTER		PAGE
XXI.	THE NEW LIFE IN CHRIST	181

1. The Holy Spirit. 2. The Life of the Spirit. 3. Faith. 4. The Life in Christ.

XXII. CHRISTIAN CONDUCT 187

1. Religion at the Basis of Ethics. 2. Christ and Ethical Values. 3. Freedom of Moral Action. 4. Concreteness of Duty. (1) The State. (2) The Family. (3) Slavery (4) Wealth. (5) Casuistry.

XXIII. THE CHURCH AND THE SACRAMENTS 194

1. The Church. 2. The Sacraments. (1) Baptism. (2) The Lord's Supper.

XXIV. THE FUTURE 201

1. The Parousia. 2. The Resurrection. 3. The Judgment. 4. The Eternal Kingdom.

XXV. PAULINISM AND THE RITUAL 209

1. The Epistle to the Hebrews. 2. The New Covenant. 3. The Mediator of the New Covenant. 4. The Sacrifice of the New Covenant. 5. Faith, the Basis of the New Covenant. 6. The People of the New Covenant. 7. The Life under the New Covenant.

PART IV. THE JOHANNINE THEOLOGY

XXVI. THE JOHANNINE SCHOOL AND WRITINGS 223

1. The Fourth Gospel. 2. The Epistles. 3. The Apocalypse.

XXVII. FELLOWSHIP LACKING 231

1. The Question of Sin. 2. The Power of the World. 3. The World Power. 4. The Antichrist.

XXVIII. FELLOWSHIP ESTABLISHED 237

1. The Knowledge of God. 2. Christ. (1) The Eternal Logos. (2) The Son of God. (3) The Lamb of God. 3. The Holy Spirit. (1) The Spirit of Truth. (2) The Paraclete. 4. The Way to Fellowship with God.

XXIX. THE LIFE OF FELLOWSHIP 246

1. Faith. 2. The New Birth. 3. Eternal Life. 4. The Law of Love. (1) The Brotherhood. (2) The Church. 5. Johannine Eschatology. (1) The Parousia. (2) "The Last Day." (3) The Resurrection. (4) The Judgment.

BIBLIOGRAPHY 256

INDEX 261

PART I

THE MIND OF JESUS

THE PLASTIC AGE OF THE GOSPEL

CHAPTER I

INTRODUCTION

1. THE BIBLE AND THEOLOGY.—From the beginning the Christian religion expressed itself in a life and a literature. The literature was nothing more than a record of its life and an instrument for its speedier and steadier propagation. As a preparation for the appearance of this literature the older body of writings current among the Jews had served a good purpose. Imperceptibly within a century from the time when Christianity was recognized as a new "Way," its literature assumed a place coördinate with the sacred writings with whose content it was affiliated and was given the significant collective title of the New Testament. Thus the Jewish Torah, Prophets and Writings came to be recognized as the Old Testament.

For all subsequent history the sacred literature of the Christians has been a Bible of two parts, vitally joined together because of their common monotheism, their common ethical ideals and teachings and their common Messianic salvation presented as a prophetic foreshadowing in the earlier and as a spiritual achievement in the later part. To both parts with singular uniformity high value was conceded, and by many unique authority. In all efforts to construct systems of Christian thought the Bible has always been recognized as a primary source. With the Reformation the Protestant wing of the church defined the place of the Bible as that of the only source and standard for Christian thought. "The Bible, the Bible only, is the religion of Protestants."

But, though the Protestant theologians from the first squarely and firmly planted themselves on this exclusively Biblical basis, it was not until long after the Reformation period that any efforts were made to deduce the Christian system from an independent and first-hand study of the Bible. The Reformers themselves found too much value in the writings of Augustine and the early theologians to discard them. They contented themselves in testing the earlier theology by their studies in the Bible and correcting it wherever it needed correction. Meantime they also studied the Bible exegetically and wrote commentaries on its several books.

The results of these studies in theology and in the Bible were given in the Confessions and Creeds and in the private expositions of the seventeenth-century theologians. Among these the best known are Turretin, Cocceius, Witsius, the Puritans in England, the Arminians in

Holland, Amyraut, Placeus and others in France. All of these aimed to present the Christian system as the teaching of the Bible pure and simple.

But with all their intensive work on the Bible and its content of thought they could only see the unity and harmony of its religious ideas. It was reserved to others who followed them to see in the harmony, the variety and the wide range of differences of point of view between its different parts. When this began to dawn on the minds of Biblical students, a new type of investigation arose, namely that of the Biblical theologian to whom the separate authors or groups of authors of the Bible were distinct and different from one another, contributing each some aspect of the truth which it was given to him alone to convey. This analytic presentation of the contents of the various books was then given the name of Biblical theology.

2. THE RISE OF BIBLICAL THEOLOGY.—The reign of this type of Biblical theology, however, was not very long. With John Philip Gabler[1] it became clear that not only were there differences between the different writers of the Bible, but that they were largely determined by the historical conditions and times in which they lived. Each employed forms of thought current in his day. Each was affected by the atmosphere and environment of his generation. In other words, Biblical theology was cast into historical molds; and the student of the theology of the Bible must approach his task as a historian.

For the hundred and forty years following this discovery and application of the historical method, Biblical theology has continued to be called by the same name, but it has practically been transferred from the group of philosophical studies into that of the historical. Together with this transfer the name itself has shown a tendency to be disused. No longer is it customary to speak or write of Biblical theology, or of the Biblical theology of the Old Testament, but of the religion of Israel, or the religion of the Hebrews. In the New Testament branch of the study works of the type of Bernhard Weiss, Beyschlag and Holtzmann have been superseded by books on The Ideal of Jesus, the Gospel of Paul, the Apostolic Message and others.

3. WHAT IS BIBLICAL THEOLOGY?—The change in the situation makes it necessary to define with clearness the limits of the new type of study resulting. It is a study which concerns itself with the religious content of the Bible historically explained and presented.

This means that all but religious ideas are excluded from the field as primary material for investigation and construction. But since religious ideas are interwoven with scientific and historical ones and better understood in the light of these associations, it is not only legitimate, but profitable that they should be taken into consideration as auxiliary subjects of research. They cannot be materials to be constructed into the religious thought but sidelights upon it.

Just as the new construction of Biblical thought limits itself to

[1] *De justo discrimine, etc.*, 1787.

religious ideas as its material, so it limits itself to the Bible as its only source and field for those materials. It cannot take into its texture religious ideas from the field of the contemporary world. Yet here, too, no ideas current in any age or environment can be viewed as totally detached from one another. They are so intimately interrelated that to understand the nature and meaning of any group of them their associated ideas in other groups must be taken into account. Extrabiblical religion thus comes to the place of an auxiliary in the study of the Biblical field.

But the most distinctive characteristic of the new construction is its thorough subjection to the historical method of investigation and arrangement. As in all history the investigation begins with the search for the facts. That its materials are ideas or conceptions of human minds does not affect their factual character. Ideas emerge in the minds of persons described in history and they are themselves capable of being described.

The historical study of ideas is primarily concerned with their actual occurrence in the minds of men. It is not cumbered with the antecedent problem of whether they could or should have occurred or not, except as the question is raised upon the lack of evidence. What a given individual might have been expected to think, history can never consent to say except on the ground of what he actually said. The first requirement of a historical investigation is a mind open to consider evidence and decide upon the evidence exactly what the facts were. There are contingencies in which antecedent probability becomes a part of the evidence, but in no case can it supersede or annul the clear verdict of known facts.

A second element in the historical investigation is the recognition of facts in their relations with one another and with the whole setting within which they emerge. While each single fact or idea must be faced and mastered in itself, it is clear that no single fact emerges in a vacuum but always into a group of associated facts. And its whole purport and meaning are affected by its setting. It can never be fully understood except as viewed in the light of its setting. For obviously the meaning of the same fact would be different in different contexts.

A third condition for the conducting of a historical investigation is the determination of facts in their chronological and genetic relationships. Just as no fact emerges in a vacuum, so no fact emerges out of vacuity. Every fact is unfolded out of an antecedent fact or facts. It presents new aspects which gradually differentiate it from its parentage and constitute it a distinct thing by itself. Nevertheless each fact or idea is always the offspring of a fact or facts, or idea or ideas, out of which it has grown. History presents in this respect perfect analogies to the realm of life. As development takes place in the world of animate nature, so it takes place in the world of historical events. And as events are never anything else but products of ideas, so it takes place in the realm of ideas. Therefore no process of historical investigation or effort to understand historical facts can be fully successful which omits to consider the whence of the events and ideas underlying historical facts.

Care should be taken, however, to avoid the exaggerated and wrong applications of this principle. In some quarters the impression prevails that to trace an idea to its beginnings is to annihilate it. This impression is based on the confusion of the notions of beginning and origin, or process and cause. No explanation of beginnings can serve also as an explanation of origins. No analysis of process can do away with the need in thought of a cause of operating through the process.

Since the Bible consists of two literatures separated not only by a gap of time but also by a marked difference in type of religious thought, the application of these principles brings into view two distinct developments. The first of these is clearly Judaism in process of formation; the second, Christianity in the making.

4. IS A NEW TESTAMENT THEOLOGY POSSIBLE?—Concerning the possibility of a historically complete account of religion in the Old Testament, no question need be raised here. But the validity of any such account drawn from the New Testament alone has been recently challenged.

The challenge is based upon (1) the ground of the insufficiency of the data, and (2) the arbitrariness of the distinction between the New Testament and contemporaneous or immediately subsequent literature.

With reference to the first of these grounds of objection it is said that the writings of the authors of the New Testament, even the most prolific from the point of view of literary activity, such as Paul and John, are only fragments. They were produced upon the presentation of specific occasions and cannot represent the whole circle of thought peculiar to these men. Being called forth by the exigencies of controversy, they are necessarily colored and give even the fragments of the systems of those men not in their balance but with undue stress upon some parts or aspects of truth present to their minds. And if this be true of the writers who have given us the most, how much more so is it of men like James and Jude and even Peter and the author of the Epistle to the Hebrews, whose mind is known to us only from single and brief writings?

That this objection is not valid against the construction of such a historical exposition of the flow of thought in the New Testament as we have already defined our science to be, is apparent from the existence of manifest progress from one stage to another in the development of New Testament teaching. No matter how inadequate the data may appear to be, when they are historically arranged, they certainly exhibit all the phenomena which we call by the single name of development. From the beginning of the study of the New Testament writings through the Biblical-theological method the line of progress has been quite visible, and it becomes more and more so as closer attention is given to the facts and a better knowledge obtained of them. We do not claim that it is in the province of the science to reach absolute and final results such as might be secured from a larger abundance of data.

INTRODUCTION 7

For its purposes even apparently indistinct indications may be sufficient. On the contrary large and voluminous productions are not always the surest guarantee of the clearest and fullest understanding of a system of thought. The historian of philosophy does not hesitate to reconstruct the systems of the early Ionians, Pythagoreans and Eleatics, even though he has only fragmentary expressions that can be authentically traced back to those philosophers. On the other hand, in spite of the apparently overwhelming abundance of materials in the writings of Plato, he is often puzzled and at a loss as to how to complete and bring to its utmost refinements the system of the great exponent of the idealistic philosophy. As far as the breadth and fullness of the sources are concerned, we may, therefore, feel assured that there is no insuperable difficulty in our way.

The second objection cited above, viz., that from the arbitrariness of the distinction between the New Testament writings and other writings of approximately the same period, has even less force than the one just considered. That the New Testament as a body of writings is quite distinct we can only regard as an unquestionable fact. Whether with good reason or without, this collection of writings won as early as the third century a unique place. This place it has kept to the present day and seems likely to keep indefinitely. These are facts that justify the examination of its content of thought from every point of view. Apart from any dogmatic considerations involving the ideas of inspiration, infallibility, authority and canonicity, and upon the single ground of the history of these writings, we may proceed to arrange and present the religious teaching contained in them. If it be said that the earliest church classed certain other productions, such as the epistles of Barnabus and Clement, and the Pastor of Hermas, with the writings of the New Testament, and that there is no valid reason why the line should be drawn so as to exclude the thought of these from New Testament theology, we would point out, first of all, that the inclusion suggested would not affect the general results of our science. But the ground upon which the inclusion is claimed is not a solid one. It was only a matter of convenience that some of the writings of the apostolic fathers were put into the same large manuscripts with the books of the New Testament. As to the character and authority of the New Testament writers, the earliest church, not excepting the apostolic fathers themselves, drew a sharp line around these and set the collection on a supreme level all by itself.

On closer examination the separation of the New Testament scriptures into a class by themselves and their exaltation to a level higher than that of all other literature is neither arbitrary nor based on superficial grounds only. Even the older evangelicalism did not do the subject justice in taking the position that the New Testament books constitute a group by themselves because they are all writings of apostles or men intimately associated with and dependent for their authority upon apostles. The term apostle is not rigidly used in the New Testament itself. If it be understood in the broadest sense in which it is found in Scripture, the very point at which the older evangelical view aims will be missed. If, on the other hand, the term be taken in the strict sense, it is quite possible indeed that all the New Testament books were written by the men of the apostolic circle. But when we consider that so many of them are anonymous and that it would be impossible at the present day to demonstrate their immediate connection with the apostolic circle, it becomes clear, first of all, that the apostles themselves were not especially intent on having their connection with these writings put beyond doubt. Else why leave some of them without the assurance that they were authorized by themselves? Neither did those who immediately followed them regard the test of origin within the apostolic circle as supreme in accepting these writings as authoritative. This does not, of course, exclude their looking upon the writings of the apostles and of those who were immediately connected with them in the foundation of the church and the first preaching of the gospel as exceedingly precious. Neither does it exclude the idea of their seeking for and cherishing letters, books, or other scraps of literature that contained the words of the apostles. It simply excludes the idea that the apostolic seal was absolutely necessary to constitute a part of the new canon that was forming.

Accordingly, we do well in not pressing origin within the apostolic circle, which is a mere external and superficial mark of a writing, as the sole ground of its uniqueness. The New Testament scriptures possess characteristics that make them unique, but they are different and are based on a far less precarious foundation, a foundation that goes much deeper than any criticism of authorship or literary form and composition can reach or weaken. This uniqueness is constituted by the supreme personality which is the source and subject of their content. The New Testament writings issued from a spiritual life that came with the incarnation of Jesus Christ, a life which was infused by him into his disciples and perpetuated by them after his ascension. Spiritual life gives vent to institutions. So did this; and the result was the church and its ordinances. It gives vent to outward conduct, and so did this, in the holy lives of the first generations of Christians, which by its contrast with the morality of the age marked them and set them apart as a peculiar people. Spiritual life also gives vent to a literature. So did this; and the body of writings that was preserved has been accepted by Christians as a part of the universal and infallible rule of faith and conduct for men. It is not so much because the New Testament writings are the works of inspired men that we believe in their inspiration as that because we know them to be inspired we believe them to have been written by inspired men.

5. THE NEW TESTAMENT AND THE GOSPEL.—Our study is based on the assumption that the New Testament gives us the answer to the question: What is Christianity? and that it gives it not in one sudden revelation coming to birth like Athena full grown and armed from head to foot, but in successive stages. Not only does the New Testament tell us what the gospel is as a whole, but also what the elements are that constitute it. These it brings into view one after another as they emerge

in history in one continuous vital process of development. Being vital and not mechanical, this process cannot be construed as one of additions from without, each distinct and detachable from every other, like bricks in a building, or pieces in a puzzle picture, but as members of an organism, which as they become maturer and more clearly defined add completeness to the living body and at the same time give expression to the formative idea of its growth.

Such a study must in the nature of the case affect the conception of the gospel. It precludes the notion that the gospel in its New Testament form is a single proposition. On the other hand, it also precludes the notion that it is a vague something which may be cast at will into any form which any individual may choose for it. It reveals it further as a fact of such a vast and momentous significance that it was necessary for many minds to perceive for themselves and to point out to the world its various implications. In its inmost core this message is that God out of his infinite love reaches out to his erring children, and not only offers them his grace but takes the evil of their sin upon himself expiating it in the person of his Son Jesus Christ.

Any interpretation of the gospel which makes it a mere ethical system, because it deprives it of its meaning as a message and reduces it into a prescription or commandment, is untrue. It is "another gospel that is not a gospel." As Schleiermacher in his day saw and pointed out, Pelagianism was just such an interpretation of the Christian religion which virtually deprived it of its essentially Christian character. Christianity is the announcement in a historic form and under precise historic conditions of the eternal fact of God's redemptive love.

Per contra, any definition of the gospel in the terms of a single aspect of it, be it the most central one in its historical presentation in the New Testament, runs the risk of failing to do justice to its richness and fullness. It is like an X-ray picture which misrepresents the reality of the whole man in the very effort at the realization of the solid central skeleton around which he functions. Such a definition, whether built superficially out of mere forms of expression, or more logically by the selection of the cross as the central fact in redemption without an adequate understanding of the real motive and meaning of the cross as an expression of God's character as love, is bound to distort the reality of the gospel.

In the New Testament the essentially Christian message of God's grace, revealed to patriarchs like Abraham, lawgivers like Moses, prophets like Isaiah, Hosea and Amos, was first revealed as "the gospel of the kingdom" by Jesus and when he had accomplished his work, by Paul and John as the "gospel of reconciliation through the cross" by the former and of "fellowship with him" by the latter.

The validity of these contentions can be tested only by the appeal to the facts of history. To the extent that historical study conforms to its ideals in principle and method, its conclusions will conform to or deviate from the truth.

CHAPTER II

ANTECEDENTS AND BACKGROUND

1. THE OLD AND THE NEW.—The gospel was preached in the first instance as a new phase of an older religion. It recognized itself at once as the offspring and in a true sense the successor of the message of the Old Testament. Accordingly from the moment of its appearance its attitude and relation to its parent became a subject of interest. Jesus himself felt the unspoken challenge of the Jewish leaders of his day toward the new element in his preaching. He repudiated any possible interpretation of his words that might put a construction antagonistic to the Old Testament. It was easy, and it has always been easy to stress the differences between the old message and the new and make them appear mutually destructive. In the second century Marcion and his disciples followed this path. Throughout the history of the Christian church Marcion's point of view has had sporadic supporters. But it has never prevailed.

Jesus' own explanation of the relations of new and old was that the former was only a fulfilment of the old. "Think not that I am come to destroy the law or the prophets. I am not come to destroy but to fulfil" (Mt. v. 17, 20; cf. xxii. 40; Rom. iii. 31; Gal. iii. 24). But what exactly did Jesus mean by "fulfilling"? The term is frequently used to express the actualization of prediction. If this were the sense in which Jesus used it, he would have meant that the law in its prescriptions and requirements foreshadowed him and the prophets in their utterances predicted him, therefore when he came, both the law and the prophets were realized, proved true, and therefore fulfilled.

But that this was not what Jesus had in mind is made clear by the illustrations he gives of the relation of his teaching to the old. After asserting the eternal persistence of the old law, he declared the greater breadth and fullness of his own. "For I say unto you that except your righteousness shall exceed the righteousness of the scribes and the Pharisees, ye shall in no wise enter into the kingdom of heaven" (Mt. v. 20). Evidently to fulfil was to broaden and magnify, to sublimate and spiritualize.

From this general characterization of the meaning of his term Jesus passes to concrete instances of the manner in which he fulfils the old system. He shows how the prescriptions "Thou shalt not kill," "Thou shalt not commit adultery," "Thou shalt not forswear thyself," "An eye for an eye and a tooth for a tooth," and "Thou shalt love thy neighbor and hate thine enemy," are affected by his gospel. In fact the whole of the Sermon on the Mount is an expansion and an illustration of the meaning of "fulfil."

ANTECEDENTS AND BACKGROUND 11

Fulfilment evidently means the development of the inner life to the utmost possible. There is an ideal of expansion toward which the inner life of the old law tends. That idea is reached in Jesus' mind.

The whole view of the Old Testament in the New is that of identity of essence with a change in form, a change that brings fully into view and into active and vital operation all the inner power of its principles. Modern forms of thought and expression have one comprehensive and significant word for this type of relationship—the word "development." All that the concept of development contains is present in the relation of New Testament to Old Testament thought.

First of all, in every instance of development there is an element of continuity. In spite of its changing aspects from stage to stage the developing entity maintains an inner identity. This is true of New Testament religious ideas as they unfold from their antecedents in the Old. The older Christian scholars embodied the thought in the observation, "The New Testament is concealed in the Old, the Old is revealed in the New" (*Novum Testamentum in Vetere latet; Vetus in Novo patet*). The unseen essence of the New in the Old is like the invisible life of the plant wrapped up in the germ. The full-grown reality as seen in the New is like the mature body of the organism which lay lurking in the seed; it was potentially present in the Old.

Among the complex of ideas which illustrate the continuity of Old and New Testament religion that of a personal God stands first and most conspicuous. Students of religion differ widely on the origin and early history of Hebrew theism. But the Old Testament writings leave no room for question on the predominance of the monotheistic conception from the days of the Exile onward. Through all the obscurations and eclipses that the idea suffered before that period it became the one definite article of the creed of Israel after it. At the opening of the New Testament age any change in religious outlook must needs come either by way of reaction against strict monotheism or by acceptance of it; and the latter was the course pursued.

But the God of the late Old Testament age was neither an abstraction nor a personality of indifferent character. He was a holy God with an intense interest in creating and maintaining a holy people upon earth. In this respect the Old Testament idea of God was unique. In the earlier form of it there appears some faint resemblance between it and the notions of the separateness of deity from all else current among other peoples. But in the later state of thought the holiness of God grew more and more into a quality of the ethical and spiritual type without parallel anywhere else.

And since in his holiness God could take pleasure in nothing unholy, the idea of the necessity of holiness in those who would seek his favor came into the foreground and assumed an essential place in the religion of the Old Testament. Israel was chosen by Yahweh to be his people. Therefore Israel must be holy. Yahweh would recognize them as his people on no other condition. Israel would be God's kingdom and Yahweh would be Israel's God. But whereas Israel could not dispense with God, God could dispense with Israel. This, too, became a permanent idea to be transmitted with the conception of God's unity and holiness to the New Testament.

From the point of view of continuity of inner content the line between the Old and the New Testament religious systems is an invisible one. It is impossible to say just at what point the one ceases and the other begins.

But besides continuity the notion of development includes the elimination of outgrown features. He who becomes a man "puts away childish things." This is the law of all growth in the sphere of all organic being.

The elements of the Old Testament religion which are eliminated from the New are its particularism and its ceremonialism. Particularism, which is the limitation of God's favor to a class or people or race, and in the Old Testament to the nation of Israel, yields to universalism, which is the inclusion in the class of subjects of God's good will of every man as man. Ceremonialism, again, which involves the approach to God through prescribed rites and inflexible forms, yields to the free approach into the presence of God as a spirit present in all places at all times. Nationalism is eliminated in the process of the development; and with the universalism which follows each individual stands alone before God. Universalism is associated with individualism because racial and institutional lines disappear. Ceremonialism is eliminated and, with the free access of the spirit, religion is driven inward. It becomes a loyal consecration of the soul to its creator and savior.

Elimination does not take place suddenly. It is not an end in itself. It was years after Jesus indicated that the kingdom of God was for all men that his followers came to realize the need of going beyond the confines of Jewry to preach his gospel. For a considerable part of the New Testament age the followers of the new way went into the temple and engaged in its services. Ceremonies dropped off only when the spirit within was ready to express itself in new ways independently of the older forms. Nevertheless, as in all growth, the old and outworn was put away.

But as a development from the Old the New Testament system includes some elements which are new. Some of these are new only in appearance and form. They are the older elements taken up and related to the whole in richer helpfulness. Religion must express itself in life, and for every form that is set aside as too narrow and inadequate a new and broader one must be devised. The best illustration of this process of reëxpression in new forms are the reinterpretations of the older ideas of the kingdom of God, the nature of the Messiahship, the work of the Holy Spirit of God and the reconstruction of the sacramental side of the Old Testament ritual. To an observer from without these features are like the new leaves, flowers and fruit produced by the plant in the course of its gradual expansion to its ideal.

ANTECEDENTS AND BACKGROUND 13

2. THE CONTEMPORARY BACKGROUND.[1]—The spiritual setting in which the gospel made its appearance has been called the Later Judaism. Generally speaking the phrase is applied to the world of thought and life constituted in Palestine and thence disseminated in the Dispersion during the two or three centuries preceding the birth of Jesus. It is distinguished from the Earlier Judaism by the emergence of certain new factors in Jewish life not strictly deducible from the Old Testament or reducible to its prescriptions. While Later Judaism, like its earlier antecedent, was, as it aimed to be, in the main a system of principles and ideals fully given in the Old Testament, the new conditions created by the Persian and Macedonian dominations introduced some powerful influences into the situation which the religious life of the day could not ignore. There arose, accordingly, certain interpretations and applications of the Old Testament system which gave Later Judaism a character of its own.

(1) *Tradition.* Even apart from foreign contacts (the Persian and Greek) the application of the Old Testament to life was bound to require some natural and necessary self-modifications by way of meeting and adapting itself to inevitable changes. When in consequence of Ezra's labors the Law became the effective guide of life, the question was bound to arise, What does the Law mean in any particular instance? To answer the question first a group of keen-minded students of the Law undertook to instruct the perplexed on the meaning of the Law and afterwards a body of concrete answers to specific questions arising in doubtful cases was elaborated and published. Those who made the study and interpretation of the Law their care were called scribes. They were considered the successors of Ezra the "ready scribe" (Ez. vii. 6; x. 11; Neh. viii. 3, 6, 11). The informal but steadily growing collection of decisions on special cases was the tradition. As time passed the body of tradition was given more and more authority, until it secured a place as high as that of the Law itself.

In the course of its growth tradition spread and intertwined itself with every portion of the Old Testament, whether historical, didactic, prophetic or poetic. It divided itself, however, into two general branches, one designed to gratify the desire for knowledge and the other to meet the need for guidance. The first was called *Haggada* (narrative) and embodied a mass of legends expanding and filling up gaps in the story of the forefathers. The second was known as *Halacha* (procedure, walking), and consisted in a number of precepts to be used by those perplexed concerning the course to be pursued in doubtful cases.

The tradition grew into a vast luxuriance. But instead of helping the spiritual life, it rather burdened and hindered it. It necessitated a complex, elaborate and not altogether consistent machinery, which at

[1] This subject must be treated here in a very brief and sketchy manner. The details which might render it fuller will be found scattered through the work in connection with the treatment of separate topics. For collateral study see Bibliography (Chap. 2). The most suggestive and modern work on the subject is Kirsopp Lake and Foakes Jackson's *The Beginnings of Christianity,* Part I, Vol. I.

times annulled and reversed the trend of Old Testament ethical instruction. It was on this ground that Jesus rejected and denounced it (Mt. xv. 26; Mk. vii. 26). As against the tradition and its intolerable and impracticable system of detailed prescriptions, the gospel came like a refreshing and reinvigorating impulse of the spirit from within, renewing the prophetic inspiration and the impulse toward the Godward life.

But the tradition did not command the unanimous respect of the Jewish people. As it slowly grew, those who wished to be faithful to the ancestral institutions accepted it and banded themselves together into a loosely organized party, and ultimately became known as the Pharisees. Those whose interests were centered more firmly in current political movements kept aloof from the more strictly religious stream and ended in the formation of another group under the name of Sadducees. When these parties were fully developed, the differences between them came to include a number of points. Josephus borrowing language used in the Hellenic world calls them "schools of philosophy."[2] The starting point of both parties and their common ground was the Law. To the Sadducees, however, the Law meant the Pentateuch. And in the Pentateuch the chief seat of authority was the office of the high priest. They derived their very name from Zadok, the son of Aaron. When the high priestly office was assumed by the Hasmonean princes, they supported and aided these princes against all disaffected elements and remained loyal to the dynasty. Thus they became the party of the aristocracy and the hereditary nobility of the Jews. Their point of view was that of the political leader. The Law was to them the adequate instrument of furthering the national life. Additions to it might arise to cumber it and prove hindrances to its right functioning. Other tenets attributed to them such as disbelief in spirits may be viewed as by-products of the same spirit of secularism which saw in the Law the sole means of political prosperity.

The so-called sect of Pharisees saw beyond the Pentateuchal Law and the political integrity and power of the Jewish nation. Without minimizing the importance of these things, they sought to realize the prophetic ideal of an Israel in perfect harmony with the will of Israel's God. Only in the Law they believed they had the divine prescription for securing the ideal, viz., the righteousness which would make Israel immune to the attacks of all their enemies. To the strict observance of the Law by all, therefore, they bent their energies. Hence, they stanchly stood by the tradition which seemed to aim at the effective observance of the Law. Through the tradition, which was significantly called the "hedge," they aimed to protect the Law from corruption and compromise. By defining its contents to the minutest details they expected to remove all difficulty in the way of perfect obedience to it.

It is not difficult to see that the standpoint of the Pharisees was favorable to the development of a broader theology than that of the Sadducees. They made their appeal to the religious intuitions. They cherished the supernatural element basing upon it the beliefs in spirits

[2] *Antiquities* XV. iii. 1-2.

ANTECEDENTS AND BACKGROUND

and in the resurrection. They preached disregard and even contempt for alliances with heathen nations and absolute dependence upon the covenant God for deliverance in times of peril. They endured foreign domination as a temporary state of tutelage during which Israel would be trained for its ideal place.

In the New Testament only three[3] party names appear distinctly— Pharisees, Sadduces, Herodians. Of these the last is of purely political significance. Another group name, however, is given by Josephus in his enumeration of "the schools of philosophy," namely, the "Essenes." But from his description of them it is plain that their classification with the Sadducees and the Pharisees is based on superficial grounds. They were more strictly a fraternal organization with a rudimentary creed and a peculiar ritual and regulations for life. By the authorities of the Jewish nation they were considered heretical. Their sacrifices were offered by themselves as a schismatic body, and they were "excluded from the common court of the temple." It does not appear that either their system of thought or their manner of life directly affected the national life. Toward the tradition they were altogether neutral. Their own tradition and rules being derived from other sources, they ignored the prevalent interpretations of the Law among the Jews generally.   קַבָּלָה

(2) *Apocalyptism.* Just as the tradition grew out of the Law, so the apocalyptic line of thought with all its outgrowths into forms of expression developed out of prophecy. The former met the need for more precise guidance; the latter, for a more intense and powerful encouragement. The prophets were great religious and social reformers. They preached the possibilities of an ideal Israel upon earth upon condition of conformity to God's will; and from time to time they drew pictures of that ideal condition. These vivid portraitures became the starting points and the models for more vividly picturesque views of the future.

In times of persecution and distress this type of prophecy vindicated its usefulness by the increased power of endurance and resistance it produced. Consequently between 150 B.C. and 150 A.D. it developed into a specific as well as peculiar method of addressing the people. It kept the torch of hope burning during the dark days. As its exponents spoke in times of oppression by unscrupulous and cruel overlords, they were obliged to exercise great caution. Therefore they protected themselves by putting their messages in anonymous books and using ancient sages as the central characters and seers of the future. They safeguarded their message also by clothing it in symbolic forms and using codes which their readers might understand but not their enemies. Both of these expedients were bound in due time to lead to obscurity and misinterpretation. But for the period during which apocalyptism

[3] A party under the name Zealots has been sometimes placed alongside of these. According to Josephus (*Ant.* XVIII. i. 6) these were "the fourth sect of Jewish philosophy." But from his description their distinctive idea appears to have been political rather than intellectual or religious. Moreover the earliest date with which the name is connected is 66 A.D. The allusion in the New Testament to them as a sect is extremely doubtful.

prevailed probably there was little misunderstanding on the part of those for whom the apocalypses were written.

The apocalyptists based their message on the conviction that God was on the side of right, and that a day was coming in which he would reveal his power as well as his mind. This day ("The Day of Yahweh") would mark the end of one dispensation and the beginning of another ("the present age," "the age to come"). Meantime those who stood for righteousness might cheerfully await the unfolding of God's plan. And this with all the greater confidence because his method of procedure would be supernatural. The prevalence of this type of thought in the background of the New Testament was far more widespread than it was realized before the recovery and interpretation of the apocalypses, which was achieved within the last half century.

(3) *Hellenism.*—Behind the tradition and apocalyptism as an indirectly producing condition stands Hellenism. This term is applied to the culture which crossed over with Alexander the Great and the Macedonians and spread all over the East. The culture itself was complex, and there were times and places where the religious strand in it passed unperceived and unresisted. Among the Jews, however, with their extreme sensitiveness to the introduction of alien elements into their spiritual life, the effort to diffuse Hellenic culture raised a storm of opposition. The aggravating condition for this was the arbitrary and blunt way in which the champion of the culture, Antiochus IV, tried to force it as a perpetual program upon his subjects.

But Antiochus was not the sole mediator between Hellenic culture and Jewish piety. In Alexandria these two principles had met under terms of freer and more cordial intercourse. And what Antiochus found impossible to accomplish the Alexandrian leaders without a definite campaign or purpose succeeded in bringing about. A synthesis was reached between the apparently unrelated and alien elements. In its most thoroughgoing form this fusion was the theory that Hellenism and Judaism are essentially identical. Philo proposed the thesis and supported it by his famous allegorical method. He undertook to demonstrate that what Moses taught was the same as the teaching of Pythagoras and Plato.

But Hellenism entered into Judaism also in a subtler and more irresistible wave of influence in indirect ways. Probably methods of living in the Gentile world all about them stirred the minds of the Jews and aroused queries the answering of which in a sincere spirit made them hospitable to ideas of non-Israelitish origin. At all events while enough Jews in the Dispersion became more rigid in their adherence to the Jewish tradition to give semblance to the contention that the Jews of the Dispersion were more orthodox than those in Palestine, a still larger number were liberalized. When the gospel was presented to them, these were evidently more eager than Jews of Jerusalem and Judea to listen to it and recognize its truth.

At its strongest the Hellenistic element in Judaism never affected the fundamental religious beliefs of the average man. Polytheism, image worship, anti-ethical conceptions and practices in religion always

ANTECEDENTS AND BACKGROUND

remained abhorrent to him. It was mainly among the learned and for purposes of intellectual coördination and formulation that Hellenic ideas were adopted. And while strict limitations to the diffusion of Hellenism, either geographical or otherwise, cannot be shown, generally speaking, the central source from which it issued was the Egyptian Dispersion with Alexandria as its headquarters. Here from the middle of the third century B.C. a powerful intellectual movement had sufficiently affected the mind of the Jewish literati to lead to the translation of the Old Testament. In no other part of the Dispersion had such a translation appeared before. All religious thought after the completion of this translation was based on the Greek text.

But as the Hebrew Old Testament continued to serve as the sacred book of Palestinian Judaism, and as its study and discussion in Palestine were based on the Hebrew text and were carried on in the older Semitic ways but slightly affected by Greek methods, two types of Old Testament interpretation arose. Both have been loosely called rabbinical. But between the rabbinism of Palestine and that of Alexandria there was a deep gulf. In fact the common ground they occupy is the acceptance of the Old Testament as the standard and source of all religious thought and the effort to make it explicit for purposes of popular use.

CHAPTER III

JOHN THE BAPTIST

Our knowledge of John the Baptist is derived from accounts controlled by interest in another and more commanding personality. Apart from his relation to Jesus, so far as we know, John's name might have been lost to history. The only allusion to him made by Josephus [1] is brief and leaves it doubtful as to whether John's career was that of a social and religious reformer or a political leader. Josephus lays more stress on his death which he alleges was due to Herod's fear of his political influence.

In the Gospel story John is viewed as a transitional personality. He combines in himself the highest ideas of the Old Testament together with the consciousness that these were inadequate and as yet unfit to be universal and permanent. From his own lips the Gospel account derives its conception of his self-subordination to a greater one to come. John is thus viewed as a stage in the process of the development of a given divine plan. There is no reason whatever why this account of John should not be accepted as absolutely true. Even Josephus' story leaves the impression on the mind that John was bent mainly, if not solely, on securing the purification of his people. And instances are not rare in history in which men have viewed themselves in exactly the same light relatively to other master spirits as John is said to have done relatively to Jesus.

1. The Life and Personality of John.—By his ancestry John was affiliated with the priestly order. His father and mother were both descended from Aaron (Luke i. 5). But his own work was to be not that of a priest but that of a prophet. Like Jeremiah and Ezekiel he combined in his person the blood and character of the priests and the office and work of the prophet. His early life and training are left untouched in our records, and his personal relations with Jesus, if indeed they extended to acquaintanceship during this period, are also unnoticed. That he was a kinsman of Jesus is distinctly intimated; but it does not follow from this that the two kinsmen were at any time before the beginning of their public labors in personal touch with each other. When John reached the age at which it was customary for the sons of the priests to take upon themselves the duties of active life, he deliberately chose to withdraw himself from the world and spend some time—how long we know not—in solitary meditation and discipline. Why did he pursue this course? Did he foresee that he would thus be equipped for a unique prophetic mission? Or was it his design to spend his whole

[1] *Ant.* XVIII. v. 2.

life in the wilderness aiming through self-denial to avoid the sin that is in the world and in the flesh? Whatever his motive, his plan of life was rigidly ascetic. He was a Nazirite. In some particulars he seems to have conformed to the customs of the Essenes. There is enough originality, however, in his mode of life to make it as a whole look like a thought of his own. The description of his asceticism is summed up in the statement: "John had his raiment of camel's hair and a leathern girdle about his loins, and his food was locusts and wild honey." He reduced his wants to the lowest limit. He allowed himself the barest and simplest necessities in order to "keep under the body," and have as few points of contact with the world as possible. Thus freed from care and labor for the sustenance of the bodily life, he could devote as much time and energy as possible to the building up of the inner man. In the wilderness through the discipline of solitude, meditation and direct contact with the source of all inspiration, he not only received life for himself, but also a special message and mission of supreme importance.

His ministry was brief but notable. He was heard by many and in a sense heeded by those who heard him. His work may be summed up in the three propositions: He preached the coming of the Messianic kingdom. He recognized in Jesus the promised Messiah. He rebuked unrighteousness in high places and low. The performance of the last part of his task brought him into conflict with the infamous Herod Antipas. Herod was living in criminal relations with his brother's wife. It was the part of Elijah to rebuke Ahab. As long as iniquity of this type prevailed in high places, and the prophet did nothing to declare God's displeasure with it, it could not be expected that the message of righteousness preached to the common people should have its clear and full sway. Without shrinking from the consequences which John must have anticipated, he fixed his face toward the residence of Herod, walked with unfaltering step into his very presence, and reminded him of the law of God. He was seized, cast into the dungeon, and there allowed to languish and suffer. The fact that Jesus was at work must have cheered his heart in spite of the darkness that faced him personally. Still, questions arose in his mind. Was it after all the Messiah whom he had baptized on the banks of the Jordan? Why did not the kingdom appear in undeniable might and glory? He referred these questions to Jesus; but whether they were answered to his satisfaction or not, we are not told. His work was done. The tragic circumstances in which his life on earth ended are too familiar to need description.

We know too little of John's education and early experiences to be able to trace with confidence any of the influences that contributed to the formation of his thought. Though he stands plainly as the connecting link of what precedes him with what he precedes, the last of the series of prophets and the forerunner of the new teacher, his figure is but an outline. He is like a peak in a mountain range, viewed from a distance. The intermediate depressions between it and the higher peaks beyond are lost to the eye of the observer and the perspective hidden in a mist. His parents were undoubtedly among those who devoutly looked and prayed for the deliverance promised to Israel. The song of Zacharias, whether or not composed by him in precisely the form in which it is given in the Third Gospel (Luke i. 68-79), shows a deep sentiment of piety as well as a clear vision of the Messiah portrayed in the Old Testament scriptures. It belongs to the purest type of the Jewish faith and thought during the age. Apart from this parental religious influence, the data given by the third evangelist, who is our sole authority on the subject, consist only in the statement that "the hand of the Lord was with the child" (Luke i. 66) and that he "grew and waxed strong in spirit and was in the deserts till the day of his showing unto Israel" (Luke i. 80). That there was personal intercourse between him and Jesus is a conjecture leading to interesting speculation in view of John i. 31, but one on which no definite conclusion can be reached. Hence whatever possibility there may be of John's having been influenced by early contact with his cousin can only be presented as a speculation.

2. JOHN'S MESSAGE.—John the Baptist is no formal teacher of doctrine. In fact he is no teacher in any sense of the word. He is a prophet with a message. But his message is enframed in a group of thoughts which, taken together, constitute a coherent whole. The center and heart of John's thought is the ethical character of the Messianic kingdom. God is about to establish his long-promised reign on earth. God's own character is a pledge that the kingdom cannot be a mere earthly and secular society with no special relation to moral and spiritual realities. On the contrary the kingdom cannot come apart from a moral and spiritual transformation among the chosen people. The transformation is needed because as things are there is no preparation for the pure and righteous reign of God. Thus the central thought of John's theology is the need of an ideally moral setting as a condition *sine qua non* of the coming of the Messianic kingdom. Without the proper soil the plant will not take root and grow. But the plant is of God's designing and the soil must be provided. If that which is ready to hand will not submit to a transformation which is necessary, the Master Husbandman will dig it up and cast it out and provide another. Whatever else men may forget, righteousness must be kept in mind as the necessary atmosphere for the life of the Messianic kingdom.

At this point it is that the theology of John the Baptist shows its dependence upon and identity with that of the old prophets. Like them he feels that above politics there stands a compelling ethics. If Isaiah and Jeremiah, Hosea and Amos, Elijah and Elisha, urged on Hezekiah and Josiah, on Jeroboam and Ahab the need of holding before their own eyes as their ultimate goal the high ideal of a morally pure people worshipping a morally perfect God, John the Baptist urges upon the people the perfection of moral life as the preparation for the coming of the ideal king among them. He does not underestimate the political factor; he does not desire a breaking away from the secular power; he does not ask individuals to follow in his steps, move out into the wilderness and aim to attain perfect righteousness by keeping aloof from the temptations of the world. He says nothing of everlasting life as a goal for the individual. He believes in the preëminence of the social element; for it is a kingdom that must come, and a kingdom is a social organization; but he insists that this must be permeated by the righteousness of God if it shall be truly the kingdom of God.

The first point of difference between John the Baptist and the Jewish teachers of his day was that to him the conception of God was that of a living being known by direct personal contact. To them also God was a living being, omnipotent in the heavens, the God of their fathers, the God of the promises and the covenants, who specially cared for Israel and was about to restore it to independence and power; but he was a God of whom they could read in their sacred books and speculate through their dialectics, not one who was accustomed to speak to them or to any men of their age directly. John felt himself to be in immediate touch with God, and therefore his conception of God was that of the immanent near person whose presence should serve as the all-dominating force in the consciousness. "The Word of the Lord came to John, the son of Zachariah, in the wilderness, and he came into all the regions round about the Jordan preaching." That this was a fundamental conception in John's theology and not a mere matter of sentiment is plain from the fact that it led him to no arrogant or fanatical claims. It is accompanied by the sanest thought of self-depreciation. When his words began to stir the multitudes and inquiry was made as to who he might be, he promptly denied that he was anything more than a forerunner of the Messiah. "I am not the Christ," he said, and appropriating the words of Deutero-Isaiah, "I am the voice of one that crieth in the wilderness" (Is. xl. 3). His sense of the nearness of God was that of the old prophets. It stripped the conception of God of all artificial mystery, and did away with the need of roundabout ways of reaching him. God was the God of Israel who spoke through the prophets, and was even now speaking by him.

The chief thing in the relation of God to his people was that he wished to be recognized as their sole sovereign. He was about to establish his reign upon earth, but his right to reign was no new thing. He had already laid down his law of righteousness and demanded obedience. To do God's will was the normal life of Israel; it was to "bring forth good fruit," to attain to the character of "the wheat and be garnered into God's garner" (Luke iii. 17).

This law obeyed, righteousness results. And righteousness in John's thought means not merely abstract morality but spiritual conformity to the ideal of God for man. It is because the kingdom of God is at hand that men must abandon their sins and lead straightforward and pure lives. No dialectic distinction is drawn between politics, ethics and religion. The unity of man, either as an individual or in his social and corporate life, is not broken into subdivisions; and yet in John's view the spiritual idea predominates and determines the ethical, just as the ethical in its turn is paramount in the political sphere. To do God's will, then, is the primary task of man; to fail to do it leads into the displeasure and wrath of God. It is sin.

Sin, accordingly, is a violent change of attitude toward God on the part of man. This is certainly assumed in the call to repentance. But how widely sin is diffused, and how deep its hold John does not explicitly state. He calls upon all to repent. He makes no exceptions in favor of any class. It is not only the publicans and the soldiers and the common people in general as they came to him, but also the Pharisees and Sadducees whom he recognizes as sinful and in need of repentance. It is the latter especially that appear to be addressed as "a generation of vipers." To be precise in ritual observances, and to claim the special mark of God's covenant in circumcision and even to have the blood of the great ancestor, Abraham, in one's veins was not a sign of exemption from the power and guilt of sin. National privileges availed nothing. And if those to whom God had extended his favor in the past and whom he was now calling to prepare for his coming reign needed remission of sins, how much more those who were beyond the bounds of this circle of favor?

The just reward of sin is quite emphatic in John's thought. His language on this point is especially vigorous and severe, though clothed in figurative form. The penalty of continuing in a sinful condition is "the wrath to come" (Mt. iii. 7; Lk. iii. 7). It is being "cut down and cast into the fire," "burned like chaff with fire unquenchable."

Sin, then, is something that must be immediately put away. And as it is a completely wrong attitude toward God, its putting away must be a complete change of attitude, repentance. John the Baptist's first recorded word is, "Repent." It is now a universally accepted conclusion of exegesis that repentance is something more than penitence or sorrow for sin. Its more exact equivalent would be conversion or change of mind. As righteousness is an inner thing that cannot be dispensed with even by those who may rightly claim descent from Abraham and as sin is an inner failure to attain righteousness, so is repentance an inner and spiritual process, which issues in complete change in him in whom it is wrought.

But repentance must be accompanied by confession of sin. All those who came to John came "confessing their sins." From the nature of the case, he said probably very little on the subject of confession; and of that probable little nothing has been recorded by the historian. It was not necessary to say much. Those who came to John in repentance were already in the attitude of confession. Their formal acknowledgment in public of such concrete sins as they most vividly felt burdening them and perhaps called for restitution could only serve to make explicit what was already involved, and thoroughly and clearly understood to be involved in their whole attitude and conduct as they came to the banks of Jordan to be baptized of John.

Furthermore repentance means a new outward life. They must "bring forth fruit worthy of repentance." And this fruit is just such outwardly correct conduct as each man may in the course of his particular private or official life be called upon to present day by day. There is no effort to define the whole sphere of duty ideally. John is not concerned with morality as morality. The rich man whose besetting sin is covetousness

JOHN THE BAPTIST

must resist the temptation to keep for himself what he has acquired in order that he may possess all the more. He must give one of his two coats "unto him that hath not." The publican whose peculiar functions make it so easy for him to be dishonest and to extort more than the just amount of tax must keep steadily before his eyes the law of honesty and restrain himself and demand only what the law prescribes. Thus in every case the righteousness preached by John is a practical one. In this view of the matter, ethics ceases from being a series of prescriptions to be observed by all irrespective of their inner disposition and motives and their outward circumstances. It becomes an inner attitude for the kingdom of God which leads each individual to express his ethical life in harmony with the conditions that call forth his action.

As a sign of repentance John administered the rite of baptism. The religious significance of baptism is inextricably intertwined with its archæology. And the question, therefore, of the origin and history of the rite becomes of importance in determining its significance. It has been a debated question whether baptism was practiced by the Jews before the days of John the Baptist in the initiation of proselytes. There is no doubt that it was in use in the second century A.D. But at that time it was quite a fixed institution of the Christian church. Of its use by the Jews earlier, the evidence is scanty and insufficient. The contemporary sources are altogether silent. On the other hand it is not credible that the Jews should have borrowed it from the Christians in the second century or later. Baptism easily affiliates itself with the Levitical lustrations. In fact, ceremonial washing is not such an elaborate and out-of-the-way practice as to demand that wherever it occurs its origin must be sought for in some precedent or example. It is likely that it appeared spontaneously among different peoples altogether unrelated with one another. When Gentiles began to apply for admission into Israel, it would be very natural to demand of them some sort of ceremonial purification. If the Jew was compelled to wash himself in order to be ceremonially clean, how much more the heathen who had been all his lifetime in touch with a defiling environment? These considerations have led the majority of scholars to adopt the view that the baptism of proselytes to Judaism antedates John the Baptist. It is easier to account for his taking up the usage as he found it than for their introducing it into their customs from the Christian church at a later period. The silence of the sources regarding the existence of the practice may be due partly to its comparatively recent origin, partly to its unofficial and informal nature, as it was not required by written law, and partly to the lack of any real occasion calling for specific mention.

The meaning of baptism in this case is beyond question that of cleansing from impurity. And in this it was similar to the ablutions and sprinklings of the Levitical law. But in John's hands it received a new and deeper significance and a broader application. It became a symbol of moral purification preparatory to the coming of the Messianic kingdom. Hence it was not limited in application to the ceremonially unclean or to the heathen, but was administered to Jews and even to

Pharisees who were scrupulous to the extreme in keeping themselves ceremonially pure. It has been objected to this view that as Jesus needed no moral purification and yet was baptized by John, moral purification could not have been the primary significance of John's act. But the objection overlooks the vicarious and corporate nature and significance of much of what Jesus does. The kingdom of God was a new order of things, coming to Israel as a body. It was to be received by Israel as a body and therefore Israel must be purified as a people, but this could be accomplished only as each member of it submitted himself to the moral regeneration necessary as a condition. And not only each member, but the head also, the Messiah himself, must symbolically represent the moral purification of this people. The idea is not unfamiliar in the Old Testament, being especially brought into view in the description of the suffering servant (Is. liii.). And this part of the Old Testament was undoubtedly carefully studied for the light it threw on the character and works of the Messiah.

But John the Baptist distinctly conceived of another and more radical step as necessary after the setting up of the kingdom. If moral cleansing is symbolized in baptism with water administered by himself, the Messiah was to administer a more drastic purification through baptism in the Holy Spirit and in fire. The second part of this language is clearly figurative. Fire consumes that which is worthless like chaff. After the wheat harvest has been finished, it burns away the perishable and weak element and leaves the strong all the cleaner and the more valuable. It has often been used as a symbol of thorough purification. It is not legitimate to press this figure, however, as some[2] do to the extent of finding in the fire the idea of the acceptance of a sacrificial covenant after the similitude of that offered by Abraham and accepted in the mysterious transaction of Genesis xv., or the idea of the accompaniment of the Israelites by the fiery pillar in the wilderness. In the thought of John it is the idea of baptism that is supreme. Fire and water are simply contrasted means of cleansing. Water is the weaker and fire the stronger of the two.

The Messianic baptism is still further conceived of by the Baptist as a baptism in the Holy Spirit. It is evident here that we are not to impute to John the Christian use of this phraseology. It is not sanctification through a personal being called the Holy Spirit that he has in mind. On the other hand, it is quite possible to empty the words of all their legitimate meaning by making them refer to a mere outward activity of the physical element of wind, because the word spirit (πνεῦμα) is primarily the equivalent of a blowing wind. The plausible feature of this view is that it constitutes a threefold baptism, that by water, that by wind (divinely appointed and working out God's holy will) and that by fire. The first of these John declares to be his own baptism; the second and third he ascribes to the Messiah as more full and complete in their effect.[3] But though the term "spirit" might be primitively the word for wind, the historical usage of the phrase

---

[2] Feather, *John the Baptist*.
[3] *Cf.* A. B. Bruce in the *Expositor's Greek Testament*.

JOHN THE BAPTIST

"Holy Spirit" had long gone beyond this etymology and settled down to a different sense when John the Baptist appeared.

The most prominent work of the Messiah is that of judging the people. He has his fan in his hand, and will by its means separate between the wheat and the chaff, consigning each of these elements to its proper place and lot. Unrighteousness was in his eyes worthy of utter and final extinction from the face of the land, and a stern and unrelenting punishment was what it deserved. He had seen too much of its effects upon human life to tolerate the thought of its continuing in the perfect order of things just about to begin. Its punishment was "the wrath to come" from which the only safety lay in flight. The Messiah could do greater work than to judge, condemn, sentence and punish wickedness. He thus stands in the Baptist's system of thought as the great enemy of sin, the stern judge and executioner with whom there is no regard for any mitigations and no possibility of tolerating evil. "Kiss the Son lest he be angry and ye perish in the way," is his golden text.

Two observations must be made on John's place in the history of gospel beginnings. First, it is to be confessed that the data in the records are few. They are given only as the chief things among many others that John spake (Luke iii. 18). On the other hand it must be remembered that the truths most vividly present to one's mind and consciousness are those to which he would naturally give utterance; and there can be little question that we possess the essential features of John's system of thought. The second remark which should be made at this point is that probably these same thoughts regarding the kingdom of God, the moral condition of the people, the necessity of moral regeneration and the work of judgment to be instituted by the Messiah were taken up by many who heard John and cherished by them as their peculiar system of thought. In any case John the Baptist became a figure observed and known of others than the evangelists and the Christians.[4]

With the death of John the Baptist the very first intimation of a gospel ("message of good," "glad tidings") was given to men when Jesus appeared in Galilee. The content of the message was that the kingdom of God was about to be established. Through his ministry Jesus expounded this message, repeating it, giving evidence of his divine commission in so doing and enduring sufferings and death in the course of the fulfilment of his task. After his death and resurrection his followers recognized him as the fulfilment of his own message, identified him as the king of the kingdom he had preached and summed up the gospel in the phrase, "Jesus is the Christ." With the accession of Saul of Tarsus to the number of Jesus' followers the questions of how and for whom the Christ accomplished his work were brought into the foreground and answered by Paul himself. Following closely in Paul's footsteps those who accepted his interpretation, especially the author of the Epistle to the Hebrews, expanded and applied that interpretation. Finally later in the second generation under the influence of a

[4] *Cf.* Jos. *Ant.*, XVIII. ii. 11.

broader Alexandrian tendency the author of the Fourth Gospel with a group of others presented the person and work of Christ in the light of its practical outworking in the spiritual life of those who had accepted him. Thus generally speaking four or five stages were gone through before the New Testament age closed. If we are to trace the course of the gospel in its plastic age, we must therefore begin with the teaching of Jesus and follow its unfolding through these successive stages.

CHAPTER IV

THE SOURCES

1. THE GOSPELS.—Obviously for all knowledge about Jesus, whether as to what he did or said or thought one would go to the four Gospels. But as soon as these are examined and compared with one another a marked difference between the first three and the fourth comes into view. This difference is seen in the vocabulary, style and content of thought.

(1) As far as vocabulary is concerned in the Synoptic Gospels a certain difference is perceptible between the words of Jesus and the words of the authors. This difference may not be of such a nature as to justify the claim that the words of Jesus are reported with absolute accuracy, but it is sufficient to show that each of the reporters aimed to quote the language of Jesus rather than to tell of the thoughts which it had aroused in his own mind. In the Fourth Gospel the author permits the words of every speaker to sink out of sight and expresses what he himself had been stirred to think, more fully reproducing only the general drift of what he had heard. This habit would be a negligible factor in ordinary cases. But it becomes necessary to take account of it when the extent and number of Jesus' speeches in the Fourth Gospel are held in view. The vocabulary of Jesus and the vocabulary of John are limited to the same range.

(2) What is true of vocabulary is equally true of style in the Fourth Gospel. In the Synoptic Gospels Jesus is the peerless master of parables; in the Fourth Gospel he constructs allegories. In the Synoptics he resorts to short well-balanced statements, conforming to the style of the Wisdom Literature. In the Fourth Gospel he enters upon elaborate discourses. Frequently he startles his listeners and mystifies them by clothing a plain spiritual teaching in material terms. Therefore he is misunderstood. In general the author of the Fourth Gospel identifies the thought of his speakers so thoroughly with his own thought that at times it becomes very difficult to draw the line between a reported speech and the comments of the reporter. This is notably so in the account of the conversation of Jesus with Nicodemus, which is followed by the testimony of John the Baptist and this again by the reflections of the evangelist. Just where the testimony of the Baptist ends and where the reflections of the evangelist begin commentators have never been able to define.

(3) The difference in content between the first three Gospels and the Fourth is twofold. In the first place John covers a segment of the ministry of Jesus which was enacted for the most part in Jerusalem and Judea, while Matthew, Mark and Luke report his labors in Galilee

and Perea. This, however, is not in itself indicative of a different point of view. On the assumption, now almost unanimously recognized, that the author of the Fourth Gospel had before him the works of the earlier evangelists and that he wrote partly with a view to supplementing and correcting their accounts, it was to be expected that he would embody in his account the story of a part of Jesus' ministry which they had not fully presented.

The other side of the difference cannot be attributed to this or any similar origin. It consists in a marked predominance of the inner and interpretative element in the fourth as contrasted with the descriptive and reportorial point of view of the first three. John's account of Jesus and his mind is that of one who has grasped his meaning as a person and who therefore brings into view more clearly the full implications of his words. The Synoptic account is not lacking in signs of an attitude on the part of the authors kindred to awe in view of Jesus' commanding personality; but they reproduce as nearly as they can in the circumstances the words he spoke and report as faithfully the deeds he did. John's account is that of a devoted disciple who has tested through a long experience the truth and power of the Master's principles; that of the Synoptists is that of men who have been impressed by the supreme value of what they have perceived but are not as yet fully aware of all its potentiality. They aim to give to others exactly what they have found. John's account is mediated through his experience. The Synoptists anticipate and aim to create experience.

This view does not impair the historically of the Fourth Gospel. It finds in that document a different design from that of the mere chronicler. The Fourth Gospel was written, as its author explicitly tells us, not with a primary view of informing the mind regarding occurrences, but with that of creating and promoting faith in Jesus and thereby implanting in men eternal life. There were many events which might have been included in the story of the primary object if it had been to give information, but they were omitted. "But these are written," he says, "that ye may believe that Jesus is the Christ, the Son of God; and that believing ye may have life in his name." John records facts in order to release the spiritual forces that are conveyed through them. If the Synoptic picture of Jesus is at all comparable to a photograph in its approximate realism, that of John is like the portrait painted by a master artist in its idealism. A parallel, with some essential differences, to the double portraiture of Jesus in the Gospels is to be found in the twofold picture of Socrates given respectively by Plato and Xenophon.

The facts brought into view by this examination make it clear that the effort to dissociate the thought of Jesus as reported in the Fourth Gospel from the thought of the faithful disciple through whose consciousness it is mediated is not historically warranted. Therefore the Synoptic Gospels and the Fourth Gospel cannot be used in precisely the same way. When the search is made for the exact forms in which Jesus communicated his mind, the Synoptics alone must serve as sources. When the place of Jesus and his thought in the minds and lives of his followers cleared and developed through years of meditation upon and practice of his teaching is the object of search, the Fourth Gospel will claim a primary place.

2. THE SYNOPTIC PROBLEM.—Our direct access to the mind of Jesus is through the Gospels of Matthew, Mark and Luke. These are commonly known as the Synoptic Gospels because they take the same view of the matters they narrate. At first glance they are independent documents. But upon closer examination they develop striking resemblances. Their subject matter, the order of its arrangement and the language in which it is expressed are in general the same.

(1) As to the subject matter they present the singular phenomenon of limiting themselves to the same section of the ministry of Jesus. They do not pretend to give an exhaustive history of what he did or said; nor do they treat of it by selecting illustrative incidents from the different portions of it. They single out the Galilean labors of the Master and passing over silently what precedes and what follows, they give a full account of his last days of suffering and of his death in Jerusalem. That there was much more than they account for is evident from the Fourth Gospel ninety-two per cent of whose material is unrecorded by the Synoptists. How do the Synoptists come to fix on this segment of the career of Jesus?

(2) The disposition of the material by the Synoptists follows the same order. This would not raise any question if the order was purely chronological. But in some instances when an incident is taken out of its natural place in the order of its occurrence by one of them and inserted in a parenthetical way in some other setting, it is found in the same displacement in the parallels. Such is the case for instance with the death of John the Baptist (Mt. xiv. 12; Mk. vi. 14-29; Lk. ix. 7-9).

(3) All the Synoptists tell their story in approximately the same language. This coincidence of expression is so striking as to call for explanation apart from any other consideration. A glance at the harmony of the three Gospels will make all comment or illustration of this fact unnecessary. What is the significance of these resemblances? The answer to this question will also answer the questions: How did these Gospels originate? and, how did they take their present form?

It is no solution of this problem, but simply a denial of its existence to say that each of the Gospels is independent of the other, and all came into being under the power of the Holy Spirit, who revealed to each evangelist just what he should write and in what forms of expression he should put it. As far as we know the Holy Spirit has nowhere else caused different productions to bear such marked resemblances to one another thus independently. This theory is, therefore, manifestly an untenable one and has at present no advocates.

It is noteworthy that although the Synoptic problem is a modern one, dating scarcely from the closing years of the eighteenth century, the interrelations of the Gospels did not fail to arouse interest in the ancient church. As far back as Augustine[1] it engaged the thought of close students. Augustine's explanation of the relation was that Matthew having published his Gospel first, Mark followed and condensed it. Mark is the *pedisseques et abbreviator Matthaei*. In this attempt at a solution we have an illustration of a number of others that followed. Their common feature is that they regard one of the Gospels as the original and the other two as dependent upon it. This may be called the interdependence theory. It is capable of six modifications according as one of the three narratives is viewed as the source and the other two as first and second derivatives. If Matthew be taken as the first, then Mark may be second, and Luke as building on these two. This was Augustine's theory as above stated; and for many years it remained the favorite with traditional evangelical scholars. But assuming still that Matthew was the first, Luke may be regarded as preceding Mark, and Mark as condensing these two. This is Griesbach's[2] famous view. But if Mark be taken as the original, Matthew may be put next in order and Luke last. This is the theory of Storr, Reuss, Ritschl, Thiersch, Ewald, Meyer, Hausrath, Schenkel and Holtzmann. Or, still assuming that Mark was first, Luke may come second, and Matthew close the series. This is the view of Wilke, B. Bauer, Volkmar, and B. Weiss. Finally if Luke be taken as the earliest of the three, Matthew and Mark may come as second and third respectively. This is the view of Buschind, Evanson, Gfrörer. Or, Luke being first, Mark may precede Matthew. This is the view of Vogel and Noack. Each of these views has, of course, been defended by its supporters upon grounds which seem to them quite convincing.

Another attempted solution of the problem finds the answer in a common source for all of the three Synoptics. They are related as they are because they all derive their accounts from the same original. But what is the original source? Is it oral tradition, or a written document or several written documents? In these three questions there are suggested the three varieties of what may be called the common-source theory.

The first of these three varieties to be propounded was that of the one-document hypothesis of Eichhorn.[3] He attributed the similarities of the Synoptics to their use of one original Gospel (*Urevangelium*) and their differences to different translations by different persons. As the process of translation was soon seen to be an unwarrantable assumption and could not account for many of the facts, Eichhorn modified his theory and put at the source of the Synoptics a Greek gospel which, however, he still insisted was a translation of an Aramaic original. Later exponents of the view abandoned this last feature of it, and proposed a primitive Mark (*ur-Markus*) as the common document at the basis of the Gospel. And according as this original Mark is viewed as nearer or farther from the present Mark, the view comes

---

[1] *De Consensu Evangeliorum*, i. 2.
[2] *Commentatio qua etc.*, 1789-1790.
[3] *Einleit*, 1794.

nearer or farther from the variety of the interdependence theory which makes Mark the basis of all the Synoptics.

The next great and distinctive variety of the common-source theory to appear in order of time was the oral-tradition theory. It was propounded by Gieseler.[4] Its essential feature is the contention that the three Synoptists adopt as the nucleus of their narratives a common story repeated over and over again through the apostolic age and thus become more or less fixed and stereotyped. That such a large mass of narratives and discourses as that of the triple tradition was preserved through many years and then independently made the basis of three different written gospels by three different authors, presents an antecedently improbable aspect. In order to remove this improbability, those who advocate it appeal to the special conditions and circumstances under which the Gospels arose. What is unlikely at present and in a literary environment created by western civilization was quite natural in the land and among the people where the gospel narrative was first heard, repeated and preserved in unwritten form. And undoubtedly for the earlier years of the circulation of the gospel story this consideration possesses very much value. But when the view which makes use of it goes to the extent of assuming such a fixity in the oral tradition as it must necessarily have possessed, if the facts in the case shall be satisfactorily explained by its assumption, it practically resolves itself into a variety of the single written-document hypothesis. For an oral tradition fixed as rigidly as this is virtually no different from a writing. At the same time the view opens itself to all the difficulties of the one-document theory. Nevertheless it was until the advent of the present generation of scholars a favorite hypothesis in England. It was supported by such men as Salmon,[5] Westcott[6] and Arthur Wright.[7]

The third of the varieties of the common-source theory has grown out of Schleiermacher's studies of the external testimony regarding the origin of the Gospels.[8] The starting point of the movement was a now familiar passage of Papias quoted by Eusebius in his Ecclesiastical History[9] that Matthew had recorded the words of Jesus (Λόγια) in the Hebrew language and that each one interpreted them as best he could, and that Mark had written down the deeds of Jesus but not in order. Schleiermacher's examination of this passage led him to believe that our present Gospels of Matthew and Mark could not be the productions alluded to by Papias. At the basis of these Gospels there must have been a number of narrations (Lk. i.). The Logia of Papias furnished the nucleus for the Gospel of Matthew, but in Mark and Luke he saw the use of other narratives in addition to the Logia. Upon the basis of these conclusions Weisse[10] reduced the documents under-

[4] *Hist.-Krit. Versuch ub. d. evv.*, 1816.
[5] *Introduction to the New Testament.*
[6] *Introduction to the Study of the Gospels.*
[7] *Composition of the Fourth Gospel*, 1890.
[8] *Studien und Kritiken*, 1832 A.
[9] III. xxxix. 14.
[10] *Evangelische Geschichte*, 1838.

lying the Synoptic Gospels into two, the Logia and Mark, an original form which was, however, not very different from its present form.

After a full discussion extending over three-fourths of a century and carried on by two successive generations of scholars, this view has practically vindicated itself. Meanwhile a vast number of modifications of it in details have been proposed and set aside as inadequate or irrelevant. Of those that have been accepted the most important is that Mark is the oldest of our Gospels and constitutes the source of most parts of Matthew and Luke. This is placed beyond doubt when the three Gospels are compared paragraph by paragraph. Matthew and Luke agree with Mark either together or separately. They never agree against Mark except in matters on which Mark has nothing to say. It may be noted further that Mark's simpler modes of verbal expression and his more primitive type of thought support his priority.

But another main agreement reached on the question is that Matthew and Luke have used a second source. This was also given in Weisse's theory. According to that theory the so-called Logia of Matthew was the second source. And according to Papias the Logia was a collection of Jesus' sayings. The comparison of the three Gospels shows that where Matthew and Luke do not take their materials from Mark they still have much in common, and that this common material consists of utterances of Jesus as contrasted with deeds of his. This has been taken to indicate that they had before them a collection of Jesus' words. How large this collection and how coherent and uniform the copies of it in circulation, it is not possible to say. Neither is it clear that the Apostle Matthew had anything to do with it. Hence abandoning the name Logia given by Papias scholars have agreed to speak of it under the symbol "Q."[11] Since there are some reasons for believing that Mark uses this document, it must have been older than Mark. If Mark is the oldest of our Gospels, "Q" is the oldest of the sources.

But both the First and Third Gospels contain much more than they have derived from Mark and the source Q. Where did each get this additional information? This question cannot be satisfactorily answered in this stage of our knowledge. This can be affirmed about it only with some degree of confidence that the additional information given by Luke which amounts to more than a third of the whole Gospel, notably the Great Interpolation in ix. 52, xviii. 18, bears internal marks of being part of a consecutive document, characteristically full of illustrative anecdotes and parables. Both Matthew and Luke may of course have incorporated some of their reports from oral tradition.[12]

But if this is the real state of the case with reference to the Synoptic Gospels, the question naturally next presents itself, What is the relation of these Gospels to apostolic authority? and What their

[11] The letter Q is the initial and symbol of the German word *Quelle* (source).
[12] Canon B. H. Streeter in his suggestive volume *The Four Gospels* proposes as a solution of the question raised the theory that underlying the third Gospel and serving as a source for it lies an earlier and briefer recension of the work which he calls the *proto-Luke*, written either by an earlier writer or by Luke himself.

THE SOURCES

trustworthiness? The key to the answer to this question is given by the third evangelist when in his prologue he lays bare the method adopted by him in the composition of his book. He tells us that there have been efforts to compose gospel narratives and that these efforts had been based upon the possession of accurate information. He identifies this information as information given by "eyewitnesses and ministers of the Word" (αὐτόπται καὶ ὑπηρέται). He does not in this particular claim a distinction between his own story and those of his predecessors. They were all based on the reports (traditions) of eyewitnesses. What he claims is that his own narrative was to be complete, correct and orderly in its unfolding. The whole question, therefore, of the sources of the Synoptics is answered when it is said that these were the reports of eyewitnesses, followers and disciples of Jesus.

That some such process as has been sketched above underlies the formation of the Synoptic Gospels has been made more probable in recent years by the discovery of collections of "Sayings of Jesus." Two groups of such "Sayings" have been brought to light during the last twenty years from the rubbish heaps of Egypt.[13] This fact indicates that in the earliest years of the dissemination of the gospel collections of the utterances of Jesus were made and circulated locally and that these collections served as materials for the Gospel writers. Together, however, with the collections of the utterances of Jesus, the writers of the Gospels did, in the nature of the case, combine incidents from the ministry of Jesus which came to them independently of such documents.

The process of gospel formation is thus revealed in its various stages:

1. Jesus, using the Aramaic, gave his words to his followers as occasion offered. His sayings were repeated by those who first heard them. Later they were translated into Greek by those who sought to make him known throughout the whole world. The disciples, furthermore, added their recollections of the occasions on which the words were spoken and associated such incidents as threw light on his sayings.

2. These sayings and associated narratives were collected together. There arose two or perhaps three notable collections—those known as "Q," Mark and the unknown source of Luke.

3. In the last stage these documents were taken up and constructed into the present Gospels by the evangelists, each of whom seems to have a distinct object in view. Mark writes for the Roman world and he forms his Gospel out of those materials which are best suited to commend Jesus to the Roman world. Matthew does the same for the Jews, and Luke for the Greek world.

Of course there remains the question of the names attached to these Gospels. On that point there can be no generalization applied to them equally. The Gospel of Luke, traditionally and from internal evidence, is evidently the work of the physician Luke, companion and friend of Paul. It is not only the Gospel "according to Luke," but the Gospel written by Luke. This may not be the case with Matthew or Mark.

[13] *Oxyrhynchus Papyri.*

"According to" (κατά) does not necessarily mean that Mark or Matthew wrote the Gospel thus linked with his name.

If criticism makes it impossible to hold that the Synoptic Gospels as we have them are the writings of their reputed authors, it only overthrows a weak and unsatisfactory position in order to plant the trustworthiness of the gospel history upon the impregnable rock of first-hand testimony. If it has not borne out the belief that the Gospel of Matthew is in its present form the work of the apostle of that name, a belief dependent altogether upon insufficient proof, it has traced the process whereby this Gospel as well as the others has been built up out of trustworthy accounts issuing from the apostles themselves. What it has seemed to deny of the verbal form of one gospel it has asserted of the essential content of all the three. It has led away from apostolic authorship only to lead back to apostolic authority.

One striking outcome, then, of the discussion of the Synoptic problem is the assurance that we are in possession of strictly reliable accounts of the life and words of Jesus, *i.e.*, of accounts in which the subjective element infused by the historians is at minimum and that minimum easily eliminated by comparing the three records. Or to speak more accurately the personal element in each case vanishes automatically when the three are used in combination. It was contended that since the accounts of the life and words of Jesus given in the Gospels were separated from the events by a period of a half century, they could not be treated as trustworthy testimony. The mentally honest student was much affected by this contention. He can now use these sources without misgivings.

Another outstanding gain of even more practical value is the discrimination with which these sources can be used. Generally speaking the sources are either primary or secondary. Mark and "Q" belong to the first class. Possibly, also, Luke's peculiar source. Such additions as each evangelist makes to the data furnished by these may in particular instances be even more accurate than the primary sources. But of this we cannot be sure. Therefore whenever we can trace testimony to the primary sources we must accept it without further questioning. Whenever we must rely on secondary sources, we are to estimate carefully the value and meaning of what is given. In doing this we shall be exercising precisely the same sort of judgment as when we conduct a process of exegesis.

CHAPTER V

JESUS

The personality of Jesus as portrayed in these histories stands out strikingly. His appearance in Judea in a lowly home, his boyhood and early manhood, his three years of public ministry as a teacher, or more precisely as a prophet, his leadership of a band of disciples, his miraculous works, his failure to meet the Messianic ideas and expectations of the leaders of the day, his betrayal, arrest, crucifixion, death and burial, his resurrection from the dead on the third day and his parting words to his followers are all briefly but vividly sketched in these narratives.

1. The Historicity of Jesus.—This picture is drawn from the primary sources. But does it represent actualities? Was Jesus, after all, a historical person? In an age when every belief cherished from time immemorial has been challenged including the existence even of the challenging mind or self, it was inevitable that the purely historical reality of an exceptional person should have been questioned. It is well that the question has been raised.

Let it be said at the outset that the gospel exists whether such a person as Jesus existed or not. It has become a power through the ages and has affected the whole human race for many centuries. If it were demonstrated that Jesus is a mythical character, the question would still be pertinent, and in some respects even more pressing than otherwise: How, when and under what circumstances did the gospel originate and assume its final form? This is a question to which the deniers of the historicity of Jesus have not given a satisfactory answer.

This fact together with what has already been said of the sources of our information will satisfy most minds of the futility of the effort to disprove the existence of the historic Jesus. Others, though few in numbers, will wish to enter more fully into the merits of the contention. For such a few words on the mythical theory may be of value.

The denial of the historicity of Jesus is an extreme development of an older so-called mythical rendering of the gospel story, first propounded by D. F. Strauss. Strauss contended that Jesus did not perform the miracles reported in the Gospels, but that his disciples and followers in the second and third generations worked up some remarkable things about his life into myths. For example the feeding of the five thousand was an elaboration of an original incident which itself was not miraculous at all. Jesus and the disciples were together on the route between Jerusalem and the northern section of the land, and a caravan of pilgrims to Jerusalem on their way to observe the feast

Whately wrote a book to show argument for non-existence of Napoleon!

gathered around him. They were delayed long enough for some of them to use up all their provisions. Jesus, by his influence on those who had not exhausted their provisions, persuaded them to share what they had with those who had none. He aroused the spirit of fraternity so that the multitude was fed. This incident was afterward transformed into the miraculous feeding of five thousand persons by means of the loaves and fishes. Similarly Jesus' walking on the water was simply an emphasized form of a very marvelous rapid trip along the shore from one point of the lake to another. The rapidity of Jesus' journey was so marvelous that in later reports it was transformed into the walking on the water.

The first to enshroud the figure of Jesus himself in a myth was Bruno Bauer. He made an advance upon Strauss in extending the mythical idea from the miraculous events to the very personality of the miracle worker and teacher. He [1] attempted to show that the life of Jesus was a pure invention of the earliest evangelist, Mark. Bauer was followed by Kalthoff [2] who explained that Jesus was the personification of the social aspirations and highest ideals of his time. At about the same time J. M. Robertson [3] aimed to resolve the entire gospel story into Hebrew and Greek mythical elements. These views were adopted some years later by Arthur Drews [4] and Wm. B. Smith [5] and developed into an elaborate and systematic effort to demonstrate that the so-called life of Jesus is the embodiment of the religious ideas prevalent among the heathen in the first century. Jesus is the *Soter* (Savior), the victim and at the same time the conqueror, the healer of disease and the great annihilator of all evil. Belief in such a person was common among the peoples of the lands surrounding the Palestine of the day. But such a person never had a historical existence. In support of this view these writers produce a large array of popular lore from the surrounding world—Asia Minor, Greece, Rome, Persia and even as far as India.

The method of procedure used in these contentions violates all the usual canons of historical investigation. It builds upon indefinite folk-lore instead of carefully sifted testimony. It plays upon conjectural etymology and uses obscure derivations to demolish the trustworthiness of reports by eye- and earwitnesses. It sets aside documents and their contents and supplants them by a priori theories of the nature of religion and life. If the Christ-myth theory be accepted on the basis of the considerations alleged in its favor, there is no reason why any outstanding epoch-making personality might not be dissolved into a myth.[6]

2. JESUS AS TEACHER.—It has been customary to speak of what Jesus thought and said as his "teaching." But to this term objections

---

[1] *Christus und die Cæsaren*, 1887.
[2] *Das Christusproblem*, 1903.
[3] *Christianity and Mythology*, 1900 and *Pagan Christs; Studies in Hierology*, 1903.
[4] *The Christ Myth*, tr. 1910.
[5] *Ecce Deus*, 1912.
[6] Case, *The Historicity of Jesus;* Conybeare, *The Mythical Interpretation of the Gospels;* Thorburn, *Jesus the Christ, Historical or Mythical?* 1912.

are raised.[7] What he said was in no sense formal. His whole attitude and bearing before his so-called disciples was unconventional. They called him *rabbi*, but his methods of conveying his thoughts are radically different from those of the rabbis. If we continue to call him a teacher, following the unanimous custom of the ages and adopting the language of his immediate followers, it must be with the understanding that the words "teacher" and "teaching" are more broadly applicable than to instruction formally given in the classroom. Teaching is also in the broad sense of the term the intellectual skeleton and substructure which underlies and gives permanent value to the message of the prophet, the immortal creation of the poet and the artist.

That Jesus was called a teacher in his own generation was due to the recognition of this inner value of his utterances. At the same time it must be borne in mind that when he began his ministry, teaching had attained to the dignity of only a half-recognized profession. There were teachers and schools in connection with the synagogues for the training of children in the elementary knowledge of the Law and the traditions (*Beth-Hassepher*). There were also rabbis and groups of disciples about them busy with the task of getting a more profound knowledge of the Old Testament. One of the three functions of the scribes was to instruct such pupils as they might secure in the meaning of the Law.[8] As the schools and teachers reached up higher and higher in the realm of study, their formal organization became less and less necessary. Larger freedom was exercised as to time, places and methods of instruction. Jesus himself was recognized as a teacher although he did not emerge from any of the existing groups of schools (cf. John iii.) and in fact he was commonly addressed as "Teacher," not only by his disciples but by the Pharisees and Herodians. (διδάσκαλε, Mt. viii, 19; Mk. ix. 17; Lk. x. 25 etc.). It becomes, therefore, a question of some importance if we shall interpret his thoughts correctly, what his method was and what his favorite forms of teaching.

The first characteristic of the method of Jesus is what we may call its occasionalism. The conventional element is totally absent from his way. He did not set forth a system consisting in propositions to be expounded and studied, but declared the advent of the kingdom of God, and sought to explain its nature as occasion offered. To say that he was informal in this way is not to say that his thought lacked coherence, or that he expressed it to his disciples haphazard and depended on accidental circumstances for the opportunity to expound his ideas. He began with some elementary points and advanced to higher teachings as those that heard him showed aptitude or preparation for them.

Another feature of the method of Jesus was its directness. In this he was radically different from the scribes who based their utterances on some text or expression of the Law, and could at the most claim that their teaching was an unfolding of the meaning of the Law. "He spake

---

[7] B. W. Bacon, *The Apostolic Message*.
[8] The other two were, first, to develop the Law, or by careful study to make explicit its implicit meaning; and, second, to act as referees or arbiters in deciding doubtful applications.

with authority" (Mt. vii. 29). He did not ignore the Old Testament, but put his own authority on a level with it. He could set his own, "But I say unto you" over against some of its temporary and superficially understood prescriptions. There was accordingly no erudition in the words he used; there was no appeal to older teachers, no elaboration of argument. He put his thoughts plainly and positively so that they might be understood by the most ignorant and allowed them to carry the convictions of their own truth unaided by quotations from literature or intricate processes of reasoning.

A third feature of Jesus' method was its concreteness. His main idea was an abstract one, that of God's reign in the hearts of men, leading them to constitute a kingdom of God on earth. But he presented this idea under the concrete form of a divine realm rather than that of the abstract rule of God. Very many of his other teachings were similarly abstract, but they are always clothed in concrete form. Principles are supreme, but they are given generally not as principles, far less as rules deduced from principles, but as cases or instances. Hence the abundance of illustration in the Gospels. In fact the great body of his parables is a result of his choice of concreteness in teaching.

Kindred with this characteristic is the fourth, that of vividness of presentation. Vividness goes beyond completeness. It is not a mere matter of style full of highly colored and sharply outlined imagery. It is a trait of thought which fastens on an important phase of truth and insists on it with vehemence to the end that it may be fully and finally impressed on the mind of the taught. As long as that aspect of truth is in question, all others are for the moment left out of consideration. There is some risk in dealing in this way. The proportion of truth may appear not to be preserved because each part of it is emphasized for the time being to the exclusion of its counterbalancing part. The complete truth may not appear to be given. But in the course of the teaching of Jesus this risk is obviated. The aspects at first neglected receive equally emphatic and exclusive insistence. The balance of truth which seems to be disturbed upon one occasion is restored upon another. Pedagogically this is a valuable principle. It is the failure to realize the fact that Jesus made use of it that has served as a source of so many wild vagaries in interpreting his thought. Its due appreciation becomes the death blow to literalism in interpretation. The words of Jesus startled their first hearers; they even shocked them and compelled them to give the new truth they conveyed proper consideration. It seemed to have been his deliberate purpose to banish indifference from the attitude of his hearers. To disturb the peace of mind of men accustomed to receive ancestral tradition unquestioningly was for Jesus a secondary evil, if evil at all, as compared with inert apathy in thought. To this end he even resorted to the paradox of making vivid impressions through obscure and enigmatical utterances. His speaking in parables is partly at least (Mk. iv. 12) in order to stir inquiry and stimulate thought.

Another feature of the method of Jesus is accommodation. In its basic principle accommodation is merely the adaptation of the teacher's forms of speech to the capacity of the pupil. The audiences of Jesus were for the most part composed of men uninstructed in any but the simplest elements of knowledge. He spoke to these so as to be understood by them. He allowed his thought to move along the level of theirs at the beginning in order that he might lead their thought to the level of his as he proceeded. Such a course required the apparent acceptance as a common basis for him and them of their views of all matters not essential to his primary teaching. It would have been neglect of economy to divert the attention from his message in order to correct their erroneous notions of historical events, their crude knowledge of the facts and laws of nature or their false theories regarding psychological and philosophical questions. As long as these errors did not interfere with what he aimed to accomplish, to enter into the discussions necessary in order to remove them would have been to confuse and not to enlighten.

The use of accommodation naturally begets a difficulty of determining just where the line shall be drawn between that which is essential and that which is not. It is not easy to decide what errors stood in the way of Jesus' conveying his great message of the fatherly rule of God and the necessity of accepting it by a supreme act of faith, and what errors did not stand in the way. But this or some such similar difficulty, we might say a more serious one, was in the circumstances unavoidable. As a matter of fact the difficulty is not as serious as it might appear; for when the individual utterances of Jesus are studied, the line above spoken of determines itself. All the interpreters do not agree on how much is accommodation and how much is not; but their differences on this point are not more radical than their differences on other subordinate matters.

From the point of view of Jesus' prophetic work his words carry what is commonly called "authority." By authority in this connection is meant independence, originality and power of convincing.

The independence of Jesus is expressed in the words, "He spake not as the scribes, but as having authority." The scribes taught what they found transmitted to them. They constantly appealed to others in attestation of the validity of their teaching. Jesus taught what he himself recognized as true and without any appeal to other teachers, whether prophets, scribes or fathers. Even the Old Testament was to him not authority, so far as its letter was concerned, but to be revered and accepted because of its content of truth. He set his own interpretation of the inner meaning of the Old Testament against all previous interpretations and found in the Old Testament much more than the literal sense. "Ye have heard that it hath been said of old—but I say unto you."

The originality of Jesus does not mean that what he brought into view had never been announced before. The Golden Rule, for instance, had appeared in some form or other in earlier times in the teachings of other leaders. The summary of the Law as given by Jesus to the rich young ruler had already been given by Hillel the elder. Various phrases in the Lord's prayer separately are found in earlier compositions. Parts of the Sermon on the Mount were similarly extant before Jesus. The originality of Jesus does not consist in creating the materials of his teaching out of nothing, but in organizing and vitalizing them and giving them their connections with one another as parts of one living thought.

The third element in the authority of Jesus is that quality in it which binds the mind and the conscience. On the essential teachings of Jesus the normal mind does not raise any objections. Nor does it question their wherefore and whence. It accepts them unhesitatingly. For that reason the apologetic for the teaching of Jesus cannot go beyond a mere comparison with accepted standards of truth and right. In a word the authority of Jesus is the authority of axiomatic teaching.

3. THE FORMS OF HIS TEACHING.—It has been questioned whether Jesus ever preached sermons or delivered consecutive discourses, which by any stretch of the term were in plan and purpose like the modern sermon. His longer reported addresses consist for the most part of briefer pithy sayings connected with each other very loosely. From this fact it has been reasoned that they are compilations of utterances spoken to different audiences upon different occasions. But a more careful examination leaves scarcely any room for doubt that Jesus did speak more at length and in consecution upon some occasions and that some of the discourses so reported represent these sermons.[*] It is quite unlikely that when audiences of considerable size gathered around Jesus he would let the opportunity pass by without giving them such expositions of truth and exhortation as are reported in connection with the gatherings on the mount or by the sea or in the synagogue.

But there is no question whatever of Jesus' having given utterance to short sayings not very different from the proverbs composed by the wise men of the older days. Proverbs, the Wisdom of Sirach and the Pirke Abhoth furnished the pattern for this form of teaching. But the saying ($\lambda \acute{o} \gamma \iota o \nu$) must not be so distinguished from the sermon as to be set over against it by way of contrast. It is a characteristic of the oriental and Semitic rhetoric that even in its consecutive address or sermon it strings together pithy proverbial sayings the connection of which with one another is not always seen on the surface. The difference lies rather in the fact that truth could be compacted in brief maxims for use in informal conversations, which maxims were particularly fitted to be repeated and circulated. In some cases they were scarcely distinguishable from ordinary remarks in conversation. They simply embodied truth in literal speech. But much oftener the form was so selected as to contain the figure known as the simile (cf. Mt. x. 15; Mk. x. 15; Lk. xiii. 34; x. 18). Very slightly different from these are those expressions which contain complete analogies or comparisons in single sentences (Mk. ii. 17, 19, 21; iii. 24, 27; iv. 21, 27; ix. 50;

[*] The case has been ably argued by Prof. B. W. Bacon in his lecture on *The Sermon on the Mount.*

Mt. vii. 16, 9; x. 24; xv. 14; Lk. xvii. 31). These similes are sometimes, as by Wendt,[10] classed with the parables or made into a variety of parable. This classification is a good one from the point of view of the ultimate nature of the simile and the parable. They both institute a comparison between the external and the internal, between the material, social and the moral, spiritual worlds. They aim to make the more external, which is also the more familiar, explain and illustrate the less-known facts of the spiritual world. Moreover the classification is one the evangelists and Jesus Christ himself seem to recognize (Mt. iv. 32; Mk. iii. 23; vii. 17; Lk. iv. 23; vi. 39). Yet for the sake of convenience and clearness it will be best to reserve the term parable for the more extended narrative similes to which it is usually applied.

Jesus' fondness for illustration led him to seize upon the parabolic form of presentation and to give it a unique dignity as well as a most effective use. As a vehicle of teaching the parable was familiar to Hebrew literature. But, like all other literary forms, it began with crude and vague rudiments and became only gradually purified and differentiated from kindred forms. Accordingly, in the Old Testament, parables of the type so frequent in the teaching of Jesus are sparingly used and not clearly distinguished as such.[11]

As already intimated, a parable is in the strictest sense a comparison (παρά and βάλλω). The terms of the comparison are a truth in the spiritual experience on one side and a transaction in outward daily life on the other side. The former which is inner and imperceptible is as if in a dramatic living and concrete form brought into the field of vision and made clearly comprehensible. The principle underlying is that of natural law in the spiritual world, understood, however, not in the strict form as identical law, but only as analogous.

While this is the chief and radical idea of the parable, an invariable feature of it as used by Jesus is realism or life-likeness. Inasmuch as the design is to impress a spiritual lesson and the truth thus to be impressed is in the human sphere, the parable is always derived from human life and experience. The beings of a lower order than man introduced into it are only such as have a natural relation to mankind, such as the sheep, the field of grain, the mustard seed, the leaven, the vineyard and vine and figtree, etc. These relations are further never pictured in untrue colors. There is a natural inadequacy in the relations of brute animals or of these of plants and stones toward illustrating human relations. Hence such inanimate and merely brute beings are never alone made the figures of the parable. And whenever such infrahuman beings are used, they are represented with absolute fidelity

---

[10] *Teaching of Jesus*, I. p. 117.
[11] The name *Maschal* (משל) which is applied to them (II Sam. xii. 1-4; xiv. 6f; I Kings xx. 30f; Is. v. 1-6; xxviii. 24-28) is also applied to fables, allegories and proverbs. In the LXX the word is translated not only by the Greek παραβολή, but also by παροιμία (Proverbs i. 1, *cf.* Wis. Sir., vi. 5, 8), θρῆνος, Heb. (Isa. xiv. 4), and προοίμιον (Job xxvii. 1; xxix. 6). In the usage of Jesus the parable is freed of these ambiguities and becomes a distinct literary form assuming a beauty and adaptation to instruction which mark the highest point of development.

to nature. At this point the parable differs from the fable with its grotesque endowment of inanimate objects with the faculties of human beings.

But Jesus' teaching was not limited to his spoken word. As Augustine has put it, *"Factum verbi verbum nobis est."* His action as well as his words was a rich source of instruction. In this connection it is helpful to distinguish between those acts of Jesus which were primarily intended to convey ideas and those in which the instructive element is subordinate and incidental. Of the former class are those symbolical acts through which he aimed to impress his followers with the importance of some virtue or aspect of ideal relation to God. Instances of this are the setting of the little child into the midst of the disciples just as they were disputing regarding the matter of precedence. There can be no doubt that coming when this act does, it was primarily designed to show them the futility of the discussion in which they were engaged and the necessity of a humble mind and a simple heart as elements of ideal character. Jesus' miracles are not only signs of the presence of the supernatural power in him, but also tokens of his attitude of mind and heart toward the evils that infest the world. They give us the values he places upon experiences in life. He considered them not only signs of power, but signs of the kingdom of God whose controlling principle is goodness; therefore when he was challenged for the signs of his Messianic claim, he pointed to the good deeds that he was performing, enumerating the healing of the blind, the lame, and the maimed, and also the preaching of the gospel to the poor. His preaching to the poor had the same motive as his healing the diseases and the infirmities of the people. His passion is a source of instruction as to the spirit in which he bore his suffering and his intention in bearing it.

Less conspicuous as mere teaching and yet scarcely less powerful in its influence on the formation of conviction was the revelation of Jesus' character in his daily conduct. It is not thinkable that he should have lived before those who came to know him and to call him rabbi without powerfully affecting them and modifying their ideas. By his relations with those of his home, by the high ideals he set on friendship, by his scrupulous regard for the rights of society and the state when these did not conflict with interest, in the higher plane of the kingdom of God, by his light estimate of merely earthly comforts and his emphasis on spiritual blessings, by his reverence for and study of the Scriptures, by his well-known seasons of prayer, by his fearlessness before the mighty of this world and his consideration for the lowliest, by his regard even for prejudices and scruples in religious matters, and finally by his absolute and consistent self-denial, he could not have failed to impress those about him, even though he had not alluded to any of these matters in his conversation. The example of Jesus, considered apart from the fact that he founded a religion or a church, was destined to be the germ of a world of thought.

Of the data given in these various ways and forms of teaching the student must depend for the most part on the explicit oral statements made by Jesus whether in direct discourse or parable. His action as miraculous or merely natural can be only tributary and incidental.

If we look at the effect immediately produced by this teaching, we shall find that not all men did understand Jesus' inner thought. The total effect of his ministry was not the enlightenment of the mass of his hearers but their encouragement in every feeble effort to please God. They received stimulus and support and were cheered and strengthened by contact with him. "The common people heard him gladly" (Mk. xii. 37) because he showed them that they could put themselves under the rule of God in spite of the discouraging theories of their leaders as to their hopeless condition. The sinful and outcast felt the revival of hope within themselves when they heard him discourse regarding the affairs of the kingdom. But all this can scarcely be considered intellectual illumination. It was rather an inspiration and elevation of life under which there lay undoubtedly intellectual conception, and out of which there grew quite as certainly clearer ideas of religion and of the spiritual life. For the real results of the teaching of Jesus we must look to the mind of those of his inner circle, the disciples who followed him constantly, and proceeded to the more advanced stages of the divine knowledge he gave them, and who cherished, remembered and recorded his words. On these the impression was profound and adequate. They did not write down all that he told them; and he did not command that they should write anything. And yet so vivid and vital was the effect on their thought that what they have recorded, scanty as it is, has had the power of a full and clear portraiture of him and of his teaching.

CHAPTER VI

THE KINGDOM OF GOD

JESUS gave expression to his mind as he found or could make occasion for so doing. He spake "at sundry times and in divers manners." His manner was not that of the modern philosopher who presents a systematic and balanced exposition of a theme from a central viewpoint. And yet he did not esteem all that he said of equal importance. He was no exception to the law controlling every mind, according to which a center and circumference exists in the individual's thought. Some matters are entirely subordinate, others are of more importance and one stands out preëminent. Wherein lay the matter of greatest interest for Jesus? What did he esteem to be the most vital matter for men to know and take as the ruling idea of their lives?

The search for the answer to this question has led some scholars [1] to fix attention upon the self-consciousness of Jesus and to ask what Jesus thought of himself and then to take his estimate of himself as the central and supreme idea in his thought. This procedure is on the assumption that since Jesus was regarded as the Messiah by his disciples and since these derived their conviction from him, the Messianic self-consciousness of Jesus must have always been the central theme of his teaching. But this line of thought is too subtle and elusive. The sources offer too slender a ground for it.

A much more obvious starting point is given in the fact that "Jesus came into Galilee preaching the gospel of the kingdom of God." While one does not always begin with what he ends, and while the center of interest may and does shift for many thinkers, Jesus evidently produced the impression upon the earliest evangelist of one primarily concerned with the coming of the kingdom. As Jesus proceeded with his work, it became clear that other great thoughts more fundamental than the formal conception of a kingdom of God claimed his attention. It was of the utmost importance, for instance, for men to know what sort of a king God was. Jesus lays stress on the fatherhood of the king. Some have fixed on this conception as central. Others realizing the inner nature of the ideal as an ethical one claim that Jesus was intent, first of all, in establishing a new righteousness among men. Harnack [2] takes the ground that the teaching of Jesus may be included in three circles which are neither concentric nor mutually exclusive. The centers of these circles are respectively: the fatherhood of God, with its correlative the infinite value of the human soul; the kingdom of God and its

---

[1] Baldensperger, *Das Selbst-bewusstsein Jesu;* Stapfer, *Jesus Christ Before His Ministry.*
[2] *What Is Christianity?*

THE KINGDOM OF GOD

coming; and the better righteousness and the commandment of love. His treatment of the subject aims to be popular and he deals with these three circles, expounding their content without striving to fuse or organize them into one system. For the sake of formal presentation, however, that would appear to be the best arrangement which follows the most prominent idea in the form of the teaching and, as has been already indicated, this is the conception of the kingdom of God. Accordingly with the great majority of those who have written on the subject, we shall put that conception into the center of our exposition.

1. JESUS' CONCEPTION OF THE KINGDOM.—The phrase kingdom of God has been used in Christian history with but slight regard to its strict meaning in the usage of Jesus. It has, therefore, acquired connotations from which it must be dissociated if what Jesus himself had in mind when he uttered it shall be realized. To this end an analysis of Jesus' usage will be necessary.

Adopting the expression as a generally current one, Jesus naturally used it without formal definition.[3] As reported in the sources his use of it is not uniform. Sometimes he calls it the kingdom of God, at others the kingdom of heaven. On closer examination, however, this difference resolves itself to one as between the reporters and not to the indiscriminate use of Jesus. Matthew reports him as using the phrase, kingdom of heaven, where Mark and Luke have kingdom of God. Jesus may have used either or both phrases. But if he did it was not with the difference between them clearly in mind. All that has been said by the older interpreters[4] by way of distinguishing between them was an importation into the facts rather than a result of the legitimate exposition of the mind of Jesus.

The question remains: Why did Matthew use his peculiar version of the phrase and Mark and Luke theirs? Was there any reason why Matthew should have used the phrase kingdom of heaven? Matthew Judaizes—adapts his language to Judaistic practice just as he does his whole method of presenting the character of Jesus Christ and his work. Judaistic practice with reference to the use of the divine name evaded, as far as possible, the word "God" and substituted equivalent synonyms or designations. The motive underlying it was reverence for God and desire to observe the third commandment as literally as possible. In other words Judaism had settled down to the avoidance of the word God in order to be on the safe side in observing due reverence toward God. Hence "heaven" became a synonym for "God," and Matthew used it as a suitable substitute in his effort to adapt his report to the Judaistic practice.[5]

---

[3] The exact language reported is: kingdom of God (βασιλεία του Θεού), kingdom of heaven (βασιλεία τῶν οὐρανῶν), my kingdom (ἡ βασιλεία μου), the kingdom (ἡ βασιλεία). The two outstanding forms, kingdom of God and kingdom of the heavens, are found in the sources over one hundred times (forty-five in Matthew, forty in Luke, fifteen or twenty in Mark).

[4] Beyschlag, Weiss, Stevens.

[5] Substantially the view of Wendt, Schürer and the great majority of more recent scholars.

The probability, then, is that Jesus, who had no superstitions of his own nor unusual respect for those of others, used the phrase kingdom of God as reported in Mark and Luke.

What did Jesus mean by the kingdom of God? His allusions to the subject, informal and figurative for the most part, are classifiable into four groups.

In one considerable class of passages, Jesus presents the kingdom as a place (Mt. xi. 12, Mk. xii. 34)—a place which may be entered into, an enclosure with an approach to it and with a fence and gate; the way to it may be thronged and the gate may be broken open.

In a second class of passages, the kingdom is represented as a possession. In the parable of the Merchantman Seeking Goodly Pearls, the kingdom is a thing of value; also in the parable of the Treasure Hid in the Field (Mt. xiii. 44-46), it is declared to be a gift (Luke xii. 32). It may be taken away from one class and given to another class. It is an inheritance (Mt. xxv. 34).

In a third class of passages the kingdom is held up as an organism. This class of passages is involved in the very language of the phrase kingdom, which presupposes kingship and a law, and a people ruled by the king. Like every other organization it has its constitution and its offices and officers (Mt. xii, 25; Lk. xxii. 29).

In a fourth class of passages, the kingdom is viewed as a dispensation, an order of things. In the phrase, "Thy kingdom come," of the Lord's Prayer, the outlook presents an order of things upon the earth which is to be. The idea of a dispensation was familiar in the day of Jesus (Lk. xxii. 18, xxi. 31, Mt. vi. 10).

In a final group of sayings not as large and distinct as the above the kingdom appears as a principle. It is an invisible spirit to which men yield. It enters into them and controls their lives (Lk. xvii. 21).

Before proceeding to deduce from these data the idea conveyed through them it is necessary to secure the light thrown upon them by their antecedents and the environment in which they appear.

2. THE DEVELOPMENT OF THE CONCEPTION.—Jesus neither invented the idea nor coined the phrase kingdom of God. How then did it originate? In the Old Testament the phrase does not occur, but the idea is dominant. It constitutes the organizing principle of the state of Israel. The nation began to exist as the people of Yahweh. It always looked on itself as the realm in which he would exercise his sovereignty. The Greek word "theocracy," which was later coined to designate all government by deity, is only a synonym for kingdom of God.

In the period of Judges Israel made as near an approach to theocracy as was possible. The tribes of Israel accepted God as king, and the "judges" were his officers. It was he who called, appointed and directed them in their work. When Israel fell away from this type of theocracy and chose to be ruled by human kings, the ideal was not regarded as outgrown or set aside but as existing and operative behind its apparent human violation. David, the ideal king, governed as the

THE KINGDOM OF GOD

executive of God's will. When he departed from the straight line, he was condemned and reproved. The line of kings who followed David illustrates even more forcibly this dominant principle. It was the function of the prophets to keep alive and nourish to its full stature the supremacy of Yahweh. When the royal house was particularly deficient in realizing this, they denounced its representative and predicted its downfall but, at the same time, they also announced the coming of a second David, a king after God's own heart that should allow God to rule through him.

So long, therefore, as the monarchy continued in Israel either united or divided, the conception of God's kingship could only exist in the shadow and background. It was eclipsed, as it were, but not destroyed. And down to the period of the Exile it persisted in this form. With the collapse of the monarchy it emerged from the shadows assuming the aspect of a vivid hope for the future. What the kings of Israel and Judah had failed to realize an ideal son of David would realize for the nation, now chastened and purified by its sufferings in exile. When the restoration from banishment was achieved by slow stages, it was the hope of many that Zerubbabel would prove this ideal king. But the years passed and the commonplace character of this prince ended in their disillusionment. Thus the Old Testament period reached its final stage with the kingdom of God idea still a dream to be realized in the future.

At no time in the intertestamental period were the conditions right for a faithful Israelite to believe that the divine rule had been or was about to be established. The Maccabean struggle culminated in the rise of a dynasty which by no possible interpretation could be identified with the expected Davidic restoration. But the darker the actual conditions, the brighter the light of the ideal grew. If the kingdom of God could not come, as seemed likely, through existing royal persons or dynasties, it should come in some other way by the interference of God himself in the affairs of the world.

Just how this interference might take place was a point of dispute. Some expected that in some obscure group somewhere in the land God would train and prepare his servant, the Messiah, and lead him, even as he had led David of old, to wonderful achievements, ending in the establishment of his kingdom. Thus the kingdom would come by a historical evolutionary process.

Others despaired of the ordinary movements and laws of life and imagined that the interference of God would be direct and from without. The apocalyptic writings expressed and at the same time fostered this idea. The kingdom would come by a sudden break in the order of history. And not only of history but of nature also. Convulsions of a terrific character would take place. The order of nature would break and be reconstituted. At the point of division between the old and the new orders would come the change from what was called the present age to the coming age (οὗτος ὁ αἰών - ὁ αἰὼν ὁ ἐρχόμενος). Between this cataclysmic theory of the coming of the kingdom and the historical one opinion wavered.

In either case, however, when the kingdom was established it would mean the independence, even the ascendancy of Israel over his enemies and oppressors, and the subjection of these to the new sovereignty. The conception was formally a political one. But the supremacy of the righteous God of Israel could, in no case, be entirely detached from ethical ideas. And, in the end, the kingdom of God meant to multitudes of faithful Jews an order of society pervaded and controlled by respect for and obedience to the righteous laws given by God himself to his people Israel.

It is reasonable to suppose that in the age of Jesus a wide variety of concrete views prevailed among different types and classes of Jews concerning the exact form in which the expected kingdom would materialize. Pharisees, Zealots, politicians, scribes and priests would naturally laid more or less stress on the political, the moral and the religious elements which all together entered into the common notion. John the Baptist was evidently, under divine leading, of opinion that righteousness was to be the dominant factor in it, and that without it no Jew would find himself better off, but even worse in the kingdom than he was in existing circumstances. Others, we know, had extravagant and even mythical ideas of abundant material goods to be enjoyed in banquets automatically on condition of pure loyalty to the nation.

To what extent the difference between the two meanings (the abstract and the concrete) of the term kingdom ($\beta\alpha\sigma\iota\lambda\varepsilon\iota\alpha$) was appreciated one can do no more than conjecture. Did the men of Jesus' day think of the kingdom as a reign or a realm? Did it mean to them the kind of rule to be exercised by the king or the extent of his dominions and the machinery of his administration? These two shades of meaning are, of course, never found apart from one another. Where there is a reign there is a realm, and vice versa. But it would help us to-day to know how far the relation of these two sides of the conception entered into the thought of the day.

In spite, however, of the uncertainties inhering in the data as above sketched, it is certain that when Jesus made use of the phrase he had in mind that order of things in Israel and through Israel in the world, in which men would recognize God's fatherly rule, submit themselves to him in faith, and enter into fraternal relations with one another, looking forward to the perfect consummation of the will of God in an ideal human society.

CHAPTER VII

THE FATHERHOOD OF GOD

THE idea of the kingdom of God as preached by Jesus is primarily a religious one. It is scarcely open to question that his object in preaching it was to illumine men's minds concerning their ideal relations with God and to lead them to accept his rightful rule over their lives. But men live in relationships to one another which, though inspired and controlled by the spiritual motive, branch out into social and political outgrowths. The conception of the kingdom of God includes a social ideal and a forward look into the future. It was as developing in these directions that Jesus preached it; and it is with due reference to them that it must be viewed.

As a religious ideal the kingdom of God is thoroughly self-consistent. It meets the demands made in every religious ideal by offering a conception of God, a conception of man and a conception of the actual and ideal relations of God and man. The relative emphasis, too, on these conceptions is that of their intrinsic as well as practical importance. The conception of God is by far the most conspicuous thought in the mind of Jesus; the other two conceptions are subordinated to it and their content is determined by its content.

1. THE IDEA OF DIVINE FATHERHOOD BEFORE JESUS.—What then did Jesus think of God? It is not a mere coincidence that in the earliest sentence recorded from his lips God is named "Father," and that in the last words he spoke from the cross he committed himself to Him as such. It is true that in both cases he thought of himself and his relation to God. But his uniform designation of God all through the period between as the Father of men leaves no room for doubting the central place that fatherhood occupies in his thought. On this point it is utterly unnecessary to invoke the criticism of the sources in order to reach the exact idea in Jesus' mind. The impression his words produced on all the reporters is that to him God is the Father.

But Jesus was not the first to use the language of fatherhood in speaking of God. A notion of divine fatherhood was undoubtedly current among the ancient heathen. The Greeks and the Romans thought of men as the offspring of semi-divine beings who were themselves of divine parentage. And in the divine sphere the individual gods were like a dynasty genealogically traced to one parentage. One God was "the father of gods and men." But when the case is thus stated it requires neither argument nor explanation to make it clear that a conception of this sort has no kind of connection with the thought of Jesus.

Jesus' thought was obviously affiliated with that of the Old Testament prophets. And in the Old Testament the substratum of the conception of God was that of creator and ruler. This differed in many respects from the heathen idea. In the latter the gods were the offspring of the same process of evolution which brought into existence the world of nature. In the Old Testament the one God existed before all and was the maker and sustainer of all things. Not only was heathen thought different from Old Testament thought on the subject of the unity of God, but also on the character and the relations of God to nature and to men. Gentile thought admitted of belief in a deity apart from the gods accepted by the common people. This deity might be conceived as an impersonal substance underlying all the elements and forces of the world. Old Testament thought was intolerant of any identification of God with the nature forces or with the world as a whole. God is one; God is holy, righteous, pure, just; God is merciful to those who keep his law. This was in substance the nucleus of what Jesus took over from his Jewish parentage and teaching.

Such an idea laid stress on God's right to rule. As creator he could do as he pleased with the work of his hands. The outstanding characteristic of his relation to men was his sovereignty. The relationship of fatherhood was not absent from the conception. But it was a fatherhood of sovereignty. In the Psalter, with all its expressiveness of the personal relation of God to the faithful and his mercy and consideration for them, the fatherhood of God is totally absent except in Psalm ciii. 13, where it is given in the comparison of Yahweh to a father ("like as a father"). In the prophetic writings the point of closest intimacy reached by man in his relation to God is that of servant.

Yet the Old Testament has its usage of the idea of God's fatherhood. Collectively the people of Israel is called God's son. "I have called my son out of Egypt" (Hos. xi. 1). Yahweh sends word to Pharaoh, "Israel is my son" (Ex. iv. 22; cf. also, Deut. i. 31; xxxii. 6). Not only Israel but the king of Israel is at times spoken of as a son of God, as of Solomon (II Sam. vii. 14) and of the ideal king (Ps. ii. 7; lxxxix. 26, 27). Whether God is ever called Father of an individual Israelite in his unofficial capacity except in a metaphorical sense is questionable. Expressions which may indicate this are always open to the interpretation which finds only in Israelites collectively the children of God (cf. Is. lxiii. 16; lxiv. 8; I Chr. xxix. 10).

In all these uses of it the expression does not as yet lead to the fixation of the word "father" as a name of God or to the discovery in it of the very essence and character of God. It is rather the sign "of his covenant relationship with the people."[1] In later Judaism the dominant tendency was rather in the direction of attributing to God a more exalted place above the world of nature and mankind. While the older usage was embalmed in liturgical expressions, and God was addressed as Father, it was with a sense of greater remoteness than before that the worshipper came before God.

2. JESUS' NEW REVELATION OF IT.—Coming out of this atmosphere

[1] H. Schultz, *Alttestamentliche Theologie*, p. 528.

into that created by Jesus is like emerging from twilight into the full glare of the day. His thought that God is primarily the Father of men is no less than revolutionary. It amounts to a new revelation equally epoch-making with the first realization that God is one for the whole world, or that he is perfectly holy and requires holiness from those who come nigh unto him. To say that Jesus used language which was familiar in making this revelation is to utter a meaningless truism with no particular relevancy to the subject. To say that he only transferred the emphasis from sovereignty to fatherhood and opened the eyes of the world to the reality of a sovereign Father where formerly men only saw a fatherly Sovereign is not enough. That transfer of emphasis brought into view the inner nature of God and perfected his revelation to men. If a sovereign exercises his rule in a fatherly way he is still first of all a sovereign, but if a father exercises authority he can only exercise it out of the whole world of thought and feeling which constitutes fatherhood.

This is all forced upon the consciousness as one enters into the spirit of Jesus' self-expression both in word and in conduct. For him it became the dominant thought of life. It explained the world of nature and of men. It filled him with trust in the dark hours and with joy in the bright ones. He surrendered himself so absolutely and completely to it that not for a moment would he permit death itself to obscure the reality of it. It stirred him to indignation as he saw his Father's house turned into a den of thieves (Jn. ii. 16). It moved him to compassion as he saw the sufferings of his Father's little ones. It filled him with absolute confidence in his own mission and message as he realized the inexhaustible source of strength his Father could furnish him.

If we now pass from his life to his words, we shall find that his thought is equally conspicuous and all-absorbing and at the same time maturely developed. It is not a mere expression of feeling; but a carefully considered idea. He discriminates in his use of language, introducing variations of meaning into it. In speaking of those who live out of sympathy and fellowship with God, whether Jews or Gentiles, he does not say, "God is their Father," using the third personal pronoun. Neither does he apply the term to designate the relation common to himself and the disciples. He never says in the first person plural, "Our Father," in speaking of God. The address in the Lord's Prayer is only an apparent exception. He is there teaching the disciples as a community how to pray, not praying with them.

This is the negative side of the significance of Jesus' usage. The positive side presents other lines of discrimination. Sometimes Jesus speaks of God as his Father individually. He uses the first person singular of the possessive pronoun. He "that doeth the will of my Father which is in heaven" (Mt. vii. 21). "Every plant that my heavenly Father hath not planted shall be rooted up," Mt. xv. 13 (cf. also Mt. xvi. 17; xviii. 10, 14, 19; Lk. ii. 49). However in some instances even the omission of the possessive pronoun does not remove the restriction to himself. The context leaves no room for questioning that Jesus speaks of his individual relation to God. "No man knoweth the Son, but the

Father; neither knoweth any man the Father, save the Son" (Mt. xi. 27). Similarly in the prayers of Jesus, the personal pronoun is omitted (Mt. xi. 26; Lk. x. 31; xxii. 32; xxiii. 34; Mk. xiv. 36).

But, at other times, Jesus applies the term in speaking of the relation of God to the members of the kingdom. As these utterances are uniformly intended to comfort the disciples, or to incite them to a more intense loyalty, the pronoun used in them is the second, either in the plural or the singular, "your Father," or "thy Father." "Let your light so shine before men that they may see your good works and glorify your Father which is in heaven" (Mt. vi. 16; cf. Mt. vi. 1; etc.; Mk. xi. 25; Lk. vi. 36; etc.). "And thy Father which seeth in secret himself shall reward thee openly" (Mt. vi. 4).

But there are utterances of Jesus in which he presents the fatherhood of God in a broader sense. In these God is seen acting the part of the Father toward all men, the good and the vile alike (Mt. v. 45; Lk. vi. 35). It is true the word "Father" is not used in this connection. But the meaning is plain enough. No mechanical rigidity of interpretation can narrow it down, for the same method of interpretation would lead to confusing results elsewhere. There is nothing to show, for instance, that Jesus in addressing his followers had in mind only believers in him and in his mission. Finally the parable of the Prodigal Son (Lk. xv. 12ff.) represents God at least under the figure of the Father of the faithful and estranged son alike. If it be said that this is a parable and, therefore, the language is purely figurative, the answer is that the whole idea of God's fatherhood is figurative. The relation of God to created beings can be only analogous not identical with the relations of human parents to their offspring.

The facts in the case cannot, then, be explained on the basis of the denial of the universal fatherhood of God in some legitimate sense. On the other hand they cannot be explained on the basis of any generalization that ignores the discrimination pointed out in the usage of Jesus. Both in the employment of phraseology and in the presentation of the idea this discrimination is too consistently carried through to be denied or disregarded; but the existence of such a discrimination raises a problem.

By way of solving this problem it has been proposed by many[2] to summarize Jesus' thought in the formula: "God is the Father of all men, but men must become his children." God is always what he ought to be; men must change in order to conform to God's ideal for them. A more particularistic variety of this conclusion is that given by Holtzmann: "God is the Father of all who will to become his children."[3]

This solution is essentially sound and true. But its paradoxical ring is likely to puzzle and, to the mind of the strict logician, it cannot but appear offensive. It makes God the Father of beings who are not his children. Strictly taken the idea of fatherhood is here so attenuated as to amount to a mere sentimental attitude. It is practically emptied

---

[2] Dr. R. W. Dale, who is followed by Prof. G. D. Stevens and G. H. Gilbert, *The Revelation of Jesus*, p. 22; Beyschlag, *Neue Testamentliche Theologie*, I. p. 79; and Wendt, *Die Lehre Jesu*, Eng. tr. II. p. 117.

[3] *Neutestamentliche Theologie*, I. p. 169.

THE FATHERHOOD OF GOD

of its rich meaning. It may be helpful, therefore, to restate its content in an analytic form.

The idea of fatherhood is a complex one. The analogy of human parentage suggests the following: (1) Origin of being. The parent is the source of life for his child. Thus divine fatherhood is like all fatherhood. God is the originator of the being of all men. And if this were all that fatherhood involved, not only human beings but all creatures would naturally be entitled to the name of children of God; for they all owe their existence to him.

But (2) the idea of fatherhood includes similitude. Every child in a measures reproduces the image of its parents. The divine fatherhood is like the human. All men are the children of God in that they are made "in his image and after his likeness." The image is not perfect and clear in any. It is more complete and distinguishable in some than in others. But it is just as really the same image in all because its essential lines are found in all. Moreover it is a function of the moral nature to aspire after the restoration of the completeness of the image of God. And to this extent it is a duty to become like their heavenly Father (Mt. v. 48).

But (3) all parenthood includes the element of affection toward the offspring. Without full love the parental relation at once becomes unnatural; and if love be totally lacking, it is even regarded as monstrous. This element, then, above the other two, characterizes the fatherhood of God. But love is itself a complex affection. Its underlying, indispensable and always present substance is the feeling of benevolence. Love tends to seek and, so far as possible, to create happiness. To love is to wish the person loved all that is possible of good. The wish, however, is completed only in the effort to secure its end, and thus benevolence becomes the root of beneficence. For one who wishes well and has the power to realize his wish, to wish well is to do well. This element of love is represented as existing in its entire breadth and full strength in God. He wishes well and does all the good that it is possible for him to do without violating his own nature or the natures of the objects of his benevolence. The great fundamental blessings of life he bestows on all his creatures without discrimination of moral character. He causes the rain to fall and the sun to shine on the good and the evil alike.

Another indispensable element in love is the desire for requittal. Love is not genuine or perfect if it leaves the heart indifferent to the attitude of the object loved. This constitutes the basis of fellowship. The desire for association and nearness are legitimate consequences of the demand of love for reciprocity. Of course, in its fullest and strongest form, love will overlook the denial of return. It is long-suffering. "Beareth all things, believeth all things, hopeth all things, endureth all things, never faileth." But it cannot forego the longing after communion and the effort to attain it. It is hardly needful to add that, in this aspect of it, the love of God is represented by Jesus as full and complete toward all his human creatures.

But still another factor in the fullest love is delight. Love takes pleasure in the person on whom it is lavished. And yet when he who loves is unable to find any ground for delight or pride, his love does not vanish. On the contrary the very absence of such ground often shows the genuine character of the affection. Love that is not complacent proves itself disinterested and enduring. Where complacency is impossible, love becomes more intensely benevolent. The yearning to help becomes more and more unselfish. And if by reason of sacrifice it succeed in bringing to its object the quality lacking, love completes itself and becomes full-orbed. It is at this point that God's love for the disciple and his love for the sinner begin to differ. God cannot take pleasure in the sinner or his sin. The formula frequently used, "God loves the sinner but hates his sin" can mean only that God lavishes on the sinner his benevolence and the longing for his repentance, but can have no satisfaction in him.

If then, the idea of fatherhood be viewed with reference to its highly complex content, it will show itself one of manifold aspects. As one or another comes into view, the idea will assume a different meaning. God will reveal himself as Father in more than one sense.

The first and most superficial sense in which the fatherhood of God is to be understood is that in which his relations to all his personal creatures are the same. They are all his children, first, because they owe him their being; secondly, because they bear his image, and, thirdly, because they are the objects of his love. He lavishes his good will upon them in an infinite number of ways, he longs for a return of his love from them, he desires to hold communion with them. This is true of all alike, the just and the unjust, the prodigal as well as the elder brother.

But within this wide circle of God's children there is a narrower one in which the idea of his fatherhood is more real and potent. There are those who respond to his love. They put themselves in perfect harmony with him. Thereby they call forth his delight and satisfaction in themselves. For them God's fatherhood becomes a full and effective one. Of them God may be said to be the Father in so much larger a sense as to constitute them into a new class.

But within this narrow circle there is another narrower still in which only Jesus himself stands. He is the Son of God not only in the fuller sense above outlined, but in a deeper one. What that sense is, is not explained in detail in his teaching. The practical conditions and aims of that teaching did not call for such an explanation of the mysterious relation of the Son to the Father, but that such a relation exists lies beyond doubt, and it is enough to say of it that it is not merely an official and Messianic one. The only adequate terms for designating it are the words transcendental and unique.

To sum up, then, this cardinal teaching of Jesus, we find that the fatherhood of God assumes a threefold form, though its ultimate principle is one. The first and broadest of these may be called the rhetorical. It presents a vague and incomplete but yet real fatherhood. It includes all men. The second is the ethical or logical one and is complete including only those who have opened their hearts to God and have given him the opportunity to perfect his love toward them. The third is the transcendental and unique one which can include only Jesus himself.

CHAPTER VIII

THE CHILDREN OF GOD

1. What Is Man?—In view of the originality of Jesus thought of God, the profusion with which he expresses it and the emphasis he places upon it, his views of the world and of man as a part of the world, are apt to strike the man of to-day as commonplace and uninteresting. Presumably Jesus accepts the cosmology and anthropology current in his day. This presumption cannot be strictly demonstrated. Yet he displays no interest in the questions of the origin and constitution of the world and of man, but proceeds to reveal such important realities as it is necessary for men to know for their guidance in their moral and spiritual relations.

The fact that he does not evince a special interest in the exact knowledge of the sphere of science does not, necessarily, commit him either in favor or against the notions of contemporaries regarding these subjects. It certainly does not commit him to these notions. It simply leaves him in the place of one who, whether he accept or reject certain views in this sphere, is too careful and sparing of his efforts to undertake enlightening others on all sorts of secondary matters.

Views of the origin of man and of his constitution are entirely subordinate to true knowledge regarding his destiny, his relation to God and the way in which he should bring to its realization God's idea of him. Moreover knowledge of God sufficient for such spiritual ends may and does come apart from accurate information on the origin and constitution of the world or man. In fact the knowledge which Jesus imparts is not affected by the substitution of one theory for another in purely scientific cosmology and anthropology.

At some points cosmology and anthropology may seem to come very close to the realm of Jesus' interest. Their bearing on spiritual life seems vital, so much so that the one could not be modified or abandoned without affecting the other. But no matter how vitally the two spheres seem to be interlaced when viewed from a distance, as one comes nearer to them they are seen to be separate and distinct. Like mountain peaks thrown against each other through perspective, in such a way that the higher seems to rest upon the lower when viewed from afar, they diverge and break away from each other, as the observer draws nearer to them, and perceives the great valley lying between them and each resting upon an ample basis of its own.

This does not mean that in the view of Jesus it is a matter of indifference as to what men think of the bodily life or of the world of nature, but rather that thoughts of these things do not determine what one ought to think of the kingdom of God and its righteousness; on the contrary the thought of God determines thoughts of other matters. What one believes regarding God and his relation to him controls and shapes what he may think of and how he shall act with reference to the material universe and his own physical life. If God be the loving being whom Jesus declares and if he care for the sparrows that fall, if he clothe the lilies of the field, if he feed the fowls of the air and number the very hairs of human beings, men may very well care for them, too, cultivate them and use them each in accordance with its own nature and laws. But in order to take this view of the flowers of the field, and the fowls of the air, and the dignity of the human body and the value of animal life, one must first be assured that God sustains the relation of a benevolent creator and an interested protector and guide of all sentient beings in the world.

This is the central and characteristic element in Jesus' view of man and the world. Hence psychology as a science plays no essential part in his teaching; and far less do physiology or cosmology. The world is only the realm in which God has a right to reign and will eventually do so; and man is a being that can and must sustain relations of intimacy, loyalty and love to God. Questions regarding the laws of the universe, the organization of the human body, the nature of the soul and even the apparently vital question whether these two are after all distinct entities, or parts and aspects of the same thing, whether man is a unit or a unity made up of two or three separate and distinct substances, all these matters may be left for philosophers and scientists to study and pronounce upon. And the results reached by them in one generation may be reviewed, corrected and improved in another generation. Meantime man as a living, acting being must learn to adjust himself to his maker and his destiny.

But Jesus' conception of man is not either neutral or barren. Neither would a negative statement of his attitude toward man and the world be adequate or satisfactory. It has a constructive side which may be condensed into a single proposition: Man is the child of God. In other words Jesus' view of man is the exact converse and correlative of his conception of God.

Simple and transparent as the conception is, it has far-reaching bearings. First of all it contradicts and excludes all views which minimize the dignity and value of human nature. Passion for God and not enthusiasm for humanity was the starting point and center of the interest of Jesus. His passion for God begets a far healthier and abiding enthusiasm for humanity. Jesus expressed this serene and all-controlling enthusiasm in his attitude and relations to those around him. To him a man was worthy of all consideration just because he was a man. He loved children because every child had in itself the potentiality of a fullblown manhood in which God might take delight. He pitied and helped the infirm and helpless because in each he saw a child of the heavenly father.

Secondly he saw in human nature not only great value and dignity but also the possibility of reaching an ideal. Even the most degraded and hopeless were in his eyes capable of recovery and redemption. The

THE CHILDREN OF GOD 57

Pharisees of the day had a doctrine of reprobation according to which, beyond a certain point, human nature becomes incurably corrupt. It cannot be saved and all efforts to save it are futile and wasted. This begat in them a sense of contempt for large classes. They called them scornfully "the people of the soil" (*Am-hāaretz*). Against this view Jesus raised an earnest protest. No one is past saving. Salvability is an inalienable characteristic of all. Human nature is instinct with good impulses, sentiments and aspirations which can be organized and constructed into the character requisite for membership in the kingdom of God.

And it is worth while to develop these instincts and impulses and lead them to their ideal fullness because for man existence does not end with death upon earth. He survives that event and continues consciously after it. There is a singular indifference in the mind of Jesus to the mere article of death. He nowhere alludes to it in proportion to the magnitude of its place in ordinary human thought and experience. When he meets it in life, it does not stir him nor lead him to moralize. Those who are affected by it among the living, parents and kindred surviving and left sorrowing, appeal to him and he comes to their rescue; but as far as the event itself is concerned, or the departed, it does not seem to interest him. Evidently he does not look upon it as the black and gloomy thing that men have always regarded it. The death of the body is not the death of the man. "Be not afraid of them that kill the body, but are not able to kill the soul" (Mt. x. 28). This does not mean that the soul is indestructible, for there is one that is "able to destroy both soul and body in Gehenna." Nevertheless it clearly commits Jesus to belief in immortality as a gift of God and explains his intense desire to bring men into the true relation with God because of the momentous consequences involved in that relation.

During the intertestamental period thought on this general subject flowed into the channel of a doctrine of the resurrection of the body (Dan. xii. 2; II Mac. vii. 9; xi. 14, 36; xiv. 46). The idea is used as the ground for the encouragement of martyrs. Their enemies might kill and mutilate their bodies, but God would restore these same bodies to their perfection. The author of Enoch li. goes a step beyond in teaching that the righteous should be raised from the dead, and also that they would all become angels in heaven.

The doctrine came into prominence and furnished one of the points of acutest difference between the Pharisees and Sadducees. It was inevitable that such an important question should have been brought to Jesus for his answer to it. It came in the imaginary case of the woman married to seven brothers. And Jesus, true to his conviction, did not evade the issue. He first showed that the supposed difficulty in this case was no difficulty at all. The conditions of a resurrection state must be very different from those of the earthly life. "They which shall be accounted worthy to obtain that world and the resurrection from the dead neither marry nor are given in marriage" (Lk. xx. 35).

Here he might have stopped. He was bent on a more constructive expression on the subject. He proceeded to show that the reality of

God's love is a bath of immortality. Whoever is immersed in that bath is free from the sword of death.

a future life is involved in the teaching of the Old Testament. For his interlocutors this was an unanswerable argument. "Ye do err, not knowing the Scriptures." "Have ye not read that it was spoken unto you by God saying, I am the God of Abraham and the God of Isaac and the God of Jacob?" "God is not the God of the dead, but of the living" (Mt. xxii. 23-33; Mk. xii. 18-27; Lk. xx. 27-38). The significant thing about this affair is that Jesus does not quote from the Old Testament words directly and indisputably referring to the resurrection of the dead, but a passage which involves the more fundamental teaching of immortality. It is because God called himself the God of Abraham and of Isaac and of Jacob that these patriarchs are to be regarded as not dead but living.

This pronouncement of Jesus is significant from more than one point of view. In the first place it shows his comparative indifference to the current doctrine of mere bodily resurrection. The more vital matter to him was that death does not end all. Whether the Pharisees were satisfied with the disposition he made of the Sadducees' objection to resurrection was of no consequence to him. The reference of their disputed point to him had given an opportunity to express himself on one of the most vital problems that have ever puzzled the human mind and he had pronounced in favor of what the great thinkers in their deepest moments have considered true.

But Jesus' answer to the question of resurrection has another significant aspect. It passes by the philosophical and purely intellectual phases of immortality and finds its root and substance in man's religious nature. Abraham, Isaac and Jacob are living because God has called himself their God. God could not call himself the God of transient, perishable beings. If he says that they are his and he is theirs, it is because they have for him meaning and value, or because he has embraced them in his imperishable love. As long as he lives and is what he has revealed himself, they also must continue to live. This is not meant to discount or supersede interest on the scientific or speculative sides of the problem. Men must investigate in all fields the unexplained facts which invite their inquisitive instincts, but a working faith in immortality must be grounded in man's spiritual nature as a child of God.

There is still another side to this declaration of Jesus. It seems to present immortality as the privilege of the few rather than the prerogative of all. God does say that he is the God of Abraham and of Isaac and Jacob, but does he say that he is the God of Herod and of Pilate and of Judas? And, if not, what becomes of their immortality? But is it clear that God does not say he is the God of his erring children as well as of those who accept his kingdom? And if this question be answered with a "No," does that make immortality the same for all? Can immortality apart from the enjoyment of God's love and fellowship be true immortality? These are questions which Jesus did not face and answer.

2. SIN.—It is certain that in the mind of Jesus all men were in need

of some readjustment of relationship to God. On the surface of it he seems to divide them into two classes, the righteous and sinners (Lk. vi. 32). But on closer examination this is only an ironic use of language. For the very class who are here called "righteous" are elsewhere (for instance in the parable of the Pharisee and Publican) found under a worse condemnation than those called "sinners." Generally he denounces Pharisees and scribes in terms of unmeasured scorn. And the so-called sinners he never either justifies or excuses. High and low, therefore, reputed righteous and open sinners, they are all in need of a radical change. If the prodigal in the parable is in need of a return to the father's home, the elder brother is in even a greater need of a return to the father's spirit and character.

Christians in all generations have called this need sin. But Jesus' phraseology is strikingly free of the words "sin" and "sinner." He prefers the term "lost" to "sinner" or "sinners." The reason is that the terms "sin" and "sinner," with the conception attached to them, were already used by his contemporaries with connotations that he did not wish to corroborate and endorse. A sinner to the Pharisees of that period was not necessarily an offender against God in a moral relationship, and sin was not exclusively a transgression of God's moral law or failure to conform to God's moral will. Pure accidental relationships and ceremonial failures to conform were regarded as sins. And men were called sinners because providentially their lot may have been thrown in other than what the Pharisees regarded as the moral, holy and righteous relation with God. A Gentile was a sinner by the very fact that he was a Gentile. And by the mere accident over which a man might have no control at all, of failing to conform with a ceremonial prescription, he might commit a sin. By avoiding this terminology, Jesus practically called clearer attention to sin as it is. He showed men its true nature and results.

Jesus calls sinners the "lost"; and by lost he means those who forget or ignore their true relation to God. Loss is twofold: (a) It means what God loses. Thus in the parables of the Lost (Lk. xv.) the coin and the sheep are pictured as lost to their respective owners, and the son to his father. There is a value that has been taken away from the treasury and so far as its inherent potency is concerned, it is useless. (b) Loss is loss to the lost being. In the case of the sheep loss means not only that the shepherd loses the value of the sheep, but also that the sheep loses its own comfort and happiness and falls into distress and danger, misery and suffering. In the parable of the sheep, particularly, the loss seems to mean something further, viz., the helplessness and inability to restore itself to its primitive condition. The son can say, "I will arise and go to my father"; but the sheep seems to be utterly unable to help itself. It has no way of putting forth effort to get back to its former happiness. Hence, to Jesus, the evil in the case of the lost sheep is a little more serious than in any of its other forms.

From this point of view sin is no light matter. It affects God, the sinner and all his associates in life. Jesus laments it and aims to neutralize and conquer it. He sees it as an evil principle deranging the inmost lives of God's own children. He does not absolve its victims of their own share of responsibility for it; but he does not intend to leave them to take care of themselves or endure the consequences all alone. Of course he also sees the varying degrees of power and hold which sin has over different men. Some deserve more stripes than others. The publican goes to his home more readily forgiven than the Pharisee. But all alike need redemption and release from its power. All alike fail to realize the precious privilege of God's fatherhood and live in alienation from him.

3. SALVATION.—The kingdom of God, whatever its exact nature and in whatever form it may be conceived, would be unreal and futile when it is established if the children of God were still left under the dominion of sin. So long as sin abides in the heart, the child of God remains in an unfilial attitude. He can neither enjoy nor claim his privileges in a world which is his Father's. Thus Jesus, though he never made sin the formal theme of any discourse, consistently and everywhere urged men to turn away from their sins and to seek deliverance from the power of sin as an absolutely indispensable condition for entrance into the kingdom.

(1) *Repentance.*—But how should sin be removed? Mark in reporting the entrance of Jesus upon his work (i. 14, 15) says that his first words were: "The time is fulfilled, and the kingdom of God is at hand: repent ye, and believe in the gospel." And always afterward the idea of repentance was an essential part of his message (Lk. v. 32; Mk. vi. 12; Mt. xi. 20); and not only a part of his own message, but also the chief exhortation of the apostles whom he sent to preach in the towns and villages of the land. Without repentance the privileges of the kingdom of God are of no avail. It is because the Pharisees and scribes will not repent that they are in peril of missing the kingdom, and that Jerusalem's condition draws from his eyes tears of compassion and from his lips the cry of anguished pity (Mt. xxiii. 37).

And just what repentance really is, the context of his preaching as well as the radical meaning of the word itself makes very clear. The word μετάνοια means change of mind. It is the equivalent of what in modern usage is oftener called conversion. It is, however, conversion not in mere conduct, but in disposition and purpose. It calls, first, for full change of the mind and will and of the outward life afterwards. It brings pain in the contemplation of the past because it naturally includes a larger or smaller sense of guilt. The tendency has been to dwell on the pain for the past and pass by the forward bearing of it on the life. It is not a solitary act but a stream or movement. They need to repent as long as there is anything in them to be repented of. It differs from regret which is a feeling resulting from the contemplation of the unforeseen evil consequences of wrong doing but has no roots in the moral nature. Judas regretted his act of betraying Jesus and was led to despair. Peter repented and reconsecrated himself to a life of sacrifice and leadership in the Master's service.

(2) *Faith.* With repentance is inseparably associated in thought

and often in expression, belief in the gospel. The word is not used with a view to the distinction between intellectual assent to a proposition and cordial abandonment to what is recognized as true. Its combination with repentance indicates that what is meant by believing is acceptance of the new order in a practical way. Belief is faith. At all events so far as the mind of Jesus is concerned no faith exists which does not commit to the kingdom of God. Hence faith is an instrument of power by which wonderful, even miraculous results are accomplished (Mk. v. 34; x. 52; Mt. xxi. 21; Lk. xvii. 6). But the chief exercise of faith asked for by Jesus was in the acceptance of himself as lord and leader. Many believed his words and even entrusted themselves to his benevolent care taking advantage of his powers to heal their diseases. But what he aimed at was to get their acceptance of his priestly leadership into the most intimate fellowship with God the Father.

(3) *Forgiveness.* Faith and repentance are the conditions, or rather together as one and indivisible inner experience, the condition of the forgiveness of sin. Without repentance there is no forgiveness; and without forgiveness no membership in the kingdom of heaven. And yet Jesus' uniform and constant assertion of the boundless fatherly love of God and of his desire to bring all into full fellowship with himself would lead to the belief that God forgives his erring children unconditionally. He enjoins forgiveness of offenses as the law of the kingdom among those who follow him. And for such forgiveness among themselves he intimates that it must be free, full and unconditional, "until seventy times seven in a day." Can the servant be expected to forgive more fully and freely than the lord? In the parable of the Great Debtor (Mt. xviii. 23-25) the lavishness of the great creditor is held up as the ideal for the servant. The law of forgiveness for men is the law which God himself observes.

What, then, can be the meaning of conditions of forgiveness? The paradox of unconditional forgiveness being conditioned on faith and repentance is solved when it is understood that the conditions are not conditions of forgiveness, but of its effectuation in life. God forgives, but there is no practical forgiveness until by repentance and faith man appropriates the gift. A gift involves two acts, the act of the giver and the act of him who receives. And until the latter is realized, the gift remains a mere offer, nothing more. Free as pardon is it cannot be forced upon the sinner. The father may be ready to receive the returning prodigal, but the prodigal must return before he can be welcomed as a member of the household. As long as he persists in his estrangement and wandering, the fatherly heart may be lacerated by grief, but it can neither take pleasure in him nor regard his offense as nonexistent. It could be no otherwise in a world of free moral creatures. He who is unconscious of his sinful condition and esteems himself righteous, appeals to the law, and the law is inexorable. He thinks he needs no salvation and can have none. To save him in spite of himself is to reduce him to an automaton.

This principle underlies the utterance of Jesus concerning the so-called "unpardonable sin." The sin of blasphemy against the Holy Spirit amounts to the utter mortification of the spiritual sense whereby forgiveness could not be made effective. In other words there is no sin which God will not forgive as such; but there is a sin whose effect on the power to accept forgiveness is such that it will prevent acceptance. And since forgiveness is not only the offer of pardon but also the acceptance of it by the person to be forgiven, because that acceptance is not possible, forgiveness becomes impossible.

The subject was alluded to in connection with the charge by the enemies of Jesus, that he was performing his holy and divine works by the power of the archenemy. That, however, was an indication of such spiritual blindness as would prevent them from seeing spiritual good anywhere. In charging the work of God to the account of the archenemy, they were showing a lack of capacity to discriminate between the gifts of God and the evil interests of Satan. This would make it impossible for them to receive the favor of God when God offered it. If, however, the very sin of mistaking God for the devil became the subject of questioning in their hearts; if they debated whether they would be forgiven for it or not; and if by any chance they should come to wish forgiveness for a sin of that kind, would they be forgiven or not? They would be forgiven. God would not hold it against them that they attributed his works to Satan. But could they desire to be forgiven for a sin of that kind? Could they ever be brought to see that they had sinned? How could they, when their distorted vision made them see Satan where God was working? And how could they wish God to forgive them for what did not appear wrong to them since, by the very supposition, they had no power to realize that it was wrong? It is a self-contradictory act for a man to see white as black and black as white, and then to realize that he is blind and must have his eyes opened. "Unforgivable" is not an apt word for the sin. God will forgive, but the question is whether the offender will accept that forgiveness.

The essence of forgiveness is annulment of offense. The subject is brought into view in figurative ways. Sin is sometimes viewed as a debt and its forgiveness as conciliation. Or it may be viewed as something to be cast off. This is inherent in the term frequently used whose modern equivalent is "remission" (ἄφεσις¹ from ἀπὸ and ἵημι). Since God, according to the clear teaching of the Old Testament accepted at the time of Jesus, is always the person against whom sin is an offense, all remission must be from him. Yet one who is in intimate fellowship with God and knows his mind thoroughly may reveal the fact that God has forgiven in a declaration, "Thy sins are forgiven thee" (Mk. ii. 5).

4. THE FILIAL RELATION.—When the sinner has accepted forgiveness at the hand of God, he enters into the ideal filial relation. So far as he may maintain himself in this relation, his attitude toward God will be that of perfect trust. Hence:

(1) *Confidence in the Father's Care.* He will gratefully recognize

THE CHILDREN OF GOD

the providence of God and find in all the arrangements of the universe round about him signs of his heavenly Father's goodness. He will live as aware of the constant care of God. He will never doubt that all his needs will be supplied and the paternal protection will shield him from harm whatever the circumstances may indicate to the contrary. Jesus urges his disciples' unreserved commitment to the providential care of the Father (Mt. vi. 19-34).

(2) *Prayer.* The filial life is also one of prayer. Prayer, as practiced in the age of Jesus, was beset by a confusion and tangle of misunderstandings and corruptions of thought. Jesus endeavored first of all to disentangle it and restore it to a healthy and wholesome practice. Inasmuch as externality was predominant and men were using forms without entering into their full meanings, he protested against the use of hard and fast forms. Inasmuch as prayer was made the vehicle of much selfishness, and led to the love of display and of pride, he rebuked the practices that were associated with this aspect of it. Prayers in public places, prayers that were offered with the intention of calling attention to the piety of those who offered them, prayers that consisted in vain repetitions of words, were to him no prayers. They violated the essential law and notion of prayer.

Over against this corrupt and confused practice, Jesus presented prayer as the recognition of an intimate filial relationship with God. It is only as God was seen to be the heavenly Father that the approach to him would become true prayer. Hence true prayer came to its fullest realization when it was practiced in secret—in the prayer closet with the door closed. Secrecy was not in itself an addition to the efficacy of prayer, but it corrected the conditions necessary for the more intense realization of the relationship subsumed. It fostered concentration and the exclusion of selfishness and of the love of display and pride. When a person was praying in secret, he could not take pride in himself or display to others his extraordinary piety. On the other hand he would realize more intently his true relationship to God as a son.

Moreover prayer is to be practiced in the right attitude, which includes faith or trust, and persistence or importunity, not, however, as if God must be wearied into yielding but as an opportunity for the development of faith. By faith in prayer Jesus does not mean mere belief that one is to receive the exact equivalent for his petitions. This is very well illustrated in the case of the one praying that the mountain might be removed and cast into the sea. To expect that that which is prayed for shall be performed in the exact terms of the petition is to mistake prayer for command and its answer for obedience. It is to assume that God has given the right to the ignorant creature to order Him the All-Wise. But this is barred out by the very figure of fatherhood. The father knows best what the child should have. The child must ask in the spirit of submission to the father's fuller wisdom.

Jesus' practice confirms, illustrates and expands this conception of prayer. His whole life was a continuous, ceaseless prayer, so understood.

The object of prayer, according to Jesus, is the enlargement of life.

In the model prayer (the Children's Prayer, commonly called the Lord's Prayer), the enlargement of life is indicated at the very outset in the use of the plural possessive pronoun, "our Father."[1] A man does not pray alone. Since he prays to the common Father, he must recognize those who are in the same relation with the Father. Prayer includes petitions for heavenly blessings. "Thy kingdom come, thy will be done on earth as it is in heaven." It includes also earthly blessings (the "daily bread"); prayer would be insincere and not the expression of the whole inner man unless it expressed also the desire and dependence upon and need for earthly blessings—the means of preserving health, vigor, and efficiency. Anything a man needs and wants must be the subject of his prayer, otherwise he would be hiding his desire for it from God, or esteeming the object of his desire beneath the interest of the omniscient. The fullness of the idea of dependence and sincerity of expression demand that even the least things and the most outward that are included in one's desires should be incorporated in prayer.

Finally Jesus' own prayer lays much stress on the recognition of the Father's will and its realization as the best answer to all prayer. "Thy will not mine be done" (Mk. xiv. 36; Mt. xxvi. 39; Lk. xxii. 42) is the phrase with which he closes the most intensely conceived desire of his human heart, because above his keenest wish there is the supreme longing that the Father's desire may prevail. Such prayer can never remain unanswered.

---

[1] This thought is not materially affected by the probability that Luke's version of the prayer omits the pronoun "our."

CHAPTER IX

THE MESSIAHSHIP

THE kingdom of God, according to Jesus, was at its core a religious ideal. But religion apart from its expressions in life is an abstraction of which nothing definite can be predicated. Moreover these expressions of religion become its means of self-protection and self-promotion. And, still further, in its emergence in life religion has always followed the channels of social activity. This is what we mean when we say that religion is always social; that no one can be religious all by himself; and that apart from its ethical and social workings, no religion can be of any value. From the beginning religion has adopted tribal, racial and national organizations and expressed its own grouping-together of men under the forms of these political working ideals.

In the days of Jesus the current form of political organization was the monarchy. The patriarchate had long passed out of existence. The democracy had had a brief career in Europe, but was scarcely known in Palestine. Its day was two thousand years in the future. In the terms of the kingdom, therefore, it was natural that the religious ideal of Jesus should be cast if it was to be understood at all and used as a practical means of self-expression as well as self-promotion.

The necessary elements of the conception of the kingdom are a king, a people and a law. These are the essentials of all organic life—headship, membership, organic law.

The headship of the kingdom of God naturally belongs to God. But in the order to which Jesus and his contemporaries were looking it was to be exercised through the Messiah (Greek, Χριστός, "Anointed"). And Jesus revealed his consciousness of being the Messiah.

This last statement, however, has been challenged recently by Wellhausen, Lietzmann, Nathaniel Schmidt and others. These scholars claim that Jesus did not aim to do more than find a place among the prophets. Like all his contemporaries he knew that a Messiah must come in fulfilment of the Old Testament predictions, but that he never identified himself with this august personage. The denial is based on the radical difference on the face of it between the hard and fast mould of the Messianic conception as held in the age and Jesus' self-revelation of his own mind concerning his supreme mission upon earth. The later ascription of a Messianic self-consciousness is based on a misunderstanding of his words, as for example, of his use of the phrase "Son of Man" in speaking of himself. According to these scholars this is nothing more than the equivalent of the personal pronoun "I."

Only a careful examination of the usage of Messianic language can furnish the data for the solution of the problem thus raised. The effort at such an examination reveals the fact that in the sources four Messianic titles are used, viz., Messiah, Son of David, Son of Man and Son of God.[1] The first two of these occur so rarely and are apparently used in such a conventional way as to be negligible in the attempt to find Jesus' own idea of what they mean (Mt. ix. 27; xii. 23; xv. 22; xxi. 9; xxii. 45; Mk. x. 47; xii. 35-37; Lk. xviii. 38; xx. 44). Of the other two Son of Man occurs oftenest and at once produces the impression of being used significantly.

1. THE SON OF MAN.—The frequency above alluded to that characterizes the use of this phrase is due to nothing else than Jesus' choice and appropriation of it as his own favorite self-designation. With the exception of the personal pronoun I, which he also uses in some contexts, he always refers to himself as the Son of Man. On the other hand no other person either speaks of him by this name or addresses him under it. Where did Jesus get the phrase and what does he reveal by it of his own thought of himself?

(1) *The Older Usage of the Phrase.*—In the Old Testament the phrase Son of Man is used: (a) As a synonym for man (Num. xxiii. 19, I Sam. xxvi. 19, Ps. viii. 4), (b) As the equivalent of a weak or frail man (so by Ez. ii. 1; iii. 3 and repeatedly through the book. Yahweh addresses the prophet thus, reminding him of his frailty), (c) as a designation of the ideal king, the Messiah in his preëxistence (Dan. vii. 13). The sense, however, in which the phrase is used here is peculiar and needs explanation. In later usage the Son of Man is a single person, occupying a place of distinction and command in Israel; in Daniel the Son of Man is the ideal Israel personified, hence the Messianic monarchy or kingdom. That the phrase is used in this sense is clear from the context. Daniel in a vision beholds, as in a moving picture, four monstrous beasts which he comes to realize are the symbols of the Assyrian, the Babylonian, the Medo-Persian and the Macedonian empires. These world powers are pictured as brutes because each one of them has a brutal aspect. The point of view of the whole vision is that of the faithful Israelite. The policy and the attitude of the world powers is determined by the ruthless and cruel use of power. The prophet's soul, deeply impressed by the exhibition of their brutalities and at the same time confident of God's goodness, looks forward to the appearance of a monarchy whose characteristic would be humaneness as contrasted with brutality. The day of brutality and unreason is doomed to end with the present age and that of intelligence to follow it with the dawn of the new age in a new world power. To this power he gives the name of the Son of Man. This which is Israelitish or human monarchy is prepared of God, held in reserve and occupies a place beside the Ancient of Days (God) ready to be revealed at the proper time and to wield eternal dominion upon earth. The vision was seen by Daniel during the bitter days of Antiochus Epiphanes. The Macedonian world power was in the person of this king carrying

---

[1] Kirsopp Lake and Foakes Jackson (*Beginnings of Christianity*, Part I, Vol. I, pp. 362ff) question the identity of the persons designated by these titles.

THE MESSIAHSHIP

out a policy of relentless oppression over God's chosen people. In the midst of the darkness the curtain is lifted for a moment so that the seer might know the truth in advance of the advent of this power in order that he should comfort oppressed Israel and encourage them with the assurance that their sufferings were temporary, and that they were soon to assume the ascendancy and hold control in a perpetual kingdom in succession to the kingdoms that shall have been destroyed and pass away. In an earlier vision of the prophet (ii. 34, 35) there occurred in a dream of Nebuchadnezzar a composite head of gold, bust of silver, body of brass, legs of iron and feet of mixed iron and clay. This frame was overthrown by a little stone cut out without hands, which took the place of the image and became a perpetual and abiding mountain. This rock is also the symbol of the Messianic kingdom. The rock of the earlier vision is the Son of Man of the later one.

The title Son of Man is in the Ethiopic Enoch adopted as the distinctive designation of the Messiah and is uniformly so used (xlvi. 1; xlviii. 2; li. 3; lxi. 17).[2] It is probable that the usage of the Book of Similitudes affected that of educated men familiar with its content. By a transition of thought quite natural to the ancient world but difficult for the thinker of to-day to trace the collective "Son of Man" (Israel) was transformed into an individual. The link of connection in this transition is the fact that the head of the tribe or king of the nation was often identified with his tribe or people and spoke of himself and was spoken of by others as if he were the nation or the tribe. The figure of the King of Israel was fused with that of Israel itself (cf. Ps. lxxx. 17 as an instance of this habit of thought). The Son of Man, then, as the emblem of the Israelite empire came to be the name of the ideal king of Israel for the period of its world-wide dominion.

In the Apocalyptic Literature the process of individualization never became popular. Neither did it acquire fixed connotations. Of all the ways of designating the Messiah it remained the most plastic.

(2) *The Usage of Jesus.*—As already indicated Jesus applied the title to himself. It occurs in his allusion to himself as given in Matthew twenty-nine times, in Mark thirteen times, and in Luke twenty-five times. A careful examination of these passages shows that emphasis is to be laid: (a) sometimes on the notion of humanity under privation and suffering. The Son of Man has nowhere to lay his head. The foxes have holes and the birds have nests in which they may take refuge, but the Son of Man is destitute. The Son of Man must needs be betrayed and delivered into the hands of men, suffer and die. (b) At other times the emphasis is laid upon the human feeling of sympathy. The Son of Man comes "to seek and to save that which was lost." He allies himself with the destitute. Though not necessarily

---

[2] The Ethiopic Enoch is, however, a composite work of which only chapters xxxvi-lxxii, commonly known as *The Book of Similitudes,* make use of the phrase in question. In another section of the book which undoubtedly proceeds from another hand (lxxxv-xc) and is generally regarded as a part of an Apocalypse of Noah, the Messiah is represented as coming to the rescue of Israel in the form of a powerful white bull.

destitute himself he casts his lot with those who are so. (c) In a third class of passages stress is laid on the glory and dignity of the Son of Man including his exaltation into supreme power. He becomes the head of a redeemed human race. In this connection Jesus speaks in particular of his resurrection from the dead, of his ascension to the right hand of God, of his judging mankind, and of his return in glory accompanied by the heavenly hosts.

(3) *The Messianic Consciousness of Jesus.*—In answer to the question, Why and how did Jesus use the title of himself? some have said that he chose it without any reference to its Messianic implications. Those who hold this view deny that the phrase Son of Man means the Messiah at all. They claim that in the Aramaic language, in which Jesus probably used the title, it is a simple equivalent or substitute for the personal pronoun "I" (*Barnasha*).

Others render Son of Man as equivalent to ideal man. Basing the interpretation on the Old Testament (as in Ez. viii. etc.) they find its main implication to be the humanity of the Messiah, but qualify the humanity as ideal or "divine." But when we test this interpretation by the process of substitution in the passages where the title occurs, it fails. For example, "the Son of Man has not where to lay his head," would become, The "divine" or "ideal man" has no place to live in. Why should the ideal man have no place to live in when the beasts and fowls have houses? That in other places the substitution would stand the test (The Son of Man is Lord of the Sabbath—the ideal man is Lord of the Sabbath) does not help the theory because these harmonize also with the Messianic sense.

Hence a larger class of interpreters have attributed a more fully and distinctly Messianic sense to the title. Among these some have made the Messianic sense very simple, pure and ordinary. When Jesus says the Son of Man, he simply means the Messiah because he wished to conceal his meaning from the public at large and reveal it only to the inner circle of his disciples. He desired his disciples to understand that he was the Messiah; but he also wished the public at large to know nothing about his Messiahship, at least until after the Messianic work was accomplished. To the inner circle it was easy to explain its meaning. The people were not familiar with it as they were with the terms Messiah and Son of David and its use would not betray his Messiahship prematurely. This esotericism is foreign to the spirit of Jesus. He never aims to conceal himself from anybody.

The best interpretation is that according to which the title is chosen by Jesus because of its plasticity or adaptation to the process of transforming the Messianic idea from a political to an ethical and spiritual conception. Jesus found the title freer than any other of association with ideas which he could not endorse. He could pour into it his own thought. This thought he found in his own self-consciousness. And in his self-consciousness he found a different content from that believed to exist in the Messiahship, though a content which was not contradictory or exclusive of the common conception.

This content includes the following items: (a) The Messiahship carries with it the functions of service rather than that of lordship. "The Son of Man came, not to be ministered unto, but to minister." He said to the two disciples who rather desired the place of honor among the heathen: "Those who hold office among the people lord it over them, but it shall not be so among you."

(b) The Messiahship is a universally human rather than a national or racial office. The Messiah was to be the benefactor of the whole world. Therefore he was not to establish a visible kingdom for the benefit of the Israelite or for the race of Israel, but an order or dispensation for the advantage of the whole world.

(c) The Messiahship was to include spiritual dominion over all spiritual forces and powers. Not merely men but spiritual powers of all kinds ("the demons") and the forces of nature (winds, waves, and diseases) were subject to the Messiah. From this point of view, those good works which have been called miracles are signs of the Messiahship of Jesus (Mt. xi. 5-7).

The reason, then, why Jesus used the title Son of Man is that it yielded itself a ready instrument to the revelation of his inner consciousness and allowed him to develop out of the political Messianic conceptions of the day the idea of saviorhood of the whole world. This interpretation does not exclude the idea that Jesus did use the apocalyptic forms of thought and expression current in his own day.

2. THE SON OF GOD.—The second significant designation of the Messiah in the Gospels is "Son of God." And like the title Son of Man this too is not a new one. It has its roots in the Old Testament. But, broadly, it may be said that the Old Testament is not constant or precise in the employment of the expression. It generally suggests a close relationship with God. (a) Those are called sons of God who because of preternatural powers or gifts seem to fall out of the ordinary classification of men. As these powers or characteristics point back to God as their source and author, the relationship which they suggest between their possessors and God is naturally designated as that of sonship (so in Gen. vi. 2, 4). (b) Again those are called sons of God who by their constant abiding in his presence or by their loving ministrations may be pictured as the members of his heavenly household (so the angels in Job xxxviii. 7). (c) Further, Israel collectively is called the "Son" of God when Yahweh wishes to indicate his special purpose of delivering him from bondage under the Egyptians. God had taken the nation under his care, adopted it so to speak into his heavenly household and was to exercise his jealous care of a parent over him. "Thou shalt say unto Pharaoh, Thus saith Jehovah, Israel is my son, my first born," (Ex. iv. 22). The thought is presented in Isaiah lxiii. 16 from the converse point of view of the Israelite. "Doubtless thou art our Father, though Abraham be ignorant of us and Israel acknowledge us not. O Jehovah, thou art our Father (cf. Mal. i. 6). (d) But if Israel, the people, is the Son of God, the name is preeminently fitting when applied to the king of Israel. From the side of the people it is fitting because the king sums up and represents them,

and from the side of God it is fitting because the king is God's own chosen one and exercises authority in his name. Accordingly even before the kingdom was established in the projected ideal of the king (II Sam. vii. 14) he is designated as the Son of God. "I will be his Father," says Jehovah, "and he shall be my Son." (e) But the kingly line was to culminate in the one ideal king held as the prototype who was to rule the people in perfect conformity to the will of God. Therefore the Messiah, the ideal king, is preëminently the Son of God (cf. Ps. ii. 7; lxxxii. 6; lxxxix. 27, 28). From these data it is clear that in the Old Testament the phrase is never the designation of the nature or qualities of those to whom it is applied, but of the relationship established by God's choice of them with himself.

In the apocryphal and pseudepigraphic literature of the intertestamental period, the Messiah is declared to be by God himself his own Son. Thus in Esdras vii. 28, 29, "For my son, Messias, shall be revealed with those that are with him, and it shall come to pass after those years that my son, Messias, shall die." And again several times in Chapters xiii. and xiv. Of the Book of Enoch, the same declaration is found upon the lips of Jehovah. "For I and my Son will unite with them, forever, in the paths of uprightness in their lives and he shall have peace" (cv. 2). In the other writings of this class, however, the title is conspicuous by its absence; but the cases already cited indicate that its meaning is no longer broad and subject to variation as in the Old Testament. Sonship of God is synonymous with Messiahship.

In the Gospels the outstanding fact is that Jesus never calls himself the Son of God, though he never disclaims the title when used by others of him. And it is frequently used by others as by those possessed with demons (Mt. viii. 29; Mk. v. ; Lk. viii. 28), by the centurion who had charge of the crucifixion (Lk. xx. 70) who, however, being a pagan must have had quite a different thought in his mind when he used it; by the high priest at the trial (Mt. xxvi. 32; Mk. xiv. 61; Lk. xxii. 70); and by the disciples at Cæsarea Philippi (Mt. xvi. 16). To these instances may be added the voice from heaven at the baptism (Mt. iii. 17) and at the transfiguration (Mt. xviii. 5), and also the words of Satan in the temptation ("if thou art the Son of God," Mt. iv. 6; Lk. iv. 9).

From the point of view of linguistic usage the phrase is expressive of a relation figured primarily in the relation of the offspring to the parent. But the figure is sometimes very dimly held in view. It is a complex figure in any case and suggests several analyses. In some instances participation in the same nature or mere resemblance entitles an individual to be called "the son of a power, principle or element." The two disciples are called "sons of thunder" when the intention is to convey to the mind that they were dominated by a stormy and passionate temperament. Similarly men are called "children of light," "sons of darkness" and "sons of disobedience." Judas is the son of perdition. Again the figure of sonship is based on a conceivable relation to antecedents and environment. Men are called "sons of the present age," "sons of the kingdom," "sons of the bridechamber." Joseph was the "son of seventeen years" (Gen. xxxvii. 2, Heb. text).

Obviously in all the cases in the Synoptic Gospels the Son of God is conceived of as no other than the Messiah. If not used in the stereotyped technical sense in which the phrase is just the title of the expected son of David, Israel's great deliverer to be from all ills and misfortunes, it conveys little more than the peculiar nearness of him to whom it is applied to God, the ruler of all. It has an ethical, theocratic content and that only. To read into it more than that would be to attribute to the high priest, to the demoniacs, to the centurion and to the simple-minded and plain-thinking disciples notions of which they betray no trace in all else they say or do. Since Jesus himself did not choose to reveal the inner content of his self-consciousness in this phrase by using it of himself, such a course is not warranted upon historical and exegetical grounds. Yet by tacitly accepting the title as given him by others Jesus confirmed in the minds of those who accepted his leadership the conviction that he was the Messiah.

3. The Messiah's Work.—It has been already intimated that by his choice of the title Son of Man as Messiah Jesus revealed to his hearers the new development of the Messianic office and work which he was unfolding in his own inner life and view. During the course of that development the Messiahship was being transformed from an outward eschatological political office and work limited to Israel into a spiritual, ethical mediation of the kingdom of God among men of all races and tribes. That the work of the Messiah would be primarily ethical and spiritual, and political only as it might superinduce social and outward changes will present itself as a subject for discussion later. Just now assuming that the ideal of Jesus was primarily inner, it may be noted that as Messiah he laid chief stress upon the work of mediation.

As mediator, however, Jesus could serve only as a representative of God to men. For if the mediator's office is to bring to mutual understanding those who stand aloof from one another since God is in no need of more clearly knowing the minds of men than he does know them, no mediatorial work on that ground can be necessary. Hence the first and foremost task of Jesus as Messiah was to bring the mind of God to men. And this Jesus did by preaching the "Gospel of the kingdom of God." He declared not merely the willingness, but the intense and eager desire of God that his erring children should accept his fatherly care and rule. This is the essence and core of the "gospel of the kingdom." By his words, by his example and by his whole life Jesus aimed to make this clear to those who saw and heard him.

In the course of the performance of the Messianic mediation as thus outlined Jesus saw and declared the necessity of suffering and death for himself. And this he saw was to come upon him not as an individual but as the Messiah. His death was to be not accidental but an essential part of his mission and work. His blood was to be shed for many for the remission of sins. Whether this conviction came as a consequence of meditation upon the work of the suffering servant of Jehovah pictured by Deutero-Isaiah (Is. lii. 12; liii. 13) or because of watching the progress of the rising feeling against him on the part of the leaders, is a question of secondary importance. It does seem very probable, however, that the experience of the suffering servant agreeing as it did with what he saw impending in his own case confirmed his consciousness of being the Messiah and his realization of what the Messiah's work would be.

Just what place suffering and death occupied in his work Jesus does not fully explain. And his allusions to the matter are indirect, leaving some room for differences of understanding. On one occasion (Mt. xx. 28; Mk. x. 45) he declares "that the Son of Man came not to be ministered unto, but to minister and to give his life a ransom for many." The meaning of the expression hinges on the significance of the word "ransom" (λύτρον). Etymologically the word means "a way of release" (from λύω, "to loose"). Originally such a means was something of value given in exchange for a forfeited life. The life might be and was predominantly, or at least very commonly, that of a captive taken in war. The warrior was held a prisoner in the hands of the enemy, and to redeem him from his captivity either a sum of money or some other equivalent for his life might be given. In case this was money the connotation of the term became commercial. In case a captive was exchanged for a captive the connotation was purely military. If Jesus had nothing more in mind than these alternatives, the question would be simply whether he looked upon his life as a military or a commercial ransom. By the time, however, that he made use of the expression both of these senses of the word had been superseded by a third, growing out of a ceremonial usage. This is traceable through the Septuagint back to the Hebrew word *Kopher* (from *Kaphar*, "to cover"), covering. The Septuagint rendered the word by the Greek λύτρον. The history of the expression in the Bible thus leads to the Old Testament ritual of the covering of sin by the blood of the sacrificial victim on the day of the atonement. In this ritual the blood of the victim (a goat) was sprinkled upon the mercy seat and was looked upon as a covering for the sin of the people. The underlying thought seems to be that the holy God looked upon the innocent blood of the sacrificial victim instead of upon the sin on which the innocent blood was laid, and viewed and treated his people as innocent.

If this be the correct explanation of the term "ransom," the emphasis is not on the manner in which it works but on the result. The word ransom thus reverts to its primitive and etymological meaning of a simple means of release. Jesus meant that his life was the means of releasing many from sin.

Another occasion on which Jesus made reference to his own death is in the words of the institution of the Lord's Supper. Here he spoke of the shedding of his blood: "the cup of the New Testament which is shed for many, for the remission of sins." The occasion as already said was the institution of the Lord's Supper in commemoration of the establishment of the new covenant. The radical idea underlying the institution is identical with the idea of the covenant between God and Israel through Moses (Ex. xxxiv.). The words "new covenant" are significant. In the old covenant the blood of the victim indicated the community of life between the covenanting parties. In the new covenant the cup containing the emblem of life indicates the life in which God and men unite.

As in the ransom passage, so in the institution of the Lord's Supper the emphatic thought is the value of the life of Jesus and not the merit of his death. His death is simply the means of securing the value of the life in its completeness. The conception of the Lord's Supper, therefore, appears to be a development of the sacrificial idea of the Old Testament ritual, and in that idea it is the offering of the life of the victim rather than the incident of his death that is significant.

CHAPTER X

THE MESSIANIC COMMUNITY

No kingdom could be imagined which did not concern itself with a more or less definite body of living men and women held together and vitally affected by it. It was necessary that in holding before his hearers the ideal of the kingdom of heaven Jesus should have either himself given them a conception of the Messianic community or stirred them to form such a conception. Since very soon after the completion of his earthly work his followers as a body used the word church to designate themselves collectively, Jesus has been called the founder of the Church.

1. JESUS AND THE CHURCH.—But Jesus very rarely employs the term church. In fact his use of this term is limited to two occasions, both reported in the Gospel of Matthew. In the first of these the term is introduced just after the Messianic confession of Peter and in response to it. When the apostle in behalf of all the disciples had declared faith in his Messiahship, Jesus said, "Upon this rock will I build my church" (Mt. xvi. 18). The second occasion is that of the instruction of the disciples regarding the treatment of offenses among them (Mt. xviii. 15-20). Both of these occur at a rather late period in the ministry of Jesus and they will be examined more carefully hereafter.

The fact that Jesus appears to use the word church only as reported by Matthew, together with the fact that he is made to associate with it the personal pronoun my ("my church"), whereas Paul knows only of a church of God, showing as this latter fact is alleged to do that the expression in Matthew must be a later and more developed form than the Pauline, has led some to deny that Jesus used the word at all.[1] Others find no difficulty with ascribing the word to Jesus.[2] As a mere question of the use of a special word, the point is of small consequence. The idea of a brotherhood of followers of his is an undisputed fact. Unlike John the Baptist, Jesus trained a group of followers to perpetuate his work. The use of the word to designate this brotherhood

---

[1] Weisse, *Evangelische Geschichte*, II. p. 94; followed by Bleek, *Synoptische Erklärungen*, II. pp. 46-91; and Holtzmann, *Neuetestliche Theologie*, I. p. 210).
[2] Ritschl, *Rechtfertigung und Versöhnung*, II. p. 299; Beyschlag, *New Testament Theol.*, I. p. 162; and Titius, I. p. 172. This last-named author urges that though at the beginning of his public work Jesus could not have thought of the separation of his disciples from the Jewish community, a little later upon his rejection by the nation he must have been driven to this position; and the words in Matthew are therefore perfectly natural.

sets in clearer light the principles that underlie and can be discovered elsewhere throughout his teachings.

Whatever, then, may be said of the utterances of Jesus on this subject, it was inevitable in the nature of things that such a revolution as his personality must make in the world should be the beginning also of a new social organization. If the revelation of God by Jesus as the Father unites men with God in an intimate relation, it also unites them with one another as brethren. Of the revolutionary character of his mission Jesus was fully aware from the beginning and throughout his entire ministry. In particular he took account of that aspect of it which would cause the sundering of existing social ties and the formation of new ones. He was conscious that he had come "to set a man at variance against his father and the daughter against her mother, and the daughter-in-law against her mother-in-law" (Mt. x. 35; Lk. xii. 51-53).

Religious organizations before the beginning of the Christian era were, in general, coincident with national lines. Each people was from the point of view of its political life a nation and from the point of view of its religion a church. Two forces, however, operating during the period which ends with the birth of Jesus tended to break up this order of things, at least in Palestine. The first was the formation of world empires of the Roman type. Under the empire of the type of Assyria each subject people was loosely associated with the paramount power and its political as well as its religious unity remained, after conquest as before, a unitary and distinct affair. A formal recognition of the suzerain power and the payment of tribute sufficed to constitute subjugation. Under the Roman type with a stronger central administration, and a truer regard for principles of justice, there was less of a spontaneous recognition of the national character of religion and a larger relegation of religious questions into the spiritual and individual sphere. The second factor is the appearance of what may be called the creed idea in its rudiments as representing the intellectual element in religion. This was due to the guiding influence of Greek philosophy. The movement went so far that Plutarch could preach religion almost without showing any consciousness that it must run in tribal lines.

In the Old Testament church and nation were at first one and the same organization. From the point of view of its religious function Israel was a *quahal* or *edhah* (assembly, congregation). The experiences of the three centuries intervening between the Maccabean generation and the final extinction of Jewish independence constitute a period of transition in which, in the midst of much apparent confusion, it is possible to trace the steady growth of the church idea. Israel might lose national autonomy, but the Israelite could not lose his faith in the God of his fathers; and since his religion must survive, it survived as the faith of Israelites. The idea of religion, however, did not because of this find itself reduced to a loose individualism. It held together in the spiritual bonds of a common faith, and transformed it gradually into a church. The rise of this Jewish church was conditioned on the one side by the separation of the religious from political life necessitated through the submergence of the latter, and the substitution of the spiritual bond for the political. But where the race and national lines became indistinct, it was natural for the religious spirit to pass over them and seek others than the persons included within them as subjects for its dominating influence. The religious organism in this way was conceived as broad enough to include men of all nations and tribes, and the church idea was fully fledged.[3]

Furthermore within the Jewish church developed just before the days of Jesus the phenomenon of men banding themselves together under the impulse of common specific religious tenets. Some of these were very loosely held together as parties. Such were the Pharisees and Sadducees. One at least was very compactly organized with a definite body of practices and institutions making up a sort of monastic order. This was the Essenes. These are the so-called "heresies"[4] of the New Testament (cf. Acts. v. 17; xv. 5; xxiv. 5; xiv.; xxviii. 22). The Jewish church was by this process prepared to be divided into branches. It became possible for any of those if they felt themselves moving too far from the main life of the organism to assume an independent existence. And on the other hand it became possible for the original body to cast out and refuse to recognize as a part of herself such as had departed too far from her norms or standards.

It was in the midst of such conditions that Jesus drew to himself a group of disciples. The term, however, is rather vague and general in its application. It includes many who accepting Jesus as their master and giving him their loyal support never appear among those who followed him in his journeys. Such was, for instance, the household of Bethany. It includes also others who from time to time attached themselves to him but for one reason or another did not stay permanently with him. It includes, finally, the narrower circle of companions and helpers called together to share with him his thought and his fortunes to the end of his earthly ministry. These are sometimes called the "Twelve."

The assembling together of the Twelve was patterned generally after the custom of the times. Every teacher (*rabbi*) who was conscious of having knowledge to impart to his contemporaries drew to himself a circle of companions and enlightened them by his teaching. These companions were his disciples, learners in his school and mediators between him and the world at large. In them the teacher multiplied himself. And upon them he depended for the dissemination of his teaching. So far as that teaching was ethical and affected character, the teacher became the example and ideal of his followers.

In utilizing this general plan and method of publishing as widely as possible his message of the kingdom of God Jesus went a step farther and definitely committed to the Twelve the task of going forth among the communities of Judea and Galilee and proclaiming the gospel. He

[3] *Cf.* Bousset, *Die Religion des Judentums*, pp. 54-56.
[4] The word heresy (αἵρεσις) is in this usage not the equivalent of a departure from a standard recognized as normal but that of a variety of the same type.

THE MESSIANIC COMMUNITY

made them commissioners (missionaries) or apostles.[5] Through these steps, accordingly, around the personality of Jesus a community was naturally formed.

What now was the idea of Jesus regarding this new organization? And in what relation did it stand to the kingdom of God? Plainly the church is not exactly identical with the kingdom.

And yet to an extent church and kingdom of God coalesce. The church, like the kingdom, is dominated by the will of God, and realizes his ideal upon earth. The church, like the kingdom, includes human souls that have recognized God's right to their loyalty and service. The church, like the kingdom, enjoys the favor of God and has the guarantee of his protection and help to the end. They both have a visible and an invisible side. The points at which they differ are extent, definiteness and aim. In the first place the kingdom is much broader than the church, and includes all institutions, principles and agencies that make for the advancement of the divine will. The church is a specific and definite influence for the realization of the ideal furnished in the kingdom. It is the chief agency. Moreover the kingdom is a vague outline, vast and expansive, like a sphere of light; the church is the embodiment and localization of this sphere, if not like the luminary from which the light issues, at least like a spot at which it is focussed, and from which it radiates anew.

How compactly did Jesus intend to have the Messianic community organized is a question sometimes dismissed with an insufficient regard to the facts given in the records. It may be true that Jesus did not legislate in this matter or in any other matter. But he expressed himself concerning the general plan and principles that might be useful in the self-development of the body of his followers as an organization. And this preëminently in a passage which has been understood in a wide variety of ways. The occasion was the confession of Peter at Cæsarea Philippi (Mt. xvi. 16). Here he addressed to Peter the words, "Thou art a rock, and upon this rock will I build my church."

What do these words mean? We may set aside without extended consideration the suggestion that Jesus pointed to himself as he used the demonstrative pronoun "this." Grammatically, without some adversative conjunction, such a transition of thought would be inadmissible. It is evidently Peter who is the rock, and Jesus could not pass to the thought that the church must be founded upon himself who is also a rock and a stronger and firmer one without at least inserting a "but"; "Thou art Peter, a rock; but upon this rock (myself) will I build my church." It is not denied that Christ is the cornerstone and foundation of his church. That thought is both implicit, and enunciated and emphasized elsewhere. It is not, however, intended to be expressed in this place.

The same reasoning, though in a different way, would hold against making the mere faith of Peter, as shown in his confession, the foundation of the church. According to this idea, Jesus on hearing Peter's words recognized in them the fundamental principle and indispensable

[5] ἀπόστολος from ἀπό and στέλλω

platform upon which all that enter his organization must stand. He further assured his disciples that with such a faith in him they might be confident of ultimate victory. The prospect might be gloomy for the community; but faith in him as the Messiah is a foundation not to be shaken. Yet it is not capable of being deduced directly from the words of Jesus. It would require a violent transition of thought from the declaration that Peter is a rock. Perhaps a paraphrase might show plainly how much it would be necessary to supply to make this interpretation natural: "Thou art the rock disciple, and upon thy faith as the strength of thy rock nature will I build my church."

Peter is the rock. That is his name.[6] But is he the rock as the individual Peter or as the type of the aggressive man who has faith and is ready to express it? The former of these alternatives is the familiar one taken by the Roman Church. Jesus in these words confers upon Peter a permanent individual primacy with a continued line of succession. He founded a special office of headship over the church, making Peter the first incumbent of it. The circumstances, however, do not warrant this conception. Even if headship were designed, as Dr. Hort observes, "some other image than that of the ground under a foundation must have been chosen."[7] Moreover other speeches of Jesus addressed to Peter make it impossible to think that he could have designated him or any other man as the primate of his church. To the twelve disciples he assigned equal honor upon twelve thrones in the judgment of the world (Mt. xix. 28). When asked who is the greatest in the kingdom of God, he did not point to Peter, but took a little child and put it in their midst, saying, "Whosoever shall humble himself as this little child, the same is greatest in the kingdom of heaven" (Mt. xviii. 1, 2), and his earliest followers evidently did not understand him as either creating such an office or calling upon Peter to be its first occupant. In the church at Jerusalem James, not Peter, was the foremost man, and when the assemblage took place at which the question of the circumcision of Gentile converts was considered, it was James who presided. Nowhere do the other apostles look upon Peter with any more deference than was due to his naturally aggressive attitude and character. They called him to account for eating with the Gentiles (Acts xi. 2, 3), and again for yielding to Jewish prejudices and declining to hold fellowship with converts from among the heathen (Gal. ii. 11).

It is, however, weakening the thought of Jesus and emptying it of its most important content to say that Peter, though not as the first of a succession of heads of the church, was still individually to be the foundation stone as the first confessed Christian. This would mean that as the first to make the open confession of the Messiahship of Jesus, he was the first to be admitted into the membership of the new community. He was the first on the list of its charter numbers. That is an honor, but not a mere empty honor. It takes greater power to

---

[6] In the Aramaic, which was undoubtedly spoken upon the occasion, the word *Kepha* was both the name of Peter and the word for stone.
[7] *The Christian Ecclesia*, p. 16.

initiate than to continue. The first to enter into a noble and worthy enterprise deserves more credit than those who later join it when the rightness of its claim is more concrete and visible or its prospect of success better assured. But it is more than a first charter member that Jesus sees in Peter. It is a type of man, a character. He calls him the rock. It is not simply a first stone to be followed by many others that he is to serve, but as the rock that is to bear the weight of a structure. The fact that he placed himself where he did caused a succession of others to do likewise. His action was in a true sense creative.

Peter was not only the first among the disciples, but the exponent of their common faith and character, their representative and leader. Both during the time of Jesus' earthly ministry and after his ascension, Peter was the head and spokesman of the whole company. And it was because he expressed the common thought of all that he was selected as the recipient of the address in question. Peter is then the rock foundation of the church because of his character; and it is as if Jesus had said to him, "Upon the type of man that thou art, as shown by thy confession, I will build my church." That character and confession are not in themselves the products of mere natural or human activity, but of the divine efficiency. "For flesh and blood hath not revealed this unto thee but my Father which is in heaven." The church of Christ is, therefore, to be built upon a type of man enlightened by God and consequently believing in Jesus as Christ, and confessing him before the world. To this church, thus constituted, Jesus also gives "the power of the keys."

2. MEMBERSHIP OF THE MESSIANIC COMMUNITY.—The sole condition of entrance into the church is the open confession of Jesus as "the Christ, the son of God." Other than this none is mentioned anywhere. But this is essential. In the nature of the case none others could be members of a Messianic community than those who accepted the Messiah in his own sense, *i.e.*, as the revealer of God the Father and the redeemer from all evil. And whosoever accepts Him clearly knowing the import of his action could do nothing else but express his acceptance before the world. Apart from this confessed faith in him the community could have no coherence and must remain an unorganized, inchoate mass.

Within the community thus constituted the dominant principle is the spirit of brotherhood. "And all ye are brethren" (Mt. xxiii. 8). "And if thy brother offend against thee, show his faults between thee and him alone: if he hear thee, thou hast gained thy brother" (Mt. xviii. 15). And nothing seems to have laid hold of the earliest disciples more firmly than this thought that in Christ they were brought to a fraternal relation with one another. During the period when they went about without a definite name and when they were unconsciously feeling for that designation which should distinguish them from all other men the term "brethren" was deemed more expressive of their mutual relations than any other word. Therefore long before the world learned to call them Christians they had called themselves the "Brethren." The idea of brotherhood was simply the consistent carrying out of the central element in the revelation of Jesus. If God was henceforth to be known as the common Father, those who recognized him as such could not fail to recognize in each other brethren of the same household.

The principle of brotherhood thoroughly appreciated and faithfully obeyed develops a type of character. The member of the Messianic community under its molding power becomes free from the faults and blemishes of a self-centered and self-seeking disposition. He grows in meekness, humility, tolerance long-suffering in a forgiving and self-sacrificing spirit. In addition to these passive characteristics he develops the more active ones of independence of human judgments, aggressiveness in service, of loyalty toward God, a prayerful spirit and constant dependence on God for all that is best for himself and for the world.

3. THE TASK OF THE CHURCH.—Jesus set before his followers a twofold work. On the one side as a body they must preserve themselves from the forces of spiritual decay; on the other, they must promote the kingdom of God throughout the whole world, or in other words the church must assimilate the human race to itself.

(1) *Offenses.*—In the performance of the first part of the task Jesus anticipated that needs for mutual helpfulness would manifest themselves among his followers (Mt. xviii. 15-20). First of all misunderstandings leading to recriminations and charges of offense would emerge. His instructions concerning these were explicit and yet scarcely legalistic and technical. He said: "If thy brother shall trespass against thee, go tell him his fault between thee and him alone: if he shall hear thee, thou hast gained thy brother." That is certainly the first victory of a genuine fraternal feeling. If love is at the base of brotherhood, it will lead to the taking of a charitable view of the offense; it will avoid publicity with its attendant misunderstandings and aggravations of the offense. It will seek for a heart to heart explanation. If this explanation is forthcoming and proves satisfactory, it will dictate the spontaneous full and free forgiveness of the offense. In the spirit of long-suffering this process may be repeated indefinitely. "I say not unto thee, until seven times, but until seventy times seven." But brotherly love must not be confounded with weak indulgence overlooking and sheltering sin because of the inconvenience of probing and removing it, or of the pain that may be caused in the effort to do this. Indeed it could not be a true brotherly love unless it were also firm in the desire for the brother's good and made every possible attempt to convert him from this error and gain him for the kingdom of God.

The next step recommended is in perfect consistency with the first. "But if he will not hear thee, then take with thee one or two more that in the mouth of two or three witnesses every word may be established." When the alleged trespass is by the refusal of its perpetrator to recognize it as such reduced to a difference of point of view, it becomes possible that it was not a case of simple trespass but a mistake on the part of the complainant. And, if so, brotherly love would require the intervention of disinterested and unbiased brethren to settle the question. With their minds unclouded by selfish interest and their hearts full of tender affection for both parties, the two or three witnesses can form a true judgment and bear true testimony in the case. Their word "is established." But there is a possibility that the case of offense may not be settled even thus. The offender may prove obdurate; or the judgment of the two or three may be considered erroneous. A third step then becomes necessary which equally with the first two is the outcome of brotherly love. "And if he shall neglect to hear them tell it unto the church." No true disciple can set his judgment in a private and personal matter against that of the church. If he have in his heart the true love of a brother, he will yield to the voice of his brethren collectively. And thus the church becomes the last court of appeal. "And if he neglect to hear the church, let him be to thee as an heathen man and a publican." His failure to submit to the finding of the brotherhood breaks the tie that connects him with them.

Authority is thus vested in the whole body of believers. "Verily I say unto you, whatsoever ye shall bind on earth shall be bound in heaven, and whatsoever ye shall loose on earth shall be loosed in heaven. For where two or three are gathered in my name, there am I in the midst of them." The words are addressed to the whole band of disciples; and to these not in the capacity of twelve apostles, for it is not at all probable that the Twelve, neither more nor fewer, were his listeners at the time, but the whole group of his followers. And this is made the clearer by the closing words that generalize the commission. Where two or three come together as Christians, i.e., in the name of Christ, his presence invests them with authority, it makes them a part, an arm of his church. It is his authority expressed through them.

But authority is a word used in more than one sense; and when it is introduced into a discussion of the teaching of Jesus it needs careful explanation. That Jesus realized the necessity of a cohesive principle to keep his followers together as a company can be assumed without fear of contradiction. That he expected the sense of brotherhood to furnish this principle of cohesion is also unquestionable. But it is also true that, among the words he is reported to have spoken to them, certain ones indicate along what lines the consciousness of brotherhood among his followers was to be developed and supported in order to be an effective means of solidarity and practically secure harmony and coöperation among them.

These are the words which he added to his direction concerning the settlement of so-called offenses among them (Mt. xviii. 18). "Verily I say unto you what things soever ye shall bind on earth shall be bound in heaven; and what things soever ye shall loose on earth shall be loosed in heaven." The language used here is Jewish rabbinical and its exact meaning must be sought for in the contemporaneous usage of the phrase "to bind and to loose." To bind according to the rabbinical usage of the day was to forbid. To loose was to allow. The church is to declare what is permitted and what is not. Lightfoot [8] thus paraphrases the words with primary reference to the Mosaic Law: "Whatsoever ye shall bind in the law of Moses, that is forbid, it shall be forbidden, the divine authority confirming it; and whatsoever ye shall loose, that is permit, or shall teach that it is permitted and lawful, shall be lawful and permitted. Hence they bound, that is forbade, circumcision to the believers; eating of things offered to idols, of things strangled and of blood for a time to the Gentiles. They loosed, that is allowed, purification to Paul and to four other brethren, etc." This interpretation is based upon the principle that the church shall make the laws which will govern her membership. She may declare what is forbidden and what is permitted not, however, in the strict terms, it asserts merely by singling out parts of the Mosaic legislation and binding them or forbidding their practice and sanctioning others, and thus loosing them, but by working out her own legislation as a social organism. As the Law of Moses was the working code with which the organization began, this legislative power was, of course, in part exercised as above explained; but the broader principle underlying the instructions of Jesus is the general one that his church has legislative authority.

In harmony with this conclusion we must understand "the power of the keys." First of all it was not to Peter as the official head of the church that the emblems of authority were delivered, but to Peter as the leader and representative of the whole body of disciples. The church has the power of the keys of the kingdom of Heaven in the sense that a declaration by her that an individual is a citizen of the kingdom may be safely taken as the statement of a fact. This, however, must not be pressed to mean that the church can use such power arbitrarily, without conscientious regard to actual realities and simply out of weak, sentimental yielding to human wishes or for the sake of securing earthly and sordid ends. For the church to do this would be to cease to act as the body of which Christ is the soul and thereby to forfeit the power of the keys. But more than in the declaratory sense the church has the power of the keys in the privilege she enjoys of bringing men to the knowledge of God and thus leading them into his kingdom. In other words she opens the kingdom to men through the preaching of the gospel. As Beyschlag very well observes, "The keys of the kingdom of Heaven are the truths of the gospel, the fact of the coming of the kingdom of God; by these Jesus himself has hitherto opened the kingdom of Heaven to men or closed it in the case of those who lacked susceptibility. He now desires to bequeath them to the first, and, as yet, the only one who has truly known him; for he only can use them according to his mind." [9]

(2) *Worship.*—Mutual interest and care in a community brought together by spiritual and religious bonds naturally develops associations not only in the relationships of daily life but in the fellowship of

---

[8] *Horæ Hebraicæ*, Oxf. edition, II. p. 237-240.
[9] *New Test. Theol.*, I. p. 175.

THE MESSIANIC COMMUNITY

common worship. In the Judaism of Jesus' day two types of worship prevailed—that of the temple and that of the synagogue—the one dignified, uniform and stately, the other free and spontaneous. Jesus took part in both. But on the whole the latter afforded larger opportunities for the expression and realization of his ideals. At all events he anticipated that his followers would come together as groups after the manner of the faithful members of synagogues. "Where two or three are gathered in my name," and "if two or three of you will agree on earth as touching anything that ye shall ask, it shall be done for you of my Father who is in heaven," are the words in which he referred to the matter. But beyond this recognition of the necessity and great value of assemblings for public worship he gave no directions as to how it should be conducted or what forms should be used in it.

(3) *Sacraments.*—This general statement will not be disputed if by public worship is meant only the periodical appearance together of the faithful for prayer, praise and instruction. But common worship has special impressive incidents and features known as sacraments. Concerning these it has been claimed that Jesus did leave explicit directions. And, per contra, this has been denied. The denial was based in earlier days on more general grounds of probability supported by exegetical considerations. In more recent days these grounds for disputing the interest of Jesus in sacraments have been shifted into the critical field.

The facts will bear investigation. Concerning the Lord's Supper they may be summarized as follows:[10] There are four accounts of the institution in the New Testament, those of Matthew, Mark, Luke and Paul (I Cor. xi. 23). These four may be reduced into two groups which are so related that they probably represent one tradition each. Matthew and Mark stand together in one group, and Luke and Paul in the other. To read Matthew and Mark alone one would not gather that in eating the last meal with his disciples Jesus was establishing a new rite. He is represented as simply taking the elements and handing them to the disciples with the words, "Take ye." The case is otherwise put by Paul and Luke. In their report Jesus is made to add: "This do in remembrance of me." According to Matthew and Mark, Jesus simply indicated to the intimate circle of his followers, as if in an acted parable, that he was about to die and that his death was to inure to their benefit. "Expecting as he did to return at an early day, he can scarcely have been solicitous to provide for the preservation of his memory—it was apparently not the institution of a memorial feast he had in mind so much as the announcement of his impending death and assurance that it would result not in evil but in good to his disciples."[11] But what Jesus did not have in mind seems to have been brought about by the time that Paul wrote to the Corinthians. The disciples very often, perhaps at every meal, thought and spoke of the Last Supper as a separate and special meal and to distinguish it from

---

[10] See Jülicher, *Theol. Abhandl.* C. V., Weizsäcker, *Gewidmet*, p. 217.
[11] McGiffert, *Apostolic Age,* pp. 68-69. Percy Gardner, *The Origin of the Lord's Supper,* also takes a similar view.

all others as a ceremony for the remembrance of the death of Jesus, ascribed to Jesus himself the establishment of it.

Perhaps (Briggs adds) on a subsequent occasion after his resurrection, Jesus being present with the disciples at one of the Passover celebrations observed by them, enjoined upon them the repetition and perpetual observance of that portion which had reference to his own death, the Lord's Supper. Thus the Apostle became the real founder of the sacrament. What he had in mind in his account of the origin of the institution was true. The words which he reported were all uttered by Jesus, but they were uttered on two separate occasions, some upon the eating of the last meal with his disciples, and some between his resurrection and ascension. He simply brought them together into one report. As they all bore on the same subject—the origin of the Supper as a church observance—it would be eminently fitting that they should be blended into unity. The difficulty however is that Paul does this without giving the least intimation that the words represent two separate occasions and there is not a shred of evidence that Jesus said anything of the sort alleged after his resurrection. Moreover, if the phrase, "This do in remembrance of me," was uttered by Jesus, whether before or after his resurrection, the institution of the Lord's Supper was after all a historical act of his own, and the traditional view on the point is reached though by a somewhat circuitous critical route.

The starting point for the settlement of the questions thus raised must be the undisputed fact that Jesus and his disciples sat together in the upper room to partake of a meal which has ever since been known as the Last Supper. All that is credibly recorded of what was done and said at this meal is of secondary importance from the point of view of Jesus' intention to institute a sacrament except the words: "This do in remembrance of me." While Mark and Matthew do not include these words in their report, no valid reason has been shown why Jesus should not, or did not, utter them. Since the Pauline account, of which that of Luke is practically a duplicate, does give them and since the Pauline practice of observing the Lord's Supper according to his own words ("I have reecived," cf. I Cor. xi. 23) is traceable to the original practice of those who heard Jesus and took part with him in the Last Supper, the presumption is all in favor of the originality of the words in dispute. Their omission from the alternate account of Matthew and Mark may be due to the very fact of their familiarity.

A similar discussion has been carried on regarding the institution of baptism. The debate here, too, is concerned mainly with the genuineness of the words in which the ordinance seems to be commanded. These words constitute the familiar Great Commission: "Go ye therefore and make disciples of all nations, baptizing them in the name of the Father and of the Son and of the Holy Spirit" (Mt. xxviii. 19). The point of attack against the Commission is, in general, its alleged lack of harmony with the plainer thought of Jesus himself and its agreement with later conditions. It is alleged that "it canonizes a later ecclesiastical situation; that its setting, the narrative of the forty days, is legendary; that a comparative study of the Synoptic texts tells against it; and that the trinitarian formula intertwined with baptism in it is foreign to the lips of Jesus." All these considerations are a priori. Over against them there lies the unquestioned fact that from the very first day new members were admitted into the Christian brotherhood by the rite of baptism. It is more reasonable to suppose that this practice is based on the known desire of Jesus than that the prevalence of the practice superinduced an unhistorical logion of Jesus. Moreover for such a practice there was a precedent in the example of John the Baptist.

But what was the design of these ordinances? There is nothing more than a loose connection between them and the rites of the Old Testament. Therefore we cannot determine their meaning by affiliating them with predecessors in the Old Testament. Evidently, however, in external form they are both suggested by older practices and institutions, traceable back to Old Testament antecedents. In the common meal of the household upon the festival of the Passover, there was a pattern ready to hand for just the expression of the ideas to be put in the Lord's Supper. Indeed Semitic archæologists now tell us that every meal in primitive times in Israel was a sacrificial one, that a portion was separated for God who was regarded as a member of the household and offered to him by the father of the household in the capacity of a priest. In later Judaism common meals were not seldom used as the occasions for the expression of common interests and religious fellowship among the pious (cf. Jos. *Ant.* XIV. 215; III Mac. vi. 35). In a similar way the form of baptism was already in existence. Jesus simply adopted it and gave it a meaning of its own. In justification of this statement it is scarcely necessary to do more than point to the custom of subjecting proselytes to a baptismal purification (*Tbilah*). In the first century of the Christian era, this was a universally prevalent practice considered almost as important and as necessary as circumcision for the admission of pagan converts into Judaism. And it grew no doubt out of the ceremonial lustrations prescribed in the Mosaic Law. Neither common meals, however, nor proselyte baptism were assigned sacramental significance in the strict sense. They were sacramental only if a sacrament is a symbolical act expressive of gracious processes and conditions already complete.[12]

[12] Bousset, *Die Religion des Judentums,* p. 182.

CHAPTER XI

THE NEW RIGHTEOUSNESS

EITHER by virtue of enactment or by the tacit self-expression in laws found convenient in its experience, every community lives under an organic law or constitution. The organic law of the Christian brotherhood is summed up in the single term "righteousness." It is a term found by Jesus in the usage of his time and inherited from the Old Testament. It signifies not any particular aspect of conduct or character, but rather the whole ethical quality of life. The righteous are those who conform to the divine law and are acceptable to God. Righteousness is a synonym for moral goodness. To discourse about righteousness was to expatiate on ethics or on some aspect of it. Jesus' teaching on righteousness in the kingdom of God is therefore practically his system of ethics.

1. THE OLD RIGHTEOUSNESS AND THE NEW.—There were several moral ideals before the minds of Jesus' contemporaries. The first was the Pagan. With this the Jewish people had little to do. They did, indeed, see it practically at work; but its failure was patent. It made no appeal to them, neither did it affect their conduct. Therefore Jesus, too, leaves it out of account with the mere intimation that it is unworthy of the aspirant to membership in the kingdom of God (Mt. v. 47, "Do not even the Gentiles the same?"). Another ethical ideal was the Pharisaic. Its adherents assumed that it was the same as that of the Old Testament. Before Jesus lay the task of leading men to see that it was different. Then there was the Old Testament ideal. It was presented in concrete precepts deriving their force from the circumstances of their delivery, but restricting its breadth and binding down to material elements its spirituality. The task of revealing the difference between contemporary conceptions and the Old Testament conception was delicate. But that of freeing the Old Testament conception from its concrete limitations and showing its essential vitality was vastly more delicate. The accomplishment of this double task constitutes the virtual revelation of another and new moral ideal to the age.

The disclosing of the vital principle of the Old Testament moral law Jesus called its "fulfilment" (Mt. v. 17). It was easy to misunderstand his attitude and his intention in dealing with it. Therefore he protested at the outset that he had no design to impair or nullify it. His purpose was rather to give it full force and freedom by cutting it loose from its temporary connections. This he explained by selecting a few instances of precept and showing that the concrete and temporary

THE NEW RIGHTEOUSNESS

elements in its delivery really held its essential principles. "Ye have heard that it was said by them of old time, Thou shalt not kill; and whosoever shall kill shall be in danger of the judgment; but I say unto you, that whosoever is angry with his brother without a cause shall be in danger of the judgment" (Mt. v. 21, 22). The mere act of taking life was but a partial index of the moral principle involved in the commandment. One might violate the letter of the law and take life, as the law itself in some of its penal provisions directed, without disobeying its spirit. On the other hand and much oftener, if one limited himself to its letter, one might be blameless outwardly, but a violator in reality. This is true of the other prescriptions used by way of illustration and, of course, with the vastly larger number which are not cited at all. The moral code of the Old Testament was framed according to Jesus with a view to the capacity of those to whom it was first given. It was not the law concerning divorce only that was given in the precise Old Testament form, "for the hardness of your hearts." And Jesus, therefore, taught that "from the beginning it was not so." That is, in the nature of things, as given in the creator's ideal, the essence of the ethical law is spiritual. It looks to the universal man as its subject and not simply to the Hebrew. And its application must set aside the Hebrew as such and strike deeper to the point where time and circumstance make no difference. So far as the Old Testament expression of it was conditioned by time and circumstance and directed to the Jew, it must yield to a new expression: "I say unto you."

But if Jesus was not quite satisfied with the form of the moral law given in the Old Testament, he was far less satisfied with the interpretation given of it by the scribes and Pharisees. Indeed upon this point his attitude can be characterized as nothing less than open hostility. His tone was calm, and his expressions free from violence; but his judgment of it is unfaltering, and his sentence amounts to a condemnation of it as hopelessly defective. Unless something better could be brought forth than the Pharisaic ideal, men could in no case enter into the kingdom of God. Its fruit as seen in its teachers was vain glory. "All their works they do for to be seen of men; they make broad their phylacteries and enlarge the borders of their garments, and love the uppermost room at feasts and the chief seats in synagogues, and greetings in the markets, and to be called of men, Rabbi, Rabbi" (Mt. xxiii. 5-7).

Against tradition as such Jesus has no word of criticism. A precept is not wrong nor is a statement untrue simply because it is a matter of tradition. On the contrary there is a legitimate place and work for tradition and when it limits itself to these, it may be useful. The framers of the tradition of his day were in a certain sense worthy of attention. "The scribes and the Pharisees sit in Moses' seat. All, therefore, whatsoever they bid you observe, observe and do" (Mt. xxiii. 2, 3). Not, of course, indiscriminately but with reference to their harmony with Moses and the Mosaic teaching. There is a deference to be paid even to the human vehicles through which the divine will is transmitted through the generations; but these vehicles must always be held open to scrutiny and if found defective, it is imperative that they should be set aside.

(1) The points at which Jesus attacked the Pharisaic ideal of morality include first of all its subordinating the divine to human authority. Of this he directly and plainly charged the Pharisees. "For, laying aside the commandment of God, ye hold the tradition of men." And he gives a demonstration of the truth of his charge in the familiar instance of the fifth commandment of the Decalogue. The Law explicitly said, "Honor thy father and thy mother"; but the teachers of the day taught: "If a man shall say to his father or mother, it is Corban, that is to say, a gift, by whatsoever thou mightest be profited by me, he shall be free, i.e., of his obligation to contribute that to the support of his parents (Mk. vii. 8-13). Here was a case of the manifest reversal of the intent of the Law. The Law was of divine authority. The tradition which annulled it was of human origin; and yet when it came to a choice between the two, the preference was given to the human rather than the divine. Such tampering with conscience as this involved would result only in the deadening of the moral nature.

(2) Another point at which Jesus attacked the current ideal was its subordination of the internal to the external. The moral law is a mere abstraction unless it issues in outward applications. And in the application of it outwardly questions must arise. A healthy, strong moral nature will strive to answer these questions for itself, but the weak have always clamored for prescriptions defining the Law in detail, and thus answering such questions beforehand. It was this that led to the development of the so-called "hedge" around the Law in the days preceding Jesus. In the *Pirqe Aboth* it is said: "Moses received the Torah from Sinai, and delivered it to Jehoshuah, and Jehoshuah to the elders, and the elders to the prophets, and the prophets to the men of the great synagogue. They said three things, 'Be deliberate in judgment; raise up many disciples; and make a fence to the Law.'"[1] That is, surround the Law with special rules and prescriptions that will guard against transgression through ignorance or inadvertence. "Impose additional restrictions so as to keep at a safe distance from forbidden ground."[2]

The building of this fence meant the multiplication of precepts covering every conceivable sort of detail. It aimed to externalize the spirit of it so as to make its observance or violation a matter of easy discernment, a palpable thing. And it effectually did so. The multitude of its prescriptions could be easily grasped, because they were outward rules. As a matter of inner right for instance, the law provided for the payment of tithes; but it was not so easy to decide what sort of product should be tithed. In building the fence the rabbis externalized the Law by deciding that even garden herbs, mint, and cummin must be tithed. The difficulty was removed, but with its removal attention was fixed upon that which was of secondary importance and "the weightier matters of judgment and the love of God" were lost sight

[1] I. i.
[2] C. Taylor, *Sayings of the Fathers*, p. 11, note.

of. Hence the severe arraignment of the system: "Now do ye Pharisees make clean the outside of the cup and platter, but your inward parts are full of ravening and wickedness" (Lk. xii. 39). So, also, when he compared them to whited sepulchers which appear beautiful without, but within are full of dead men's bones (Mt. xxiii. 27), *i.e.*, from the point of view of the Pharisees' loving and boasting of ceremonial purity, they were full of uncleanness.

(3) Akin to the defect of laying undue emphasis on the outward is that of depriving the moral of its true significance by ignoring its motive. The Pharisaic ethic judged all action as such, paying no heed to its motive. Worse still it approved of actions apparently good even when they sprang from selfish and unworthy motives. In either case morality ceased to exist. If good is done perfunctorily from constraint, it has no ethical character because it has settled to the level of mechanical action. If it is done from other than the motives furnished by the conscience, it is not the offspring of the moral nature, but of the intellectual. It becomes a matter of calculation and self-interest. The state of things which Jesus found predominant in this respect partook of both of these weaknesses. The prescriptions of the Law were performed either perfunctorily by the common people, or by the more zealous Pharisees from love of ostentation. And for this latter reason they were most unsparingly exposed by him. (Mt. xxiii. 5-7).

(4) Still another fault of the moral system of the Pharisees was its breaking into a vast multitude of disconnected precepts. This was an inevitable consequence of the development of the so-called "hedge." It sprang from the laudable desire to be exhaustive. If the Law needed fencing, it were well that the fence should be adequate. Every portion of it should be carefully protected with rules, making it impossible for the loyal Israelite to transgress it. But the result was a burdensome code with an enormous number of specifications impossible to grasp and unify in one vivid governing principle. In the attempt to make it easier to know the bearing of the Law, the fence had led to the greater difficulty arising from this impossibility of grasping and holding its innumerable prescriptions. Jesus in speaking of its advocates says: "They bind heavy burdens and grievous to be borne and lay them on men's shoulders" (Mt. xxiii. 46). For himself when asked what is the chiefest of the commandments, he does not hesitate to sum it all up in one great principle, that of love with its two natural phases, toward God, and toward man.

The method and point of view of Jesus are those of the Hebrew prophet rather than of the classical or modern philosopher. Therefore he does not give his ethical teaching in academic propositions, but embodies it in the call to reform, starting from the existing evil condition. The glaring defects of the current system could not fail to be seen in the fruit it bore in the characters of the most sincere and enthusiastic advocates. They were notorious for the vices of hypocrisy, vanity, self-esteem and contemptuousness. Because their minds were fixed on the performance of mere outward acts without regard to the motives from which they should spring, they became accustomed to measure their qualities by the judgment of those about them. They did their righteousness to be seen of men, and they had their reward. When they had secured the approval of a shallow and superficial public, they readily gave their own approval to themselves and settled down to a self-complacency that rendered growth impossible. Then judging those who failed to come up to their standard, they looked down upon them as hopeless reprobates. They constituted a moral aristocracy practically equivalent to a caste. They regarded the common people as the profane rabble (*am hâaretz*). They thanked God that they were different from other men. And lest they should be assimilated by contact with others, they refused to associate outside of their own class. Jesus denounced this type in scathing terms. He warned his own disciples to beware of those "which love to go in long clothing, and love salutations in the market places and the chief seats in the synagogue and the uppermost rooms at feasts, which devour widows' houses, and for a pretense make long prayers" (Mk. xii. 38-40; Lk. xx. 46-47). He pronounced them worthy of condemnation and justified the penitent publican before the Pharisee of this type. He was roused to the highest point of indignation as he thought of their evil influence (Lk. xviii. 14; xvi. 14; xi. 42ff.).

In one particular on which later thought has departed from the ethics of Pharisaism Jesus found no fault with it. This was the intimate association of the moral and religious elements in life. Pharisaism had its origin in an effort to conserve the old religious ideals of Israel; but these were embodied in a ritual with specifications regarding purity, fasting and prayer. As it grew in power, it was inevitable that it should lay stress on ritual details. But the line between ritual prescriptions and ethical rules is never clearly drawn. The Pharisaic conception of righteousness came to be that of a comprehensive rule of life involving both the religious and the moral natures. And so intimately were the two blended in profession and conduct that the effort to separate was bound to fail either by growing into a pedantic and useless analysis or by way of resulting in a fictitious line in human conduct where nature has not provided one.

In the mind of Jesus ethics and religion are not separate spheres loosely connected with one another or, worse still, altogether disconnected. They are rather one stream combining healing and thirst-appeasing qualities; one beam of sunlight, with illumining and warming power. Religion without morality is void and useless. The man who under the religious impulse will take his offering to the altar, but is conscious of a moral offense of which he is chargeable even though he may feel that he is innocent of the charge, must first go and make an honest effort to remove it, and then come to perform his religious service (Mt. v. 23-24). On the other hand the moral life apart from the religious is not complete. The order is, first, "Thou shalt love the Lord thy God with all thy heart," and then "thou shalt love thy neighbor as thyself." Righteousness should not be done as unto men only. "Take heed that ye do not your righteousness before men"; that is, not merely before bystanders as witnesses. That might be a very easy

THE NEW RIGHTEOUSNESS

thing to avoid; but before men even as beneficiaries of it. "But when thou doest righteousness, let not thy left hand know what thy right hand doeth, that thy righteousness may be in secret; and thy father which seeth in secret himself will reward thee openly" (Mt. vi. 4).

2. THE ETHICAL IDEAL OF JESUS.—The ethical ideal of Jesus is the righteousness of God, and it is inextricably interwoven with his kingdom (Mt. vi. 33). It is the chief end and ultimate aim of the disciple to approve himself a worthy child of the Father which is in heaven, to "be perfect even as his Father which is in heaven is perfect."

Therefore, like his heavenly Father, he should "love his enemies, bless them that curse him, do good to them that hate him, and pray for them that despitefully use him," for the Father "maketh his sun to rise on the evil and on the good, and sendeth rain on the just and on the unjust." In other words the law of right conduct is according to Jesus at its root religious. It finds its normal expression in the character of God. To be perfect morally one must begin by knowing God aright. And the righteousness of God must serve as his measure and source of inspiration.

The phrase itself, "righteousness of God," is liable to be misunderstood because it is used by the Apostle Paul in a slightly different sense. It is not, however, on that account to be assumed as not used by Jesus at all. It certainly expresses his genuine thought. Here, too, the contrast between the ethical teaching of Jesus and that of the rabbis of his day is apparent. They conceived of God as a lawgiver, and of the relation of man to God as essentially a legal one. According to them obedience out of proper regard or without proper regard to the personal element in the case was the essence of righteousness. His conception of God as Father involves the retirement of law into the background in favor of the more potent and effective consciousness of divine sonship. The new motive achieves all that the law aims at and much more.

But if the consciousness of filial relation lies at the root of the moral life, the moving and shaping force of it can be nothing less than the principle of love (Mt. xxii. 34-40; Mk. xii. 28-31). The effort to be perfect like the heavenly Father is actuated by the desire to please him and at the same time to imitate him. To be moved by love in all things is to be godlike. Love is not a virtue among other virtues, but the life of all the virtues. In a certain aspect of it, love is broader than righteousness.

The qualities of the morality which Jesus inculcates are, therefore, lofty ideality in combination with regard for common, practical ends. (a) First, and above all, this morality is a spontaneous outgrowth. Commonly this feature of it is called inwardness. But if innerness is to be understood as pointing back to a hidden source within man, a mysterious something beneath the surface that cannot be probed, the term spontaneity describes it better. Yet it must be clearly understood that spontaneity is not causelessness, but rather freedom from constraint from without. Moral conduct is, from this aspect of it, not mechanical obedience to an external law, but the glad expression of a willing spirit. Compliance to the will of God makes up the essence of righteousness.

Spontaneity, moreover, means not merely inwardness as freedom from external restraint, but also positive ability to determine one's own moral course. Jesus would have his disciples decide the questions of conscience for themselves without asking for authoritative pronouncement upon them by rabbis whether living or ancient. None should have the name and authority of a rabbi among them. "Do not be called Rabbi, and call no man your father upon earth," does not, of course, mean that the mere calling men by such titles is in itself evil; but that where it means the recognition in those so called of a binding authority, it cripples the moral nature and to that extent deprives it of its vitality. This accounts for the independent attitude which Jesus assumed and imparted to his disciples in all matters pertaining to the outward practices of fasting and prayer, of ceremonial purification and abstinences and of the observance of the Sabbath. These practices are, to be sure, more ceremonial than moral; and yet the principle involved in them and in his judgment of them is equally applicable to the purely moral sphere.

(b) Because the moral ideal of Jesus is spiritual in its essence and moves from within outward, it is also all-pervasive. It penetrates the whole tissue of the human being and diffuses itself into its minutest interstices. There is no part of conduct which can escape its presence or fail to feel its influence. If the tree is sound in its inner life, it will send forth healthy sap into all its branches and twigs and produce healthy leaves and the right kind of fruit. If the spirit of brotherhood fills the heart, it will rise into the mind and give birth to brotherly thoughts and intentions; it will pervade the hands and feet and lend to brotherly deeds. It will affect every action Godward or manward. The distinction between great things and little does not disappear in the moral ideal of Jesus; but both great and little are controlled, each according to its importance by the desire to bring it into subjection to the same law of the divine household, the law of brotherly love.

The Pharisees, too, had realized the need of giving heed to the little things and of defining the duty of man toward God; at least they were applying the law of tithes to minute garden herbs—mint and cummin. In commenting upon this, Jesus did not declare that such trifles were exempt from the application of the principle underlying the law of tithing. On the contrary he said that they were not; because in the spiritual and, by parity, in the ethical sphere there are no trifles. "These things ought ye to have done." It was not because they condescended to little matters, but because they allowed the weightier matters of righteousness and the love of God to pass unobserved that they had failed. There is little risk of man's overdoing and much in his underestimating his duty. In the effort to include the less obvious matters men may let slip the more obvious ones. To Jesus any omission is a failure of the ideal.

It is in these principles that Jesus gave his disciples what in the schools is commonly called his ethical system. But he aimed to speak in concrete terms which the minds of his untutored followers could grasp; and he frequently gave utterance to expressions that sound like rules. These, however, are never to be taken as hard and fast legislation applicable under all conditions and in all circumstances. The applicability of every rule depends on the breadth and universality of the principle it aims to practicalize, and also on the typical or generic nature of the conditions under which it is given. But the great majority of the precepts ("sayings") of Jesus are easy to translate into the terms of universal life for all generations. The Golden Rule, so called, in particular, has appealed to men of all ages and races. It comes as near as any formula can to reducing the most universal principle of ethics into a practical precept. Its essence is nothing more nor less than the commandment, "Thou shalt love thy neighbor as thyself."

3. THE SOCIAL TEACHING OF JESUS.—In the domain of social life Jesus does not propose concrete measures for the reform or the organization of society or the purification of its institutions. This might lead to the impression that he was not interested in the knotty problems presented by human society. But on the other hand because his teachings invariably terminate in some practical good to man as a social being, it is possible to classify him among the great social agitators and reformers. The fact is that social and ethical are terms whose content can only theoretically be kept apart. If Jesus' teaching was essentially ethical, it was by that very fact essentially social. Without dealing with sociology as a science he effectually furnishes the key to the solution of all its problems. And this all the more effectively because he did it by inculcating principles and not by promulgating proposals of reform.

Chief and foremost among the institutions of society was the household. And the condition of affairs in his day did not leave Jesus the option of speaking or keeping silent upon the subject of the household. The question was fairly thrust before him. Among the Romans the household had ceased to be what it once had been, a sacred unity. The moralists and poets of the age give a sad picture of the situation. The Christian writers of a century or two later may be considered as looking upon it from the point of view of higher standards, but the heathen philosophers, whose minds one might suppose had been more or less hardened to the evil, speak in unmistakable terms.[3] But in the nearer circle of Judaism also the spirit of laxity appeared. By adopting a liberal interpretation of the Law of Deuteronomy, the rabbis had inculcated loose views of the marriage tie and without theorizing about the matter the Jews had in practice settled to the modern-day doctrine that marriage is a civil contract. To Jesus this was contrary to the will of God the Father, and in violation of the principle of brotherhood. He did not hesitate when the occasion offered to state his view in the most explicit terms.

And, first of all, he taught that the home was no institution of man's making, no mere result of a gradual development during the course of human history. If that were the case, there would have been a time

[3] Cf. Döllinger, *The Gentile and the Jew*, xi. 230ff.; Friedländer, *Sittengeschichte der Römer*, I. 5.

when the human race lived and fulfilled the will of God without it, and there might be a time, in a different stage of evolution in the future, when the family should be antiquated and outlived as a matter of convenience. There is no denial in all this either explicit or implicit of the evolution of the home as it now is from simpler and cruder beginnings. There is only the assertion that at the very outset it was a divine institution in all its essential features. "He who made them from the beginning made them male and female and said, For this cause shall a man leave his father and mother and cleave to his wife" (Mt. xxix. 5). Marriage, then, which is the bond that establishes the family is one of those matters that God has not left to man to arrange for himself according to his notion or to establish or abolish by his laws and statutes in accordance with changing custom or difference of temperament. He who created them had a definite plan on this subject, and it was a plan to prevail and last as long as mankind should.

That plan involved the union of one man with one woman. Violations of this rule Jesus considers as violations of the ideal. To this same general conclusion the age of Jesus had settled down, and it could interpose no objection to his insistence on them. Polygamy had become obsolete. With very few exceptions no Israelite wished to take advantage of the precedents so abundant in the earlier history of the Old Testament and maintain a household of many wives. There was, however, another practice which amounted to virtual polygamy, viz., easy divorce. What was practiced by the ancients under the form of legal marriage with more than one wife at the same time was practiced by Jesus' contemporaries, under the guise of divorcing one wife on slight grounds and marrying with another. Thus the appearance and responsibility of a polygamous household were avoided; but at the same time the essential principle of the family as divinely instituted was just as effectually set at naught. In denouncing easy divorce Jesus did not even await a specific opportunity to express his condemnation. In the Sermon on the Mount he almost seems to go out of his way to denounce the practice (Mt. v. 32). "Every one that putteth away his wife, saving for the cause of fornication, maketh her an adulteress; and whosoever shall marry her when she is put away committeth adultery" (Lk. xvi. 18).

Subsequently he was approached with the definite question, "Is it lawful for a man to put away his wife for every cause?" This was done in order to ensnare him. But instead of evading the issue or modifying his expression, he repeated his judgment with greater emphasis: "I say unto you whosoever shall put away his wife except it be for fornication and shall marry another, committeth adultery: and whoso marrieth her which is put away doth commit adultery" (Mt. xix. 9). This teaching was a bold departure from what was believed to be a divinely enacted law. Moses had prescribed that if a woman had found no favor in her husband's eyes because he found some uncleanness ("a matter of shame") in her, he should "write her a bill of divorcement and give it in her hand and send her out of his house, and when she is departed out of his house, she may go and be another man's wife" (Deut. xxiv. 1, 2). This was interpreted by the liberal school of Hillel as permitting the husband to put away his wife upon some very flimsy grounds, as for instance, if she had spoiled his dinner.

The later law as set forth in the Mishna explained the Mosaic provision in a still more lax spirit. A man might divorce his wife if some other woman pleased him better. A woman could not only be divorced at the will of her husband, but she might even lose her dowry therewith if she transgressed "the Law of Moses" or "the Laws of Israel." Under the former ("the Law of Moses") were included such things as failure to obey the prescriptions regarding tithing, or setting apart the first of the dough, or those regarding purifications. Under the latter ("the Laws of Israel") came such offenses as going out in public with uncovered head, spinning in the public streets, entering into conversation with men, to which others added the misdemeanor of brawling or disrespectfully speaking of the husband's parents in his presence. This was the state of thought and practice to which the mind of Judaism at the time of Jesus had practically settled down, though it may not have shown itself in its full results. Jesus unwaveringly set his face against it. He declared marriage to be irreversible, and divorce by law contrary to the will of the creator and the design of the creation.

"Why then," said they, "did Moses command to give a writing of divorcement?" Jesus did not deny either the genuineness of the law or the competency of Moses to legislate on the subject. He appealed rather to the principle that not even an ideal legislator, yea, not even God himself, could give an ideal legislation to a people unprepared to receive it. It must be more or less tempered to their condition of heart. The Law of Moses was given "for the hardness of their hearts." To an infantile race only such laws can be given as will at once restrain abuse and bring them out of their infantile condition by a gradual process of education. What they needed was the mellowing of their hard hearts. When that came, they could receive, appreciate and obey more perfect laws. Meanwhile the evil which they could not do away with might be kept in check by accommodated legislation.

Between the family, which is the most elementary social unit in the world, and the whole race of mankind, which is the most comprehensive, there stands the organized nation or state. And toward the state Jesus maintained a silence all the more noteworthy because it is in such contrast to his explicitness regarding the family. This silence, however, was neither accidental nor due to lack of interest in matters political. It is rather the result of a firm determination to preserve his freedom and spare himself for the higher affairs of the spiritual realm. Jesus could have easily implicated himself in the difficulties of the political situation of his day. The air was electric with the intense feeling prevalent on questions of government. But his own conception of the Messiahship contrasted with that of his countrymen made him careful to keep out of the main stream of political discussion. To do otherwise would have been to open himself to misunderstanding and to imperil his entire mission. Only by a complete silence on the political issues could he disengage the Messiahship from its political associations and present it freely as the spiritual office and function which he knew it to be. And even thus carefully as he avoided the subject, in the end his being put to death was based upon a trumped-up political ground. Jesus' reticence concerning the state then can only mean the subordination of its problems to the spiritual and moral. Not the disregard but the right approach to the question of the state was the most important thing in his mind.

The only definite utterance of Jesus on the question of the state is found in his words in answer to the question of the tax levied by the Roman government (Mt. xxiii. 18-22). The case of the tithe paid by a miraculous finding of coin in the fish (Mt. xvii. 27) does not bear on the subject. The organization which claimed this tax was not the state but the religious body. Jesus submitted to the authority of this ecclesiastical organization of the legitimacy and the rights of which when in its purity there was no question. The tax collected by the Roman government raised a different issue, that of the legitimacy of that government. "Is it lawful to give tribute unto Cæsar or not?" Is the supremacy of Cæsar over the chosen people of God rightful? Must a faithful Israelite recognize it as such? This was the essence of the question. And it must be said at once that the answer given by Jesus is affirmative without equivocation. It is not categorical in form, but none the less definite. In modern discussions of the subject it has been alleged that the opinion was given hypothetically, as if Jesus adroitly sought to escape committing himself. He asks regarding the coin, "Whose image and superscription is this? They say unto him, Cæsar's. Then said he unto them, Render therefore unto Cæsar the things that are Cæsar's, and unto God the things that are God's." If, that is to say, this coin belongs to Cæsar upon the principle that everyone has a right to his own, Cæsar has a right to receive it back. But this is entirely superficial. There are principles involved which it manifestly ignores. It is not because Cæsar issued the coin and it belonged to him that he had a right to collect it; but because he had the right to issue it, which very right was called in question. Jesus' answer is not hypothetical but parabolical. It means: "Since you recognize the right of Cæsar to issue the coin, a right acquired by conquest under the providence of God, the duty of obedience and support inevitably follows. But the right of the God by whose permission Cæsar holds his right should not be neglected." The question is not, Is any government right and legitimate? On that all were agreed. But is a pagan government over Israel to be accepted by the pious Jew and tacitly approved by the payment of the tax? Jesus shows that for the time being that question had been providentially settled.

Equally free from the entanglements of local and temporary interest and equally on the lofty plane of the permanent and universal are Jesus' teachings regarding property. This too, is a means toward an end, viz., the advancement of the reign of God in the inner man, the predominance of love and fraternity as the human correlative of the recognition of God as the Father. On the question, Is property in itself a violation of human rights?—a question which was not distinctly before the mind of his day—it is quite safe to say that Jesus would have given an emphatic negative answer. A man had a right to hold and to administer wealth. For wealth was a trust committed into his hands. By his faithfulness in its administration he may be tested. "For unto everyone that hath shall be given, and he shall have abundance; but from him that hath not even that which he hath shall be taken away" (Mt. xxv. 29).

The test of the proper administration of the trust is the promotion of the kingdom of God. "I say unto you, make to yourselves friends by means of the mammon of unrighteousness." And this mammon who is to serve for building up the higher and enduring life is simply earthly riches. It is the rich man, not as such, but as he has used his riches in a hard-hearted way, contrary to the will of God and in an unfraternal spirit toward his fellow man, who finds himself separated by an impassable gulf from the beatific presence of God. It is to test fidelity that all trusts are given. "He that is faithful in a very little, is also faithful in much; and he that is unrighteous in a very little is unrighteous also in much" (Lk. xvi. 9-10).

In his personal relations Jesus did not discriminate in favor of the poor or the rich. He associated with either class according to circumstances, encouraging both to use themselves and all they had in the service he was preaching. He invited himself to the house of Zachaeus. And when Zachaeus declared his intention to do right with and in matters pertaining to his money, Jesus heartily commended him. On the other hand the courtesies of hospitality did not prevent him from gently reproving the loveless politeness of the Pharisees who were also "full of extortion and wickedness" (Lk. xi. 39) and to urge them in the person of his host to give alms.

But Jesus saw plainly that wealth was attended with fearful perils, and he sounded distinct notes of warning against this aspect of it. So vivid indeed was his apprehension of the dangers of great wealth that he seems at times to have set his face against the rich as such. "Woe unto you that are rich," he is reported to have said (Lk. vi. 24), and to the young man who claimed to have kept the commandments from his youth up, "If thou wilt be perfect, go and sell that thou hast, and give to the poor, and thou shalt have treasure in heaven." And when the young man turned away because he had great possessions, Jesus said unto his disciples, "Verily I say unto you, that a rich man shall hardly enter into the kingdom of heaven . . . it is easier for a camel to go through a needle's eye, than for a rich man to enter into the kingdom of God" (Mt. xxix. 21-24). Jesus does not specifically name the moral snares that invariably accompany the acquisition and possession of wealth, but, without bringing them formally into the foreground, he shows that he felt their presence and allowed them to mould his expressions. "Lay not up for yourselves treasures upon earth, where moth and rust doth corrupt and where thieves break through and steal: but lay up for yourselves treasures in heaven, where neither moth nor rust doth corrupt, and where thieves do not break through nor steal: for where your treasure is there will your heart be also" (Mt. vi. 19-21). The primary danger pointed out here is the absorption of time and energy in the effort to acquire, preserve and increase one's earthly gains, crowding out the more profitable pursuits of spiritual and eternal treasure. Others, such as the temptation to use methods inconsistent with brotherliness in the effort to accumulate riches, the risk of developing a proud, contemptuous and tyrannical temperament because of the consciousness of power attendant upon the possession of wealth, the gradual disappearance of the tenderer feelings and the growth of hard and unsympathetic elements in the character, the reduction of the whole of life to the rigid and mechanical measures prevalent in commerce and industry, all these things underlie and actuate Jesus' warning cry against wealth. Nevertheless nowhere does he declaim against it as such. It is manifestly its perils to the higher man that stir him to pronounce his beatitude over poverty and his woe over riches. It is better not to have riches than to have and misuse them. But to have and use them for the advancement of God's reign upon earth is, after all, the ideal.

CHAPTER XII

THE KINGDOM IN THE FUTURE

UNQUESTIONABLY John the Baptist announced the kingdom of God as a divine project about to be realized in the immediate future. In doing this he did not speak of an unfamiliar matter for he found among his hearers a certain readiness to accept his message. When Jesus entered upon his public ministry, he also began by preaching the coming of the kingdom as an event to be expected. Did he, during the course of his ministry, retain the view that the kingdom was to be established at some later date? Or did he look upon it as already established upon earth and destined to grow into larger proportions in the future? If the former then he must have entertained an idea of the kingdom identical with that of his contemporaries. He must have thought of it as the result of a political upheaval and reorganization of the world order, culminating in the domination of the world by the Jewish nation under the leadership of the Messiah. If, however, Jesus thought of the kingdom as a living reality that had already begun an existence to be prolonged into the remote future, his conception was very different from any entertained either in his day or ever before.

1. THE KINGDOM IN PROSPECT.—The difference between the alternatives just stated has been developed in recent years into an acute antithesis. The first has been rightly called the apocalyptic and eschatological conception, the second the ethical and spiritual one. The two conceptions are different not only in their presentation of the nature of the kingdom, but also of the time and manner of its realization. Since the controversy based on their difference is waged on the ground of the facts as given in the sources, the best way to examine the merits of the two views is to state each with the support claimed for it.

(1) In favor of the apocalyptic and eschatological view it is claimed that it was the one generally held by the Jews of that time. From the Book of Daniel (ii.) they had come to learn that the fifth or Israelitish world empire would be established by a grand divine act. In that vision the establishment of the Messianic empire was symbolized by a stone cut "without (human) hands" from the mountain side, which would roll down and smite the feet of the image, causing it to crumble and disperse in a cloud of dust, while the stone grew into a great mountain.

At least during his Galilean ministry and perhaps all through his lifetime Jesus believed that this great event was to take place in his own lifetime. He sent his disciples to preach the coming of the kingdom and warned them in so doing that it was unnecessary to provide as if for a long journey (Mt. x. 6, 7, 10). He instructed them to reduce their stay in any special place to a minimum length (vs. 11-15). If persecution should break out, they were to withdraw to other cities. They were to waste no time; for time was short and precious. The kingdom would come before they had done going the round of the cities of Israel (v. 23). The death of John the Baptist was simply a foretoken of the advent of the kingdom.

But the opposition of the chiefs and the hardness of heart displayed by the people, forced Jesus to abandon the hope of a sudden change. He understood that much seed falls upon soil not quite ready for its reception, and that the generation in which he lived was far from prepared to accept the kingdom of God. Baldensperger compares Jesus to a hunter who is chasing game within sight, but is delayed by the necessity of opening a path through an impassable thicket which bars his way. The inevitable prospect of death loomed up before him; and the coming of the kingdom, therefore, receded somewhat into the future. He prepared his disciples for faithfully continuing the work begun by himself. As for himself at the proper time he would return, no longer under the guise of the poor, humble, unknown and unrecognized preacher, but "with power," "in the glory of the Father" (Mt. xix. 25-28; xxv. 31; Mk. x. 37; ix. 1; Lk. ix. 26).

Thus was the idea of the suddenness of the return incorporated into Jesus' expectations and preaching. And with this was the further expectation that he would find both the good and the wicked servants at their natural employment; and still further that this consummation would take place during the lifetime of the generation which was listening to him (Mt. xxiv. 45; xxv. 14; Lk. xii. 40; xvii. 20; xxi. 36; Mk. ix. 13, etc.).

But though to occur during that generation, its day and hour are known to the Father alone (Mk. xiii. 32). These two statements of a return during the lifetime of the generation to which he was speaking and of his ignorance as to the day and hour are not contradictory or mutually exclusive; they rather supplement and support each other. Jesus is not concerned with mathematical statements but with general principles. He dwells upon the certainty of the event without fixing on the minuter details of its time and manner of occurrence. The prediction of his rising from the dead is, moreover, made to mean the same thing as his return. The three days' period to be spent under the power of death must not be taken in the literal sense. That would be a contradiction of Mark xiii. 32. The meaning of "the three days" is rather similar to that of Hosea vi. 2. Jesus himself used parallel phraseology when he sent word to Herod (Lk. xiii. 32) saying, "Go ye and tell that fox, Behold I cast out devils and I do cures to-day and to-morrow, and the third day I shall be perfected."

This return was to be bodily and, therefore, visible. It would come as a sudden break into the order of earthly affairs as if from heaven. Its object, however, is not that he might wage war against the enemies of Israel and establish its universal ascendancy over the world powers (so fondly cherished by the Pharisees and Zealots), but in order to

THE KINGDOM IN THE FUTURE

judge all of the peoples of the earth and gather his own followers into eternal life (Mt. vii. 21-23; xvi. 27; xix. 28; xxv. 31-46; Mk. viii. 38; Lk. xvii. 30). His conception of the manner of the Messianic coming does not appear, therefore, to have differed in its general outline from that of his contemporaries, but his idea of the work of the Messiah after the kingdom is established is radically different.

As a confirmation of these conclusions, it is alleged that Jesus' second coming is foreshadowed always in the very body in which he was to die. For him, as for the Pharisees, the kingdom of God is a heavenly state upon earth. If he is to realize it in spite of his death, since he has not only consented to his death but has accepted it as an inevitable step on the way to the establishment of the kingdom, he must be raised from the dead, and that before the forces of decay had rendered it impossible for him to use the body in which he was at the time of the utterance of these predictions.

All of this is based upon the supposition that the conceptions as well as the language of Jesus were simply and purely those of his environment, that he did not transcend it in expression or in thought. The apocalyptic imagery of the day had become an integral part of his system. To see any other view in his teaching is to read into it what the events later proved to be facts rather than what he himself had in mind. And to do this is to spiritualize, or in other words to lose historical perspective and substitute ideals for facts.

But Jesus was evidently much concerned about the course of life of his followers and took pains to instruct them in the "new righteousness" of the kingdom. Why if the time was so short, should he take the trouble to elaborate and hold before them ethical ideals apparently of permanent value and validity? The question is answered by the school of apocalyptic interpreters by the assertion that ethical conduct is of the utmost importance. Even for the short interval of the duration of the old age it was worth while that the men expecting the coming change should live lives in harmony with its principles. All of Jesus' ethical teaching is just *"interim ethics."*

This general view agrees substantially with the old chiliastic eschatology. According to that system the kingdom of God as a political organization was by Jesus proposed to the Jewish leaders of his time. Had they accepted it, he would forthwith have established the kingdom. But since they rejected it, he held it in abeyance until the world in general should become conscious of its desperate need and God in his wisdom and justice saw fit to break into the course of affairs and establish it finally. When this moment arrived Jesus would make his appearance ($\pi\alpha\rho o \upsilon \sigma i \alpha$, "presence") in a second coming.

The differences between this earlier (chiliastic) eschatology and the modern eschatological rendering of the teaching of Jesus is that, according to the former, Jesus knew that the offer of the kingdom would be rejected by the Jews, and that his idea of the kingdom is literally accurate; according to the latter, he was mistaken in his expectations about it, that what truth there is in his teaching inheres in the essence not in the form of it, and that mentally he readjusted himself to the new light that came to him as his work advanced. But he proceeded to the very end of his earthly work with the same fixed notion that God would intervene preternaturally to establish the kingdom. As for himself until God did intervene, his work was to be prophetic and after the intervention he was to assume the new duties of king and judge in the established kingdom. To his keen mind, however, it became clear quite early in his ministry that his prophetic work must end in suffering and death. In this conviction he was reinforced by the remembrance of the fact that suffering and death had been frequently the lot of the prophets before him (Mt. xxiii. 37; Lk. xiii. 34). The figure of the suffering servant of Deutero-Isaiah, (Is. lii. 13; liii. 17) too, stood before him still further strengthening the conviction that as Messiah his death must be an integral part of his redemptive work, with all vicarious and atoning significance.[1]

(2) As against the purely apocalyptic construction of the kingdom of God, those who hold to the ethical and spiritual interpretation contend that it does not explain much even of the phraseology used by Jesus. In a series of expositions of its nature he seems to represent the kingdom as in process of growth. At times this growth appears to be slow. Most striking in this respect are some of the parables. The parable of the Mustard Seed is based on the fact that the mustard seed and the kingdom both begin with apparently insignificant and small origins and grow to a large maturity. Aside from this what could possibly be the meaning of a comparison between that "which is less than all seeds" and the kingdom of God? The parable of The Leaven is exactly of the same nature and import.

Equally clear is the tendency in this direction of the parable of The Wheat and the Tares. The wheat and the tares, sown by different parties, grow side by side at first scarcely distinguishable from each other but becoming more and more so until their incongruity in the same field becomes quite manifest and they are finally separated at the harvest time. If the apocalyptic construction were the one intended by Jesus, he must have compared the kingdom not to the sowing of the wheat as he does, but to the harvest.

In his direct teaching, too, Jesus touches upon an aspect of the kingdom which is irreconcilable with its merely apocalyptic coming, namely, that it eludes the outward observation. "The kingdom of God cometh not with observation." The force of this consideration is, however, denied by those who render "observation" ($\pi\alpha\rho\alpha\tau\acute{\eta}\rho\eta\sigma\iota\varsigma$) as "close scrutiny." If this rendering be correct, Jesus must have meant that when the kingdom comes, it will come with a clear and unmistakable flash. The kingdom needs no signs; it is its own sign. It is not a matter to be observed as the result of close and careful examination. But all this is inconsistent with the words that announce

---

[1] With variations in subordinate details the above view was propounded by Johannes Weiss (*Das Reich Gottes*) and has been advocated by numerous scholars most vigorously and from the extreme radical viewpoint by Albert Schweitzer (*The Quest of the Historic Christ*, 1910, tr. of a work entitled *Von Reimarus zu Wrede*).

the kingdom as already in their midst."[2] Exactly the opposite, then, is the real sense of the title. They asked him, "When cometh the kingdom of God?" and he answered, "The kingdom of God cometh not with observation; neither shall they say, Lo, here, or there, for lo the kingdom of God is in your midst" (Lk. xvii. 20, 21).

So clear is this teaching that even J. Weiss, most strenuous advocate of the purely eschatological conception of the kingdom of God, felt compelled to explain it as meaning that the social principles and the beginnings of the kingdom are already, to the mind of Jesus, present in the world by way of anticipation. But even were this passage to be interpreted in harmony with the sudden and apocalyptic advent of the kingdom, the parable of Mark iv. 26-29 would still stand as an evidence of the elusiveness of the process of the kingdom's coming. In that parable the man who has cast the seed into the ground is represented as going to sleep and rising up and being occupied with other things while the seed springs and grows up "he knoweth not how." It is only when the fruit is brought forth that he realizes what has taken place.

It is striking and certainly not without significance that the teaching regarding the growth of the kingdom should be embodied especially in parabolic forms. The parable, less than all other vehicles of instruction, is capable of being transformed in the transmission or corrupted in passing from a fragmentary source to a complete gospel narrative. Its story form makes it easy to retain and reproduce it as heard. At any rate the principal teachings of a parable must be preserved in the repetition, otherwise the whole of it failing to accomplish its end, would be lost. That the idea of growth, therefore, should plainly appear in so many of the parables points with a greater degree of probability to the fact that Jesus propounded it.

(3) Even a cursory glance at the data disclosed in the above discussion must convince the impartial mind that Jesus spoke of the kingdom both as a present reality and as a future event. The severest critical treatment of the sources cannot eliminate either the apocalyptic element from his discourses or the ethical. All efforts to explain away the one in favor of the other have proved futile.

When, for instance, the advocates of the apocalyptic view have tried to show that the ethical, spiritual utterances attributed to Jesus were imported into the records by his disciples at a later stage of the development of thought, they have cumbered their argument in a way which greatly weakens it. That an intellect of such obvious originality and independence as that of Jesus should have slavishly adhered to the letter of the apocalyptic tradition while untutored minds such as those of the Galilean peasants of his circle should have realized the magnitude and power of the ethical and spiritual ideals which they attributed to him is a proposition that strains the credulity of the most uncritical.

Moreover the ethical and spiritual element in the teaching of Jesus is embodied in the parables, which from the literary point of view are the most consistently characteristic of the productions of Jesus, so far

[2] The ἐν ὑμῖν is evidently here not equal to "in you," but "among you."

at least as subject matter is concerned. To extricate it from the records as a later interpretation would be to practice a sort of criticism which in any other connection would be branded as absurdity itself.

But if the ethical and spiritual teaching cannot be eliminated from the sources, neither can the apocalyptic. It is true that this element could be more easily imagined an interpolation of the reporters. For they were surely men of their generation, steeped in its ideas and controlled by its thought currents. They looked upon the world through the eyes of their age, saw the powers at work, despaired of their being overcome and were probably ready to believe that only by a divine interference in a cataclysm, the promise of a better age should be fulfilled. To men of this mind it is conceivable that foreshadowings of the transformation of an unrighteous into a righteous world made in plain terms might in the course of time and transmission be altered into apocalyptic terms. While all this is conceivable as a matter of theory, when the sources are carefully examined, the supposition becomes untenable. The eschatological element is so thoroughly interwoven in the discourses of Jesus that only by serious violations of the canons of criticism could it be disentangled and cast out of the sources.

That the reports of his utterances may have brought matters of different kinds together with consequent confusion and misunderstanding of unessential details to the reader of the Gospels in later times is quite possible. When for instance the "little apocalypse of Jesus" (Mt. xxv., Mk. xiii., Lk. xxiii.) is said to contain parts of speeches of Jesus on three different subjects—the fall of Jerusalem, the collapse of the Jewish nation, the end of the world and His own second coming—this may be true or not. But even if successfully carried out, the analysis does not help in eliminating the apocalyptic element from the words of Jesus as given in the Gospels.

But if both types of representation are genuine, can it be that they belong to different periods in the teaching ministry of Jesus? Did Jesus begin with declaring the coming of the kingdom as conceived by the apocalyptists, and later develop his own spiritual view of it? The facts do not justify an affirmative answer to this question, much as such an answer would relieve the situation. Nowhere does Jesus show any signs of change of mind. On the contrary some of the most pronounced apocalyptic utterances of his occur in the reports of the latter days of his ministry. That in the natural growth of his human understanding of which the evangelist testifies (Lk. ii. 52) Jesus saw more and more in his mission and ministry, we are bound to believe; but that he abandoned one point of view and adopted another is not probable.

But are the two points of view as inconsistent with one another as it has been assumed in the controversy? In the negative answer to this question lies the solution of the problem. Jesus did resort to the apocalyptic modes of thought and expression current in his day. This was inevitable if he were to establish contact with the mind of the day. But his own world view far transcended the apocalyptic system. His deepest interest was in the inner and personal relations of men to God.

THE KINGDOM IN THE FUTURE

Outward events whether cataclysmic or natural in the manner of their occurrence were nothing but means of the promotion or the hindrance of inner movements. If, in harmony with the thought of the age, he conceived of a sudden change in the world issuing in the coming of men under the direct and loving rule of God, it was not the suddenness or any other incidental feature of the change that interested him, but the result.

His keen insight into the processes of the world both human and divine revealed to him changes of a gradual and slow character. The kingdom of God might follow the processes of nature. It was probable that it should, even if it were established at one stroke. In fact if it were so established, that would only bring into visibility what was already inherently the vital principle within it. "The kingdom of God is within (among) you." In the end the kingdom of God must grow and thrive as any other living organism does. The apocalyptic mode of thinking of it can apply only to its inception; and in that field it is not inevitable, but only a possible way, a mere matter of method of reaching a result. For Jesus the necessity of using a vehicle which would adequately carry his thought to his hearers' minds, much as the adoption of the current language of the geocentric view of the world, made the use of apocalyptic ideas and expressions imperative. But it did not bind him to their absolute reality and their indispensability to his message.

2. THE PLACE OF JESUS IN THE FUTURE OF THE KINGDOM.—Whether the kingdom of God were conceived as portrayed in its apocalyptic form or as a vital ethical reality the Messianic consciousness of Jesus never permitted him to dissociate himself from it in its future. And though his place and part in it must naturally be thought of harmoniously with its precise character, upon a close scrutiny his utterances on the subject present the same comprehensive aspect that has been found in his view of the coming of the kingdom. Outwardly much of what he says is apocalyptic in language and form; but its inner purport is centered about ethical and spiritual values. What he says concerns in general two items of interest of practical importance to those he immediately addressed, namely, his own real and active share in the life of the kingdom and his special function as ruler and judge.

(1) *The Parousia.*—The occasion for any references to Jesus' real presence in the new order he had announced was the apparent disaster threatening him personally in the intense and bitter hostility of the leaders. Assuming that he was right about God's purpose to assume the reins of government in the world, how was his death consistent with his having a share under the new regime? He answered the question both for his disciples and for his enemies by firmly declaring that his death would cause only a brief interruption in his relations to the world. When the kingdom was established, he would reappear. To his disciples he gave this assurance in its most clear and distinct form in the little apocalypse (Mt. xvi. 27; Mk. viii. 38; Lk. ix. 26). To his enemies he

held it up as an intimation of the futility of their opposition to him (Mt. xxvi. 64; Mk. xiv. 62; Lk. xxii. 69).

The event is in the First Gospel called the presence ("parousia"), elsewhere it is identified by description. The common designation of it as the second coming ("advent") has no parallel in the usage of Jesus. The detail may appear a matter of verbal importance; but it indicates, at least, that the emphasis in the original thought of it was not on the manner of its occurrence or on the relation of it to Jesus' earthly life, but on the fact of his actual presence and participation in the affairs of the kingdom of God.

(2) *The Judgment.*—The Messianic work of Jesus is foreshadowed as preëminently that of the judge of the world. The mode of its presentation here is even more distinctly apocalyptic.

A vivid picture of universal judgment is given in the Old Testament in the vision of the Valley of Decision (Joel iii. 13, "the Valley of Jehoshaphat"). It evidently impressed the mind and stimulated the imagination of later Judaism. It serves as the basis of Jesus' portraiture of his universal Messianic function of judge (Mt. xxv. 31-46) presumably at the very beginning of his rule. That such a function belongs to the Messiah's office is ultimately traceable to the Old Testament doctrine of the Day of Yahweh. In incorporating it into his own ideal of the kingdom, however, Jesus has in mind the just and merciful character of God.

The significant aspects of Jesus' picture of the Messianic judgment are, first of all, that it takes into account "all the nations" of the earth, secondly, the test applied in it and, thirdly, the surprising results.

(a) The circle of the judged would consist of the Gentile world. The term "nations" must be taken in this connection as the equivalent of Gentiles. That among the Gentiles those only are meant to be included who came into relationships with the followers of Jesus (as Wendt contends) is not indicated by anything in the context. That the Jews are not to be made subjects of judgment because they were not named in the passage is also an unwarranted inference from silence. The Gentiles are named undoubtedly because their relation to the kingdom of God was a problem to the Jewish mind. In making them subjects of a judicial procedure Jesus designates just how they stood in reference to himself as the Messiah and how their place in the Messianic age is to be determined.

(b) The test applied in the Messianic judgment is that of the special attitude of the subjects of judgment to the Messiah's aims and purposes. At first glance the test may appear to be that of works. "Inasmuch as ye *did*"; "inasmuch as ye *did not.*" But this leaves out of account the more important words which follow, "unto me." Moreover the Messiah intimates that kindly conduct or the brotherly disposition which is shown in feeding the hungry, visiting the sick and imprisoned, etc. is just the expression of the inward spirit which is the Messiah's own and characterizes the Messianic rule of life. In the end those who are approved are approved because of their inherent affinity and affiliation to the Messiah.

(c) The judgment is, at the same time, a means of revelation. The tests which both Jews and Gentiles applied to their own lives were so far misleading that many who esteemed themselves right in their relations to God were utterly wrong and vice versa. This was because they thought of racial distinctions rather than ethical principles as the grounds of the divine judgment. The Messianic verdict will show the mistake and confusion in this view. When that verdict is announced, it will surprise both those who are approved and those who are disapproved if they still expect to be justified or condemned on other than purely ethical grounds of the conformity or lack of conformity of their minds to the Messianic ideal.

Incidentally the verdict reveals the fact that the relation of loyalty to the Messiah which will win approval at the judgment need not be a conscious one. Those who may say to him, "When saw we thee hungry?" etc. were none the less members of his band because they had accepted his leadership without a clear knowledge of his personality, of his saving sacrificial work for them or even of his name.

(d) The issues of the judgment are "everlasting life" on the one hand and "the outer darkness" on the other. There is no new revelation, in the words of Jesus, on these matters. He simply accepts the thought forms of his day as means of conveying to his followers the truth that between those who live in the right relation to God and those who do not there is an eternal difference. Not only as they are, but as they shall be in the future they are infinitely apart from one another.

PART II
THE EARLIEST APOSTOLIC MESSAGE

CHAPTER XIII

GENERAL VIEW

Less is known upon first-hand testimony about the interval between the ascension of Jesus and the beginning of the ministry of Paul than about any other portion of the period covered by the New Testament writings. And yet enough is known to put it beyond doubt that during that interval the followers of Jesus, beginning at Jerusalem, disseminated through Judea and adjacent regions a definite report of what Jesus had done and experienced. It was during this interval, too, that the disciples of Jesus were drawn together in a compact organization to which the name church was at once given.

1. Sources of Information.—The estimate of our sources of information concerning the apostolic preaching of this interval will depend somewhat on whether we make the effort first to determine by critical processes which of the New Testament writings either intentionally or incidentally present pictures of the time unaffected by later development, or accept the whole group of documents unconnected with the names of Paul and John and by a process of sifting secure as nearly as we can the knowledge desired. The condition of New Testament critical research at the present day quite decidedly compels the adoption of the latter course. Accordingly out of the Acts of the Apostles, the Epistle of James, the First and Second Epistles of Peter and the Epistle of Jude we shall endeavor to reconstruct as best we may the course of thought in this transitional age.

That this method of procedure is open to objections may be freely admitted. None of the documents named originated before the beginning of Paul's career, unless the Epistle of James be dated, as has been done by some scholars, at 44 A.D. This does not seem probable; and even if granted, it would not alter the case so far as the other writings are concerned. And yet it is not the date at which a document was produced which determines its value as a source, but the intention vividly or dimly held in view by its author to treat of subjects within certain limits. A late document often presents facts regarding an earlier period whereas a much earlier dated writing may contain information concerning a later time. On this unquestionable possibility the five writings named may be in general brought together. Yet the grouping must be made only tentatively with qualifications to be indicated upon a separate examination of each.

(1) *The Book of Acts.*—At the outset it must be noted that not the whole book of Acts, but only the first section of it (i.-xii.) can be used as a source for the pre-Pauline period of Christian thought. This is so obvious that the mere mention of it should suffice to accredit it. Per contra, the thorough and critical study of the whole book has

issued in its acceptance as a trustworthy source of information throughout. The author is unquestionably the third evangelist, Luke, companion and fellow worker of Paul. He was the only originally Gentile writer whose works have found a place in the New Testament collection. His world view was not free from the influences which in the Gentile world of the day were accustomed to color the thoughts of even the clearest-minded men. But he has written enough to enable critical scholarship to form an adequate estimate of his mental habits. Accordingly it is not difficult to see through the atmosphere in which he paints his world and to identify the facts he describes quite correctly.

His literary methods as seen both in the Third Gospel and in the Acts are those of the historian. His Gentile training had evidently equipped him for orderly and methodical investigation and composition. He made use of trustworthy witnesses, whether living men and women or documents. Among the latter are clearly recognizable (1) a journal or itinerary (the "we-passages") interspersed through his narrative; (2) letters such as that written by Claudius Lysias to Felix the procurator at Caesarea reporting the case of Paul and that drawn up by the conference at Jerusalem regarding the circumcision controversy (xv.); (3) speeches of various leaders as nearly realistically reported as it could be expected in an age when stenography was not common. Notable among these are the summaries of Paul's preaching during the missionary journeys and his series of defenses after his arrest. These are evidences of pains and care in the writing of history which inspire confidence.

The credibility of Luke has been confirmed by comparison with contemporaneous well-attested history, at least so far as Paul's labors are concerned. There is no reason to suppose that his story of the pre-Pauline period of the church is in any way inferior in trustworthiness. He had undertaken, according to his own statement, to write a sequel to the Third Gospel, tracing the progress of the new faith in Jesus from Jerusalem through "all Judea and Samaria and unto the uttermost part of the earth."[1]

---

[1] This view of the design of Acts differs from other views as (1) it is a mere sequel to the Third Gospel in pointing to the more exact intention of the sequel which was not simply to follow up what had been given in "the former treatise," but so to follow it up as to show that from Jerusalem the faith in Jesus Christ spread until it reached Rome and thence as from a center the whole world. (2) The earlier theories of Acts as a vindication of Paul against suspicions raised against his authority by the Judaists. According to this view the author shows Paul's right to leadership by balancing his services with those of Peter. He shows that for every miracle that Peter performed Paul performed one of the same type. (3) It was designed to reconcile the Pauline and Judaistic parties by an appeal to the Paulinists to recognize Peter as equal to Paul, paralleling Paul's great missionary labors by Peter's services to the Jerusalem church. (4) It aims to give an account of the deeds of the Holy Spirit as a continuation of the deeds of Jesus (reported in the Gospels) as if there were an antithesis or distinction between the labors of Jesus himself and the works of the Spirit. (5) Acts was of the nature of an apology addressed to Theophilus, whose favor as a magistrate the author desired to win in behalf of the followers of the new way. None of these views of the aim of Luke accounts for the plan and contents of the book as fully as the one pointed out in the text.

GENERAL VIEW

(2) *The Epistle of James.*—Reasons have been given why we should believe that the Epistle bearing the name of James is the oldest of the New Testament writings.[2] If these reasons were more convincing than they are no further explanation would be needed of the appearance of the document among our primary sources of information concerning the state of mind of the pre-Pauline Christian community. But instead of furnishing a clue to the time of its composition, this Epistle is so elusive on this matter as to have given ground to many of the most recent scholars for asserting quite positively its post-Pauline origin.[3]

But while the writing of the Epistle is subject to dispute, the type of thought it presents is not. It is freer from Pauline influence than any other New Testament writing of its compass, though one cannot say that it betrays no knowledge of the Pauline teaching. The author has not allowed Pauline ideas to affect his thought, and in his effort to keep himself independent of Paul has actually assumed an attitude of opposition to Paul's ideas at best as preached by Paul's followers. But this very attitude of putting himself on his guard against Paulinism gives him the right to speak of the pre-Pauline type of Christian thinking.

Thus far the way appears clear. But when some go further and present the document as a tract designed to drive Christianity back into Judaism—the instrument, as it were, of a backward propaganda—they certainly attempt to build a larger edifice than their materials warrant. Upon the whole the Epistle is a writing expressing the mind of a disciple of Jesus thoroughly committed to the religious and ethical teaching of the Lord, but free from the deductions which some other disciples of Jesus had made concerning his personality and the significance of his work.

Tradition has identified the author as the brother of Jesus bearing the same name. In view of the fact that James the son of Zebedee was put to death by Herod Agrippa before 44 A.D., and that James the son of Alphaeus is passed over in the New Testament with no distinct note of any service he may have rendered, the identification of the author of the Epistle with the brother of Jesus seems well supported. The suggestion of J. H. Moulton that James the brother of the Lord wrote it but for non-Christian Jews and, therefore, he deliberately avoided using distinctively Christian language in it deserves fair consideration. On the other hand the doctrinal barrenness of the writing from the point of view of Christian theology has been overemphasized. Too many negative conclusions have been drawn from it. No man with the definite object in view of affecting the conduct of his readers rather than instructing their minds should be expected to present all or most of the ramifications of

---

[2] Among those who support this position are Alford, Stanley, Renan, Neander, Weiss, B. Zahn, Beyschlag, Dods, Mayor.
[3] Those who have done this are Bain, Zeller, Hausrath among the older critics, and Jülicher, Von Soden, Harnack, Bacon, E. F. Scott, and others. These place it some time between 70 and 150 A.D.

his system of doctrine in a document of as small compass as is this writing.

The best view of the purpose and purport of the Epistle of James is then that it was addressed to Jews whether Christians or non-Christians with a view to leading them to find in the person of Jesus their lord and leader and in his social and moral ideals the consummation of the best that Judaism had meant in the world.

(3) *First Peter*.—That a "Pauline" strain cannot be strictly excluded in the selection of sources for the pre-Pauline stage of Christian thought is made clear by the consideration of First Peter. But the opinion has gained ground in modern times that this claim, which so far as tradition is concerned is amply sustained, is inconsistent with the facts of the letter itself. Most striking among these is the Pauline color of its thought. The tendency to build upon this feature which was very strong in the last years of the nineteenth century has largely disappeared upon later examination. Moffatt's view commends itself as the most reasonable when he admits the Pauline influence but declines to classify the author as a disciple of Paul.[4] The strain regarded Pauline is drawn from "the common practical consciousness pervading the churches—consciousness which was prior to Paul, and in which Paulinism operated for the most part as a ferment."[5]

This view of the case fits in admirably with the other facts available for a full estimate of the date and conditions under which the Epistle originated. In general these grow out of the Neronian distress in Rome ("Babylon," v. 12). The object of the writing was the encouragement of the refugee Christians who had fled the capital and were scattered in various parts of Asia ("the Dispersion in Pontus, Galatia, Cappadocia, Asia and Bithynia," i. 1). While for our purposes the Petrine authorship of the writing is of secondary importance, there seems to be no real ground for questioning the traditional testimony to that effect.

The apparent inconsistency of using a document showing traces of Pauline influence as a witness to a pre-Pauline condition of thought stands in no need of justification or even explanation. What is needed is rather some correction of the conception and use of the term Paulinism. Hitherto Paulinism has been viewed as some reality carved precisely with mechanical accuracy as if out of marble. Such definitions are invariably contradicted by the facts of history. Paul did not invent the whole of Paulinism. He developed its pronounced form out of preëxisting ideas. While some of these must be always associated with the system he worked out in the course of his ministry, others are rudimentarily contained in the thought and life of the Christian community which antedates his appearance in it. First Peter is a transitional document. It was produced during the period of the inception and first propagation of the Pauline system. It embodies Pauline ideas, but whether derived from Paul himself, or not, these are not the dominant ones in it. It contains far more prominently ideas

---

[4] "The writer is by no means a Paulinist," *Introd. to the N. T.*, p. 340.
[5] Moffatt, pp. 330, 331.

representing the common stock of the thought of the primitive church.

(4) *Second Peter.*—Whether Second Peter is available at all as a source for any stage in the growth of thought in the New Testament period must depend on two previous questions: (a) Was the document produced during the New Testament period or soon enough after the end of that period to give fresh and first-hand testimony concerning its facts and conditions? and (b) If not, does it incorporate sources of information otherwise inaccessible but capable of identification through careful critical processes?

The first of these questions has been the subject of debate all through the history of New Testament criticism. The grounds for the belief that Second Peter was written by the Apostle himself are very meager. As compared with those for First Peter, or for the genuineness of any other book of the New Testament they are almost nothing.

The earliest mention of the letter in Christian literature occurs toward the end of the third century. Even as late as the days of Eusebius the work was classified among the Antilegomena (controverted writings) of the New Testament. Ardent defenders of the traditional views have adduced earlier allusions to it; but on closer examination these prove illusive. The external evidence is thus very precarious.

Turning to the internal evidence we find (a) that the unusual eagerness of the author to be recognized as the Apostle Peter arouses suspicion. There is a series of passages in Second Peter that is said to indicate an exceptional desire on the part of the author to be known as Peter. He begins by calling himself Simon Peter, which is not unusual, but later he aims to identify himself as the man who was with Jesus on the Mount of Transfiguration. Still later he speaks of a first epistle that he has written, and claims to be on terms of intimacy with the Apostle Paul. (b) The second group of internal indications is centered around the total unlikeness between its content of thought and that of First Peter. The first epistle aims to create hope. The second aims to correct bad morals. It is directed against corrupt teachers whose teaching is degrading from the ethical point of view. (c) Another consideration of the internal kind is found in the linguistic peculiarities (choice of words, the formation of sentences, and general literary color) all of which are different from that of First Peter. (d) There is still a fourth consideration drawn from the allusion to Paul's letters, which are placed on a level with the Old Testament scriptures, and ascribed canonical authority. This would indicate that Second Peter was written considerably after the death of Paul. For it was not till then that Paul's writings were collected and read and misunderstood because of their inner difficulties, and by some (perhaps by the majority of) Christians lifted to a place of canonical authority. But in order that all this should have taken place, it was necessary that some time (perhaps one hundred or one hundred and fifty years) should have passed and afforded the opportunity for it.

This is in general the argument against the genuineness of Second Peter. In defense of its genuineness, it is first necessary to account for the lateness of the earliest allusions to the epistle. The only solution of this difficulty is to show how the Epistle may have escaped notice for two hundred and fifty years. In the treatment of the internal evidence, each consideration is turned into account in favor of genuineness.

The interest in the genuineness of Second Peter exists mainly because it is thought to be implicated in that of canonicity. The evidence has been in the past measured and weighed with a certain prejudice in favor of a theory of canonicity which is not beyond challenge. The effort has been made, in other words, to defend the Petrine authorship because of the belief that unless that were done the canonicity of Second Peter, i.e., its place in the Rule of Faith and therefore its spiritual authority and value, would have to be abandoned. This, however, is neither necessary nor reasonable.

In the first place the canonicity of this writing might be preserved upon the theory that the letter was in the main the work of Peter's but largely interpolated. Grotius of the seventeenth century, a great jurist and theologian, propounded the view that Second Peter was written by a certain Simeon in the latter part of the first century, and that a later scribe, supposing this Simeon to have been Peter the Apostle, added the name "Peter" after that of Simeon. Thus arose the superscription Simon Peter. Then to justify and clear up this supposed Petrine origin other details were interpolated, perhaps by others. This may be the origin of the letter's doubtful Petrinism. If that view were correct, all objection to the canonicity of Second Peter would disappear. The problem would be reduced altogether to one of textual criticism.

But, secondly, even if that view be not correct, and it should be found that the letter was composed much later and put forth in the name of the Apostle Peter, there would be nothing to interfere with its acceptance as a part of the Rule of Faith, since that Rule is constituted, not on the ground of the authorship of the writings entering into it, but on that of their internal spiritual authority as recognized by the spiritual sense of the normal human community upon presentation of the writing itself as a whole. Therefore we need not hesitate if we find the reasons convincing that the letter issued from another man, and at a later time than the Apostle Peter, to accept that view upon any historical ground on which it may rest. The value of it would not be affected.

Against this position the objection is frequently made that if the author pretended to be the Apostle Peter, he was untruthful. But can a work issuing from an untruthful man, one who in the very first line of his writing makes an intentional misstatement, be dignified by a place in the canon? Why can we depend upon the word of our literary men (Charles Dickens, Nathaniel Hawthorne) who in their manner begin by stating things as facts that are not so? The answer is that these men did not mean to deceive. Everybody knows and understands their statements to be forms of a literary device. They are using the apparent misstatement as a means for carrying their thought. They are not working upon our credulity. They are not trying to palm off their misstatements as exact statements of fact. They are using a literary device familiar in our own day. Similar literary devices were resorted to when this writing was put forth, either by Peter or under the name of Peter. Among these the attachment by authors of the names of older notable men to their writings was considered legitimate and practiced. An author was not consciously and intentionally falsifying when he practiced this device. He did not look upon the procedure with reference to its bearing upon the law of veracity. His aim was not to deceive, but to promote the good he had in mind in writing. And if discovered in the act, he was not judged as an untrustworthy man. Since neither he nor those for whom he wrote raised the question, it seems irrelevant to raise it now and to base upon it an objection to his general trustworthiness.

The question of genuineness may then be left aside as of secondary importance. The fact that, in general, the tone and type of thought of Second Peter harmonizes with those of this group of writings warrants our using it as a source along with them.

(5) *The Epistle of Jude.*—The main interest in the Epistle of Jude lies in the fact of its duplicating the thought of Second Peter. Three theories are possible: (a) Either that Jude borrowed from Second Peter; (b) or that Second Peter borrowed from Jude); (c) or that both borrowed from a common source. It is useless to enter into the discussion. It is little more than of literary value. The well-nigh unanimous view of scholars today is that Second Peter borrowed from Jude. An intermediate or modified form, of the view (a) above has been proposed, to the effect that Second Peter ii. 1—iii, 2 is an interpolation and that the original of Second Peter was the basis of Jude. This explanation, however, makes too much use of unnecessary conjecture.

2. From Jesus to the Church.—That the withdrawal of Jesus from the midst of his followers would make a difference in their lives and labors was to be expected. But just what this difference would be could be determined only by the event. The meagerness of light furnished by the sources on this point has led to extreme positions. For the most part the difference between his explicit teaching and their preaching has been exaggerated. So far as the evidence throws light on the subject, the disciples aimed to be loyal not only to his person, but also to his conceptions of God, of the world and of the law of Israel as they understood him to hold them.

It must be borne in mind that all of these disciples were Jews, thoroughly devoted to the traditions and ideals of their race and dominated by the spirit of their age. Jesus spoke to them in the language and modes of thought of their day. They saw the new element in his teaching through the atmosphere of their former training and experience. Jesus rarely, if ever, denounced existing ideas or practices. When he did so, it was not the general thoughts of the Jewish people, but the particular interpretations and practices of false leaders (the scribes and Pharisees) that he attacked. Consequently the men and women of his company clothed him and his thoughts, metaphorically speaking, in the garb of Jewish prophetic and legal and moral forms.

The result of these conditions and forces was that when the disciples were left without his personal leadership they allowed their thoughts to crystallize in Jewish moulds. The conception of the gospel they present is simple. Its core is the proposition, "Jesus is the Messiah." To this they add the practical ideas: Faith in Jesus binds his followers in a divinely approved, therefore divinely ordained, brotherhood. God signifies his acceptance of those who commit themselves to him by granting them his Holy Spirit. The lives of such are purged and sanctified. They are filled with power, but more distinctively, with holy purposes and ideals and conform in outward conduct to Jesus' own supreme pattern.

CHAPTER XIV

THE PRIMITIVE CHRISTIAN CONVICTION

WHETHER the conviction that Jesus was the Messiah brought together the church, or the church already in existence as a group of companions admirers and followers of Jesus was imbued with the faith that he was the Messiah must be left an open question. Happily for practical purposes the question is of secondary and for the most part of academic significance. The fact is that Jesus before his ascension left a group of followers quite firmly fixed in their minds about his personality and persuaded by his words of the imminent coming of the kingdom of God. Jesus' resurrection from the dead, superadded to the magnetism of his personality as a living leader, had so affected their minds that they accepted him as their Lord and Savior without the slightest reserve and were ready to give up everything and dare everything out of devotion to him.

1. THE FIRST PREACHING OF JESUS AS CHRIST.—One of their earliest experiences was without question that recorded in Acts, i.e., the implicit or perhaps explicit challenge to explain their course to their neighbors and friends in the community. Those who accept the account in Acts as absolutely trustworthy in every detail believe that this took place in Jerusalem. Those who have critical doubts about the minuter circumstances think that this challenge must have been met in Galilee. Wherever it was met, it called upon them to give reasons for the faith that was in them. In either case, also, the course they pursued would be precisely the one reported in Acts.

Substantially the answer they gave was as in Acts (ii. 36; viii. 12b; iii. 18; v. 28; xiv. 22): "Jesus of Nazareth whom ye (the Jews) put to death was (and is) the Christ promised by the prophets of the Old Testament." But an answer like this is not self-evident. Assuming that it explains their behavior, it demands justification because this Jesus was so far from conforming to the expectations of the best-informed leaders of the day. His life had not been lived as the life of the Messiah was expected to be lived if the accredited interpreters of the Old Testament prophecies were to be trusted. Above all, his death was not included in the expectation. No one who had allowed himself to be overpowered by an unjust government and had suffered an ignominious (and according to the Deuteronomic Law "accursed") death could be the Messiah.

This was the view by which the disciples found themselves confronted. No doubt they had considered the force of these considerations and had fully felt their weight for themselves. But they had overcome the power of these objections and were ready to give the reasons which convinced them. They gave them as follows:

(1) The current interpretation of the prophecies was wrong. The prophetic picture of the Messiah was precisely the one fulfilled in the person of Jesus. Jesus had been predicted as a prophet (Ac. iii. 22-26). Moses had said, "A prophet shall the Lord raise unto you from among your brethren like unto me" (Deut. xviii. 18). And Jesus impressed his hearers as authoritative like Moses. This might have been granted and yet not have sufficed to establish his Messiahship. The disciples went further. They claimed that the Messianic picture in the prophets included his death (Ac. iii. 13-15). And since the idea of his death was especially obnoxious, they reasoned that the death was only a necessary precondition for the resurrection which was also prophesied. The special appeal on this point was carefully worked out upon an exegesis of Psalm xvi, and it was in full harmony with the usual method of quoting and applying Old Testament passages to current events. Assuming that David was the speaker in the original, Peter points out the fact that he cannot have used the words as claiming for himself exemption from permanent subjection to death since the event proved that he had died, had been buried and no one ever thought of his rising from the dead. But if David in the spirit of prophecy spoke as the representative and type of the Messiah, then since Jesus had surely risen from the dead the prophecy had been fulfilled.

Thus the first line of answer given to those who might dispute the thesis, Jesus is the Messiah, was an appeal to the Old Testament. But it was not the only one.

The resurrection which had served as the ground of an appeal to prophecy was in itself an independent and, if possible, even stronger ground for their plea. It is not unreasonable to suppose that the disciples' own faith was more strongly entrenched on this ground than on any other consideration. When the crucifixion came, according to all expectation, as well as according to the testimony of all the evangelic accounts, the disciples of Jesus found themselves a dispirited, demoralized, disintegrated group. They were brought together again by rumors of his having appeared alive to some. Even then they held their conferences behind closed and bolted doors for "fear of the Jews." Not long afterwards, however, they were seen completely transformed. Instead of fear their conduct showed confidence and courage dominant even in facing persecution and hardships at the hands of their enemies.

And the confidence which they found when they were assured of his resurrection became the fountainhead and material for a line of reasoning as they came to face the world round about them. He who had risen from the dead could be no other than the Messiah of God. The resurrection of Jesus assumed a central place in the gospel. "Jesus is the Messiah," and "God raised him from the dead," became twin and inseparable articles in the first creed (if the expression may be allowed) of the primitive Christian community. Paul was expressing

THE PRIMITIVE CHRISTIAN CONVICTION

neither an individual belief nor a thought original with himself when he later put it to the Corinthians, "If Christ hath not been raised, then is our preaching vain; your faith is also vain."

For the central nucleus of the group this belief was not the result of testimony but of personal experience with the risen Jesus. It is frequently asserted even by the best scholars that the accounts of the resurrection appearances are beset with problems some of which are, in the condition of the evidence available, insoluble. But whatever these problems may be there is no doubt that in the days which followed the crucifixion and after the first panic and desertion which that calamity occasioned, many of them came together again assuring each other that they had seen Jesus alive. It is not necessary to insist that in saying this they referred to one or another sort of personal experience. They may all have had the same kind of experience that Paul testifies for himself; or it may be that some had a clearer perception of the bodily presence of their teacher and friend. The result was in either case a full assurance upon grounds which in good conscience their hearers could not reject as illusive. They were convinced that Jesus was living.

Hence, in those first days of their readjustment to their new situation, they made the resurrection the corner stone of their reconstructed thought. In the early chapters of Acts it recurs at every new development of the community's life. It is like the refrain of a song or the theme of a piece of music, ever present under all the accidental narrations of the separate occasions that called forth any expression of their minds. They declared themselves "witnesses" of it. In the choice of a successor to Judas that was to fill up the number twelve in the body of apostles, it was a condition prerequisite that the candidate should be able to testify to the fact as one who had seen the risen master (Ac. i. 22).

But while the resurrection assumed this central place in the thought of the disciples after the event, it was not an unfamiliar conception before. Jesus had foreshadowed his death to them and since he assured them of his real Messiahship he signified to them that his death was to be followed by his resurrection. When the resurrection actually occurred and they had occasion to report and explain its meaning, they could add, "He has risen as he *said*."

But just what bearing the fact of the resurrection would have on his Messiahship was not clear to them. A question, therefore, has been raised on this point mainly in our own days. It has been said that by the fact of his death endured as a means of purging Israel of their sins, he had accomplished his prophetic work; and by restoring him to life God had owned his work, and as a reward had made him the Messiah. His Messiahship did not begin until after his resurrection. This, however, gratuitously assumes that between his work before death and that after the resurrection there was in his mind and in that of his followers a sharp cleft; that whereas he and they viewed his earthly work as non-Messianic, they thought him constituted and appointed Messiah by the very fact of resurrection. For such a difference between the two portions of his work there is no sufficient evidence.

All that he said about his death and resurrection is rather given as in a unified and connected outlook. He died as Messiah and rose again in attestation of his Messiahship. The resurrection was simply the sign by which his Messiahship was to be recognized, the triumphant proof of the divine character of his mission and of his accceptance by God as his representative in the kingdom just established. The Messiahship was not attained by the resurrection but vindicated and illumined. The dignity which had been with him through his ministry of teaching and, *de jure,* belonged to him was brought into visibility and became his also, *de facto.*

Again by an easy transition and not by an abrupt and sudden flash, the exact nature of Jesus' Messiahship became known to the disciples. It has been already shown that though Jesus used the apocalyptic forms of thought of his age and spoke the language of his generation, his inward thought of the kingdom and Messiahship was essentially ethical and spiritual; that when he visualized a kingdom of God as in process of establishment with himself as king, his desire and aspiration were not fixed upon the political features of the prospect but upon the religious. To him the kingdom was the rule of God in the hearts of men and the Messiahship the office of the Mediator and representative of God's inner rule.

This was, however, an ideal which his followers could not grasp all at once in its fulness. They saw more of the shell than of the kernel of the reality. The post-resurrection developments gradually brought within view the true relationship of kernel and shell. If they said: "Jesus is the Messiah," they could also say: "Jesus, the Messiah, is Savior and Lord." For them this transformation of the ideal was a natural corollary of the resurrection of Jesus and of its obvious consequences. Jesus had indeed risen from the dead, but this fact evidencing, as it did, his Messiahship, had not been followed immediately, as their apocalyptism would have led them to expect, by the seizure by him of political power and the overthrow of the existing social order.

Whether at first the new ideal did away altogether with the old one is unessential. In all probability the change from Jesus is the Messiah as political ruler to Jesus is the Messiah as ethical Savior did not mutually exclude each other. That Jesus was believed to be now the Savior, and that later he was to be the visible king of his people is the form in which the conviction appears a generation later. And it abides as such permanently.

2. THE FIRST INTERPRETATION OF JESUS' MESSIANIC WORK.—Again it may be asked how broadly was the Messianic work of Jesus conceived by this first group of his followers? Did they think of him as the Savior of Israel or of the world? The account in Acts, written somewhat later than the very first days after the resurrection, produces the impression that Jesus as the Messiah was interested in the human race as a whole, that his Messianic work was that of a Savior, and the only Savior from sin of every man (Ac. iv. 12). But whether this

THE PRIMITIVE CHRISTIAN CONVICTION

is the primitive or a modified form of the conviction developed just a little later it certainly prevailed in the pre-Pauline church.

But since Jesus was, for the time being at least, not bodily present among his followers, how was his Messiahship to be promoted? And how, in particular, were individuals to be drawn into his kingdom? This very practical as well as pressing question soon found its answer. And it was a simple and practical answer to a practical question. To become a member of the kingdom of God one must commit himself by an act of self-surrender to the Messiah. This could be done by believing in his power to do what he had declared. Every public or private declaration of the Messiahship of Jesus closed with the exhortation to accept him as proclaimed and enter the band of those who had already committed themselves to him. The words "repent" (inherited from the Baptist), and "believe" and "be baptized" entered into the vocabulary and received a distinctive and characteristic application (Ac. ii. 38; iii. 19).

What the benefits of entrance into the relationship of faith would be for the convert is also clearly given. The first was a blessing in anticipation, namely, the privileges of the kingdom of God. Jesus was to make his appearance as the head and founder of the new order of the world, and those who believed in him were to enter with him into the new order as a reward for their loyalty and faithfulness.

But a more immediate and certain benefit would accrue to all believers in the forgiveness of their sins (Ac. ii. 38; iii. 19, 26). Since all those who were invited in this stage of the preaching of Christ were Jews, the promise of forgiveness could carry no obscurity with it. The typical Jew of sober and devout mind had been trained by generations of prophetic teaching to think of his God as a lover of righteousness and hater of iniquity. He had thought of the national reverses and misfortunes as signs of the displeasure of God at the social sins controlling the life of the people. He had been urged as an individual to contribute his quota to the return of God's favor to his people by forsaking his own sins. To be told that the acceptance of Jesus as Messiah would have the effect of purging him of his sins and commending him to God was to put before him an inducement of the strongest type of appeal.

To the future good of a Messianic reign the present one of a relationship with God free from the curse of sin came not merely as an addition of some importance, but from the first as equally desirable. And from the level of equality it was not long afterwards raised to the level of a higher good. Whatever the developments might show concerning the nature, the time and the manner of the coming of the Messianic reign, the boon of forgiveness of sin could at any rate be appreciated and enjoyed. Thus naturally, as in the unfolding of the blossom from the bud, the spiritual and ethical element in the gospel broke out of the temporal and political.

Fairly may this be called the transformation of Messianism into Christianity, and of the Messiah into the Christ. The words Messiah and Christ are from the etymological point of view exact equivalents. But some time in the obscurely known years of the early apostolic age they began to part from one another. The newer term, derived from the Hellenic strain of thought, came to convey the more fluid and vital element in the complex idea. The Hebrew term gradually ceased to be used and the Greek one took its place. The Jewish connotations of the whole Messianic conception receded into the background and the Christian, ethicized and spiritualized idea of a Christ who saves the world from sin, was conceded the supremacy. Messianism proved to be the soft germinal spot in Judaism out of which grew Christianity.

Those who are inclined to draw lines sharply (a process always of questionable value and validity in investigations carried on in the historical field) would say that the change was not only significant but revolutionary, that the religion of Christ was here changed into the Christian religion, that the message of Jesus was lost in the unfolding of the answer to the question who Jesus was. Like all efforts to condense into an epigram a complex and many-sided truth, this pronouncement errs in excluding from each branch of its antithesis the phase of thought carried in it from the opposite branch.

That the person of Jesus is brought into the foreground, even placed into the center of the gospel, is true. But this is done in order to bring into view the rich and full content of the message of Jesus. Again the idea of the place of Jesus in his own proclamation of his message is never absent. "What think ye of Christ?" "Whom say ye that I am?" was implicit in his own view of the kingdom. The question, "Has Jesus a place in his own gospel?" could never be answered in the negative. The acceptance of Jesus as Messiah was not a barren and dogmatic formula, but always carried with it the acceptance of what he proclaimed concerning God and the life of man before God as true and binding.

And yet while Christ was from the beginning in his own gospel and his mind remains in the first preaching of him as Messiah an essential even supreme element, it would be unfair and unhistorical even to minimize the significance of the change of emphasis from the one stage to the other. Christology begins with the apostolic community. Christianity is Christ, is a formula that could not have been used in the earthly lifetime of Jesus. It begins to have a meaning from the day of Pentecost onwards. And while it may be freely granted that its meaning expands and deepens as time goes on, it is never a new thing again, because it has taken its place permanently in the consciousness of Jesus' followers. Even in the account of Paul's conversion the risen Jesus could be addressed by the surprised Saul as "Lord." Just how much and what was involved in the application of the term lord to Jesus, will be discussed at a later stage in our study. For the present it is sufficient to point out the exaltation and spiritualization of the Messianic office in the earliest presentation of the gospel as Jesus the Christ the savior from sin.

CHAPTER XV

THE SPIRIT AND THE CHURCH

1. THE HOLY SPIRIT.—The idea of the Holy Spirit appears with such suddenness and vividness as we pass from the Gospels to the Acts that at first it strikes the reader of the New Testament as a new, or at least a newly revealed reality in religion. One, however, recovers from this impression as he remembers the various occasions on which Jesus himself made reference to the Spirit of God. Further thought enables him to bring into his view the fact that the Old Testament allots a prominent place to the work of God's Spirit on the life of Israel. In fact the conception of a spirit working on the minds of men has been traced by some to extra-biblical animistic religious systems.[1] In these primitive roots of the idea the so-called "divine spirit" is viewed as an independent demonic power, taking possession of men and changing their nature in a preternatural manner. "But," as E. F. Scott points out,[2] "this primitive conception could not maintain itself alongside of Hebrew monotheism."

Through the Old Testament God has a mind and spirit corresponding to the mind and spirit which is in man. In fact the spirit which is in man is inbreathed by God and continues to actuate man as long as God is pleased that man should be a living being (Gen. ii.; Ps. civ).

Man as a rule is under the dominion of his own human spirit but in exceptional instances the Spirit of God (Yahweh) enters into him. The signs of his doing this are naturally actions and words of miraculous character, feats of extraordinary physical strength (in the case of Samson, Jdg. xiv.-xvii.) or signs of wisdom and skill (in the cases of Bezaleel and Aholiab, Ex. xxxi. 2ff.) and utterances and conduct in an ecstatic condition associated with the prophets of the earlier period (I Sam. x. 10; xi. 6; xix. 20, 23).

There is, however, a well-marked change, though it is neither sudden nor to be attributed to the agency of any single person or event, between the manifestations of the Spirit in the earlier and the later stages of Old Testament religious life. And it is of the nature of a progress from the outward to the inner, from the physical and intellectual to the ethical. More and more the presence of the Divine Spirit in man is perceived in the mind that appreciates and tends to promote the righteous will of Yahweh. The prophets speak under the inspiration of God, but no longer need to point to ecstatic experiences as a sign of their inspiration. Furthermore they predict a time in the future when the gift of the Spirit would not be limited to a few privileged individuals

[1] Volz, *Der Geist Gottes*, pp. 10ff.
[2] *Beginnings of the Church*, p. 63.

but become the endowment of faithful Israel as a whole (Joel ii. 28, 29). Yet the Messiah as the ideal head of faithful Israel was to be especially possessed and equipped for his work by the presence of God's Spirit in him (Isa. lxiii.).

It is with this prophecy that the New Testament takes up the conception. The public appearance of Jesus in the Nazareth synagogue served as the occasion for the declaration of his consciousness that he had been equipped as the Messiah. Even if, as is probable, the words are placed by Luke out of their chronological order, they indicate the conviction that the kingdom of God was to be ushered under the guidance of the Spirit of God. Throughout his ministry Jesus gave proof of the initial claim he made in his sermon in the Nazareth synagogue that the Spirit of God was working in and through him.

He unquestionably cast out demons. The Pharisees, unwilling to have their idea of the Messiahship disturbed, attributed this to an alliance with the prince of the demons (Mt. xii. 24ff; Mk. iii. 22; Lk. xi. 15f). In repelling the charge Jesus called attention to the absurdity of such an alliance in itself. Then turning the argument against them he claimed that the fact of his casting out demons was evidence of the coming of the kingdom. To carry the thought to its logical conclusion he proceeded to point out the spiritual insensitiveness of attributing a good deed to an evil cause—an impulse and an action of God to the archenemy of God and good could end in a hopeless alienation from God, a sin that "hath no forgiveness either in this world or in that to come."

The pervasion of the whole personality and work of Jesus by the presence and power of the Spirit superseded the necessity of explicit teaching concerning the nature and work of the Spirit as a separate source of energy or personality so long as Jesus himself was carrying on his earthly mission. When he committed the continuation of his work to his disciples, the very first condition of their success was the assurance that the power they should need to this end was with them. Accordingly the thought of the Holy Spirit flashed into a full blaze from the very beginning of the independent existence of the brotherhood of believers in Jesus as Christ. No amount of critical sifting of the account given by Luke in the early chapters of Acts will eliminate the certainty of the conviction dominant through the first days that God had in a special manner made known his plan and purpose to bless and direct the efforts of the brotherhood in making Jesus known and recognized as the Christ. And more specifically no matter what interpretation is put upon the story of the day of Pentecost, the whole gist of the events following requires as its ground a vivid conviction that the essential facts given in the account are historical.

What then was the conception of the Holy Spirit with which the apostolic age began and by which it is pervaded? First of all a growingly clear distinction dawned on the mind of Christ's followers between God as creator, preserver and ruler of the world, the Father of human beings and the rightful object of their affection and loyalty, and the Holy Spirit working in this body of disciples committed to the cause of Jesus the Christ. That this distinction was thought of in the terms of philosophy and may be called a personal distinction would be too much to affirm in the light of the data accessible. That a separate being fitly called by a separate name, the Holy Spirit, was clearly in mind is unquestionable. The group which used this name consisted of Jews and could not entertain the notion of a second, or third God under the separate name. But it was also a group to which consistency in a philosophical way was not the primary requisite in thinking. Thus we may leave the problem of a personal Holy Spirit as one not calling for an answer in the age.

There is clearer light on the work of the Holy Spirit. First of all the presence of the Spirit was seen in results requiring the use of extraordinary power. Later thought has distinguished in the body of these results between the natural and the so-called "supernatural." To the latter it has given the name of "gifts" ($\chi\alpha\rho\iota\sigma\mu\alpha\tau\alpha$). Of the charismatic manifestations of the Spirit's power again two varieties have been recognized—"healings" and "tongues." Of these the first manifestly fall into the same group of occurrences as the miracles of healing performed by Jesus and properly best discussed in the investigation of the historical course of the life of Jesus. The gift of tongues constitutes a special type of spiritual energy distinctive of the apostolic generation though not limited to it. Just what was it?

(1) *The Gift of "Tongues."*—About the exact nature of the gift of tongues as described in Acts, however, there is considerable obscurity which must be dispelled by light to be derived from without the book. When the investigation is limited to Acts, the facts do not seem altogether harmonious. Whereas on the day of Pentecost, the first impression is that this gift consists in the ability to speak in languages not previously learned, later on the same gift seems to leave the men that possessed it just as helpless in the matter of speaking foreign languages as they were before. Paul and Barnabas preaching in the cities of South Galatia (Lystra, Derbe, Iconium) did not understand the language of the people when they were discussing their plan of sacrificing to them, taking them to be gods. And when they found out by watching their actions they were horrified (xiv. 19-14). If they had possessed the gift of speaking in languages which they did not learn beforehand, how were they so surprised? Why did Paul speak and preach in the language he had known all his life?

Light is thrown from without the book on this matter by Paul (I Cor. xii-xiv.). The gift of tongues here seems to be the power to utter impressive but unintelligible (perhaps inarticulate) speech under the power of a high emotional excitation, and not the power to speak in language not previously studied or learned. If that be taken as a basis, the phenomena of Pentecost become quite clear. The facts in the account of Pentecost are that upon the coming of the Holy Spirit the disciples became emotionally exalted. In that state they gave utterance to language vigorously and clearly. This brought a great crowd around them. In that crowd there happened to be men from different parts of the Orient, mostly Jews assembled to observe the feast of

Pentecost. The author enumerates people from fourteen or fifteen different localities, but different languages spoken by these could not have been more than three or, at the most, four.

Moreover the use of the word "dialect" in this account points to the fact that it was not distinct languages but dialectic differences that had to be overcome. Hence the conclusion seems to be inevitable that under the influence of the high emotions of the exaltation these disciples of Jesus spoke the common language known to the great majority in the audience in such a way that the dialectic differences were submerged, and they understood what apart from such an experience as they had had would have passed altogether unnoticed.

The gift of tongues was apparently the most striking of the manifestations of the Spirit because it was the least familiar to the men of the day. Though in a complete view of the physical experience it is capable of classification with others under the general group of ecstatic phenomena, its outbreak in the special form it took rendered it not easily recognizable. Consequently it attracted more attention and occupies relatively a larger place in the record than the gift of healing or miracles in general and much more than the non-charismatic manifestations of spiritual power. These latter must in the end have bulked larger in the full life of the early Christians than the extraordinary outbreaks. For life consists of the commonplaces which because of their familiarity fail to find a place in the records; whereas the spectacular and uncommon occupy an illusively important position in the foreground of all pictures drawn for the benefit of future generations.

The ethical results of the Spirit's power in the primitive Christian community were quite distinctly marked. They were from the beginning what Paul, only a few years later, summed up in the concisest possible description of the varied "fruit of the Spirit,"—"love, joy, peace, long suffering, kindness, goodness, faithfulness, meekness, self-control." Through the predominance and intensive cultivation of these characteristics a new type of manhood made its appearance. The first sphere within which this type showed itself was the circle directly affected by the presence of the Spirit. The disciples of Jesus were drawn together even before the full and abundant influx of spiritual power noted in the occurrences of Pentecost. They were thoroughly knit into a unity under the influence of that event. But what the men of the Spirit meant to one another was only a partial outcome of their whole meaning to the human society within which they moved. Everywhere the man "who had been with Jesus" was marked and distinguished from the crowd round about him. He dared stand for his convictions against all efforts to restrain or suppress him. He was known for his love of truth, of purity and of kindness toward all.

2. THE CHURCH.—It has already been observed that whether Jesus used the term church or not, and whether he may be strictly called the founder of the body which for two thousand years has borne that name, he unquestionably gathered about him a group of disciples to

THE SPIRIT OF THE CHURCH

share with him in the work of proclaiming the kingdom of God. When his work culminated in his condemnation and death, these disciples were apparently thrown into a panic and were dispersed. Not many days afterwards, however, they returned to Jerusalem,[3] and were made aware of his resurrection. Having put away all their fears they now stood as a firmly knit-together band or fraternity and soon took to themselves the name church (ecclesia, ἐκκλησία).

For this association, or if one prefers to call it organization of the followers of Jesus, into a body there were sufficient and natural grounds and precedents in the life of the day. From one point of view the existing religious sects or parties (Pharisees, Sadducees, Zealots, etc., and preëminently the Essenes) furnished a suggestion to any group drawn together by community of religious interests and ideas. Inwardly, too, looking at the conception given in the prophets of the ideal Israel as the remnant within the actual Israel there was nothing strange in a group of Israelites, conscious of divine enlightenment and guidance, assuming to itself the right to look upon itself as a society within the society of God's chosen people and so designating itself. Thus the ecclesia or church came together as an ideal society within Judaism, the nucleus of the new people of the kingdom of God aiming to assimilate the whole of Israel to its own life.

The name church (ecclesia) was primarily derived from the Old Testament. The Greek term undoubtedly represents an original Hebrew word used in the theocratic usage of the earlier days. This term is rendered in the English versions of the Old Testament by "congregation," and is the word *Qahal* (Num. xvi. 3; xx. 4, etc.; II Ezr. x. 12-14; Neh. viii. 2, 12). There was no written constitution in Judaism defining the membership of the congregation or safeguarding the rights of those who belonged to it. It was constituted upon the emergence of an occasion requiring popular support and coöperation. It was informal and yet powerful in its ways of working and evidently commanded the respect and called for the affection and loyalty of the faithful Israelite.

The Greek equivalent brought over through the Septuagint was not very different in its antecedents and connotations. Of the two synonymous expressions—"synagogue" (συναγωγὴ) and "ecclesia" (ἐκκλησία)—the latter was applied to the actual assembly in session and the former to the ideal body of individuals that might upon occasion meet in convention. In classical usage the ecclesia was the body of citizens entitled to vote upon measures of public importance. It was constituted upon a summons or call, hence "the called" (from ἐκ and καλέω). While these distinctions are not maintained with strict uniformity throughout the entire history of usage, they exist in the main and they indicate the content of thought put into the term "church" in the first stage of its existence.

The church was then the body of God's people separated from the rest of mankind by a definite mind and life and destined to serve a

---

[3] Or, according to some, found one another in Galilee. E. F. Scott, *Beginnings of the Church*.

purpose in the unfolding of God's plan in the world. This association of the ideal with God's mind and purpose makes of the church from the outset a consecrated body. Its members as individuals were called "the saints." It was under the guidance of God. It was to it and through it that the Holy Spirit was given. One of the consequences of entrance into its membership, or from another point of view, one of the conditions of such membership was the possession of the Holy Spirit.

Its object was the furtherance of the kingdom of God. It was not only the nucleus of the society which would in its completeness constitute the kingdom, but it was the instrument for making the coming of the kingdom known and spreading its sway as widely as possible.

Every one who joined the church was asked to and cheerfully complied with the request to be baptized. Though it has been said confidently that "the rite of baptism was not instituted by Jesus," the long debate on this point resolves itself into a mere controversy about words. It is certain that from the very first day of its existence the church has initiated members to its fellowship by the rite of baptism. The true relation of Jesus himself to the ordinance is undoubtedly given by the fourth evangelist who says: "Jesus himself baptized not, but his disciples" (Jn. iv. 2), i.e., they did so with his knowledge and approval. Neither Jesus nor his disciples had need to invent such an ordinance, nor was a formal instruction on his part called for directing them to adopt it. John the Baptist had already given the rite its place and significance in the new order of the coming kingdom. Repentance and a clean life being indispensable in the kingdom, washing with water was adopted and, so far as adaptation was necessary, also adapted to the gospel of the kingdom as preached by Jesus.

The meaning of baptism thus practiced was nothing else than purification as a preparation for the righteous rule of God under which only the righteous could obtain any standing. The objection that since the first members of the church were Jews and since the Jews were accustomed to baptize proselytes from among the Gentiles in token of the putting away of Gentile filthiness, no Jew would submit to such a rite, loses its force when it is borne in mind that multitudes of Jews did admit their need of cleansing under the preaching of John the Baptist.

Yet between the baptism of John and that of the primitive church a vital difference developed. John himself signified that his demand for baptism was in the interest of an ethical commitment to a future event. In a manner it was the putting away of a former condition in favor of a future one that was not as yet a factor in the life of its subjects. Christian baptism became associated with the gift of the Holy Spirit. It was by this sign that Paul discovered the insufficient enlightenment of a group of believers at Ephesus who, on the strength of their baptism as disciples of John the Baptist, thought themselves to be Christians (Ac. xix. 2f). How constant and indispensable the gift of the Spirit was, however, to every individual may be open to question. In many instances, no doubt, either the contagion of group action or the psychological conditions present on such a pivotal occasion as one's public profession of faith formed favorable conditions for spiritual quickening and the emotional flow therefrom culminating in exceptional lines of conduct.

If baptism was the rite that ushered into the community of believers, the external sign of the bond which kept believers together as a body was another ordinance which they called the "breaking of bread." It is needless to seek any other identification of what is meant by the phrase than the sacrament later called by the names of the Lord's Supper, the Eucharist, the Holy Communion. The endless speculations of later days on the meaning of this sacrament and even the question whether it was attributed any strictly sacramentarian efficacy in these first days need not detain us. Suffice it to note that it would be a mistake to find in it the fullness of meaning which the church of the following centuries has placed there. Religious exercises which become habitual have a tendency to develop into rites. And rites as a rule accumulate significance from generation to generation. Frequently while the outward observance of the ceremony remains the same, the meaning of it is changed by additions or modifications.

The fixed point of departure so far as the "breaking of bread" is concerned is that it was based upon an event or act so associated with the inmost thought of Jesus as to remind his followers of him. It is in the "breaking of bread" that he had revealed his identity to the two on the way to Emmaus. There was only one scene in his life when the breaking of bread was by himself used as a sign of attaching his companions to himself, namely, at the last meal he partook with them. On that occasion he had told them that the bread signified his body offered as a covenant sacrifice binding them to himself and binding them together as the new covenant people with God. What the Lord's Supper then meant for the primitive Christians was that through the death of Jesus they were knit together into a brotherhood with him as their head and with a new spiritual life pervading and controlling them.

So vividly was it appreciated that its observance was a daily affair. Only later was it reduced to a weekly service. Moreover it was not necessary for the whole ecclesia to meet in order to make it valid; but groups meeting from house to house engaged in it. And, finally, it was an occasion not for sad memories of a Savior gone from them, but of glad experiences of communion with him and with those who loved him. In these simple ordinances the apostolic church found its means of spiritual edification and strengthening.

A life acceptable to God.

CHAPTER XVI

THE CHRISTIANITY OF JAMES

1. RELIGIOUS TEXTURE.—Never after the first distinct presentation of the new order as essentially rooted in the relation of men to God did the thought of the earliest Christians revert into the purely political or even the merely ethical ideal of a kingdom of God. The Epistle of James which is usually looked upon, at least since the days of Luther, as the least evangelical of all the New Testament writings, rises out of a background thoroughly committed to the religious element in life and to the institutions created by religion.

Through its whole extent the thought of James implies the existence of a church. As to what the form of organization of this church is it gives no hints. But it evidently had its meetings ("synagogues," ii. 2); it had its elders ("presbyters," v. 14), who were not mere elderly men, but officers of a well-defined body known as the church (ecclesia); it believed in and practiced prayer (v. 13ff.); it had conceptions (not to say doctrines) of God, of Christ, of man, of sin and its forgiveness, and especially of the duties of those who belonged to its membership. If the author is mainly interested in the moral and social tone of the conduct of his readers, he finds himself unable to write to them except as he visualizes them enmeshed in this network of religious thoughts and practices.

In fact underlying his thoroughgoing ethicism, James has an idea of an inner power, "a wisdom that is from above" (iii. 17), a subtle, diffusive, presumably irresistible life, revealed most clearly in its fruits. By these it may be recognized as "pure religion"[1] and "undefiled before God." The inner existence and outward manifestation of this religion renders its possessor acceptable to God, though it is itself the most "perfect gift coming from above." It is a principle of life "received" as the "implanted word which is able to save your souls" (i. 21). Those who have this living principle may say "Of his own will he brought us forth by the word of truth that we should be a kind of first fruits of his creatures" (i. 18).

The idea is essentially Christian. The occurrence of the term <u>wisdom</u> at once raises the question of the exact connotations of it in the author's mind. Before the synthesis of the primitively Hebrew concept of wisdom with the Stoic word (logos), which took place in Alexandria, the term designated the divine energy (spirit of God) which operates in creation, revelation and providential protection of the chosen people. Whether James has this in mind is not easy to say. The contexts in which he uses the word indicate rather a complex of mental and emo-

---

[1] θρησκεία, i. 27, the technical word for religion.

tional energies constituting an urge toward an ideal. Such an urge may be of divine origin, "heavenly," but it may be also the very opposite in source and objective (iii. 15, 17).

2. THE PERSON OF CHRIST.—But the centrality of the person of Christ already noted in the thought of the earliest apostolic church is here absent. The conventional Messianic terminology has been either left behind or it has not yet emerged into prominence, probably the former. Jesus is the Lord, but in what sense this formula so common in the Pauline stage of the development is to be taken remains a difficult problem to solve. Twice only is the term Lord associated with the name of Christ (i. 1; ii. 1). And in general it is certain that so designated Christ stands above the level of the rank and file of the community and has a unique dignity found in no other.

Yet what is this dignity and exaltation? (1) The term Lord (Κύριος) has in later Greek a purely honorific sense. It may be applied to a person just above, but not much above the level of a common gentleman. In the vocative the word may be used in addressing such a one as the equivalent of "Sir" (Κύριε). Evidently this is too barren a sense to fit in the context of James.

(2) In a higher sense a lord is one who holds bond servants by right of ownership. He may be master of those who constitute his estate, who work upon his lands or obey his mandates. Evidently this meaning of the term lord would only apply to Jesus figuratively. If his right to the Messiahship were recognized, it would naturally carry with it his being referred to or addressed as the Lord or authoritative ruler of his people. It is open to question, however, whether the author of James has exactly this in mind. He does not show signs of thinking in terms of Messianism except in the vaguest form of it.

(3) In the Greek translation of the Old Testament the term *kurios* was used to render the Hebrew *Adhonai*, as the uttered equivalent of the written name of God *Yahweh* (JHVH). So far as the Christians of the first days as converts from Judaism had occasion to speak of God in harmony with the habits formed in pre-Christian days they must have called God "the Lord." But it is unthinkable that as monotheists of the most rigid type they could have placed the man Jesus on an equality with the Jehovah of the Old Testament or that they could have identified him with the Lord of the universe enthroned in the highest heavens.

(4) But the word lord was at this time used in still another sense, viz., as the designation of heroic figures entitled to divine honors. In some contemporary cults the term *kurios* was current with this type of religious significance and applied to superhuman beings to whom divine homage was conceded and worship offered. Such were Serapis in Egypt, Mithra in Asia Minor and Adonis in certain portions of the Syro-Macedonian world. It was only a few years later that Paul wrote, "There are gods many and lords many" (I Cor. viii. 5). One of the manifestations of the growing Cæsar worship, which after the days of Caligula and Nero presented such a difficult problem to the

church, was the use of the term lord in connection with the emperor's name. In these latter instances of course no sincere belief in the deity of him who was called lord could have existed. Yet the accession to the meaning of the word of an approach to divinity is distinctly to be seen.

That these several senses of the term lord were kept clearly separated from one another is improbable. The common notion, underlying them all, of superior authority easily leads the mind to shift its view from one to the other and to make a variety of syntheses of them. In such a synthesized sense Festus used the word when he called Nero his lord (Ac. xxv. 28). Since none of them by itself harmonizes perfectly with the mind of the follower of Jesus, such as the author of James was, it is reasonable to suppose that the Lordship of Jesus was to him his Messianic supremacy over the Church.

The association of the Lordship with the vaguely conceived Messiahship of Jesus is borne out by the more extended form in which the title appears in its parallel use in ii. 1. Here the term "glory" signifies the light and majesty in which God dwells which belongs also to the Messiah.[2] The difficult phrase, if this identification be accepted, would be paraphrased as a whole, " the Lord Jesus Christ of the Messianic glory."

Though the Messianism of James is not sharply drawn, the above evidence of it is still further substantiated by the eschatological reference in the closing portion of the Epistle (v. 7, 8). The Lord (undoubtedly the same Jesus Christ who has been so designated) is to come again. And his coming must be awaited with patience and expectation of reward. In the usual manner of the generation this coming is to be in the near future; it "is at hand."

3. THE ROYAL LAW OF LOVE.—But if the religious texture of the thought is suffused by the acceptance of the Lordship of Jesus, its ethical contents are determined by the principle of brotherhood so characteristic of the teaching of Jesus. It has been contended by some that the Epistle of James is affiliated with the Wisdom type of writing in the Old Testament. However near the truth this may be in some respects it is more accurate to say that the writing breathes out the prophetic rendering of the Law. In essence it aims to make known the will of God. In form it makes use of the literary style of the Wisdom Literature. And in terminology it allies itself with the Law.

But the law it holds out to view is not the terror-inspiring system of the older codes. It is a new and genial principle. It is a law because it is prescriptive, definite and authoritative. It is not to be judged but to be obeyed (iv. 11). It is a royal law (ii. 8) presumably because it issues from the will and represents the authority of a king. On this ground it may be called royal also because of its excellence and dignity.

[2] G. B. Gray, art., "Glory," in Hastings, *Bible Dictionary* and A. von Gall, *Die Herrlichkeit Gottes*. The interpretation of Bengel, Mayor, according to which "of Glory" is here in apposition to Christ, is not sufficiently supported.

But its authority is not inconsistent with the liberty of those who are under it, for it is a "law of liberty." Of course this is not because it is to be obeyed by a voluntary act on the part of the subject. That is true of all law. It means that the law of liberty (ii. 12) is also a law of love. The liberty it assumes encourages no attitude of discontented or sullen acquiescence in it merely because disobedience might bring condign punishment. It works a glad and appreciative acceptance of the results it aims to secure. It stands in contrast with the Mosaic Law because its action is creative rather than restrictive, and altogether ethical rather than partly at least ceremonial. And yet it is continuous with the Old Testament system as is evidenced by its bringing into fuller operation the ancient precept according to the Scripture, "Thou shalt love thy neighbor as thyself."

The royal law is further an organic unity. Its parts and phases are interrelated in such a way that its violation at one point affects its whole content. "Whosoever shall keep the whole law and yet stumble in one point is become guilty of all." This is because one personal will stands behind it and is expressed through it all. An offense against the mere letter of the law would be a blow at a mere abstraction. But an offense against the royal law reaches the will of him who expressed himself in all of its parts (ii. 11).

4. SIN.—Primarily any disregard of the royal law is in itself sin. But sin is not the mere act of disobedience or transgression. It becomes an inner power holding together and giving unity to a series of acts (i. 14, 15). As such it is viewed in the light of an organism with a birth, growth and consummation. This vital principle, however, is in James a life within the life of the individual rather than within the life of the race. Accordingly it is not traced from its absolute beginnings in the history of man. In the individual its genesis and progress are traced with psychological minuteness. An inner urge (whose exact nature however is not defined) or "lust" draws and entices the will; it then develops into actual transgression and when it reaches the limit of its development it brings on its own end in the death of the sinner. From the point of view of the standard given in the royal law which as the expression of God's will is "the truth," sin is a departure from the truth (v. 19). The main evil in it is its offense against God (iii. 2).

But if the inner nature and psychology of sin are not in the center of interest, the concrete manifestations of it are always before the mind. It leads into all manner of excesses and disturbances in the private and even more seriously in the public life of men (i. 19). Some of these are wrath with its offspring, the unbridled tongue (iii. 1-12; iv. 1); pride and vanity (ii. 2); a servile spirit (ii. 3); envyings and strife (iii. 4); covetousness (ii. 4); injustice and oppression. The rewards of all forms of sin are misery (v. 1), confusion (iii. 16), condemnation (v. 9) and death (i. 15; v. 20). Lastly the non-performance of a known duty is sin, presumably because it is always the result of excessive self-love (iv. 17).

5. CHRISTIAN SALVATION.—From the evils of sin there is a way of escape. Fundamentally this way involves the abandonment and extinction of sin itself. If salvation (σωτηρία from σώζω) be viewed as (1) rescue or (2) preservation from sin, the tendency of James is to stress the latter rather than the former of these aspects of it. But they are not mutually exclusive and a conception of it in its comprehensiveness underlies the thought and is assumed as familiar to his readers.

In fact the question of the way of salvation as a distinctly Christian system is present to the mind of James. It constitutes one of the few subjects that divert him from the practical to the theoretical arena. The question presents itself in the simple form, "What saves, faith or works?" The discussion of the question is carried on as if the doctrine of justification by faith alone as preached by Paul were the butt of an attack. So far, however, as Paul personally is concerned it is almost certain that the author of James does not refer to him. But it is not unlikely that some extreme and garbled form of Paul's peculiar doctrine may have come to his knowledge and stirred him to point out the weakness of it in the form in which it was pressed.

Furthermore a contradiction between the doctrine of justification by faith as Paul had it in mind, preached it and safeguarded it by his explanations, and the position taken by the author of James is an altogether superficial and unwarranted inference from the facts. A careful examination of the phraseology used in the so-called controversy reveals the fact that each side to it uses the cardinal words "faith" and "works" in a different sense. These are words each of which has a narrower and a fuller meaning.

Faith may be used as the equivalent of mere belief which is the assent of the mind to the reality of a proposition held before it. It is a purely intellectual and involuntary act. But faith may be the assent of the mind along with the consent of the will. It may be essentially an act of self-surrender to that which has been believed. The difference between faith as belief and faith as self-surrender is made up by the voluntary element of trust included in the latter conception. Belief alone is what the "demons" have and "they shudder."

Likewise the term "works" may be taken in a narrower sense as a synonym for deeds. In such a case the motive and underlying intellectual processes leading to their performance are left out of consideration. But works may be viewed as the culmination and necessary vital outcome of belief accepted and allowed to mature into their full consequence in outward conduct. Again the difference between outward works (or deeds) and works as the preferred and voluntary expression of thought is to be found in the element of trust. "Abraham offered up Isaac his son upon the altar," because he trusted God as good.

The contradiction between the Pauline doctrine and that of James vanishes as soon as it is realized that each of these has a different idea in mind when he uses each of the terms. To James faith is mere belief while works are the reasoned out result of an inner process ending in trust. To Paul works are deeds irrespective of the consent of the heart and mind to what is done, whereas faith is essentially the commitment to what has been believed. Accordingly both the Pauline argument and that of James are able to rest on the same illustration from the Old Testament—the case of Abraham. No genuine Paulinist of the day of James could have objected to the conclusion in which the matter is summed up: "For as the body without the spirit is dead, even so faith apart from works is dead" (ii. 26). But he might have reversed the figure and insisted that "works apart from faith are dead."

6. THE GOSPEL IN LIFE.—A full appreciation of the principles held supreme by James would lead to a full-orbed and well-proportioned ethical idea. It would present to the individual as well as to the body politic not only the pattern of conduct most consistent with the highest interests of humanity but also the rationale underlying it. The special conditions of the time, however, called for special emphasis on some matters. These are naturally given a larger prominence in the exposition of the ideal. In other words the ideal is not drawn up *in thesi*, but with a view to a situation confronting the leader of the day. It is certain also that the leader's own personal point of view, as controlled in large measure by his native qualities, and his training enter into the forces that have given direction to his exposition.

The chief questions before James were those of the social relations of Christians among themselves. Granting that the key to their conduct in all circumstances should be the consciousness of brotherhood, they were coming short in some ways because they failed to conform to ideal brotherly attitude.

One of the sources of the evil was an actual or imaginary advantage of some over their brethren. These supposed that they were better instructed and therefore competent to assume the rôle of teachers among them (iii. 1). They are reminded that a heavier responsibility awaits them and that in the nature of the case their qualifications for the rôle of teacher are relative and imperfect.

Another source of unbrotherliness was the possession by some of wealth. This fact was the occasion of stumbling both to those who did and to those who did not have the wealth. It affected the latter because it led them to lose their self-respect and adopt the attitude of servile obsequiousness toward the more prosperous. That one should be honored and preferred to others because of his money was especially offensive, since outward success and prosperity were precarious and detrimental to the spirit of dependence upon God which should be held in view in all planning for the future (ii. 5-7; iv. 15).

In another way the poor were stirred to jealousy and uncharitable judgment of the conduct of the rich. There were strivings and jealousies between "classes and masses."

But wealth was also a snare to the wealthy because its possession inspired a sense of superiority and led to unjust as well as unkind treatment of the poor. On this point James is especially pronounced and severe (v. 1-6). Perhaps he bears in mind the warning of Jesus himself to the rich and the difficulty of their securing a place in the kingdom of

God. The sin of contemptuousness together with its numerous progeny of oppressive and unjust ways of dealing with the poor was not the only offense of the wealthy. They easily fell under the power of litigiousness, dragging their brethren before the courts and causing the name of Christ to be evil-spoken because of their unworthy exemplification of its influence (ii. 7).

Another virtue held up as of supreme importance by James is that of self-control, especially in the most difficult form in which it can be exercised, namely, in the matter of the use of the tongue. A Christian should be "swift to hear, slow to speak, slow to wrath" (i. 19). Inability to bridle one's tongue is a sign of defect in religion (i. 26). And the seriousness of it and of its consequences so impresses James that he recurs to it over and over again. He names it in urging restraint and simplicity in making assertions (v. 12, "swear not") and he takes pains to depict the unforeseen and unpremeditated latent possibilities of unrestrained speech (iii. 1-12).

In general James is the exponent of the form of thought presupposing the Jewish conception of God as the creator and judge but developing it toward the side of benevolence and grace. He looks upon man as a frail being who falls into snares and temptations lying about him, who may be victimized by forces impersonal or personal (demons) and who must seek his highest good in loyal submission to his creator through Jesus Christ the Lord.

A life in Christ.

CHAPTER XVII

THE PETRINE TEACHING

Between the type of religious thinking given by the author of Acts in the speeches of Peter and that discovered in First Peter with the two secondary Petrine writings (Second Peter and Jude) there is a distinct difference. So long as criticism is not as yet able to segregate with trustworthy precision the original words of Peter from the form in which they come to us through the reporters, the most reasonable way of accounting for the difference is to attribute it to Luke's methods as a historian. One characteristic of this method is the effort to reach as nearly as possible the primitive facts and describe them with reasonable correctness. In reporting Peter's discourses he has evidently gone back to the mind of the church as far as he could ascertain it and made Peter its spokesman. The result is that the New Testament now contains two varieties of ostensibly Petrine thought—the one in Acts and the one in the writings claiming Petrine authorship. Of these the first is Petrine only as Peter is the mouthpiece of the primitive Christian community; the second aims to express the Apostle's maturer individual views as a leader as given somewhat later and repeated by a group of followers after his death.

The Petrine thought of the Epistles of Peter is an advance on the primitive apostolic undifferentiated type. It grows out of a more comprehensive and thoroughgoing acceptance of Christ, a fuller understanding of the mystery of his personality and a more intimate interweaving of his redemptive work into the practical outworking of religion in life. Its controlling idea, translated into modern terms, is best expressed in the phrase: The new life in Christ. As in the Epistle of James much stress is laid in it on the practical results of the new faith; but that faith is seen more directly rooted in the person and work of Jesus Christ. The salient points of the Petrine thought appear to be determined by the questions: Who is Jesus Christ? How does he enter into the lives of men and affect them? And what naturally does the acceptance of him mean for those who accept him?

1. Who Is Christ?—The Petrine literature makes use of the same term "Lord" which called for explanation in the Epistle of James. (I Pet. i. 2; II Pet. i. 1, 8, 11, 14, 16; ii. 10; iii. 18; Jude 4, 7, 21, 25). And the same comprehensive sense is attached to the title as in that writing. Apart from the ascription of Lordship to him, however, Jesus occupies here a far more distinctly outlined position than in the Epistle

139

of James; yet not as clear an affiliation is given him with divinity as in the Pauline system. The Petrine Christology thus stands intermediate between the primitive more technical Messianic and the Pauline theological Christologies. In a real sense it is transitional.

One expression in First Peter has occasioned a spirited debate. It is the expression "foreknown before the foundation of the world but manifested at the end of the times" (i. 20). The contrast between "foreknown" and "manifested" in this passage has been understood as necessarily implying the preëxistence of him to whom the words refer. This inference is apparently supported by the words used previously in v. 11, where speaking of the prophetic word concerning the gospel of salvation the author alludes to "the spirit of Christ" which was in "the prophets testifying concerning the sufferings of Christ." If in this last-named place the Spirit of Christ is to be understood as the person of Christ himself or an entity so identified with the person of Christ, the thought of the preëxistence of Christ would, of course, be put beyond question. To this consideration could be added the additional one of the assumed late date of First Peter and its subjection to Alexandrian influences. For it is through these that the thought of the preëxistence of Christ was developed among Christians.

There is, however, in all this reasoning a strain of artificiality. The allegation, for instance, of Alexandrian influence in First Peter will not bear the test of the full light. Neither is it consistent with the conclusion reached from all the other considerations available that the letter was written from Rome about 66 or 67 A.D., and was dictated in substance by the Apostle Peter himself. Furthermore the exegesis of i. 11 does not commend itself to the critical sense. The phrase "Spirit of Christ" can only mean in the light of the historical situation, the Holy Spirit, the mediator of revelation. That the divine Spirit, later uniformly called the Holy Spirit, was the illuminator and guide of the Old Testament prophets was a conviction of the later Judaism as well as of primitive Christendom. And the preëminence of Christ in the latter easily suggested the substitution of the phrase Spirit of Christ for it. Finally the antithesis of "foreknown" and "manifested" in i. 20 is rhetorically ill-balanced if by "foreknown" were meant preëxistent. Had the thought of the author been that of preëxistence, he must have used some such word as ὄντος instead of προεγνωσμένου.

The real intention of the author is not either to assert or deny the metaphysical and philosophical idea of Christ's person, but to impress his readers with the greatness of their salvation. Naturally this could have been done by calling attention to the exalted rank of the redeemer as a preëxistence being. But only just a little less forcible is the thought that this redeemer was a subject of God's preknowledge and care. It is not, therefore, as foreknown as an existing being, but as ideally foreseen by God in his eager desire and determination to provide a Savior that Christ is presented.

Who then is Christ? The question is answered in the proposition, He is the God-appointed Savior who even before his earthly birth and manifestation had been assigned a glorious place and distinguished career. In this respect the person of Christ is unparalleled among men. Of no other prophet or martyr, king or priest could the same words be used.

But equally unique is the life of Christ upon earth. It was a life of unparalleled moral perfection. "He did no sin, neither was guile found in his mouth" (ii. 22). It might be questionable whether this phraseology was intended by the author as a sweeping assertion covering the whole course of Jesus' conduct "in the days of his flesh," or as an assertion of his blamelessness in the matters which occasioned and led up to his death. If the latter is the case the author intended to say, he was treated as a criminal even though he was absolutely free of any criminal act or intention. In view of the earlier characterization of the dying Savior as "a lamb without blemish and without spot" (i. 19) it is fair to infer that even if in the special context the more precise sense of the words is the restricted one, lurking in the background stands the absolute sinlessness of the man Jesus. Without such sinlessness the sacrificial function he undertook to perform would lose its meaning.

But Christ's uniqueness is most clearly manifested in his resurrection from the dead. He was rejected and put to death (I Pet. ii. 2; iii. 18; iv. 1-13; v. 1). But, as in Peter's speech at Pentecost, the emphasis is laid on the fact that "it was not possible that he should be holden of death" (Ac. ii. 24). Peter holds up the resurrection fact as the ground and source of the Christian salvation (i. 3). He points to the fact as a token that God distinguishes between the risen one and all others by giving him glory. Especially does he associate the fact of the resurrection with the assurance of believers that their "'faith and hope are in God" (i. 21).

And the resurrection was both confirmed and rewarded in his exaltation to the highest place of honor at the right hand of God (iii. 22). Of what his work as the exalted Savior is there is no intimation; but that his exaltation is not an empty honor is indicated by the additional note that through it all superhuman beings created by God according to the Jewish idea—angels, authorities, powers—are made subject to him.

This exalted idea of the Savior reaches its highest and fullest expression in the opening words of the Epistle in the tracing of the salvation to the threefold grace of "the foreknowledge of God the Father," "the sanctification of the Spirit" and "the obedience and sprinkling of the blood of Jesus Christ" (i. 1). To this is to be added the use of the term Father (applied to God) in the singular as of Jesus alone—"the Father of our Lord Jesus Christ" (i. 3). The question "Who is Christ?" may then be answered upon the Petrine basis with the least possible margin of speculation and inference and the largest dependence on the explicit words of the Petrine writings. Christ is the Messiah, chosen of God and standing in the most intimate, even transcendent relationship with God. God has honored him by raising him from the dead. He is to be accepted as the Messiah and obeyed as the Lord.

2. How Does Christ Save?—The question is large and may be divided into two parts. What has Christ done for men? and, How do men benefit by what he has done?

(1) In general the first of these questions is answered in the familiar formula: Christ has died for men. At this point Peter enters the field of theology. He undertakes to give an explanation of the way in which salvation was achieved. Without taking from Paul (as has already been intimated) the conception of the redemptive efficacy of the cross, he expresses the thought of his fellow believers that Jesus by submitting to the death of the cross had assumed the rôle of the servant of Yahweh (Is. lii. 13; liii. 12). For this thought in the mind of the primitive church there was some ground in what Jesus himself had done and had, though vaguely, intimated in his words.

The Petrine thought links the death of Christ with the sacrificial ideal of the Old Testament. It contrasts the life of Christ as offered in his death with the corruptible things ("silver and gold") which were sometimes offered as the price of redemption, and points out that the life was "the precious blood as of a lamb without blemish and without spot." But though the expression leads the mind back to the Old Testament ritual, the reference cannot be to the lamb of Isaiah liii. 7; for it does not appear that the lamb in that case was ceremonially blameless, the content of thought in the figure being rather the non-resisting conduct of the victim led to the slaughter than to its spotless perfection. But in the sacrificial system the only use of the lamb is that of a burnt offering; and it serves as the expression of the offerer's aspirations in presence of the altar of God. That its blood may signify the annulment of sin is not to be questioned. But upon what principle remains unexplained. It would be natural to assume that the writer had in mind a comprehensive and not sharply outlined conception of the efficacy of Christ's sacrificial death.

Even more ambiguous and subject to a variety of interpretations is the other reference to the death of Christ which is made in ii. 24, "who his own self bare our sins in his body upon the tree." The word ἀναφέρειν (to bear or carry up), is frequently used in the LXX of bringing up a sacrifice and laying it upon the altar. But the word ξύλον (tree) is incongruous if the offering of the body of Christ on the cross is literally meant, for the cross is not an altar. Accordingly a multitude of explanations have been suggested to reconcile the inconsistency. Another difficulty arises from the fact that the sin-offering is nowhere in the Old Testament burnt on the altar. But though the expression presents these difficulties, no casual reader is ever misled by Peter's words. The evident intention is to present the crucifixion as in some way analogous with the bringing of the victim to the altar loaded with the sins of the people and doing away with sin by this act.

(2) The effect of the death on the cross is more prominent in the thought than the method of its working. That effect is explicitly described as "being rid of sin" (ἀπογενόμενοι); and being rid of sin is in turn the means toward "living in righteousness." Sin is a principle dia-

metrically opposed to and destructive of life. Salvation is the freeing of the life principle in order that it should function unhindered. The same thought is given in iv. 12. The suffering and death of Christ must issue in the cessation of sin in the lives of those who accept him.

The practical meaning of salvation is given also in other ways (1) The blessing which Christ brings is a rescue from a "vain manner of life" (I Pet. i. 18; II Pet. i. 4). Sin according to this way of thinking renders life futile. It reduces it to a bubble destined to break and disappear. Christ by eliminating sin gives it substance and value. Pursuing the figure further it converts the empty bubble into a ball of solid gold.

(2) Salvation is in another light shown to be the process of purification from sin. The thought is familiar. It is brought into view in unfolding the meaning of baptism (I Pet. iii. 21; II Pet. i. 9). Working out a suggestion which the mention of the case of Noah at the time of the deluge gives him, Peter points out the spiritual significance of baptism as a cleansing not of material pollution but of spiritual, which issues in "the interrogation of a good conscience toward God." The sinner cannot appear as such before God. Through Christ he is enabled to do so, but only as by the washing away of his sin signified in his baptism.

(3) Again salvation is a rebirth (i. 3, 25; II Pet. i. 4). The emphasis in this mode of presentation is not on the evil from which the saved is delivered, but on the blessing which he comes to enjoy when saved. Yet the figure of a second birth may be associated with the thought that the first birth was in a manner a failure; that the subject of it had permitted himself to become misshapen and that only by a reconstitution in a second process could he achieve his ideal. In any case, as in the Johannine teaching, regeneration is from above. It is "God who in his great mercy begat us again," "not of corruptible seed, but of incorruptible."

3. How Men May Benefit by What Christ Did.—In all these ways of thinking of Jesus' saving work and in others less vividly portrayed, the object is to show what God through Christ does for men. They are all primarily brought to the attention of believers in order that these may the more fully appreciate their privileges and cling to them. They are aimed to impress the exceeding greatness and preciousness of the Savior's work. How men become sharers in this saving work is assumed to be a question on which no additional light is needed. The Petrine type of thinking is not addressed to unbelievers with a view to inducing them to believe, but to Christians already convinced of the necessity of faith but in need of having that faith fortified.

Yet the questions: "Who may be saved?" and "When?" are treated by Peter in a way unparalleled elsewhere in the New Testament. For in his exposition of the full career of the Savior as he follows him from his earthly sufferings and death to his resurrection and exaltation up to the right hand of God, he inserts the incident of his preaching to "the spirits in prison" (I Pet. iii. 18-20; ii. 24). The total absence of any other reference to this account of Christ's work in the New Testament invests the words of the text with much obscurity. It becomes necessary to answer three questions, as follows:

(1) When did Christ preach to the spirits in prison? The words of the passage seem to answer that this was between his death and resurrection. This, however, has appeared to many to be rather superficial. These shift the emphasis from the question of time to that of the agent through whom Christ preached. Christ died in the flesh, but the spirit, which in him did not die, was the same that in the days of Noah had preached to the disobedient souls of Noah's day. Between these two interpretations it is not difficult to choose. The latter forces the grammatical construction so violently that it cannot be admitted.

(2) To whom did Christ preach? The answer, "to the spirits in prison" of all who had lived before his day seems to have the support of iv. 6, "the Gospel was preached even to the dead." But the fuller statement of iii. 20 singles out a special class of disobedient spirits who are elsewhere (Eth. En. vi.-xi.) also singled out and given prominence. The words of iv. 6 are not inconsistent with the rendering which finds the primary reference to this notorious group of offenders. And it is to these that the preaching must have been addressed.

(3) But for what purpose did Christ preach to them? The answer may be and has by many been supposed to be: In order that they might know what they had missed and must miss. God's grace which had provided such a wonderful salvation for mankind as a whole was withdrawn from them. This appears harsh and illogical and contrary to the author's own thought in iv. 6 where he says that they heard the gospel in order "that they might live according to God in the spirit."

It appears, then, that the Petrine doctrine of the gospel of salvation admitted its acceptance by one class of spirits at least, whose earthly lives had closed leaving them under condemnation. Whether this was a special and exceptional occurrence, a declaration of amnesty as it were in celebration of the completion of the work of redemption or only an exhibition of a principle always operative no intimation is given. If it were the former no further theological or even religious significance could be attached to the idea. If the latter it certainly shows in the Petrine type of Christian thought a distinct individual conception which nowhere else in the New Testament emerges into view.

An ingenious way of clearing the obscurity of the text has been suggested by J. Rendel Harris, which is based on a conjectural emendation of the text. If the Greek of the passage be read ἐν ᾧ χ' ἐνώχ ἐκήρυξε instead of as it stands ἐν ᾧ καὶ τοῖς it would mean that Christ was put to death according to the flesh, but was raised according to the spirit in which Enoch also had preached (in his day) to the spirits who are now in prison. To say nothing of the difference between ἐν ᾧ and ἐνώχ there is no evidence, that such a corruption of the text exists and, therefore, the proposed emendation has found little favor among scholars.

THE PETRINE TEACHING

4. Development and Manifestation of the Redeemed Life.— Upon any theory of their strict authorship the writings of the Petrine group have been placed together by the intuitive judgment of later Christendom because they represent the thought and life of the believer in the incomparable salvation wrought by Christ. They do this as mutually complementary to one another. First Peter aims to strengthen the faith of Christians and fortify them against the danger of backsliding under stress of persecution. Therefore it has a larger element of intellectual light in it. Second Peter and Jude aim to preserve them from confusion in mind and corruption in life. Therefore they are more replete in warnings against the moral dangers and pitfalls that are met in the everyday experience. But all point clearly the need of spiritual guidance.

In common they strengthen and develop the conviction that spiritual energy from God himself has been in the past and is in the present available to the believer. God's spirit (the Holy Spirit) has worked first of all in enlightening the prophets concerning the salvation to be accomplished by Christ (I Pet. i. 10-12; II Pet. i. 19-21). But, in the circumstances, it was not possible for the human minds of the prophets in spite of their great desire and effort to understand the fullness of the redemption revealed in Jesus Christ. This only was certain that they were actuated by the Spirit.

Next to his revealing work the Spirit of God moves the subjects of salvation to sanctification of life. This indeed is so vital that it can be named along with the foreknowledge of God the Father and the redemptive work of Jesus Christ as the chief good designed for the people of God's choice (I Pet. i. 2). And without distinction between the Holy Spirit and the Father as in a developed Trinitarian doctrine, God's efficiency in the lives of believers either as God or as Holy Spirit is recognized in a number and variety of ways. His power guards (as by a garrison set up around them) the spiritual welfare of his people (I Pet. i. 5) and helps those whom he has called making them perfect, supporting, strengthening and grounding them (I Pet. v. 10).

The life of Christians must be a progressive, growing movement reaching out to a broader and fuller ideal of which the perfect fulfilment is nothing short of Jesus Christ's earthly career (I Pet. iv. 1). Its beginnings may be feeble as those of human infancy. But it has its means of being nourished (I Pet. ii. 2), and may attain to fuller stature and virile power. It must grow from less to more, even as a building which is constructed by the addition of successive stones. In the process of growth the growing individual has a part. He can by conscious effort add virtue to virtue, holding what he has already gained and augmenting its proportions (II Pet. i. 19-21; iii. 18).

The tests of approach to the ideal are constancy to the faith (I Pet. i. 6), steadfast purification from sin (I Pet. i. 22; ii. 1, 11; iv. 3; II Pet. ii. passim; Jude passim), the prevalence of brotherly love in the community of believers (I Pet. i. 22; iii. 8; iv. 8) and the peaceable disposition (I Pet. ii. 13; iii. 8).

5. ISSUES OF THE CHRISTIAN LIFE.—Of these there are two, specifically distinguished from each other and yet very closely, one might say inextricably, linked with each other.

(1) *The Parousia,* "Presence" of the Lord (I Pet. i. 7-13; iv. 13).—The presence of Christ is viewed as a revelation ("manifestation"). He was raised from the dead and ascended on high, he is hidden from the outward eyes of his followers, but he will in due time become manifested.

(2) *The End of the World.*—The topic is quite prominent in Second Peter, particularly Chapter III. The mode of presentation is perhaps the most typical apocalyptic passage both in form and content to be found in the New Testament outside of the Book of Revelation. It is deduced from the older prophetic portraitures and is highly imaginative. It makes use of the figure of a final cataclysm in which the world will be destroyed by fire. The moral significance is the important thing in this portraiture. That is the purification of the world of mankind and the restoration of humanity to its original ideal as it was at the creation.

Both the parousia and the end of the world are clearly and intensely apocalyptic in form. But while they undoubtedly express an expectation of events in the outward physical sphere, it is not as occurrences in the material universe that these events interest the witness, but because of their inner spiritual and moral significance. The new heavens and the new earth to which the eye looks forward are worth while only because in them "dwelleth righteousness." And the revelation (parousia, or second coming) of the Lord is of value only as it will be the means of personal fellowship with him for the believer.

PART III
THE GOSPEL OF PAUL

CHAPTER XVIII

PAUL THE WRITER AND THE MAN

1. The Writings of Paul. —The modern world has ampler and more direct means for knowing the mind of Paul than that of any person in the age of the church's beginnings. Needless to say this does not exclude Jesus himself. For whereas Jesus wrote nothing, Paul found it necessary in his doing his share of the fundamental work to express his ideas with emphasis and fullness. In this respect Paul and Jesus stand in complete contrast with one another. The work of Jesus is creative and inspirational, that of Paul constructive and promotive. Jesus brought the materials of thought into being, or at all events, into the light; Paul shaped and fitted them together for the best use to which his own generation and all future generations could put them.

Much is given in the Acts of the Apostles by one who knew Paul in intimate personal relations. The world would have had a good understanding of him if nothing more had been preserved than Luke's account of him; but it is not dependent on Luke and the Book of Acts for its ideas of Paul and his teachings. His own Epistles give such abundant light on this subject that the parallel account in Acts could have been spared, although it must be admitted that this would have resulted in a large impoverishment of our knowledge of the great Apostle. To the Epistles, therefore, with such accessory light as the account of Acts may add we must go for our study of Paul's Gospel.

But what is an "epistle" in this connection? Deissmann [1] has pointed out a distinction between a letter designed primarily as a private communication from one person to another or to a group or community of persons, and a writing meant from the beginning to be a public document. Even when letters of the former class are given to the public (as is frequently done in the case of leading men in the type of book usually entitled "Life and Letters of, etc.") their style and content is characterized by an informality and genuineness lacking in the epistles as a literary production.[2]

Paul's Epistles are strictly personal letters, free from the artificialities and affectations of literature. This position has been recognized by the best of the most recent writers on Paul.[3] Though not of cardinal importance, this understanding of them adds something to the modern sense of the practical value of Paul's writings.

[1] *The Apostle Paul*, trans. by Lionel R. M. Strachan, ch. i.
[2] Junius, *Letters;* Pascal, *Provincial Letters;* Erasmus, *Epistulæ Virorum Observorum.*
[3] H. A. A. Kennedy, *The Theology of the Epistles;* A. H. McNeile, *St. Paul, His Life, Letters and Christian Doctrine;* David Smith, *The Life and Letters of St. Paul.*

The Epistles of Paul constitute a group in the New Testament concerning whose precise scope and content the judgment of those interested has differed. From the earliest days to the dawn of modern criticism the tendency prevailed to attribute to the Apostle every writing that by any direct or indirect line could be traced to his pen or to his influence. The distinction between Pauline and Deutero-Pauline was unknown. Accordingly more writings were called Epistles of Paul than he actually wrote. Among these were the Epistle to the Hebrews and the Epistle to the Laodiceans (a compilation of excerpts from the other Epistles).

In 1804 Eichhorn introduced the critical method into the study of the Epistles and reached the conclusion that the pastoral Epistles were not writings of Paul. This view was made the basis of an interesting discussion lasting till 1831, when Ferdinand Christian Baur began the new movement, dominated by the Hegelian philosophy, known as the Tübingen criticism. The characteristic position of the school founded by Baur was, so far as Paul and his work were concerned, that only four Epistles could be regarded as genuinely Pauline, namely Galatians, 1st and 2d Corinthians and Romans. These were called the "cardinal" Epistles because upon them the constructive work of the historical study of Paul must be based. They were also called the "doctrinal" Epistles from the predominantly doctrinal nature of their content. In 1850 the Pauline authorship of all the Epistles was denied by Bruno Bauer. The critical process thus reached the extreme possible limit of denial. And though in 1884 Rudolph Steck[4] and later the Dutch critics, Loman, Van Maanen and Pierson reasserted the denial, the tendency to reinstate the majority of the Epistles set in and has moved steadily to the present day.

This rehabilitation, however, has never reached the form of a unanimous or even predominant judgment that Paul wrote all the thirteen letters assigned to him in the New Testament. The pastoral Epistles and the Epistle to the Ephesians are still made exceptions to this judgment. But those who cannot see Paul's hand and mind in these writings are by no means agreed in denying some share of his influence or even of his work in them. Some contend that they are compositions of disciples of Paul who put forth what they believed Paul thought on problems arising after his death concerning the government and distribution of the Christian community. Others hold that a certain nucleus in each (except Ephesians) was actually put forth by the Apostle himself, but that additions and interpolations by Pauline Christians brought them to their present form.

Thus the conception and name of Deutero-Paulinism has been brought into use. Deutero-Paulinism, however, is a conception of variable compass and should not be used without caution. In its broadest sense it is made to include the thought of such writings as the Epistle to the Hebrews along with that of the pastoral Epistles and Ephesians, and even First and Second Peter.[5] In this sense it practically loses all

[4] *Der Galaterbrief.*
[5] E. F. Scott, *First Age of Christianity,* p. 207.

distinctiveness and ceases to be a help toward clearness of thought. If used of the type of thought so coherent and definable and yet so manifestly allied to and growing from Paul's system as is to be found in the Epistle to the Hebrews, it is eminently suggestive and reasonable. It will, therefore, be best to reserve it as the designation of the interpretation of the Gospel found in Hebrews, leaving the secondary Pauline element in Ephesians and in the pastoral Epistles as auxiliary material in the generic exposition of the Gospel according to Paul.

The author of Second Peter was perhaps the first to express his experience of difficulty in following Paul's thought in his Epistles (II Pet. ii. 16, "wherein are some things hard to be understood"). His latest interpreter reëxpresses the same experience. "He is no easy author. Homer is simpler, and Plato's thought plainer to follow." [6] Yet every student of Paul's writings will concur with Glover in his judgment that "Paul stands among the greatest of the Greeks." He always transcends his disciples and commentators, and not only suggests, but actually reveals in his own mind new phases of thought and experience. No mere linguistic grammatical study of the Epistles will be sufficient for the understanding of Paul's fullest thought. We shall need all the light we can secure on his life and the formative elements which determined his ideas and gave them form.

2. PAUL AND HIS BACKGROUND.—The first mention of Paul in the New Testament occurs in the story of stoning of Stephen. He was a young man evidently much interested in the spiritual life of his people. From the ample data later disclosed we are able to trace this interest to his parentage, his early life at home and his training in the schools of his day. As his life proceeds from that day onward, his interest in religion is affected first by his conversion on the road to Damascus and afterwards by his experience as a preacher of Christ. It is in the light of these factors in his experience that we must seek to get the bearing of Paul's background upon his thinking.

(1) *Paul's Parentage.*—Physically Paul was without question a man of sensitive temperament, quick to feel and to react toward the influences of his environment. Whether this was an inherited trait or one individually developed it is not possible to say. One can only surmise that his parents, too, were refined and sensitive, since they occupied an honored position in society. This fact is well established by what he says of his inherited Roman citizenship and his place in the Jewish world as a Pharisee and an Israelite of high social rank. Such privileges are usually accompanied by keenness of mind, strength of will and emotional responsiveness. Paul himself intimates that he had been qualified by his heredity for his work when he traces his call to a prenatal stage (Gal. i. 15).

Whether his highly strung nervous system was responsible for his

---

[6] T. R. Glover, *Paul of Tarsus*, p. 1.

bodily infirmities, especially the "thorn in the flesh,"[7] can be only matter for speculation and conjecture. Whatever these signs of a less than perfect constitution were, and whether his lack of ruggedness was hereditary or acquired, Paul accepted the situation as a challenge for the exercise of his inner manhood and as a ground for dependence upon the spiritual help he might receive from God himself in rising above them and achieving the work to which he was called.

The social environment of Paul's home in Tarsus was highly conducive to widely diversified, if not exactly symmetrical development of mental and spiritual life. Tarsus was a commercial center, the meeting place of many types of men from widely separated parts of the Mediterranean world. Upon its streets and in its markets, Paul would come in touch with representatives of many human interests. The influence of this diversity on the mind of a sensitive young man can be easily imagined. The ability to "become all things to all men" which Paul later exercised undoubtedly got its first start and impulse at a very early period of his life in such an environment.

The modes of thought of the market, of the stadium, of the theater and of the harbor became familiar to him. The language, too, which was to serve Paul as the means of his largest and most permanent contribution to the world's life was learned by him in this center of civilization during the very years when, in one's life, language is best mastered.

(2) *Paul's Education.*—Whether Paul received any school training in Tarsus or not is not clear. The probability is against his having entered upon formal courses of education there. It is true that Tarsus was one of the great seats of Stoic philosophy; and the discussions carried on there together with the dissemination of interest in and acquaintance with philosophy in general was sufficient to attract worldwide attention and lead to the rather inaccurate assertion that a "university flourished in the city." Paul's methods of intellectual work have given good grounds for the predominant belief that he came in touch with the leaders of the Stoic school of philosophy in Tarsus. Upon the whole, however, there is no evidence of his having been drawn any more fully into the current of Hellenic influence than one who comes to know about its existence, and who, so far as does not clash with his moral and spiritual ideals, finds attraction and value in it. Paul's early subjection to Greek education did not go beyond the breathing of such atmosphere as Greek learning had created in his native city.

Whether this acquaintance with it was such as to entice him in later

[7] The phrase has aroused considerable discussion and provoked various explanations. Some identify it with some weakness of eyesight, such as ophthalmia or some other disease of the eyes. Others, associating the physical infirmity with Paul's tendency to fall into ecstasy, suppose that he was subject to epileptic seizures. Sir William Ramsay, not satisfied with this, suggests that the thorn in the flesh was a variety of fever that disabled him, and at the same time rendered him loathsome in the eyes of strangers.

The question of Paul's physical health belongs to his biography and is amply treated in the lives of Paul—Cf. David Smith, *The Life and Letters of St. Paul*, p. 664ff.; Deissmann, *St. Paul*, p. 62; A. H. MacNeile, *St. Paul, His Life, Letters and Christian Doctrine*, p. 2.

PAUL THE WRITER AND THE MAN

years into further studies in Greek literature and philosophy has remained a question in dispute. The grounds for a judgment in the case point rather to a negative conclusion. If Paul ever became a student of the major Greek writers of the classic period, he certainly did not permit them to mould his thought or method of expression. The Greek writers from whom his very scanty quotations are made are not such as Plato, Aristotle or Æschylus, Euripides and the prose writers, but the lesser lights. Of these Aratus and Cleanthes have both been claimed as the originals of one (Ac. xvii. 28). This duplication of source is due to the fact that the phrase quoted by Paul is given by both Cleanthes and Aratus and it is not possible to determine whether in using the words, "certain of your own poets," Paul had in mind either one or both together. The quotation in Titus (i. 12) is from Epimenides. But the uncertainty of criticism as to Paul's being the author of the passage in Titus casts a doubt on the value of it as an evidence of his Greek learning. Finally in I Cor. xv. 33 there is an exact reproduction of a line in a comedy of Menander.[8] But it would be building too large a structure upon a small foundation to say that Paul was acquainted either with Menander's works or even with the comedy in question. He may possibly have found it as a floating maxim in common use.

But if Paul's acquaintance with Greek philosophy and literature was casual and informal rather than the result of study, was his knowledge of Greek and Asiatic cults and institutions more thorough? And did it affect his views and teachings in any vital way? This question is of recent origin and has aroused much interest and discussion.

At Athens the classical idolatry appears to have struck Paul with the force of a shock (Ac. xvii. 16). It is impossible to resist the impression that, in spite of all he may have seen of polytheistic institutions in Asia, he had scarcely realized the strength and manifoldness of Greek religion as commonly held and practiced.

But between the popular idol worship of Athens and the religion of Asia there was a wide difference. The latter took into itself certain ideas from some ancient cults such as the Orphic and Eleusinian rites. It permitted itself to be revitalized by them and transformed beyond recognition. The result was a new type of cults commonly called "mystery religions." The type flourished in more than one variety but the essential features were the same in all. The essence of the type is the representation to the mind in symbolic forms of the realities of the invisible ideal world. The most prominent place in the system was occupied by the life after death. The object in all cases was to deliver the souls of the votaries from the corruptible elements of the material sphere and make them sharers of immortal life through actual union with deity.

This type of cult utilized the social nature of man by bringing indi-

[8] Κρῆτες ἀεὶ ψεῦσται, κακὰ θηρία, γαστέρες ἀργαί, Cretans are always liars, evil beasts, idle gluttons. See note on Tit. i. 62, in Lock, "Pastoral Epistles," in *International Biblical Commentary*.

[9] φθείρουσιν ἤθη χρηστὰ ὁμιλίαι κακαί. Evil companionships corrupt good morals. Jerome (Com. on Gal. iv, 24) finds this in Meander, *Thais*.

viduals together into fraternal groups (θίασος) —the individual member being called θιασώτης or μύστης). The association of votaries was constituted by the possession of the common saving knowledge of eternal realities. The knowledge was imparted to each member as he joined the association through solemn ceremonies of initiation, but carefully withheld from the public at large. This feature of the cult gave it the name "mystery religion," as it also gave the member the name μύστης.

At the same time it served as a source of fascination to initiates and profane alike. At a time when other ties were beginning to break and races and small city states were disintegrating under the crushing weight of imperialistic and international forms of administration, men were eager to find each other and band themselves together through affinities they recognized as belonging to a higher realm of realities. Furthermore the very secrecy enshrouding the interests which brought the membership together, as well as the ritual they practiced and its meaning, added to the spell exercised by the organization. Even the Christian church has been by some supposed to be an imitation of the mystery fraternity (θίασος).

In the nature of the case the vows of secrecy by which the votaries of the mystery religions were bound at their initiation have resulted in a scarcity of materials for the historian of later days. Very little material has until now been found from which trustworthy accounts of the inner life of mystery cults can be constructed. Much of our information comes through those who were out of sympathy with them and misunderstood them.

The possible points of contact which Paul may have made with the mystery cults of his day are the sacramental rites of baptism and the sacrificial meal and the peculiar terminology used either in expounding their content or in alluding to their ritual practices. It is certain that some form of baptism was practiced in the ritual of the mystery cults. One especially known as the ταυροβόλιον in which the blood of a bull just slain was made to drip through a lattice floor upon the candidate for initiation, standing in a booth under it, in token of his being enswathed by the life of the deity and rendered immortal, is demonstrably of post-Christian origin. It cannot be traced further back than 150 A.D.[10]

The truth about a sacrament of eating and drinking is that from the earliest days such a ceremony was not peculiar to the mystery religions. The Eleusinian and the Dionysiac-Orphic, and also the later rituals included acts of eating and drinking symbolic of participation of the divine life. But the sacrificial meal of the tribe, so common in the religions other than of the "mystery" type, also carried the idea of communion of life between the god and his worshippers. And this communion of life was supposed to enlist the favor of the god. Wherever these common practices appear, in order to prove that they are due to the influence of one upon the other, it is necessary to show

---

[10] Cumont, *Les Religions Orientales*, p. 98ff.; Kennedy, *St. Paul and the Mystery Religions*, p. 94. Other references pertinent to the matter in earlier sources are obscure and indecisive.

not only that the practices resemble each other, but also that the meanings found in them are identical and that they stand related as derived one from the other or from some common source. So far as Paul's relation to the mystery cults is concerned, this is precisely what no one as yet has succeeded in doing.

The phraseology of the mystery religions does contain many terms which also occur in the vocabulary of Paul. The word "mystery" itself is used by the Apostle in the same sense as in the cults, viz., as something withheld from the world at large and revealed to the limited number of the privileged circle (μυστήριον). Other words such as spirit (πνεῦμα), soul (ψυχή), knowledge (γνῶσις), glory (δόξα), together with some metaphorical phrases, are quite doubtful in their bearing on the question before us. Some of them are clearly affiliated with and sufficiently accounted for by Old Testament antecedents. Others are general and may be traced to common usage distributed over a wide geographical and racial area.

Altogether that Paul was vitally affected by his early Hellenistic environment and that he carried into his Christian thought any cardinal ideas or practices from the religions of the day seems improbable.

Whether Paul's education was or was not begun at Tarsus, it was certainly carried on and completed at Jerusalem. To that extent it was typically Jewish. The only definite item we possess at first hand concerning his schooling in Jerusalem is the one he gives in his speech in the temple area informing his audience that he was brought up at the feet of Gamaliel (Ac. xxii, 3). Indirect information is conveyed in some other facts revealed in his various references to his past life. These items enable the careful student to estimate the value of his experience as a student. Gamaliel II, the grandson of the great Hillel, was the leader of the more liberal wing of Pharisaism in his day. From him Paul must have learned to look for, though not always to find, the inner principles of Old Testament teaching. To Gamaliel's school however he carried the zeal of his father as a Pharisee. His development in this was in his own eyes one of the most striking aspects of his early life (Gal. i. 14; Ac. xxvi. 4, 5).

To this intense loyalty to the standards and traditions of his race all that he saw in Jerusalem in the impressive years of his school life no doubt materially contributed. For Jerusalem was the center of Jewish life, teeming with sacred and inspiring associations. Its Temple, its David's city, its other historic monuments not only threw light on the writings of the old covenant, but filled the heart with enthusiastic devotion to everything Jewish.

(3) *Paul's Conversion.*—The Book of Acts contains three detailed accounts of Paul's conversion—one by Luke and two by Paul himself (Ac. ix., xxii., xxvi.). All of them give essentially the same story. Paul was self-consistently opposed to the Christian movement. It was nothing less to him than a blasphemous rebellion against all that he held sacred and dear. He had assumed an attitude of aggressive hostility to it, to which he gave expression when he joined the group that secured the death of Stephen, its first advocate among the Jews of the Hellenist class. From the death of Stephen he proceeded to a more active part in the plan of suppressing the new heresy.

While occupied with the execution of this part he experienced the great change—one of the most striking and familiar events in the history of all religion. That the change came with stunning suddenness, that it was radical and permanent and that its determinative feature lay in the depths of the spiritual nature where only the divine Spirit can reach, are amply attested by all the narratives.

The psychologist of the present day offers his help to a fuller understanding of the inner movement of Paul's soul. He suggests that the outward suddenness of the conversion was true only of the crisis, that the change was prepared for by a series of psychical steps for the most part taken beneath the consciousness of the subject. Among these he finds the fact that to Paul's essentially sincere mind the character of those he persecuted presented a puzzle. What they did was noble and praiseworthy, even though the cause they espoused was unpatriotic and impious. What he may have heard from their lips about the life and personality of their Master must have struck him as inconsistent with his conventional idea of the Messiahship. But if by any chance Jesus was such a man as they portrayed, there was no incongruity in his being a prophet of God. As a Pharisee he could not look upon the claim that Jesus had risen from the dead as absurd. Finally the bearing of Stephen as he faced martyrdom, his confidence, his ready endurance of the worst that men could inflict, must have stirred his admiration. The possibility that acquiescing in the stoning of Stephen he had consented to the death of a blameless man may have entered into his thoughts. This complex of thoughts and feelings, even though faintly and subconsciously pressing upon his reason, needed only an external occasion of a startling character to intertwine its strands into a conviction that he was wrong. And this occasion was offered in a thunderstorm of peculiar violence. His vague suspicions and surmises crystallized into a clear purpose.

Such an account of the hidden processes of Paul's preparation for his conversion will be welcomed by many today as a help. It is not in any way inconsistent with belief in the reality of the supernatural cause of the experience. It aims only to trace the submerged connection between the antecedent conditions and the after life of the Apostle. On the other hand the explanation is not a necessity to the acceptance of the account. The crucial element is, after all, the conviction of Paul himself that God was the active, interested and gracious cause of the change. And concerning the reality of this conviction he leaves no one in the slightest doubt. This conviction was not only clear and strong, but also in due time well reasoned out. God had done what he had done for Paul because he had a work to commit into his hands (Gal. i. 15, 16).

Such an experience was bound to affect not only the content of Paul's thought but also its form. He not only believed and gave himself up to what he had previously considered a pernicious falsehood, but the character and tendencies of his faith were determined by the experience in many traceable lines.

(a) His view of Christ and of what Christ means for men found its center, as it had its starting point, in the resurrection fact. His first view of Christ was that of the risen Lord. This was a fact to which all other considerations must yield. That Jesus had been put to death could no longer stand in the way of his being accepted as the Messiah. He was living and would assert his Messiahship in due time. Whatever he had given his disciples in his earthly teaching and his human example and in his miracles must be interpreted in the light of his death and resurrection. Just as his religion became Christocentric, his Christology took the death and resurrection of Christ as its center.

(b) The suddenness of his conversion impressed him with the truth that in all salvation it is God's grace that is effective, therefore the prominence in his system of thought of God's sovereignty and the inclusion in God's plan of all, even the minutest details of human experience. Doctrines of predestination, foreordination, divine decrees and of election, which were common enough in the Pharisaic theology of the day, received light and confirmation in his mind through his own experience. He could not attribute his sudden change of heart to any determination of his own. So far as his own tendency and motive were concerned, they were leading him in a direction entirely contrary to the mind of Jesus Christ. When he found himself in an extraordinary manner asking for directions from Jesus Christ ("Lord what wouldst thou have me to do?") it must be because this was decided apart from his own will, by a superior divine fiat.

(c) In another direction this same suddenness and supernaturalness of his conversion undoubtedly put an end in his mind to the idea that one could find acceptance before God by doing good works and opened his eyes to the reality of salvation by grace. The favor he was receiving at the hands of God was undoubtedly not due to his previous conduct. His previous conduct had merited nothing but condemnation; but, instead, he found himself a special object of God's favor. That fact must needs be explained not upon the ground of his previous works, but merely as a free gift of God. His part in the affair could be only that of receiving the gift. A righteousness not his own was the ground of his acceptance by God.

(d) In another direction the universality of the gospel doubtless presented itself to Paul. Since he, the most determined foe of the faith of Christ, could be suddenly transferred from the camp of the enemies to that of the followers of Christ, there was no obstacle that could stand in the way of the same transposition in the case of any one. The case of the heathen was even more favorable than his own, because his own enmity to the plan of God was active opposition, whereas the difficulty with the heathen was not an active enmity, but an inert attitude that grew out of ignorance rather than out of wanton rejection of the light. It is much easier for heathen men to become disciples of Christ than for such a man as he had been.

(4) *Paul's Missionary Experience.*—With his conversion the apostle Paul also associates his own commission of preaching of the gospel to the Gentiles (Ac. xxii. 17-21). But the full development of the

mission of Paul was a matter of slow progress and required time and reflection on his part. Eventually it became an additional factor in the formation of his theology. Paul came to the service of the gospel after the broadening of the field which resulted from the evangelistic efforts of Stephen and Philip, especially after the death of Stephen and the scattering of the first Christians. Strictly speaking there was no missionary effort before Paul. While all Christians preached as they travelled, an aggressive campaign for the sole purpose of preaching the gospel was first undertaken by him. And wherever Paul went he first preached Christ to the Jews in the synagogues. And, if perchance, at first proselytes and afterwards Gentiles were drawn within the circle of his hearers, he was ready to regard them as favored by God to receive the offer of the blessings and privileges of the gospel.

There came, however, a definite point of time in his experience as a missionary when he realized that the Gentiles were readier to receive the gospel than the Jews. This was at Antioch of Pisidia. Here his preaching met with strenuous opposition on the part of the Jews. Consequently he definitely turned from them declaring that they had "judged themselves unworthy" to receive the glad tidings and that he would address himself now to the heathen directly. This was a pivotal experience. It indicated to the apostle more clearly than ever what he had already perceived, in more than one way, viz., that the gospel of Jesus Christ was to be separated from the old forms of Jewish religion and to have a direct access to the hearts of the Gentiles because it was an eternal and universal gospel. The bearing of this experience on his thought scarcely needs comment. It confirmed and expanded the idea which was already assuming a dominant place in his mind of the world-wide significance of faith in Christ.

CHAPTER XIX

PAUL'S RELIGIOUS PHILOSOPHY

Was Paul a consistent logical thinker or was he a mystic and a dreamer? Was he a theologian or a prophet and an orator? Did he have a well-thought-out philosophy of religion or was he interested only in the practical values yielded by abstract thinking? These are questions to which diametrically opposite and mutually exclusive answers have been given. But questions of this class are always apt to provoke extreme and misleading answers. While there are rare individuals concerning whom it is true that they belong to either one or another of antithetic and mutually exclusive types, the great majority combine differing and contradictory tendencies in themselves. Paul is in this respect more like the normal than the exceptional man. Essentially he belongs to the mystic group. By training he was moved to the point of view of the dialectic and even technical theologian. He lived the life of the mystic; but he expressed his thought in the terms of the theology current in his day.

1. IDEA OF RELIGION.—He had a definite conception of religion. And he held it consistently through the pre-Christian as well as the Christian period of his life, though as he grew he added new features to it. He might not perhaps have given a formal definition of religion satisfactory to the scientific student, but he knew what religion should be and what it should mean in human life. In his own experience religion had been the effort to get the approval of God. His Pharisaic affiliations had fixed it in his mind that God gives his approval only to those who do his will. And to do the will of God perfectly is to be righteous. Righteousness, then, was the objective of all religion that is worth the name and, therefore, the cardinal idea in it. Every religion, true or false, the Jewish or any of the Gentile variety, was a method of righteousness.

Before his conversion the deepest yearning of Paul's heart and the goal of all his efforts had been to be found righteous at the judgment bar of God. After his conversion he claimed that he had found the object of his search. Yet he had found it not as a result of his search but by revelation from God. Before, he had aspired "to be found having a righteousness of his own, even that which is in the Law"; after, he had given up this effort and was content to accept the righteousness "which is through Christ" (Phil. iii. 9). And if righteousness secures the approval of God, it is not to be sought for any other purpose than to secure the favor of God. No man can be righteous who seeks for righteousness in order to excel among men, or to "win heaven," or to have peace of conscience. All these may come with righteousness, but they are not its objects.

2. IDEA OF RIGHTEOUSNESS.—In its long history this term has suffered the fate of many others of the same importance. It has been assigned a variety of meanings.[1] The special meaning which Paul attaches to it is derived from the courtroom. One is righteous who can be pronounced at the bar of the judge innocent of offense against the law. Essentially the conception is moral. It is inconceivable that the righteous and true God would declare any one free of guilt who is not really innocent. Yet is is not the inner character of the soul that the term designates but its relation to the law. It is then commonly a forensic term with a legal meaning.

This idea of righteousness assumes an underlying conception of God as supreme judge. He is the champion of right and insists upon it upon all occasions and in all relationships. He does this because right is the expression of his character and will. He himself is supremely righteous. He is not only judge, but also lawgiver. He is lawgiver because he is sovereign ruler. His right as ruler is based on his antecedent right as creator. Thus, by a chain of links each of which is indissolubly forged into the other, the conception of God is involved in that of righteousness. Righteousness is the only and indispensable core of religion because God is God, sovereign, present in and over all things.

The thought of God as judge and ruler Paul took over from the creed of the Pharisees. To the Pharisees of the day, however, the thought was nothing more or less than the revelation of God in the Old Testament. It was deducible from the Law and from the Prophets. And when the typical Jew of Paul's age thought of the prophets, he drew no distinction between the elder type of prophecy and the later apocalyptic. Accordingly so long as Paul's mind was filled by and fixed upon the idea of a righteous God requiring righteousness from all men, after the manner of apocalyptism, he magnified the future appearance of God as judge of all to dispense to all according to their deserts the rewards due them. In some form or other the Great Day of Yahweh was in the background of his religious creed.

That the apocalyptic conception remained with him through his Christian life in the main features in which he had held it before his conversion there is no doubt. It is also true, however, that his thought penetrated deeper and laid hold on the underlying values which the apocalyptic system aimed to conserve, to promote and to express. When the idea of God as Father, not altogether strange before his acceptance of Jesus as Lord, showed its real inner truth to him and he realized its bearings, he was willing to add its implications to those of the judgeship. He used the figure of the home as well as of the courtroom as a source of data for his theology. The forum and the home are after all but emblems of two modes of conceiving of the

[1] Cf. *Standard Bible Dictionary*, s.v.

social constitution of the world—the political and the domestic. Is the primary relationship of personalities, whether as creatures among themselves or as creatures to their creator, of the political or of the household type? Paul in his Christian period gave larger emphasis to the latter, though he allowed the former to persist in his thinking. Increasingly he looked upon men as members of God's household and on God as the Father.

3. IDEA OF SIN.—Paul's thought of sin naturally and inevitably grows out of his conception of righteousness as the supreme good. If righteousness commends the soul to God, sin alienates it from him. If righteousness is conformity to God's will given in the Law, sin is the absence of conformity. It is the lack of righteousness.

But to the mind of a man like Paul the definition of sin as a mere lack of righteousness could never be satisfactory. The preciousness of righteousness, the difficulty, the impossibility of attaining it as he discovered later, by his own efforts, the vast and complex bearings of it upon the doctrines of men, all bore down upon his mind forcing it to search for an understanding of its beginnings, of its true nature, of its fatal issues and of the effective way of overcoming it. Sin, therefore, (ἁμαρτία) came to be one of the cardinal words of his vocabulary and the fact of sin one of the chief subjects of his thinking.

(1) *Nature of Sin.*—First of all he gave his attention to the nature of sin. The mere negative explanation of it as the absence of something did not satisfy him. (a) He was convinced that sin was a positive principle or power. So vividly did he speak of it as an active principle that many have imagined that he believed it was a living entity, a hypostasis, or personality belonging to a class of "principalities, powers, rulers, angels and demons."[2] Those who hold this view, however, admit that Paul uses the term sin to designate two aspects of the reality, i.e., the cause of a phenomenon, and the phenomenon itself, and that it is only the cause that Paul believes to be a monstrous living existence. They do not deny that in many instances he uses the term sin only of the phenomenon of transgression of the divine law. But they hold that sin in Paul's mind is preëminently the living being, not the effect of its work in man.

The truth contained in the view is that Paul sees behind the concrete and individual acts of sin an energetic principle of which he speaks in terms of its personification. To say that he goes beyond this is to read into his language an extreme apocalyptism in which Paul was not interested. Expressions to the effect that sin "enters" into the world (Rom. v. 12), "dwells" in man (Rom. vii. 20), "reigns" over him (Rom. vi. 21), holds him in slavery (Rom. vi. 7), and "dies" (Rom. vii. 18) are obviously figuratively meant.

For the view that Paul conceived of sin as an energy with a quality and continuity of its own there is better ground furnished by his familiarity with rabbinical doctrine of the "evil principle" (*Yetser ha ra'*

[2] Cf. Everling, *Die Paulinische Angelologie;* Dibelius, *Die Geisterwelt d. Paulus.*

—spirit of evil). This was not imagined as a mere abstract tendency to wrong doing but as a power dwelling within man and prompting him to evil courses of action. Paul's language conforms to the usage of the schools of his day.

(b) Still another type of thinking whose native soil was Persia finds sin inherent in matter. Is Paul's idea to be affiliated with the dualistic philosophy of this system? The use of the term "flesh" points to an affirmative answer. But on closer examination this derivation of his notion proves illusive.

Paul's use of the term "flesh" is consistent. In general he means by it the "evil nature." The usage is due to the obvious fact that sin manifests itself most strikingly in the bodily constitution of man. It appears to find this the easiest and readiest ground and instrument for its nefarious work. But "flesh" in the vocabulary of Paul is not always sinful human nature. In certain connections the term reverts to its primitive sense of mere body. When, for instance, Christ is said to have "reconciled (men) in the body of his *flesh*" (Col. i. 22), or that he was "born of the seed of David according to the *flesh*" (Rom. i. 3), it can in no way convey the thought that he was tainted with sin. Furthermore human nature is capable of and destined to purification. At the resurrection it will not be evil and yet it will retain its own nature as flesh (I Cor. xv. 59). Paul, in other words, is not careful to distinguish between body (σῶμα) as the bare physical constitution and the flesh (σάρξ) evil human nature, but uses the terms with a subconscious awareness of the difference between them. Body is not the equivalent of flesh, but flesh is always at least body.

(c) But if sin is neither a separate subsistence invading the nature of man nor a necessary quality or energy of matter affecting the personality of man by the very fact of its association with it, it must be an inner disorder or disease of the soul. The peculiar effect of the disorder is that it stimulates inordinate, extravagant currents in the soul. The body then claims from the whole self a place not naturally and rightfully its own. The spiritual aspirations, cravings and longings are deprived of their rightful satisfaction. In the ideal human nature the spiritual should have first claim and should be first normally satisfied before the bodily desires have their satisfaction. The appetites and tendencies of the body should be restrained and directed by the superior nature. In the sinful order the predominance is usurped by the appetites of the body which then become lusts. The same desires and tendencies are "appetites" in the body, but "lusts" when the body has become transformed into flesh. Since the change of body into flesh is due to sin, it is possible after this predominance has taken place to speak of sin as flesh.

Ultimately the answer to the question of what is sin resolves itself to the simple formula, the predominance of the lower nature of man over the higher, which prefers self to God. If the higher nature were given free reign, and natural and normal satisfaction, man would always act in harmony with God's will. When the lower predominates, he acts contrary to God's will asserting his own selfish will. From this point of view selfishness and sin become equivalent, and all sin is selfishness.

(2) *Origin of Sin.*—Paul's interest in the origin of sin is more apparent than real. In a passage familiar because it has been used as the common arsenal of contending parties in theological warfare, he does trace the evil to Adam (Rom. v. 12, 21). But it is often forgotten that he refers to the subject in order to show the greatness of Christ's redemptive work and not in order to answer the question how the race became sinful. In fact it is the superabounding grace (v. 20) that is the objective toward which his arraignment moves; and the fall through the act of Adam is named only to enhance the greater breadth and power of the act of redemption through Christ.

Nevertheless it is true that Paul has expressed a belief which was not only his but that of many others. The passage just referred to is not the only one in which he mentions it. In the discussion of the resurrection he brings it into the argument once more as a parallel to the rehabilitation of humanity by the power of Christ (I Cor. xv. 21, 22). That the idea was current in the Judaism of his day is evident from references to it in the apocryphal Wisdom books.[3]

(3) *Universality of Sin.*—That sin was present in the person of every member of the race Paul both states as a dogma and argues from premises. He not only clearly declares that "all sinned" (Rom. v. 12, 18), but also dividing the race into the two conventional sections familiar in his day, "Gentiles" and "Jews," he demonstrates by their respective characters and their manner of life that the Gentiles were all under condemnation (Rom. i.); and then passing to the other branch of the dichotomy, he shows that the Jews were no better off (Rom. ii., they "are without excuse"). By implication also his idea of the origin of sin as in the first man's act of disobedience carries its universality. If sin came into the stream of human life at the very fountainhead, it must needs pervade and diffuse itself through the whole extent of its flow.

At this point, however, is raised the question of how sin is transmitted. To say that he believed in the solidarity of the race and, therefore, assumed that all its members had shared in Adam's sin and also in its penalty[4] is to build a larger structure than the foundation will bear. To find in the headship of Adam and Christ (referred to in I Cor. xv. 45, 49) a federal relationship is to assume what Paul does not say. That Adam and Christ stood in an analogous relation to the sinful and the redeemed world respectively Paul does assert. As to Christ he distinctly discloses that this relation is constituted by the self-commitment of the redeemed to Christ in faith. As to Adam he declares nothing explicitly. If the analogy were worked out logically it would carry the conclusion that the headship of Adam was also constituted by some self-commitment of each man to the sinful pattern

---

[3] Wisdom of Solomon, ii. 24, "by the envy of the devil death entered into the world." Wisdom of Sirach, xxv. 24, "From a woman was the beginning of sin; and because of her we all die." Cf. also IV Ezra. vii. 118.
[4] Cf. H. R. Mackintosh, *Christianity and Sin*, p. 80f.

given in Adam, in some mystical, or, at any rate, mysterious way. But did Paul work out the analogy in this way? It is a question that cannot be answered. In any case the Old Testament had a distinct idea of the connection of the sin of the parents with the suffering of their children ("visiting the iniquity of the fathers upon the children, upon the third and upon the fourth generation of them that hate me," Ex. xx. 6) which may have been in the background of Paul's thought on the subject.

(4) *The Results of Sin.*—Paul's view of the consequences of sin is comprehensive. It includes the consignment of the world to the domination of Satan and his company of evil spirits. Even the material creation is involved in this condemnation. For it, too, is under the bondage of corruption. It "groaneth and travaileth in pain together until now" (Rom. viii. 20ff.). The demonology of the day, which Paul never contradicts but freely uses as a means of explaining the application of his religious creed in many directions, furnished the background for the thought that sin issued in the reign of Satan over the world. But why God permitted Satan, his own adversary, to have such a reign over the creatures of his hands Paul does not say. Whether he had come to believe that God's goodness would be better vindicated if the suffering justly deserved by transgressors was not directly inflicted on them by God's own hand, or for some other reason, God for a season allowed "the course of this world to the prince of the powers of the air, of the spirit that now worketh in the sons of disobedience" (Eph. ii. 2). All individual offenders may be handed over to Satan for condign punishment and chastening (I Cor. v. 5; I Tim. i. 20). Part of the task of the Redeemer is to end this evil dominion.

But so far as the individual sinner is concerned, the whole effect of sin is expressed in the formula "the wages of sin is death" (Rom. vi. 36). That death was the consequence of man's wrong doing is a peculiarly Hebrew conception. The Babylonian cosmogony represents man as naturally mortal. Immortality is within his reach, but he fails to get it either by a mistake of his own or as a result of deception by a god.[5] In the Genesis account he is created presumably for immortality but loses his chance by his disobedience (Gen. ii. 17; iii. 2). With the prevalence of the portraiture of religious and spiritual transactions in the terms of law, death came to be viewed as the penalty for sin. Sin and death are thus inextricably associated. Where sin is, death reigns; and where death is, sin is the ground for its being.

But what is death? To the pre-Christian Jew it was nothing else than the natural dissolution of the physical being. And Paul no doubt began his religious thinking with this belief. But he could not have gone far in his Christian experience before discovering that death as a mere physical event could not be the penalty for sin. For even after the penalty was remitted, as it was in the case of all Christians, physical dissolution supervened in one form or another. The time had not yet arrived for the interpretation which makes death as the penalty of sin the spiritual dissolution of the relation between

[5] See Legend of Adapa in Wardle, *Israel and Babylon*, p. 188f.

God and the soul. Accordingly there arose a distinction between two forms of death, the death of the sinner in his sin, and the death of the believer whose sin is forgiven. The latter could not strictly be called death. The Christian world had already come to the same conviction. It fell into the habit of speaking of it as "sleep." The saint did not die; he slept.

Real death then, death as the penalty of sin, is an experience interfused by a complex of associated feelings and thoughts. These taken in their complexity constitute its sting. They are the fear, the horror, the anguish and suffering in anticipation of what may be. In nature these do not accompany physical dissolution. Without them as its "sting" death is not death.

4. IDEA OF LAW.—If righteousness is the central requirement which God makes of man, it was proper that He should have revealed to him the way of complying with it. And as a matter of fact, God has revealed it.

(1) First, God gave his law to all mankind in the revelation of "his eternal power and Godhead." Paul does not stint his expression on this subject. "That which may be known of God is manifest in them; for God hath showed it to them," and "they are without excuse." The Gentiles are sinners against adequate light. They have a law in their own members, inscribed in their own hearts which excuses or accuses them (Rom. ii. 15). It is not given in the same terms as the Law given to Israel, yet it is a law, conformity to which would have ideally at least brought them the approval of God.

The right to attribute to Paul the sense of the term law, according to which it is the revelation of God's will to the primordial man, might have been questioned if he had not himself sanctioned it by his own example. "For when the Gentiles which have not the law do by nature the things contained in the law, these having not the law are a law unto themselves; which show the work of the law written in their hearts" (Rom. ii. 14). It is true that the usage is quite exceptional. It is true also that the Apostle predominantly applies the term to the Mosaic legislation; but the exception shows that his conception of the law of God was not a hard and fast one. While its nucleus consisted of the body of prescriptive precepts given in the Mosaic legislation, all around it there is a penumbra of variations more or less clearly carrying the thought of revelation from God designed to serve as a guide for men. Possibly either at the beginning, or in the course of the progress of his Christian thinking Paul's mind had seized upon and developed the primitive germ of the Hebrew concept of Torah as instruction. At all events he believed in a worldwide revelation of God's will intended to bring to men his desire that they be righteous.

(2) To his universal revelation God had been pleased to superadd a special one given in the Law of the Old Testament. This was Israel's privilege. "Unto them were committed the oracles of God." (Rom. iii. 2). But what did this Law include? The typical Sad-

Torah - Heb. "instruction"

ducee's answer would have been the system of legislation given in the Pentateuch and nothing more. The Pharisee would have replied that it included that together with and as interpreted by the "traditions of the fathers." Paul as a Pharisee had held this broader view. But in his Christian period, without losing sight of the general outline of Mosaism, he had still further broadened his idea making of the Law of Israel primarily an ethical ideal of life given by God to his own people.

Such an ethical ideal must needs have specific value. And in getting this value consists the "advantage of the Jew." From this point of view, also, Paul is able to say that the law is "holy" and "good" (Rom. vii. 12, 16), and that it is not made "of non-effect," neither should be, but rather "established" (Rom. iii. 31). Its inner content is not abrogated but spiritualized by the Gospel. Yet much that has been developed out of it by men was only of temporary significance and has lost its authority (Cor. iii. 14) with the coming of Christ (Eph. ii. 15; Rom. x, 4). Evidently Paul came to entertain a highly complex notion of the nature and function of the Law.

In the endeavor to get a clear idea of his notion it will be well to begin with the fundamental thought that all law is promulgated in order to show what can and what cannot be, what ought and what ought not to be done. Law is a means of revelation. Just as the law written in the works of God and the hearts of the Gentiles so the Mosaic Law was given (a) first of all in order to make righteousness known. But just as light cannot reveal anything without at the same time revealing its opposite so the law brings into view the righteousness of God and the sin of man. For reasons which the further examination of Paul's ideas will bring into view the revelation of sin is practically of greater importance. For righteousness can be shown only through the law; but man's interest goes deeper; it is not only knowledge that he needs but inclination and ability which the mere revelation of righteousness does not bring to him. It is otherwise with sin. It becomes really sin when the light of the law falls upon it (Rom. iii. 27). What had the outward semblance of sin lacked its power and effect before the law came (Rom. v. 13). This is accomplished by the kindling of the moral impulse which automatically takes place when knowledge comes. Hence "Where there is no law neither is there transgression" (Rom. iv. 15), and "I was alive apart from the law once; but when the commandment came sin revived, and I died" (Rom. vii. 9).

(b) The revelation of sin leads to its restriction. The second function of the law therefore is "to check transgression." It has no power to make a man righteous, but it has the tendency to keep him from multiplying transgressions. A transgression is an individual act of sin. The law cannot efface sin, but it can diminish (by discouraging) the commission of new ones. Prevention and cure are entirely different. If the law could have prevented sin altogether it would have accomplished the end of salvation. But as an antidote of sin it is impotent. No matter how much it may diminish the amount of sin by preventing, it cannot reverse what has been done.

(c) Does the law, then, do nothing to promote the righteousness it reveals? It surely does. It does not merely confess its impotency but it shows where the potent remedy for sin is to be found. It does this by leading the sinner to Christ. Paul presents this thought in the well-known figure of the Law as the "tutor" that brings men to Christ (Gal. iii. 24f). The tutor (παιδαγωγὸς) in the system of education familiar to Paul was the slave in the household upon whom it devolved to lead the child from the home to the school and to the schoolmaster. The primitive pedagogue's task was to afford protection and guidance to the pupil during the daily trip to and from the school. When the law has brought men to Christ, its whole task has been accomplished. It is ready to retire.

5. IDEA OF THE PROMISE.—Yet while the world was waiting for the coming of salvation through Christ men were not completely cut off from the possibility of getting righteousness. Paul is too strong a believer in the divine origin and beneficent object of the Old Testament to admit such a pessimistic thought. What the Law could not accomplish God made possible through another medium, *i.e.*, the acceptance of the promise. When, however, his exposition of the promise is closely examined, it appears that this way is nothing other than that of the Gospel.[6]

The superiority of the promise to the law is argued from its precedence in time, the argument being based on the case of Abraham. Every Jew believed that Abraham was accepted of God if ever any man was. He was the friend of God and the father of the faithful. But Abraham lived long before the Law of Moses was given. To clear the case of any possible implication in the later post-legal developments, Paul points out the fact that Abraham's acceptance by God preceded even the adoption of the sign of circumcision. The law of which in his day circumcision had become the distinctive badge and symbol had positively nothing to do with Abraham's being declared righteous by God.

Whether Paul saw all the far-reaching implications of his illustration and its bearing upon the salvation of others than Jews who may have lived the life of faith typified in Abraham is not clear. He believed, as he showed in the case of the heathen world, that the mere revelation of righteousness to them had not resulted in the living of the righteous life. He believed that God would offer Christ to them as also to the Jews and accept them on the same condition of faith in

---

[6] In the Greek the identity of promise and gospel is suggested, even in the etymology of the words used. Promise (ἐπαγγελία) and gospel (εὐαγγέλιον) both have the idea of a message at their foundation. The promise came before Christ foreshadowing and declaring beforehand that which was to be, the gospel is the announcement of the accomplished fact. In both cases the basis is the word of God and the message reveals His goodness. In both cases also the righteousness of God becomes effective not through obedience to the law, but through the acceptance of His word by faith.

his Son. Did he believe that God had somehow offered the promise to them and accepted those who received the promise? He does not say; but the logic of his thought would indicate that he did.

6. IDEA OF SCRIPTURE.—God's revelation of righteousness had been made in a body of writings including the Mosaic legislation, the prophetic oracles and other documents. Paul accepted these as canonical. He cites them and appeals to them in his discussions with the Jews and he tacitly uses them as normative in his expositions of the gospel to his Christian audiences and to the readers of his letters. In his education the reading and explanation of Old Testament passages had been the chief method of instruction. He had taken over from the rabbinical teachers of the day the idea that God himself had spoken through Moses and the prophets. Like them also he could by metonymy, call the books of the Law (Pentateuch) "the Law" and the books of the prophets, "the prophets." When his mind reverted to the method in which the Law and the prophets came into being, he conceived of the process either as a direct one or as mediated through angels (Gal. iii. 19).

Yet between his attitude to the Old Testament and that of the rabbis of his day there is a great difference. This was perhaps imperceptible either to him or to them. Both went to their canon not to get from it the materials for constructing their religious views, but to take to it for purposes of corroboration the views which they had come to hold. Neither of them had regard to a science of hermeneutics. It is true that the general system of thought they held had been built up by predecessors by slow and easy steps out of the Old Testament; but their own use of the text of the Old Testament was of the nature of an appeal to substantiate some shade of opinion, and not primarily to deduce a meaning. Accordingly as men became affected by some phase of new thought in their day they tended to vary from the common traditional interpretations. The whole system of allegorism is an outcome of this attitude.

It gave Paul the opportunity to find the truths of the gospel in the Law and the prophets. At the same time it obviated the necessity of his denouncing the interpretations of the Old Testament by his opponents as false or having his interpretations formally repudiated as distortions of the obvious sense of the sacred writings. The nearest approach to expressing dissent from the current views of the Old Testament to be found in Paul's letters is the assertion that "a veil lieth upon their hearts" when Moses is read (Cor. iii. 15).

Upon the common basis of the current view of his time on Scripture rises his own doctrine. Its dominant characteristic is interest in the spiritual values conveyed by the "oracles of God." The divine origin of the content of the Old Testament is never lost to sight; but the human authorship of its several parts is also always in mind. It is Moses, David and Isaiah who "say" (Rom. x, 5, 19; ix. 27, 29; x. 16, 20; xii. 16; Rom. iv. 6) the words. But alternating to these reputed authors of the utterances Paul attributes to the divine source of all authoritative oracles the words he quotes by using the formulæ, "Scripture saith," or "it is written," or "it saith," all of which carried to the minds of his contemporaries the idea of divine origin.

In the matter of the interpretation of Scripture, Paul is very free. He uses the allegorical, typological and rabbinical-literal methods according to his convenience, but always with a view to getting the spiritual values contained in and conveyed by them. In other words interpretation does not mean the art of finding the original intention of the human authors, but the art of so applying the sacred text as to secure throughout spiritual results. Therefore the spiritual results which he aims to attain and the spiritual values which he finds in the Old Testament are always in the foreground; and the discovery in a stricter way of the meaning of the human writers is secondary and incidental. Instances of such conventional use of Old Testament words in his writings are the allegorization of Sarah and Hagar (Gal. iv. 21f) or the use of Deuteronomy xv. 1 as referring to the right of the preacher to be supported (I Cor. viii. 9), the reference to the Messiah as the seed (Gal. iii. 16), and the use of Isaiah liii in I Corinthians xv. 3, 4.

The key to Paul's thought of the Old Testament as a revelation of divine truth is undoubtedly his own consciousness of possessing the Spirit of God in his own heart. He knew that new light had burst into the world. He had received by revelation a distinctive form of the new knowledge concerning God's purpose which he could call "my gospel." In fact the possessive pronoun in this phrase implies that Paul had been given a revelation which was not given even to the other apostles of his day. Such a position implies the possibility of advance over the Old Testament. It further implies that the new truth was just as much from God as the revelation given in the Old Testament. It implies, finally, that the new message was mediated through the same kind of mind as the old.

But the fact that he received a revelation from God did not make him omniscient, or even accurate in all things. It did not fortify his memory so that he could remember all things with precision. Speaking of how many persons he baptized at Corinth he uses approximate language, and even openly confesses that he cannot remember. Speaking in other connections, he admits the possibility of having either overstated or understated his case.

But such revelations as he has received are authoritative. They were words of God. They cannot be broken. But their authority does not inhere in the form of the expression. Paul rarely alludes to the epistles he had previously sent to his readers. His gospel is authoritative as spoken orally (I Cor. iv. 20; I Thes. ii. 5). To the Galatians he takes particular pains to denounce those who preach a different gospel from himself and to pronounce condemnation upon them; even if "an angel of God preach another gospel, let him be anathema." But this denunciation had in view the perversion of what he had said, rather than of what he had written.

CHAPTER XX

THE GRACE OF GOD IN CHRIST

THE righteousness which Paul viewed as the supreme good in the world and core of all religion, he found he could not attain through his own efforts. Before he saw Christ on the way to Damascus, he was perplexed and troubled by his failure. He did not despair because his faith in God was all-prevailing. He would serve God at all events. It was clear that whatever the truth about salvation might be, and he was sure that his own was the right view of it, one could not lose by giving God all the service he could. It is while in this frame of mind that the revelation of Christ as the true and only way of righteousness came to him. No doubt it took a long time and much patient and intensive meditation to reconstruct his thought and to readjust his life to the new revelation. When he was fairly advanced toward this goal, it became clear that he must trace his salvation to the grace of God revealed and made operative through Christ.

1. THE GRACE OF GOD.—All that Paul had believed about God before his conversion and all that he saw in the manner of his conversion led him to magnify the part which God took in bringing men to himself. God had never consented to leave men in and to their sins. Their failure to conform to his righteous will did not come as a surprise to him. And his purpose to rescue them and reinstate them was not an afterthought. Indeed the gospel antedates not only the Law but also the appearance of sin itself as an actuality in the world. Since it appears in the unfolding of the affairs of men in the midst of events planned by God, it must have been present in his mind from the beginning. To God, then, must the initiative in salvation be traced.

For this view Paul's mind had been prepared both by his Pharisaic antecedents and training and by what he had unconsciously imbibed from his Hellenistic environment. The prophets had stressed God's supremacy as means of raising the ethical level of life. The rabbis, like the Stoic philosophers of Paul's age, were inclined to develop God's causal efficiency in all things into an article of speculative philosophy. Thus predestination, election and reprobation made their appearance in Jewish and later in Christian theology.

Paul saw the bearing and value of the thought in the explanation of the gospel. He used it in his apologetic against Jewish critics. They were saying that if his idea of the inclusion of Gentiles in the plan of salvation is true the distinction between the elect people (the Jews) and the non-elect would disappear. Paul answers that God is sovereign and may do as he pleases (Rom. ix.). He is not accountable to man, as the potter is not accountable to the clay he shaped into many forms. Yet he proceeds to show that (a) election is not arbitrary, but is designed to serve higher ends passing beyond the vision of human reason, and (b) that the rejection of the Jews (by parity of reasoning also of the Gentiles) is conditioned on their failure to meet God's requirements (Rom. x., xi.).

In another direction Paul used the idea of God's initiative in salvation in the inducing and strengthening of faith. In preaching to Gentiles it was a great help to be able to say that God in his infinite goodness had provided a glorious salvation for them as well as for the Jews "before the foundation of the world" (Eph. i. 4); that the gospel was a mystery, i.e., a secret, hidden, which God hath foreordained before the world for our glory" (I Cor. ii. 7). It was also a ground for confidence and perseverance in the faith to be assured that God's care was all around the believer, protecting him from all evil and leading him to a glorious victory (Rom. viii. 28-39).

2. RIGHTEOUSNESS THROUGH CHRIST.—Christ and his work constitute the pivotal point in Paul's spiritual experience and every survey of his thought must include answers to the questions what he thought of Christ and how he conceived of Christ's work.

(1) *The Person of Christ.*—To say that Paul accepted Jesus as the Messiah of prophecy is to use a formula which needs much and careful explanation. The final estimate of Jesus' Messiahship in Paul's conviction is expressed in his indiscriminate use of the terms Lord, Christ and Jesus singly and in their various combinations.[1] With whatever ideas he may have begun his allegiance to his master as the Messiah, in the end Christ (or Messiah) ceased for him to be an official designation and became equivalent to a mere personal name. From such a usage one can only infer that the mere eschatological conception of Jesus as the Son of Man, the supernatural person mentioned in apocalyptic literature, who was to come with the clouds of heaven and usher the kingdom of heaven was yielding to a far more comprehensive ideal, which without losing all of its eschatological content was to take on itself connotations of spiritual leadership and supremacy.[2] Paul's ideal of the Messiah after he came to know

---

[1] His favorite designation for his Master is Jesus Christ (with the order reversed, Christ Jesus). He uses this nearly one hundred and eighty times. The frequency of the forms Jesus Christ and Christ is approximately equal. The plain form "Jesus" occurs about forty times. This usage shows that Paul had come to regard the title Christ (Messiah) no longer descriptive of function or office, but of personal identity. To this designation he attaches the additional characterization "Lord" ("our Lord") nearly one hundred times. The plain official title "the Christ," however, occurs about eighty times.

[2] For the reality of the eschatological element in Paul's Messianism, see Shailer Mathews, *The Messianic Hope of the New Testament*, p. 163ff. But the author overemphasizes this element when he interprets Paul's system as revolving around this as its center. It would be more accurate to say that while Paul began and continued through his whole life to believe in the eschatological Messianism, he was more vitally attached and committed to the redemptive Messianism wrought out through the Spirit's transforming work in the heart of the believer. This point of view is approximated by Mathews in the next two chapters of his book. And his statement of the relationship of the eschatological to the spiritual in Paul's theology cannot be surpassed. It is in the words: "Eschatological messianism is not the material but the form of Paulinism." p. 206.

Christ was a transformed, spiritual and glorified ideal. Christ was not merely to exercise his Messiahship at his return, but he was actually exercising it in a most vital form of Lordship indisputable and effective.

Just how Paul came by this vital and vitalizing conception of Christ has been a subject of ingenious reasoning and animated discussion in recent years.[3] In general no theory which makes of Paul's mind a passive melting pot for mixing heterogeneous notions of Jewish, Greek or Oriental origin into artificial unity finds support in the historical data. Nor is any view satisfactory which finds in Paul's mind a mere vehicle for the transmission of ideas poured into it by the Palestinian Apostolic Church, derived in turn by this body in an esoteric, unrecorded way from the mind of Jesus himself. Paul's mentality was too virile and creative to be satisfied with the mechanical task of making a synthesis of apocalyptic, sacramental, legalistic or philosophical ideas, or of simply receiving and passing over unchanged the thoughts of others. In the absence of clearer and stronger proof that he did either, critical study will remain unstable until it gives him credit for his own contribution to the Christology of subsequent times.

It is clear that Paul never came into contact with Jesus during his ministry. If he did the contact was of an outward kind, leaving his soul movement entirely unaffected. His knowledge of Christ as a source of spiritual energy so far overwhelmed and mastered him that no mere acquaintance in the body would be worth considering (II Cor. v. 16). He did not, therefore, receive from the Master ideas directly before his death and resurrection.

On the other hand Paul by his whole attitude and in all his words never lends any countenance to the contention that he consciously added to or altered the teaching of Jesus in any vital respect. He did not mean to depart from what he had received (I Cor. xv. 3). To call him the real founder of Christianity is to use a glittering but empty epigram. He is not even the originator of the change of emphasis from the words of Jesus to his person. In this he does not differ from the other leaders of the apostolic Church. Even if answering the question, "What think ye of Christ?" is going beyond the mind of Jesus and becoming responsible for Christianity, Paul could not properly be called "the first Christian," far less the "founder of Christianity." Peter and Stephen would be in a class with him in that, even if his answer is fuller and more evident as a factor in subsequent development than theirs.

Nevertheless in a true sense the Pauline Gospel transcends that of Jesus and that of the early preachers of his Messiahship. It transcends it as the more fully developed blossom transcends the bud. In two respects, especially, Paul sees the truth about Jesus and the kingdom of God as no one before him saw it and expounds it with clearness. First in the necessity and centrality of the cross and second in the reality and realization of the personal relationship of the disciple with Christ. Both of these will come under consideration later.

What now did Paul think of Christ? To begin with, he knew of his

[3] Cf. J. G. Machen, *The Origin of Paul's Religion*.

THE GRACE OF GOD IN CHRIST

human life. He refers to his birth "of a woman" (Gal. iv. 4), to his being "of the seed of David according to the flesh" (Rom. i. 3). He appeals most clearly of all to his crucifixion and death; thus evincing a well outlined earthly human life of Christ present in his mind.

But this is only the hard nucleus of concrete facts in the conception. Antecedent to the birth of Jesus Paul thought of him as a preëxistent personality. There was some preparation in Jewish thought for belief in the preëxistence even of less exalted souls than that of the Messiah. Apart from Philo's teaching of an archetypal man (cf. Gen. i. 26) even non-personal beings of importance (the Tabernacle, the Altar, etc.) had an existence before assuming their material forms upon earth. Be that as it may, Paul's view of the preëxistent Christ is given in language that admits of no question (Phil. ii. 6-8; Rom. i. 4; viii. 3; Gal. iv. 4; II Cor. viii. 9). In this preëxistent state Christ occupied a place of high dignity and had the right at least to a place beside God himself (Phil. iii. 6). But it was not an empty honor he had at God's right hand; for an active part in the creation had been assigned him. (Eph. i. 10; I Cor. viii. 6; Col. i. 16, 17). That the thought is not casual and of secondary importance is shown from its introduction into an argument meant to meet a philosophical (Gnostic) theory of the constitution of the universe in the Epistle to the Colossians.

The belief in the preëxistent Christ renders the belief in the incarnation logically inevitable. But in bringing the incarnation of the Christ into view Paul refers to him as the Son of God (Rom. i. 4; II Cor. i. 10; Gal. ii. 10; Eph. iv. 13). To one who descends from such an exalted position as does the Son of God incarnation is a humiliation. Christ took on the "form of man," i.e., "the likeness of sinful flesh (Phil. ii. 7). But the context in which this thought occurs is as a whole of practical significance. It was intended to inculcate the Christlikeness of self-abnegation to Christians inclined to insist on their rights. It points to the example of Christ as an ideal and pattern ("Have the mind in you which was in Christ Jesus"). In view of this it is questionable whether subtler distinctions as to what and how much the humiliation involved can be based upon the surface value of the words. The fact itself of the humiliation in the incarnation is really present in Paul's mind. But is it sure that the implications of it in all directions could have been carried in a statement not designed primarily to reveal a theological doctrine?

The final and most incontestable item in Paul's view of Christ as well as the one which bore more heavily than any other on his thought of his person is the fact of his resurrection and exaltation to the right hand of God. This was the sign and seal of God's approval of him and the means of attesting to the world his supremacy. From the eschatological point of view resurrection meant confirmation in the Messiahship and certainty of the completion of the Messianic work. But ascension means withdrawal from the outward sphere and, to that extent, a postponement of the completion of the work. But it also shifted the attention and the interest from the eschatological to the spiritual side of Christ's significance for life.

(2) *The Work of Christ.*—The first and most fundamental fact to be taken into account in the study of Paul's view on this subject is the breadth and complexity of it. This is the first but not the most obvious feature of the work of Christ if one might judge from the alluring simplicity with which some portraitures of it invest it. Apart from the Pauline conception of it the work of Christ may be viewed as what he has done, what he is doing or what he is to do in the future. Since Paul was not so much interested in it as a theme in constructive theological science, but as a ground for liberating life energies to build men up Godward, he has nowhere given us an exhaustive statement of his view. He has pursued the course of the practical leader who clothes his thought in metaphorical language adapted to popular understanding and imaginative approach.

Accordingly looking at the work of Christ in the past, in the present, and in the future as securing salvation for men through his words, through his example, through his life, through his death and through his resurrection; as salvation from the power of Satan and the demons, from sin and the flesh, and from the bondage of the law, Paul has given expression to such a multitude and variety for the most part of figurative utterances as renders it difficult to reconstruct his thought without doing injustice to some phase of it.

(a) There are traces in Paul's references to salvation through Christ of an idea of liberation from a state of bondage to Satan and the demons by an act of Christ's overpowering and dethroning them. The time and circumstances of the deliverance he leaves indefinite; but the manner of it he clearly represents as one of "despoiling the principalities and powers" wherein "he made a show of them openly triumphing over them" (Col. ii. 14, 15). The same thought is in the background in the allusion to the "over-reaching" of the "rulers of the world," through which they brought their own overthrow upon themselves (I Cor. ii. 8).

(b) But Paul also looks upon the sinner's deliverance as the result of a transaction in which he is ransomed. Again it is Satan apparently that holds men in bondage but by the payment of a ransom he is redeemed (λυτρόω, ἀπολυτρόω). Those who are in slavery are purchasable; and they are purchased by the precious blood of Christ (ἐξαγοράζω), Gal. iii. 13; iv. 5).

(c) But since to redeem is not necessarily a purely commercial matter, the conception suggests the figure of exchange of prisoners taken in battle. The general conception suggested in this method of explaining salvation is that in the course of the enmity between God and the evil powers men, originally on God's side of the warfare, have been captured by Satan and Christ offers himself as their ransom (Rom. iii. 24; Eph. i. 7; iv. 30; Col. i. 14).

(d) Again the sinner is viewed as a prisoner of the state under the government of God, found guilty of offending against the law. He is under condemnation but acquitted by the annulment of the sentence. The whole language of justification involves this mode of thinking of redemption. God "condemns" sin (Rom. viii. 4) according to the

THE GRACE OF GOD IN CHRIST

law; but he imputes to him the righteousness wrought out by Christ and absolves him from the penalty on that ground.

(e) A more favorite form of conception is the explanation of sin as an offense to God by way of refusing or neglecting to give him the religious reverence and honor which is his due. Such an offense creates an alienation on the part of God. To win back his favor a sacrifice is necessary. The sacrifice of a life on the altar serves as the ground of expiating the guilt and offense of sin. This was probably the most common way of thinking among the Jews as well as among the heathen in Paul's days. Its application by Paul to Christ's doing away with sin follows the general line suggested in sacrificial expiation. Christ's offering of his life is accepted by God and sin is thereby cancelled. The terms Paul uses in this connection are ἱλαστήριον (Rom. iii. 25) θυσία and προσφορά (Eph. v. 2b).

(f) But Paul frequently speaks of salvation through Christ as a reconciliation. Sin in this method of thinking is a cause of alienation. Christ removes the cause and thereby becomes the mediator between those who were separated. He makes atonement in the strictest etymological sense of the term. The figure of reconciliation has furnished some of the clearest expressions of Christian salvation found in Paul's writings (Rom. v. 11, καταλλαγή; II Cor. v. 18; Col. i. 20, 21, cf. also Col. i. 20; Eph. ii. 14, 15, 17, εἰρήνην ποιέω, "to make peace").

(g) Laying stress, however, on the resurrection of Jesus as a factor in salvation, Paul resorts to still another mode of presenting Christ's work. In his death, he alleges, we have died and in his resurrection we have a new life free from the sin which was indwelling in us as sinners. Salvation is thus achieved by union with Christ and participation in his death and his life (Rom. vi. 5; II Tim. ii. 11). His death obliterates sin and his deathlessness becomes the source of immortal life to those who are identified with him.

These widely divergent views are based on as many possible relationships of life such as the commercial, the military, the judicial, the social, the religious, the mystical, etc. Each of these relationships furnishes a figure in which one may cast the thought of the change of relationship with God effected by Christ in salvation. The enumeration is not meant to be exhaustive. A more careful scrutiny might result in the discovery of other terms in which Paul has seen and spoken of the work of Christ. This, however, is true of all his metaphorical portraitures that he does not work out any of them to its implications in its details. When the effort is made, as it has often been made, to single out one (such as the forensic or the sacrificial) and to elaborate it into its possible fullness of outline, the result is a contradiction and annulment of what he suggests in some other, if not in all the others. Neither is it possible to say which of these implications Paul himself would accept as legitimate. Evidently no constructive interpretation of Paul's thought of the atonement can lay claim to finality or completeness.

On the other hand it would be equally untrue to say that Paul's thought of Christ's work was confused and inconsistent, or that each and every way of his presentation is of the same value. There is a center and an approximately definable circumference to his view. And on the whole it is not difficult to discover what is essential and what is unessential in his theory.

At first glance the dominant idea in the complex concept is the efficacy of Christ's death. Paul says, "the Gospel which I preached unto you . . . how that Christ died for our sins according to the Scriptures" (I Cor. viii. 11). Yet Christ's death is what it is (the efficient ground of salvation) because Christ is who he is. The death itself is nothing more than the experience of a person, and apart from the personality it can mean nothing. It is Christ who saves. "We preach Christ crucified" (I Cor. i. 23; cf. also I Tit. i. 15; I Cor. ii. 2). No interpretation of Paul's theory can, therefore, be adequate which loses sight of the person of Christ by isolating some experience of his and laying stress on its importance. Such a treatment of the subject would be analogous to the examination of the heart of a living organism and explaining its various functions independently of the associated manifestations of its energy.

Accordingly the nearest approach to a satisfactory view of Paul's thought of Christ's work will be reached if the salvation he accomplished be regarded as achieved by him as a person through his whole experience in his death, in his life and in his resurrection.

(i) Christ makes away with sin by his death. The manner in which he died is significant. Since he was crucified, he incurred the curse pronounced by the Mosaic Law upon any one who was hung "upon the tree" (Gal. iii. 13f; Deut. xxi. 22, 23). This mode of execution though different from crucifixion had the public branding of the offender in common with it. And the effect of the curse upon him who was thus branded was that his presence defiled the land. His body was to be done away with by burial or burning. The law annihilated him. Just so Paul seems to reason Christ by the operation of the law had been ideally put out of existence and passed beyond the reach of the law. But since he died for sinners, the sin for which they were accountable had disappeared with him and the law could not again claim them as its objects. Thus the claim of the law being cancelled they were free from condemnation.

(ii) Christ's work operates through the offering of his life. This means not merely the conduct of moral conformity to God's will which he was able to present. It includes this. Christ's life was one of obedience to the will of God and his obedience was a means of making many righteous (Rom. v. 19; Phil. ii. 7, 8). Christ's life is more than a series of acts; it is an energy that issues in manifold activities. And as such he offered it in behalf of men.

The sacrificial mode of speaking brings this into view clearly. In the ritual of the Old Testament it was the life of the victim (symbolized by the blood) that is the efficacious means of "covering" the sin of the offerer. Presumably its sprinkling on the mercy seat, the symbol of God's presence, was an expression of the worshiper's aspiration to be what the victim actually was, pure and free from sin. But the life of Christ was in a more real sense unspotted by sin; and in presenting it at the altar, or mercy seat, he was using a means well adapted to please God. The article of death (the bare experience of dissolution of body and soul) was only a means of securing the whole life as a complete offering of the life (Eph. v. 2).

Not only in the sacrificial form of presenting the thought, but in the commercial and forensic as well, the efficacy of Christ's death dwells in the expiation of sin, the propitiation of God and the reconciliation of man to God. The first of these terms (expiation), however, does not occur in the Pauline usage. The second appears once in Romans iii. 25 (ἱλαστήριον) where it is a question whether it refers to Christ as the victim or the mercy seat. Both of the senses of the term are supported by the usage of the LXX. The third (καταλλαγή from καταλλάσσω, reconciliation, to reconcile) is of frequent occurrence but is not connected with the sacrificial system. Moreover it is never used of any change of attitude on the part of God toward men but of a change on the part of men toward God. God is propitious and needs not to be reconciled. It is his love taking the initiative that motivates the whole process of salvation (Rom. v. 8. "God commendeth his own love toward us, in that while we were yet sinners Christ died for us." cf. Rom. viii. 32). His propitiation, necessary as it might appear to make his reconciliation from an attitude of enmity to one of friendliness, must be a change in himself of a different nature such, for example, as the natural transformation of his inward pain or just intolerance of sin into a joy or into a complacent mind toward the sinner when freed from his sin.

That Christ gives his life as a sacrifice either in the ritual sense of the term or in the sense of a ransom involves the idea that he does this not for his own sake but for others. This is explicitly brought into view by Paul in those references to the death of Christ which find it to be a fulfillment of the prophecy of Isaiah liii, and in many other more direct ways (II Cor. v. 21; Rom. v. 19). The death of Christ is in these ways clearly shown to be vicarious.

But the notion of vicariousness admits of two forms. It applies to cases in which men share each other's experiences either by the substitution of one for the other or by the identification of one with the other. Whether or not Paul kept this distinction in mind his words do not make clear. That he ever thought of Christ's work as purely substitutionary is, to say the least, exceedingly doubtful. It would be safe enough to say it is utterly improbable. The argument in favor of his doing so is based on the questionable proposition that the doctrine that righteous men atone for sinners seems to have had some currency among the Jews of his time. In support of this proposition IV Mac. (xvii. 22; vi. 29) is quoted. Per contra, Paul's use of the distinctive prepositions (Greek ἀντί and ὑπέρ)[4] is overwhelmingly against distinctively substitutionary idea. In seventeen statements of the subject he uses the preposition ὑπέρ, "in behalf of." The paraphrase

[4] Also περί in Gal. i. 4; I Thes. v. 10.

of his thought in the formula "Christ dies instead of us" is a gratuitous shifting of the emphasis from the form of vicariousness which seems most in harmony with his usage of language to the one which is not.

From this point of view Christ's offering of his life may be said to consist in a gift to men rather than to some one else in their behalf. For it means entrance into human life in order to take upon himself the evil of sin so far as this can be done, and relieve the sinner to that extent and to impart the power through which the dominion of sin shall be broken.

Both the view that Christ works out righteousness through his death and the view that he works it out through the offering of his life are suggested in the more general statements of the Apostle regarding the cross and the crucifixion. The Gospel is "the word of the cross" (I. Cor. i. 18); it is the means of reconciliation between God and man (Eph. ii. 16); it is the emblem of the new faith and an occasion for glorying in it (Gal. vi. 14); it is the sole and supreme content of the Apostle's preaching (I. Cor. ii. 2) and in general, it represents the central fact in salvation for man.

(iii) But the death of Christ viewed in either aspect of it (viz., as death pure and simple or as the offering of his life) is not to be separated from his resurrection. Paul joins the two items together and presents them as a unity (Rom. iv. 25; vi. 2-4; vii. 34; xiv. 9; II Cor. iv. 10-14; v. 15; Col. ii. 12; I Thess. iv. 14; v. 10). The resurrection is, in fact, indispensable to the efficacy of the death. If it is not a reality, then the death of Christ loses its power and faith in him becomes vain (I Cor. xv. 13, 14).

(1) The resurrection somehow perfects the life of Christ and renders it not only the offering which God accepts in behalf of sinful mankind but also a new source of power for the future. It is the ground of Christ's becoming the second head of humanity in analogy to Adam. Men are joined to him, and by so doing share in his death and also in his resurrection (Rom. vii. 4-6). The power of the resurrection is the ultimate goal and sequel to the movement begun by his death and must be reached and attained by the believer (Phil. iii. 10). It balances the fall of mankind in Adam by a restoration to the original standing designed for him (Rom. v. 12; I Cor. xv. 12, 45).

(2) Within the new humanity the headship of Christ is made visible in the constitution of a new body tending to ideal soundness of life. This is the church and Christ is the head of the church by virtue of the fact that he lives in the present and in constant communion with those who believe in him. He is the head; and the life which organizes and fits together the membership issues from him (Eph. iv. 15, 16).

(3) The resurrection places Christ at the head of the whole creation. There are indications that Paul believed this to have been the case before the incarnation; but he is more interested in the thought that his work of redemption is consummated by the exaltation of the Redeemer to the supremacy of the cosmos. (Eph. i. 20-22; Phil. ii. 10, 11; Col. i. 20). That the thought is here of a cosmic and not merely of a racial or earthly supremacy is shown from the mention of "princi-

palities and powers, things above and things beneath," which terms were used in the cosmic philosophy of Paul's readers.

(4) The application of the saving power of the resurrection in the individual's experience is that he can know himself to be in immediate present fellowship with Christ. To Paul this was the most natural and real of all experiences. His touch with Christ began with his vision of the risen Redeemer. There was no experience of loss and recovery as in the case of the other disciples of Jesus. He attained and maintained the sense of fellowship and cherished it as his supreme privilege. For all Christians he holds this relationship to be natural. The phrase "in Christ" ("in the Lord," Phil. ii. 14; II Tim. i. 9) indicates not only their intimate relation to Christ, but the ground of their privileges. These include forgiveness (Eph. i. 7; Col. i. 14), redemption (Rom. iii. 24), freedom from condemnation and law (Rom. viii. 1; Gal. i. 14). But these privileges are grounded in the present life of the risen Christ.

While it is quite true that Paul makes no theoretical construction of his view concerning the work of Christ, it is clear that his mind was naturally keen and well trained in analytic study. What he had to struggle against in facing the problem of how divine grace works out forgiveness for human sin was the fullness of his own experience. And here he found in the end the purest and most appealing thought to be what he expresses in the words: "God in Christ reconciling the world unto himself not reckoning unto them their trespasses" (II Cor. v. 19). The initiative was with God, the mediation through Christ and the result the obliteration of the guilt of sin.

3. JUSTIFICATION.—The last stage in the unfolding of the grace of God in Christ is reached in the transference of the sinner from the category of condemnation to that of acquittal. Since to be found righteous before God was the supreme good and since Paul had made it the chief goal of all his efforts, the achievement of it through Christ, when the law had failed, was the infallible test of the true way to God. Justification then is the culmination, as it is also the vindication of the gospel of grace. It is the achievement of righteousness. "Now apart from the law a righteousness of God hath been manifested" (Rom. iii. 21).

Justification is "a decision in favor of" the accused at the bar of judgment. It is the act of pronouncing "not guilty" those who by reason of their conduct would be deemed punishable. Consequently it is a purely forensic act. Every effort to interpret it as anything else is based on the confused and inadequate assumption that in it Paul condenses his full thought of what God has done for the sinner. While, as a Pharisee with all earnest Pharisees, Paul strove to earn forensic acquittal at the judgment bar, when he found Christ, he realized that religion was a fuller and deeper matter than the relationships of the courtroom could portray. But he never gave up the language of the courtroom in explaining the gospel. And, in the language of the courtroom, justification is equivalent to acquittal.

Objections to it, as such, drawn from the grammatical structure of the words used in setting forth the doctrine prove illusory. It is said, for instance, that etymologically "to justify" (δικαιόω) is "to make just," *i.e.*, inwardly in character. If so, justification must be the ethical transformation of character. This assumes that all verbs in όω carry the idea of rendering what the adjectives or substantives from which they are derived mean. But this, while generally true, has its exceptions. Xenophon uses [5] the word ἐθανατώθη (from θανατόω) of the judicial act of declaring worthy of death. Strict grammatical interpretation would have required the rendering of the words as "was put to death." But at the time when this was said of the subject, he was leading an army against the Persians. He was not put to death but judicially condemned as worthy of death.

The last application of the legal metaphor in bringing into view the full meaning of the gospel is made by Paul in the doctrine of adoption (Rom. viii. 15, 23; ix. 4; Gal. iv. 5; Eph. vii. 5). But in the language of adoption the apostle has resorted to the Roman law of the day. The law provided that one born in a different household might by means of certain formalities be made as if born in the household of the adopter. He would then have the standing and the rights of an own child. The figure brings into view the value of the privileges of the believer. But it has always been recognized as a figurative mode of presentation and rarely overemphasized either as a whole or by insisting too rigidly on the analogy between the legal form through which adoption was operated and the spiritual process by which the Christian secured his rights in the household of God.

[5] *Anabasis*, ii. 6, 4.

CHAPTER XXI

THE NEW LIFE IN CHRIST

WHEN Paul was making his strenuous efforts to secure righteousness by obedience to the Law, his mental conception of the structure of the spiritual universe was that of an organization determined by laws and statutes. But in his heart he found another principle whose presence there prevented him from getting perfect satisfaction in this belief. But of this other principle he probably gave no account to himself. His conversion stimulated this principle and liberated a new mysterious energy. At the same time it opened his eyes to the fact that personal relationships are governed by something higher than legal arrangements. Hence righteousness acquired through Jesus Christ as a gift of God could not remain a mere matter of relationship to the law. It must work inwardly as a life and outwardly as conduct. And his theology started on a new growth in which the thought of the Spirit of God loomed large and dominant.

1. THE HOLY SPIRIT.—That Paul before his conversion had an academic conception of a divine spirit working in the world is not only probable but may be taken for granted. The idea was one of the commonplaces of religious thinking in his day. But it is equally certain that his conversion crystallized and clarified his thought on the subject. The very experience of conversion he was later accustomed to trace to the inworking of the divine Spirit. His vision of Christ, his consent to accept him as his Lord, his new insight into the nature of the true righteousness and of Jesus as the Messiah he recognized as undeniable evidences of the Spirit's work. Whatever his pre-Christian notion may have been of the nature and method of operation of this factor in religious experience, as a Christian he came to hold that his own inner life was nothing less than the effect of the Spirit's power in his heart.

And accepting the testimony of his own heart as the standard for all Christians he made the reception of the Spirit the test of the true Christian. According to Luke's account in Acts (xix. 1, 2) finding "certain disciples" at Ephesus who thought themselves Christians because they were baptized, he put to them the test question "Did ye receive the Holy Spirit when ye were baptized?" To the Galatians he wrote (iii. 2), "This only would I learn from you, Received ye the Holy Spirit by the works of the law, or by the hearing of faith?" In other words, he asked them to verify their conviction of genuine Christianity by the reception of the Holy Spirit (cf. also Rom. viii. 9b, "If any man hath not the Spirit of Christ, he is none of his.").

So far then as the gospel was a new thing under the sun its distinctive characteristic was the manifestation of the Spirit in power. Not that the ages of Moses and the prophets were actuated by some other principle, but that the new Messianic age was made clearly aware of the Spirit's presence and workings. Paul could not ignore the agency of the Spirit in anything which brought God's will to men. The Old Testament dispensation as a whole was full of its power. But in Jesus Christ, the risen Lord, its revelation was so irresistibly forced on the minds of men as to produce a new consciousness of power.

Accordingly in Paul's mind the person of Christ was in a certain fashion identified with the Holy Spirit. "Now the Lord is the Spirit" (II Cor. iii. 17). When the Spirit of God dwells in anyone it is because the Spirit of Christ is in him (Rom. viii. 9; Eph. iii. 16, 17). Unless this means that there are two spirits, that of God and that of Christ, there is an unmistakable blending of the personality of the Savior with that of the Spirit. Again the Spirit which teaches believers to cry "Abba, Father" is "the Spirit of God's Son" (Gal. iv. 6). Christ as "the last Adam became a life-giving Spirit" (I. Cor. xv. 45). It is possible, of course, to take these expressions too literally. Others perhaps more numerous could be cited in which the distinction between Christ and the Holy Spirit is held by Paul clearly in mind. The benediction in II Cor. (xiii. 14) is a most pronounced instance of these. But while the fusion of Christ and the Spirit is not complete, the association of the two is so intimate that where one is the other also makes himself known and felt. This mode of thought is no doubt the result in Paul's mind of his first vision of Christ. As risen and glorified the Lord made himself known to the prospective apostle as spirit. Thenceforth Christ could be to him nothing else essentially than spirit; and the Holy Spirit nothing else than a person mysteriously made visible in the form of Christ, the Lord. In all this the personality of the Holy Spirit is always felt in the background though Paul's practical aim in all his writing furnishes no occasion for a clear and direct pronouncement on the question.

The aim of Paul in setting forth his thoughts further called for a fuller expression of them so far as they concern the work of the Holy Spirit. And on this subject his point of view is identical with that of the primitive church pictured in Acts. The most obvious phase of the Spirit's presence is ability on the part of those influenced by it to do wonderful works of power. Through these the preachers among them were able to convince men of the truth of their message. Paul enumerates this class of the Spirit's effects as "miracles, tongues, healings, knowledge, interpretation of tongues, prophecy" (I Cor. xii. 4-12). He does not draw a distinction between normal and supernormal activities; nor does he face the problem of whether they were "natural" or "supernatural." The distinction was not known among his contemporaries. He knows that the Spirit achieved these effects by a divine energy. Paul was more concerned with the utilization of the forms of this energy (the "gifts") in building up human souls after the type of Christ. The "Psalm of Love" (I Cor. xiii.), inserted in the midst of the discussion of their value, shows that he is anxious to keep the attention of his readers fixed rather on the marvel of God's love and the need of fostering it in the heart than on the marvel of the "gifts."

The Holy Spirit is preëminently the source of all holy and uplifting traits of character. Love itself he classifies among the gifts; and he gives it first place in the class ("a more excellent way," I Cor. xii. 31). When men are "led by the Spirit" not only are they "not under the law," but they abound in the "fruit" of the Spirit which is "love, joy, peace, long suffering, kindness, goodness, faithfulness, meekness, self control" (Gal. v. 22, 23).

2. THE LIFE OF THE SPIRIT.—All vital religion is the result of the Spirit's indwelling in man. It is the Spirit that initiates the movement of the soul toward God. The aspirations and desires of the saints for the better things which God reserves for them in future are due to the Spirit's stimulation. "We ourselves who have the first fruits of the Spirit, even we ourselves, groan within ourselves" (Rom. viii. 23). The prayers of the believer are stirred and directed by the Spirit (Rom. viii. 26). The impulse to overcome the evil that is within and cast it out comes from the same source (Gal. v. 17). The Spirit is a flame of fire within giving out light and heat which must not be quenched (I Thess. v. 19). The Spirit is a sensitive friend who must not be grieved (Eph. iv. 30). Finally all assurance whether of freedom (II Cor. iii. 17; II Tim. i. 17) or of ultimate triumph over all that hinders absolute communion with God (Rom. viii. 31-39) comes from the Spirit.

3. FAITH.—The life of the Spirit begins with the exercise of faith on the part of the disciple. The idea of faith in Paul's thinking is the bridge that connects the two parts of his system which at first sight strike the modern student as separate and unconnected. It is by faith that the soul appropriates the righteousness of God in Christ. It is by faith also that the soul receives into itself the indwelling Christ (the Spirit) and thereby becomes the ground and beneficiary of a new life. Paul's legalism and mysticism, wide apart as they appear, are united into a consistent whole by his doctrine of faith in the disciple.

What then is faith? Primarily it is persuasion.[1] But Paul never allows himself to lose sight of the specific truth of which Christian faith is the persuasion. Though the foundation upon which his conception is built is the Old Testament notion that God would be true to his word either when given in an established covenant or in a promise uttered through an inspired prophet, yet the main value of faith to Paul was that it allied the soul with Jesus Christ the Lord. Through this alliance faith brought into visibility the whole world of realities woven together into one supreme good in the person of Jesus Christ. To exercise faith was, therefore, to accept the Lordship of Jesus Christ. Faith then is "the complete response of the self to the glad tidings of salvation through Christ."

This reaction of the human soul, of course, begins with a perceptive element. He who believes must become aware; in fact, he must get a clear mental presentation or knowledge of the content of what he is

[1] πίστις, from πείθω "to persuade."

called upon to believe. But the mere perception of it is not enough; for it is conceivable that what is presented to one may appear to him unreal. He may find himself unable to accept it as true. The warp of faith is belief; and until belief has come into being faith cannot exist. Thus far faith is equivalent to persuasion. But in order to realize the fullness of Paul's conception of it we must go a step further and include in the idea the movement of the will which develops belief into an act of trust. For faith is energized by love (Gal. v. 6).

Faith thus conceived finds its culminating function in appropriating the righteousness wrought by Christ (Rom. iii. 26; v. 1; Gal. iii. 24). It seizes upon objective righteousness, the forensic relation with God, and transmutes it into the subjective righteousness called by Paul holiness. It saves freedom from the law from degenerating into opposition to the law. It ends by becoming something more than a means of justification for self; for it leads to a life of service in behalf of others. Faith thus becomes active as well as reactive, productive as well as receptive. Yet this aspect of it is in Paul's exposition rather implicit than explicit. For, in general he traces activity in the believer to the supernatural working of the Holy Spirit.

4. THE LIFE IN CHRIST.—Before, however, faith could become the means or source of new activity it must issue in a new relation with Christ. All relationships of trust presuppose and promote mutual understanding and dependence. But the one between the believer and Christ transcends the mere manifestations of such understanding and borders on (or as some would say, enters into) the realm of the ineffable. It becomes a mystical union. Christ lives in the believer. Christ's death, resurrection and heavenly life are shared by the believer.

Although the thought of a mystical union with Christ established by faith is not a modern discovery, the prominence of it in Paul's thought was brought into view by Deissmann's booklet on the New Testament formula "in Christ." [2] Deissmann interpreted the preposition ἐν in the phrase in a local sense inclining to a literal view of it. Subsequently he (and others) added to this investigations of the phrases "in the Lord" (ἐν κυρίῳ), 'through Christ" (διὰ Χριστοῦ), "with Christ" (in phrases where verbs compounded of the preposition σὺν are used), "in the name of Christ" (ἐν τῷ ὀνόματι Χριστοῦ), "in the blood of Christ" (ἐν τῷ αἵματι τοῦ Χριστοῦ), and some others. The generalization he reached from these investigations was that Paul viewed the communion of the believer with the Savior as a vital one best symbolized by the body with all its organs and parts.

This generalization which very many scholars have adopted and supported by independent investigations "is too broad to rest on the use of the preposition ἐν. As every student of Hellenistic Greek knows, the prepositions are loosely used by those who resorted to the use of Greek at all. And Paul is not more careful in this matter than his contemporaries. "In Christ" may be a simple equivalent of "through Christ."

[2] *The Religion of Jesus and the Faith of Paul.*

THE NEW LIFE IN CHRIST

But the case for an intimate personal ("mystical") union with Christ does not rest on the mere use of prepositions. Paul has a well-defined idea of the indwelling of Christ in the believer. "I live; and yet no longer I, but Christ liveth in me" (Gal. ii. 20). This indwelling is not a mere matter of passive enjoyment for the believer, but becomes the starting point of a stream of activities impossible to him apart from it. Paul's preaching is traced to it (Gal. i. 11; ii. 2; II Cor. xiii. 3). While in some expressions the Apostle appears to speak of the working of Christ through him as a peculiar privilege due to his calling as an apostle, there are others in which he appeals to his readers as also possessed of the same power. "Know ye not as to your own selves that Jesus Christ might enter into and have free course in their hearts?" "I am again in travail that Christ be formed in you" (Gal. iv. 19). The glory of the mystery of the gospel is "Christ in you, the hope of glory" (Col. i. 27).

The same thought is involved in Paul's explanation of the sacrament of baptism. The form of words used in administering the rite in itself suggests the idea of communion. But more explicitly those who were baptized "did put on Christ" (Gal. iii. 27). Still more clearly the sacrament is at least utilized, and is possibly understood as primarily signifying the believer's identification with the Redeemer. "All we who were baptized into Christ, were baptized into his death" (Rom. vi. 2-6). Being reduced into oneness with Christ the believer becomes a participant of his complete experience, his death, his burial, his resurrection and his imperishable life. "Christ being raised from the dead, dieth no more." "So reckon ye also yourselves to be dead unto sin, but alive unto God in Christ Jesus" (Rom. vi. 9-11). By this union Paul aims to become conformable to Christ's death and to know the fellowship of Christ's sufferings that he may attain to the resurrection of the dead (Phil. iii. 10-12).

But identification with Christ does not destroy the individuality of the soul. Identification is not absorption. Individuality is not extinguished but revitalized by it. As in the engrafting process the inferior is ennobled and filled with new value which it derives from the superior element. The new life is "in Christ" and implies the life of Christ in the believer. But at the same time it enjoys an independent development of its own. It has a beginning and a growth, a character and a task, culminating in a goal.

(a) *Regeneration*. From this point of view, whoever is in Christ is a new creature, old things are left behind for him (II Cor. v. 17). Outward forms fade into insignificance because of his entrance into a new career (Gal. vi. 15). He is clothed upon with a new manhood (Eph. iv. 24) which is destined to grow to a larger fullness as every living organism does (Col. iii. 10). Paul makes little use of biological imagery in portraying spiritual realities; but what he has in mind is not very different from the thought of other New Testament writers who more clearly call the beginning of the Christian life the new birth. If, however, the word regeneration in Titus, v. 6 is his, he associates the new birth with the cleansing signified in baptism as the symbol of renewal. Aside from the general description of it as renewal Paul resorts to his favorite idea of resurrection with Christ and to the figure of the erection of a building in referring to the initial stage of Christian experience.

(b) *Sanctification.*—The progress of the new life is, according to Paul, a process of growth in holiness. The thought appears to have been suggested to his mind when he realized the misapplication that might be made of his doctrine of justification by faith. If righteousness at the bar of God's judgment is not attained by conduct the logical inference might be drawn that one might continue in sin. He indignantly repudiates the inference. He even claims that the true logical inference from his doctrine would be not the repudiation of good works, but a new and stronger incentive to a holy life. Justification means death to sin. How can one who dies to sin continue to live in it? (Rom. vi. 1). In order to make this appeal to logic, however, he shifts his ground from justification to the gift of the new life which in his mind justification inevitably brings.

Sanctification, moreover, has two sides, a negative and a positive one. On the negative side it is mortification to sin; on the positive vivification to righteousness. By dying unto sin is meant the weakening and final extinction of the desire for sinful indulgence. This the apostle considers as a process in which the human will has an active and potent function to perform. It is something which can be controlled by a determined effort and a fit subject of exhortation. "Put to death, therefore, your members which are upon the earth, fornication, uncleanness, passion, evil desire and covetousness . . . put them all away: anger, wrath, malice, railing, shameful speaking out of your mouth" (Col. iii. 5-8). To the voice of temptation to sin the new man in Christ can and must turn a deaf ear like the ear of a dead man.

Living unto righteousness is the converse of dying unto sin. And Paul does not spare his words in urging Christians to stimulate and foster it. The motive for sanctification is double; it has an inner source and an outward allurement. As a force from within it is the consciousness of the indwelling Christ. The outward allurement is the pattern of holiness furnished by Christ. Paul beseeches his readers to walk worthily of the calling wherewith they were called (Eph. iv. 1), because he has already informed them (Eph. iii. 17) that he is praying for them and is assured of the answer to his prayer that "Christ may dwell in their hearts." He reminds them that they were "raised together with Christ" (Col. iii. 1), and urges them for that reason to "seek the things that are above, where Christ is seated at the right hand of God." He places much value on the very contemplation of the things that constitute and promote a holy and Christ-like character. The study and the adoption of the mind of Christ he singles out and holds up as not only desirable, but incumbent on all disciples of Jesus. "Have this mind in you which was also in Jesus Christ." And to the same readers to whom he addressed this injunction he also wrote: "Whatsoever things are true, whatsoever things are just, whatsoever things are pure, whatsoever things are of good report, if there be any virtue and if there be any praise, think on these things" (Phil. iv. 8).

CHAPTER XXII

CHRISTIAN CONDUCT

THE transition from the life of holiness to conduct becoming a Christian among men in Paul's thinking was an easy one. In fact it is questionable whether he ever saw any line of distinction between them. As he began with the religious interest predominant in all things, so he continued to the end. The point of view of the Stoics, who considered ethics a separate sphere with an independent interest of its own, was either unknown to him or it failed to make an appeal to his mind. Since man's chief business was to please God and his permanent happiness depended upon securing a favorable verdict at the final judgment, everything he did upon earth was to be brought to the revealed will of his maker for a just estimate of its value.

1. RELIGION AT THE BASIS OF ETHICS.—The first characteristic, then, of Paul's idea of conduct was its unitary aspect. There is no line of separation between religious and ethical conduct. Man is responsible to God both for his spiritual and his moral life. There is one law to govern him in his relations with his creator and with his fellow creatures. True this law is not revealed with equal clearness to all men. Neither is it given in the same form. To the great world outside of Israel it is made known in the works of God in nature (Rom. i. 26; I Cor. xi. 14). To the Israelite it is given in the "oracles of God" (Rom. iii. 2). But the content of both of these revelations is the same.

As the rule of life does not discriminate between the Godward and the manward conduct, neither is there any discrimination in the sanctions by which it is validated. The rewards and punishments of good and evil action respectively are presented and administered by the same God. "From the Lord ye shall receive the recompense of the inheritance" (Col. iii. 23f.). "Whatsoever good thing any man doeth, the same shall he receive of the Lord whether he be bond or free" (Eph. vi. 8; Gal. vi. 9). Likewise the law of retribution is executed by the supreme ruler of all. The sins of the heathen are noted and punished by God (Rom. i. 26ff.; Eph. v. 3-5; Col. iii. 25).

But though religious and moral conduct are covered by one continuous code, Paul does distinguish on the religious side between the merely formal and the essentially spiritual; and he not only minimizes the value of, but actually excludes the former from the class of obligatory activities. "In the Lord Jesus," he says, "nothing is unclean in itself" (Rom. xiv. 14); "meats for the belly and the belly for meats; but God shall bring to nought both it and them" (I Cor. vi. 12ff.). This was the principle that determined his attitude on the question of the circumcision of Gentile converts; and making this discrimination he was conscious of following in the footsteps of Jesus himself. "The kingdom of God is not eating and drinking but righteousness and peace and joy in the Holy Spirit" (Rom. xiv. 17).

2. CHRIST AND ETHICAL VALUES.—What has been said so often with unquestionable correctness concerning Paul's theology is preëminently true of his ethics—it is Christocentric. The moral conduct derives its value and power from Christ, and it finds its measure and test in Christ. It is the love of God that constrains the Christian to a life that shall be pleasing not unto himself but unto Christ (II Cor. v. 14). The exhortation: "Have this mind in you which was also in Christ Jesus" (Phil. ii. 5) was not given as a means to the cultivation of a mystical relationship with the Savior, but in order to develop the rare virtues of humility and altruism among men. This the context makes very plain.

And as love of Christ is the central and dominant motive in the moral life so is love towards fellow men the most beautiful and fruitful source of good in the world. In fact no contrast between the love of Christ and love towards men should be permitted. The love of Christ is nothing more than love centered and rooted in the person of the ideal for all—men, angels and God. Nothing that is said in the Psalm of Love (I Cor. xiii.) can be untrue of Christ's love or of the love of the Christian for Christ. Love emanates from and flows back to Christ. In its course of circulation it suffuses and pervades all those who may open themselves to it and transforms otherwise dead and useless deeds into the "fruit of the Spirit." It does even more; it makes the conduct begotten by it immortal. "Love never faileth." "And now abideth faith, hope, love, these three; but the greatest of these is love."

3. FREEDOM OF MORAL ACTION.—But if the moral conduct of the Christian is the offspring of Christian love, it follows that the Pauline conception of moral quality in action makes spontaneity an indispensable element in it. No action coerced by superior power can have any moral value. This is true not only of the limitation of freedom by superior power in the form of physical force, but also of all constraint of the will by improper, *i.e.*, non-moral influences. Superstitious fears, for instance, militate against freedom. So does arbitrary authority on the part of men claiming rights over the conscience. Even the ceremonial law may be turned into a tyrant imposing blind obedience to its precepts. "Touch not, taste not, handle not; which all are to perish with the using after the commandments and doctrines of men" (Col. iii. 21, 22). "With freedom did Christ set us free; stand fast, therefore, and be not entangled in a yoke of bondage" (Gal. v. 1). The obedience which the believer yields to Christ is not extorted, but joyfully offered by him as the result of a spontaneous impulse of the heart.

In the sense which the term "law" does not exclude this "liberty in Christ" it is quite true that the will of Christ becomes a new law to the disciple (Gal. vi. 2). Yet this law is nothing more than the inner spiritual principle of the old law. Paul repeats on this point in free and somewhat fuller form the summary of all the commandments given by

Jesus (Mat. xxii. 40). "For this, thou shalt not commit adultery, thou shalt not kill, thou shalt not steal, thou shalt not covet, and if there be any other commandment, it is summed up in this word, thou shalt love thy neighbor as thyself" (Rom. xiii. 9).

Furthermore, if the essence of all morality is love and if love is imperishable and unchangeable, the expectation that the present age was hastening to its end could not affect the distinction between good and evil, right and wrong. Therefore, the question why Paul should be so strenuous in his insistence upon the purest and loftiest ideals of morality when he was looking for the end to come so soon, falls out altogether as meaningless. It is surely irrelevant to ask why the Christian should cultivate goodness if goodness is the desideratum not only for this age but for the age to come. Paul's ethical principles thus push the apocalyptic eschatological world view into the background. He does not himself cease to hold it; but his attitude towards it prepares the way for its loss of practical value.

4. CONCRETENESS OF DUTY.—On the whole the ethics of Paul is limited to the working out of the problem of conduct. Its constructive idea is loyalty to Christ. Its outline is furnished not by a theoretical survey of possibilities, but by the concrete problems which arise in the average man's contacts with his fellow men every day. Paul does not, therefore, face such matters as the nature of virtue, the metaphysics of oughtness, the philosophy of duty and of the supreme good. How man has come to be a moral being is to him a simple question. God made him so. But whether God did it by a single act or trained and directed him to his present knowledge of right and wrong by a slow process is not a question that he either directly or indirectly confronts.

On the practical solution of current questions of conduct while his principles are identical and invariable for all cases there is a visible line of demarkation between his treatment of purely individual and social ethics. Where the conduct of an individual in his relations with other individuals is concerned the apocalyptic view of the world which he brought into his Christian thought makes absolutely no difference; but when organized society and its institutions are brought into the relationships, he bears in mind the speedy dissolution of the social machinery and frames his ideals accordingly.

(1) *The State.*—Paul's attitude toward the government of Rome is unexpectedly lacking in patriotic Jewish hostility. This may be due to the fact that Paul's Roman citizenship, inherited as it was and cherished from boyhood onward as a safeguard against unjust treatment at the hands of the civil authorities, predisposed him to look upon the imperial government with different eyes from those of the Zealots. It is certain that he recognized a divine appointment and authority in the State. (Rom. xiii. 1-10). This must have been somewhat of an unaccustomed view among Christians. They had received from their Jewish antecedents an idea of the Roman supremacy as an evil temporarily permitted and to be done away with when the new age dawned. In substance Paul shared this belief of his fellow Christians as it appears

in the sequel to his exposition. But so far as the main idea that the government was altogether ungodly and harmful is concerned he enters a total denial of it. On the contrary he calls it "a minister of God for good." In his own experience he had found that it had interfered with unjust and unlawful procedure designed to harm him and hinder his work. He even attributes to it, under God, the checking and arrest of destructive activities ("the mystery of ungodliness," II Thes. iii. 7) whose unrestrained operation would lead to the collapse of the order of the world.

(2) *The Family.*—Paul's idea of the family shows more distinctly than any other portion of his system the presence in and influence on his mind of the approaching change of world order. His attitude toward marriage is one of more than indifference. He would do away with it (I Cor. vii. 1, 8). Yet it is not because he believes in the virtue of asceticism, but because he expects the speedy end of the age that he takes this view. In fact he realizes that the practice of asceticism might result in immorality, unconsciously anticipating the modern psychoanalytic psychology in deprecating the suppression of natural impulse. "It is better to marry than to burn" (I Cor. viii. 9). On this ground he tolerates marriage as conducive to a higher type of character.

He even sees that persistence in the married relationship might become a means of promoting the spiritual welfare of those already married and forbids divorce on the purely religious ground of difference of faith. Considering the practice in the Roman world in the matter of divorce it is an evidence of the strength of his conviction that he reminds his readers of Jesus' attitude on the subject (I Cor. vii. 10b), adding his own argument in support that persistence in the married relation would tend to win the non-Christian member of the family to Christianity.

Within the family the observance of the law of Christ resolves itself to a matter of individual ethics. Husbands, brothers and sisters, parents and children are to be governed by mutual regard for each other's highest, i.e., spiritual welfare. Infidelity in the sexual relations like all impurity of life called from Paul special and severe condemnation. It was one of the sore spots of pagan society and an evidence of God's displeasure with the Gentiles because of the disregard of his natural revelation to them (Rom. i. 26, 27). He never neglects an opportunity of proclaiming the soul-destroying power of this type of sin (cf. I Cor. v. 1-8); and is anxious to warn those also who lived in the midst of constant temptation from it (I Thess. iv. 3; Eph. v. 3f; Col. iii. 5b).

(3) *Slavery.*—A feature of the household in Paul's day was the inclusion in it in many instances of slaves. The hortatory sections of his epistles generally include among those to whom he appeals for mutual helpfulness among the members of the family "masters" and "servants." (Eph. vi. 5; Col. iii. 22). The status of the servant (slave) as a member of the household is often forgotten by those who find Paul's view of slavery unsatisfactory from the standpoint of modern ethical ideas. The practice of slavery is removed into a different sphere when instead of an article to be bartered in the market for his mere value-producing quality, the slave is viewed as a person adopted

into the group to be not only a source of profit but also an object of affectionate regard. It is not to be denied, however, that under the best conditions outbreaks of inhumanity would occur where slavery is recognized as legitimate.

Paul takes up the institution at the point where it appears as a phase of household relationships and lifts it to the level where its distinctive character as slavery totally vanishes. This is clear in his treatment of the case of Onesimus. First of all he brought this runaway slave to the knowledge of Christ. Then he persuaded him to go back to his old home with Philemon. But Philemon at Colossae had already accepted Christ as Lord. When Onesimus returned to him to resume his life of slavery, Philemon must treat him as a brother, the only kind of treatment that any Christian can offer to any human being not to say a fellow Christian. If master and slave can live in the relationship of brotherhood, that relationship is evidently stripped of all the possibilities of injustice and oppression. Slavery in such circumstances is left an empty name. Add to this the converse that in Paul's ideal the slave also treats the master as a brother. It is inconceivable that Onesimus as a Christian can withhold from Philemon the fair and cheerful helpfulness which a brother deserves and gets. If men, as they coöperate for common ends, must divide their tasks in such a way that one takes an easier and another a harder part; and if he who takes the harder part must receive directions from his brother of the easier part, it is Paul's judgment that they "have the mind of Christ" in them. Thus their coöperation under whatever name they carry it on is a fraternal combination. The sting of evil is extracted from it. On the other hand there is a servility which is perfectly consistent with outward civil freedom. He who submits to the dictation of men when he should assert his birthright as "the Lord's freedman" makes himself a "slave" (I Cor. vii. 22, 23).

(4) *Wealth.*—Another occasion which always presents a difficult problem in the realm of thought is that of the distribution of this world's goods. Apparently this is not an equal distribution. And those who have the lesser portion are always tempted to exchange places with those who have the larger. Their desire, however, is in most cases not for an even exchange in which the goods of the more prosperous will come into their hands together with the burdens and labors which condition the possession of wealth, but simply an exchange of poverty with riches, a simple transfer of wealth into their hands apart from the labors that brought the wealth together and the responsibilities that accompany its possession. Paul's doctrine on this subject is given in his condemnation of covetousness which he brands as "idolatry" (Col. iii. 5; Eph. v. 3).

The remedy for covetousness is application to profitable labor whereby one may earn the means of helping others. "Let him labor with his hands the thing which is good that he may have to give to him that needeth" (Eph. iv. 28). To have is good, but only as the foundation of the ability to supply some need of self or of a brother. Paul looks upon work as an obligation upon all. When some Thessalonians under the excitement of the expectation of the parousia gave themselves to fanatical idleness, he rebuked them and urged their associates to withhold their support from them. "If any will not work, neither let him eat . . . them that are such we command and exhort in the Lord Jesus Christ that with quietness they work and eat their own bread" (II Thess. iii. 10-120).

(5) *Casuistry.*—Paul's treatment of questions concerning moral conduct in the concrete rather than in theory is clearly to be seen in the special attention he has given to the solution of doubts about matters commonly regarded morally indifferent. The word "casuistry" has been applied to this method of throwing light on the path of duty. It is a word that has never found favor among idealists and philosophers. This is due to the abuse of it by some teachers of ethics, who have so expounded it as to confuse and blunt the moral sense. Paul's way is designed rather to train and strengthen the conscience. Paul undertook to discuss the matter because it had assumed a considerable importance in the practical life of his day. What he teaches has permanent value because under changing conditions the demand for the solution of doubts recurs in all generations and must be met by the religious leader.

In the moral sphere the solution of doubts, or casuistry, means simply the application of moral principles to individual cases. Every decision called for in life falls into one of three classes. It is either right without qualifications, or wrong without qualifications, or it is right under some conditions and wrong under others. There is theoretically a neutral zone in which action may be morally good or evil according to the circumstances. Practically nothing is indifferent. For as soon as action is taken the conditions color the indifferent case with the tint either of right or wrong. The problem for the moral sense, then, is just how to use the light one possesses so that he may render in every indifferent case a right decision.

The zone of morally neutral action for Paul was for the most part that in which the religious practice, either Jewish or heathen, included ceremonial observances. The problem of conduct in this sphere became very acute because in the young Christian communities the matter of one's attitude to the old religious ceremonies was viewed from such a variety of angles. The more conservative spirits in these communities found much value in these rites, some even deemed them obligatory. Others saw their futility and not only abandoned them altogether but denounced them as harmful. Still others realized their proper place in religion but wavered in conduct, not being able to formulate a clear rule about them. The situation was aggravated by the divergent antecedents and habits of Jewish and Gentile converts to the gospel.

The Apostle was confronted with this situation by the experience of the Corinthian and Roman Christians. He discusses the problem in Romans xiv. and I Corinthians viii.-x. But while the class of cases directly in view in Paul's day were mostly of the ritual type, the principles he enunciates for dealing with them are the same for all morally indifferent matters in all ages. So far as the Christian conscience is concerned it makes no difference whether the problem it faces is that of partaking or not partaking of the flesh of an animal sacrificed at the altar of a heathen idol or that of engaging in amusements which the past generation considers improper for and the present permissible to a good Christian.

The principles which Paul lays down for the decision of doubtful cases are the following:

First: Every man should decide each case for himself. No other man has any right to tell him whether it is good or bad for him to do or not to do the thing about which he is hesitating. Men have no right to judge each other in such matters (I Cor. x. 30; Rom. xiv. 3, 4).

Second: Every man should have a clear conviction upon the basis on which he decides. "Let every one be fully persuaded in himself" (Rom. xiv. 5). It is the duty of each man to act according to the light that is clear to him.

Third: In every case the believer should be teleologically, not impulsively, governed. He should have an end in view rather than give vent to his feelings and appetites. A man is more nearly right when he works out a line of conduct because of some good he wishes to achieve than when he simply follows his impulses unreasoningly. The Apostle would have men look to the effect his course may have upon others, especially the weak in knowledge or feeling.

Fourth: It is safe to choose the course that involves self-denial, because there is always an insidious temptation to prefer self even when indulgences lead to sin. A man is always better off when of two courses that appear equally just to him he chooses the one that calls for the sacrifice of self to the interest of others. "If meat make my brother to offend, I will eat no meat."

Fifth: In all cases the believer should be moved by loyalty to the kingdom of God, which in the end is the same as acting from loyalty to Christ.

CHAPTER XXIII

THE CHURCH AND THE SACRAMENTS

The trend of critical work in recent years has been toward the creation of doubts as to Paul's interest in questions of organization and administration. These doubts have worked their way into the problem of his literary relation to the Epistles in which ideas of church administration play a prominent part. By a sort of circular movement the denial of the direct Pauline authorship of Ephesians and the pastoral Epistles serves as the ground of ignoring their bearing on Paul's conception of the church together with its workings and its work. So far as the question thus raised is a literary one it must, of course, be answered upon literary and historical grounds. So far as a negative conclusion is reached from the consideration that Paul was too intensely interested in spiritual realities and their general intellectual vindication and promotion to give much attention to details of government and discipline, history furnishes too many demonstrable instances of persons who combined the talents of spiritual and intellectual leadership with conscientious attention to the minutiæ of administration to let the conclusion stand. A good theologian and a consummate ecclesiastic are not necessarily incompatible.

Be that as it may there is enough evidence in the unquestionably Pauline letters to furnish materials for a doctrine of the church and whatever may be added to these from the so-called "deutero-Pauline" sources most probably (almost certainly) represent ideas which Paul's immediate disciples took over from him in germinal form and elaborated into their present detailed exposition. It would be allowing too much weight to conjectural criticism ("critical divination") to refuse to build a Pauline doctrine of the church in the present condition of our knowledge of our sources.

1. The Church.—Paul at his conversion found a more or less compact body of believers who called themselves "brethren," "disciples," "saints," but also collectively "the church." Into this body he was formally received by the rite of baptism. By this experience he was brought into touch first with a local congregation which he along with all others called the church. But he could not have been connected with this group very long before he came in contact with many others of the same kind. How these groups stood individually and collectively to the people of God, the Israel of the prophetic ideals, must have soon engaged his interest. When he began to write his letters he had already found the answer to the query. "He is not a Jew who is one outwardly, neither is that circumcision which is outward in the flesh; but he is a Jew who

is one inwardly, and circumcision is that of the heart, in the Spirit, not in the letter" (Rom. ii. 28, 29; cf. also Gal. iii. 7; Phil. iii. 3, 4). Other groups within the Judaism of the time also were banded together with the hope that in them the ideal Israel might revive. All such, no doubt, looked upon their own group as the Remnant through which God would reconstruct his holy people.

How was this special nucleus constituted? What was the vitalizing force and integrating principle of the church? Paul was not slow in coming to a clear judgment on this point. The church consists of those who believe in Jesus Christ and are by him saved. It is just the fellowship of believers (I Thess. v. 9). Therefore the bond of union among the members of the church was the saving grace of Jesus Christ in its comprehensive sense, i.e., both as an objective ground of their salvation and as an inner spirit and life moulding them into the peculiar type of manhood common to them all. It is not in order to be saved that believers entered the church, but because they were saved. Accordingly all who were saved without distinction of race, nationality, social rank, sex or age were admissible to the church. "There cannot be Greek and Jew, circumcision and uncircumcision, barbarian, Scythian, bondmen, freemen, but Christ is all and in all" (Col. iii. 11; cf. also Gal. iii. 28).

In its broadest and most inclusive form the church is not a temporal but a spiritual reality. For it is brought together by a non-material power, and its unity is maintained by a living principle that actuates all its members. Yet the favorite designation of the Apostle for the church is the body of Christ. This is, of course, a figurative expression; but its frequency in the usage of Paul leaves no room for doubt that he found between the constitution of a living corporeal organism and that of the church more than one striking analogy. Some of these he brings into view in their details.

First and most striking of all he notes the indispensableness of unity of aim to its manifold and diverse lines of simultaneous activities (I Cor. xii. 12-27). Each member in a healthy body functions in a different way from every other, but the result of the manner in which it functions inures to the benefit or detriment of all the others. No member disconnected from the others in a body is of any value or can have enjoyment by itself. "Whether one member suffereth, all the members suffer with it, or one member is honored, all the members rejoice with it" (v. 26). Hence, above all things, strife and contention among the members of the church were special sources of grief to Paul. At Corinth and at Philippi he found dissensions and most vehemently, even though affectionately, warned his friends against them. "I beseech you, brethren, through the name of the Lord Jesus Christ, that ye speak the same thing, and that there be no divisions among you; and that ye be perfected together in the same mind, and in the same judgment" (I Cor. i. 10). And "make full my joy, that ye be of the same mind, having the same love, being of one accord, one mind" (Phil. ii. 2). The supreme test of true membership in the church is the presence of the mind of Christ which the Apostle distinctly says is the spirit of mutual service and helpfulness illustrated in the life of an organism. The members coöperate.

The second analogy between the body as an organism and the church is the dominance of the type which is manifested in and determined by the head. The head of the church is Christ (Col. i. 18; ii. 19; Eph. i. 22). Whether any member is genuinely related to the whole body must be made manifest by his showing in his outward life the signs distinguishing the type. The spirit of Christ must be working in him. To change the figure from the animal to the vegetable kingdom, he must bear the "fruit of the spirit" (Gal. v. 22).

A third analogy between a body and the church is the dependence of the outward organism upon the principle of life which animates it and furnishes it with the energy necessary for its right functioning. In the figure of the growing body Paul finds the best imagery through which to picture the need of keeping in vital connection with Christ as a condition of healthy spiritual growth. Only as the channels of communication between them and Christ, the source of their life, are open and his power is freely conveyed through them can the members of his body have their natural growth in God (Eph. iv. 16; Col. ii. 19). It would be very easy to press this figure so far as to read in the Apostle's mind the idea of a mystical view of the church's relationship to Christ. In fact it is hard to resist the impression that that was his real thought. But it must be borne in mind that he is making use of a metaphor.

Still another analogy given in the body's life as a figure of the church is the mechanical structure of it. The body acts as a machine moved by a mind. In the church the moving mind is that of Christ but the church itself as a mere body must have a mechanical structure. Though the Apostle does not lay much stress on this analogy, that it is present in his mind is abundantly evident from the fact that he organized individual communities of Christians, created offices (the presbyterate and the diaconate) and appointed their incumbents. Whether he looked upon the special definitions and mode of administration of these offices as permanent is not clear. There are some indications of his viewing them as conveniences rather than sacrosanct and exclusive means divinely appointed for all time. He never doubted their divine appointment but his enumeration of them leaves the impression that he did not consider divine appointment as carrying permanent and unchangeable value (and therefore validity) for all of them equally. "God hath set some in the church, first apostles, secondly prophets, thirdly teachers, then miracles, then gifts of healing, helps, governments, divers kinds of tongues" (I Cor. xii. 28). The difficulty of identifying some of these means of administering the grace of the Spirit and his manifest lack of zeal in enforcing his ideas of administration show that while he looked on mechanical structure as necessary in general the type of it he would leave to be determined according to changing conditions in a changing world.

On the whole Paul's conception of the church presents two aspects, an external and an internal one. As a body consisting of spiritual beings the church was a real entity transcending its outward manifestations and only partially describable in the terms of the world of sense. It was, therefore, a mystical body with a mystical life. But as an organization in a visible world that must needs function through visible agencies it could and must be realized, visualized and understood through symbols and figures drawn from the natural world. Accordingly what is said of it is primarily figurative. This is seen in the employment of a variety of metaphors. Besides that which figures the church as the body of Christ, Paul also uses the figure of the building (Eph. iii. 21; I Tim. iii. 15). From another point of view the church is the spouse of Christ in the marriage relation, for marriage is the figure of the union of Christ and the church (Eph. v. 32).

2. THE SACRAMENTS.—By some Paul is regarded the creator of the church's sacramental system. He is said to have taken over the whole conception of sacramental religion from the Asiatic mystery cults and imposed it on the Christian community. Or if this is putting the case too baldly, he is said to have read into the primitive and simple rites practiced by the apostolic community, into which by his conversion he was adopted, the meaning commonly found in the mystery rites of the cults of the day.

The fact is, however, that as a Jew Paul was very familiar with ordinances already full of the sacramental idea. If that idea is in its essence the thought that by a symbolical action a worshipper or a body of worshippers appropriated a mysterious grace or power from God or that a channel was opened between the source of all grace and the suppliant in this way, then every performance of a ceremonial service in Judaism was a rudimentary sacrament. But if by sacrament is meant more narrowly the actual identification of the life of the votary with that of his deity in acts of significant self-consecration, then Paul himself found this identification not in any sacramental act but in the inward self-surrender of the Christian to his Lord Jesus Christ. And there is no evidence that he saw in the so-called Christian sacraments anything more than the outward expressions of an experience already realized by the soul. This becomes clear as one scrutinizes his thought concerning the sacraments more carefully.

(1) *Baptism.*—First of all it must be noted that though Paul entered the Christian community by baptism and practiced the rite himself, he drew a line of distinction between baptism and preaching and considered the latter the superior means of introducing men into the Christian life; at any rate he deemed it a greater privilege to preach than to baptize (I Cor. i. 17). So far as this reveals his mind, it shows that he looked upon the ordinance rather as an expression of an inner condition than as a means of securing a radical inner change. Every expression has a value both by what it does for the expressing soul and by what it may accomplish on those who are impressed by it. To that extent Paul would be the last to deny the usefulness of baptism.

But what did baptism express? The answer must be found in the act itself and in the accompanying form of words. Taking the latter first, much has been made in recent years of the use of the words ἐν and εἰς (I Cor. i. 13; vi. 11; Rom. vi. 3) with the name of Christ. So far as the prepositions are concerned, it is certain that they are interchangeable. The use of the name has called for speculations with regard to parallel uses of the name of a person (man, god, or demon) among the ancients as a means of securing his power in one's behalf.[1] Underlying this use there is the belief that the pronouncing of the name magically binds its possessor to the service of the pronouncer. In the case of Jesus the later practice of exorcism among Christians implied the belief that the utterance of it terrified Satan and his emissaries to take flight. This would interpret baptism as a magical spell. But in Paul's usage the use of the name of Jesus is incidental. He does not seem to consider it always necessary to mention it, as when he speaks of being "baptized into Christ" or into the death of Christ directly (Gal. iii. 27; Rom. vi. 3).

A sidelight on the subject is thrown by the usage of James (ii. 7) "the name by which ye are called" (lit. "which was invoked upon you"). Whether this represents exact contemporary practice to the Pauline or a slightly later one, it leaves no room for doubt that the name of Jesus was pronounced by the baptizer (cf. also Mt. xxviii. 18-20). But there is no reason to suppose that it signified more than the association of the subject of baptism with Christ whose disciple he professed himself to be by the rite. The traditional notion that he made a confession at the time of his acceptance of Jesus as his savior and Lord would harmonize with this view.

What did the act signify? First of all the entrance of the baptized into the fellowship of Christ's disciples. In this respect it was the act of initiation into the brotherhood of believers. As the possession of the Holy Spirit was the distinctive characteristic of these, Paul specifically names it as the real means of uniting the baptized into one body and every additional individual by implication uniting with the body in the same way. "For in one Spirit were we all baptized" (I Cor. xii. 13). Those who believe in Paul's having come in touch with and yielded to the influence of the mystery cults see in this a clear evidence of that influence. The evidence however only justifies the verdict "not proven."

Baptism as understood and practiced before Paul was a sign of cleansing. In Paul's usage and experience it does not lose this significance (I Cor. vi. 11). Nor does it lose the additional meaning of a cleansing (bathing) as a means of entering into new relationships. Such bathing was very frequent in the equipment of priests for entering upon their official lives, as also upon those who entered into the married relation.

But characteristically Paul looks at the inner aspect of even the symbolism of cleansing and brings into view the regeneration (without which mere cleansing is but a negative matter) as the most important element in its meaning. At this point it may be said that he takes a step in advance of his predecessors. Naturally he connects the new

[1] Heitmuller, *Im Namen Jesu, Taufe und Abendmahl im Urchristentum*, p. 12.

THE CHURCH AND THE SACRAMENTS

life signified by baptism with the mode of it in his day, and shows its appropriateness as a symbol of the new life of him whose union with Christ made him a sharer of his death and resurrection (Rom. vi. 2-12; Col. ii. 12). This Pauline addition to the meaning of baptism transcends the original content of the ceremony and prepares the way for many freer and broader interpretations in later days.

(2) *The Lord's Supper.*—The theory that Paul is the creator of the Christian idea and practice of the sacraments receives a severe jar from the fact that he refers to the Lord's Supper only once in all the range of his writings. Out of the thirteen letters bearing his name, or if one accept the more rigid critical way of speaking, out of the nine now recognized as wholly his compositions only I Corinthians (x. and xi.) contains any mention of the sacrament which is preëminently so called. And the reference in this Epistle was called forth by the need of correcting a misunderstanding of the nature of the ordinance and the abuse of it in practice. Had the Corinthian Christians remained true to the primitive conception and usage, in all likelihood we should have had in it as little information about his mind as we have of that of John or even of Peter and James. For one interested in sacraments as much as Paul is said to have been, this is a strange situation indeed.

The abuse aimed at in the church at Corinth was one issuing in disorderly conduct involving intoxication. The misconception from which this could arise must have been serious indeed. Whatever its exact nature, it led to the degeneration of the Lord's table to the level of some festivals in pagan religions accompanied by revelling and immorality. Paul recalls the misguided Christians to the original intention of the sacrament as he had received it upon entering the Christian brotherhood, "For I have received that which I also . . ." (I Cor. xi. 22).

How literally he aims to repeat the words and describe the details of the first institution of the ordinance has been the subject of much discussion and study from which some clear conclusions appear to emerge. First the four accounts of the institution that we now possess are to be reduced to two more primitive ones. Matthew's is dependent upon Mark's and Luke's upon Paul's. This leaves the question as to which of these two is a more precise description of the facts. The difference between them is reducible to the appearance, in the outline account of the distribution of the bread, of the words: "This do in remembrance of me." In Mark's story the words used are simply: "Take, eat, this is my body." The natural explanation, and the more commonly accepted one at present among scholars, is that Mark's is the original; that he reports correctly what Jesus said; and that what Jesus had in mind was not an ordinance to commemorate him and his work, but just a simple fellowship meal. Paul in such a case must have added the words that signify the repetition and perpetuation of the sacrament.

But when one pauses to consider the phrase: "This is my body" in Mark's account, the query at once arises, what is meant by it and whence is such language derived? As an expression usable on a single occasion it is incomprehensible. If derived from the usage of some ritual either that of a mystery cult or appropriate to the sacrificial system current in Judaism, it affiliates itself with a recurrent practice; and Paul's addition of the words, "This do in remembrance of me," only makes explicit what is already there. Of the two alternatives the one which associates the brief form of words with the Old Testament sacrificial system is vastly more in harmony with the historical conditions.

This conclusion is further supported by the second part of the account, viz., that which pertains to the distribution of the cup. Here Mark reports: "He said unto them, This is my blood of the covenant which is poured out for many." Paul reports: "This cup is the new covenant in my blood." Again the difference is obviously nothing more than a clearing and explicitation of what lay more or less concealed in the older statement. The sum total of the light of these investigations amounts to this: that Paul's account merely stabilizes and makes more quickly effective the knowledge of the original facts.

The relation of Paul's thought on the Lord's Supper to contemporary sacramental religion among the pagans is interesting. But from the scanty details regarding the latter that have survived no broad conclusions can be drawn. That sacramental banquets were held in connection with heathen cults is fully attested. There were "tables of demons" as well as "the table of the Lord" (I Cor. x. 18ff.). In a papyrus known to have been written in the second century the following invitation occurs to such a banquet: "Chæremon requests your company at dinner at the table of the lord Serapis to-morrow, the fifteenth, at nine o'clock."[2] In the worship of Mithra, too, participation of the flesh of a bull sacrificed to the god plays an important part. Paul evidently knows of these banquets. He warns Christians against the temptation to connect them with their own sacramental meal. Presumably his mind is not hospitable to the thought of importing their meaning into the memorial of the sacrificial death of Christ.

Yet whether consciously or unconsciously, the experience of an inner union with Christ which may be strengthened and nourished by the symbolism of eating and drinking is conserved and utilized by him. In particular he looks upon the "communion" (κοινωνία I Cor. x. 16) of the blood and of the body of Christ as a reality. And by communion he evidently means the fellowship which believers have with one another as members together of the church as well as the fellowship which as a collective body they hold with the Lord.

Finally, as always elsewhere, Paul holds to the Lord's supper as a sacrament not magically producing communion but expressing it as it exists and promoting and developing it as an adequate expression must and can. "Ye proclaim the Lord's death." It is a testimony and a declaration of faith, and not a magical means of securing immortality. Of this last idea there is not the least vestige in Paul's words anywhere.

[2] James Baikie, *Egyptian Papyri and Papyrus Hunting*, p. 313.

CHAPTER XXIV

THE FUTURE

Paul's sense of the future was extraordinarily vivid. By this is not meant that he had an uncanny faculty of prevision. So far as the knowledge of what was to occur was concerned there were times when he could look forward, anticipate and predict events. This is clearly the impression conveyed by the reporter of his experiences during the fateful trip to Rome (Acts, xxvii.). Yet there were times when he could not penetrate the darkness enshrouding the day ahead. What is meant is rather that in the government of his conduct he was guided by what he saw of its outcome both in this life and the hereafter.

Apart from this outlook his life would be an insoluble riddle. When he endured the numerous privations and sufferings which he recounts in II Corinthians xi. 24-31 his steadfastness would be inexplicable except for the sustaining power of hope. His aggressive efforts in behalf of the gospel, his aspirations for growth in every grace and virtue derived their vitality from the expectation that there was a crown of rejoicing awaiting such labors. Many a man with a less vivid confidence in the inevitable triumph of truth and right would have given up the apparently unequal struggle and followed the current with the multitude.

This sense of the future not only affected Paul's course of conduct, but it also entered his intellectual life and led him to constructive thinking about the "last things." Problems which many pass by as beyond the ability of man to solve had an alluring aspect for him. But in the solution of such problems, unlike many modern men similarly sensitive to the attraction of them, Paul had no expectation of getting light upon them from ancient predictive oracles. His recourse was to the Spirit; and the guidance of the Spirit came to him apparently for the most part through the exercise of his natural powers.

The question relative to the future which was uppermost in the minds of Paul's age was that of the Messianic advent and the establishment of the kingdom of God. For Paul after his conversion this assumed the form of the reappearance of Jesus upon earth in power to assert the dominion of God and his righteousness.

1. The Parousia.—Jesus had completed his sacrificial work and withdrawn from among men after his resurrection. But to Paul, as to all his fellow Christians, the work accomplished by Jesus was only a part of his whole task. And his withdrawal from earth meant only the temporary concealment of his personality. It was an absence to be

followed by a presence (παρουσία). While because of the resurrection and his existence as the Spirit Christ held communion with those who belonged to him, yet his relation to the objective world was not in the range of visibility but must enter it in the future. Similarly while his sacrificial work on the cross secured for believers forgiveness of sins, this did not make superfluous his conferring upon the world the privileges of a temporal reorganization in a glorious order.

If one were to ask why Jesus did not at his resurrection immediately establish the new order, Paul's answer might be (though it is nowhere explicitly given) that the exact moment for the coming kingdom was the moment of transition from the old age (αἰών) to the new. That moment was held secret from the whole world; and even Jesus must await the pleasure of God the Father for the signal. At all events the parousia according to Paul would flash upon the world suddenly and unexpectedly (Phil. iv. 5; I Thess. v. 2, 3).

Yet, though the exact moment of the parousia is unrevealed, there are large movements which can be traced and whose courses point to it as their fulfillment and consummation. These are the Messianic "birthpangs" (ὠδῖνες Μεσσίου). Among them is a certain predominance of one or more evil forces. The symbol of this was the figure of "the man of sin" (II Thess. ii. 3, 4), arrogating to himself a place of supreme honor and authority. This evil genius, also called "the mystery of lawlessness" (II Thess. iii. 7), was restrained and kept in check by the Roman imperial government, a very precarious and temporary force, indeed, according to the apostle. Its withdrawal would precipitate the cataclysm of the change of ages.

But if the Apostle is unable to fix the exact moment of the parousia, he can foreshadow the manner of it, at least in symbolical terms. It will take place to the accompaniment of the sound of a trumpet, a fiery flame and the breaking in to the human sphere of a host of angels (I Thess. iv. 16; II Thess. i. 7; I Cor. xv. 51, 52). The presumption is that the very presence of the Messiah will automatically transform the old order into the new. But there are indications of a positive infliction of force to cut off all opponents. "They shall not escape" (I Thess. v. 3). These may be the last vestiges of imagery surviving in Paul's mind as the result of familiarity with Jewish apocalyptic representations in which a Messianic war of "blood and iron" was vividly pictured (cf. Rev. xvii. 14 and Jude xiv. from Eth. En. lx. 8; xciii. 3).

But the culmination of the parousia is the establishment of the new order in which Christ is recognized as supreme over all human affairs. Of a second withdrawal of Christ after the lapse of a thousand years (or any other period of time) Paul knows nothing. On the contrary Christ's supremacy will extend over all creation ending only in the absorption of his official functions into the absolute sovereignty of God himself at the final consummation.

This doctrine conceived as a separate conviction, like the whole of the apocalyptic complex plan, was for Paul the first but not the end of all thoughts about the future. Underlying were spiritual and ethical values and interests which it was to bring into view. Among these the most vital were the direct consequences of the parousia, the resurrection, the judgment and the consummation of all things.

2. THE RESURRECTION.—When the idea of a resurrection dawned on the Hebrew mind, it brought a flood of light on some problems of interest in the field of moral and religious values. Its first practical use was the basis of the justification of God's ways in permitting the persecution and martyrdom of his faithful ones (Dan. xii. 2). Those who had appeared to have labored, suffered and died in vain were, after all, to be rewarded. Death did not end all. They were to return from the grave.

An idea of immortality was loosely held before this light dawned, but it gave no hope of blessedness beyond the grave. The dead were supposed to be cut off from fellowship with God; and without that no joy could be perfect to the Israelite. No wonder, then, that during the interval between the persecution under Antiochus Epiphanes and the days of Paul the notion of the resurrection was rapidly diffused, being adopted as one of the most distinctive articles of the Pharisaic creed.

Of course the doctrine of the resurrection did not cancel or contradict that of immortality. On the contrary it furnished for it a clear outline and substance in which the Hebrew mind could realize its importance. For just as the Greek mind was inclined to put out of the field the notion of a bodily resurrection without examining it (Ac. xvii. 32), so the Hebrew mind viewed a bodiless immortality as inconceivable and futile. Coming into Paul's mind first through his Pharisaic training, and then through the experience of his vision of Christ on the road to Damascus, it not only lost all its abstract aspect but it also loomed into a clear visibility. One could reason about it with confidence, and even describe its actual conditions.

Furthermore, Paul placed the idea into the central area of his thinking. He could revert to it over and over again (Rom. i. 4; Phil. iii. 10) and make it the special topic of a practical dissertation (I Cor. xv.). The occasion for this last treatment of it was the appearance in the Corinthian church of some who denied bodily resurrection altogether, and claimed that as a spiritual experience it had taken place already. Paul meets this position by citing the resurrection of Jesus as a proof that resurrection is a physical and not a bare spiritual experience. He further strengthens his argument by pointing out the fact that the resurrection of Jesus is a necessary article of the Christian gospel, which he assumes the errorists would not deny. If now they denied or explained away the resurrection of believers they must look upon the experience of Jesus as entirely exceptional, even unique, thus isolating him from all others.

Upon the basis of these facts the Apostle builds his idea of a law of resurrection. This phrase is of course a modern expression. There is, however, no other in which Paul's thought can be better summarized. Among its other current senses the term law is also used of a series of facts which emerge in the visible sphere from an assumed inner necessity. Paul's conception of the resurrection is that it occurs as a series of facts in a given order. "Christ the first-fruits; then they that are Christ's at his coming." "Each in his own order." And the series is without question constituted by the one principle of a common life with Christ. The inner necessity for the separate resurrections of believers is the energy of his indwelling in them.

Paul next takes up objections to the idea. His mode of meeting these objections is that of analogy. Analogy is the mode of reasoning from one sphere to another. In this case it means that for the difficulties met in this particular region there are equally strong difficulties in other regions into which we do not allow doubt to enter. Paul cites as an analogy the objection that might be raised by one who did not know the process of the organic development of the stalk of wheat from the grain. If he were given a description of the process, he would find it difficult to believe its reality. Apparently to him it would be impossible. Yet it is true. Similarly the resurrection life is true even though it looks incredible to the one who may look at it superficially.

But Paul finds the positive ground for accepting the doctrine in the confusion that would result from its denial. Here he alludes to the loss of meaning in baptism for the dead (v. 29). The allusion is obscure. The practice referred to is nowhere else mentioned. But whatever it was, evidently those addressed believed in its efficacy; and he appeals to them on the ground of self-consistency to accept the corollary.

Another and much more universally prevalent belief which Paul finds would collapse and leave Christians confused and in despair is the sacrifice of the present for the future implied in all suffering for the faith. If there is no resurrection, there is no possibility of rewards for such experiences as his own "fighting with beasts at Ephesus." The wreck of morality in such a case would be in the predominance of the maxim: "Let us eat and drink for to-morrow we die."

Throughout the discussion Paul presumably speaks of the resurrection as a physical experience, i.e., the return in bodily form into the relations of the earthly life of those who had died. But concerning the relation of the bodily form after the resurrection to the body before death he introduces an idea entirely unprecedented [1] in the previous history of the subject. This is the notion of the "spiritual body." The resurrection body is in one sense identical with the full mortal body; but from another point of view it is an entirely different body—the same body, and yet not the same. This is something like a paradox. But the Apostle does not offer it as such.

By "spiritual body" he means such a body as was made visible to him in the person of the risen Christ at his conversion. In all likelihood Paul conceived of this body as made out of a finer form of substance, free from the limitations and repulsive features of common matter. But what was of more importance is the complete subjection of

[1] The idea, however, that the body at the resurrection will be transformed for the better is found in the Apocalypse of Baruch (1. li), a writing contemporaneous with Paul's letters. The converse of it, also, i.e.. that the bodies of the wicked will suffer a change for the worse is given.

THE FUTURE 205

this body to the spirit. Such subjection whether of an organism constituted out of ordinary matter or of some other unknown [2] kind of substance could be properly called "a spiritual body." And it was because Paul believed that a supernatural substance would better respond to the control of spirit that he conceived of it as such.

What Paul says of the resurrection he applies to believers only. With the resurrection of non-believers he is not concerned. His doctrine of a universal judgment involves some sort of a return of them to a state in which God's sentence of retribution may be made effective, but the object of his writing was not to expound a doctrine *in thesi*, but to show its bearings on the conduct of a well-defined class. And for the members of this class the resurrection of the body was assured by their union with Christ. "In Christ we are all made alive" (I Cor. xv. 22).

3. THE JUDGMENT.—The sources of Paul's thought concerning the judgment are (1) What he read in the Old Testament prophets; (2) What he found in the rabbinical theology of his day (ostensibly based on the prophetic utterances, but in reality a mass of imaginative speculation); (3) What he felt in common with all men of sensitive conscience to be the demands of justice; and (4) the mind and spirit of Jesus as he understood it together with the assured results of the work of Jesus as Savior.

The tendency of the first two of these sources was to fix upon a definite occasion—a "day"—on which all men without distinctions of race, belief or even relationship to Christ would appear before the judgment seat of God and receive the just deserts of their conduct. From the last of his sources comes the addition to this picture of Christ as the judge. "We must all be made manifest before the judgment seat of Christ" (II Cor. v. 10). The third, the cravings of the healthy conscience, contributes strength to the conviction that Christians must appear at this judgment as well as non-believers. But the assurance of justification, on the ground of Christ's work received by faith, leads him to the belief that no further judgment can be passed on the Christian. "There is now no condemnation" (κατάκρισις, judgment, Rom. viii. 1). Is there here a real inconsistency, a paradox or a twofold conception of judgment?

The answer seems inescapable that the apostle unconsciously moves from one to another of the branches of his paradox by resorting to the notion of two ideas of judgment. There is a judgment in life constantly unfolding and manifesting God's justice. "Whatsoever a man soweth that shall he also reap." But this does not exclude the gathering up of all judgments into one in a final display of God's glory and a justification of his ways. Much of Paul's language that seems inconsistent with the legitimate implication of the gospel concerning the immediate salvation of believers and their consequent exemption from

---
[2] Surely no scientific-minded man of our day can object to the possibility of an "unknown" entity, seeing that our metaphysical word, substance, has totally lost its erstwhile meaning in the light of the electronic explanation of matter.

the great final trial, must be understood of divine judgment as a constant process. The remainder of what he says about judgment refers to it as a final act.[3]

A great final judgment, however, though assumed substantially under the same form as it was conceived before Paul is never brought by him into the foreground of thought. He mentions it as "the day" (I Cor. iii. 13); "that day" (II Thess. i. 10); "the day of our Lord Jesus Christ" (I Cor. i. 8); "the day of Christ Jesus" (Phil. i. 6); and "the day of Christ" (Phil. i. 10; ii. 16). All of these phrases point back to the prophetic "Day of Yahweh," and Paul's usage indicates his characteristic tendency to see in every permanent element of the Old Testament system the figure of Jesus Christ. Therefore when he employs the term day as the equivalent of the event (the judgment) he includes in it the notion of relative time. Because it is "the day of Christ," it is to come at his manifestation. And Christ would be the judge.[4]

When the relation of the judgment to the place and work of Christ loomed clearly in Paul's mind its purpose, too, was illumined more fully. That purpose included two mutually supplementary and yet independent aspects. First it was to bring into view "the goodness and severity of God." In the last analysis this means the vindication of God as just. The thought is identical to that underlying Abraham's question, "Shall not the judge of all the earth do right?" (Gen. xviii. 25).

God's justice is vindicated in the punishment of the wicked and the reward of the righteous. The age-old question: Is God really just? is occasioned by the apparent failure of the natural order to secure justice in all cases. It is, however, a reality and needs only to be brought into view. That the failure was not real will be shown by the equitable visitation of penalties. But this very fact will also enable all to realize that instead of a sign of weakness the apparent failure was only the token of the forbearance of God. His restraint and patience would thus enhance what was known of his power.

And the thought that sometime God would visit the iniquities of wicked men with just punishment strengthened the righteous in his course and had a tendency to deter the lawless from indulging freely in unrighteousness. For Paul the thought was of the greatest importance. So keen was his idea of the offense of sin that he could not be satisfied with anything less than the certainty of God's full execution of his righteous will upon sinners. However one may conceive of the wrath of God in its essence, to Paul it was a real reaction toward evil, which taken in view, must fill the evil-doer with the "terror of the Lord" (II Cor. v. 11). The actual details of this punishment Paul nowhere works out; but he warns Christians to live consistently with their

---

[3] That Paul had changed his mind on this point, passing from the thought of a final to that of a perpetual judgment, is argued by Holtzmann, *Neutestamentliche Theologie*, p. 192; Teichmann, *Die Paulinische Vorstellungen von Auferstehung u. Gericht*, pp. 81-83.

[4] It is a refinement not justified by the facts to say with Volz, *Jüdische Eschatologie*, pp. 232, 234 that Christ would be the judge of angels but that God would judge the world of mankind.

justification on the ground of Christ's work, for otherwise the reality of that justification would be only apparent and they would fall under the terrible condemnation of those judged by the law. God's character of justice must be vindicated at all hazards.

Besides vindicating the character of God the judgment is to result in the renovation of the world preparatory to the eternal kingdom of Christ. The great defect of the present age is the existence in it side by side of evil with good. This is why it should not and cannot last. Only a world entirely free from evil can be permanent. If, therefore, the parousia was to usher in, either immediately or by initiating a movement which should culminate in a new age, the evil must be swept away. This means, at least, that the incorrigible souls from whose being evil cannot be eliminated must somehow be cast out of it. And only the judgment can accomplish the complete separation of such from those who shall survive ("attain to the resurrection of the dead").

To this end the judgment must be complete and thorough. The righteous must be completely freed from all the temptations to evil and the hindrances to the life of the spirit that now make their course a struggle; and the wicked must be completely put out of the way. Exactly what the former of the branches of this dichotomy means is given in the word σωτηρία, salvation. The destiny of the unrighteous is similarly summed up in the single contracted word ἀπώλεια, destruction. But does destruction mean annihilation, consignment to eternal suffering outside the kingdom of God or a middle condition from which they may and will at the end be restored? The question was never faced by Paul. All that he is interested in is that the eternal kingdom of God will not be disturbed by the presence of evil-doers. If an unbeliever in this age enters it, it must be as a believer on the same conditions as these who are found in it at the judgment.

4. THE ETERNAL KINGDOM.—It is customary to speak of the permanent condition of the world as presented by Paul as the Consummation (of all things). His own designation of it is given in I Corinthians xv. 24 when he looks forward to the last visible limit of the future, "Then cometh the end when he shall deliver the kingdom to God, even the Father." The new and final era begins with the transfer of the kingdom of God from the hands of the Messiah to the hand of God himself. There is a difference between the kingdom of God under the Messiah and under God. Just as there is a difference between the kingdom of God before the Messiah and under the Messiah. The consummation of all things is, then, the return of all things under an ethical principle to him from whom they issued under the physical principle of creation.

This is a conception found nowhere in the New Testament outside of Paul's thinking. It transcends the purely Jewish outlook and borders on the Hellenic effort to think of things in the terms of the absolute and ultimate. But Paul's interest in it is not philosophical but religious. The motive for his directing his eye to the eternal goal of the gospel was his loving devotion to Christ. He feels that somehow his Lord must have a share in the supreme object and end of all creation and he finds that share in the supreme act of subjecting all things to God and extending the kingdom of God over all.

The "all," too, is absolute. It includes not only the human world but the world of angels and principalities and powers. Just as "all things were created by him" (Col. i. 16b), whether thrones or dominions or principalities or powers, "so in all things he is destined to have the preëminence." Thus just as Paul looking to the last moment of time found there Christ supreme, so as he looks to the totality of created beings imaginable, he sees Christ over them all. It may be truly said, without the least accommodation of his language, that he sees the kingdom of God through Christ extend over all the cosmos. He gives the gospel a cosmic significance.

CHAPTER XXV

PAULINISM AND THE RITUAL

(The Epistle to the Hebrews)

1. THE EPISTLE TO THE HEBREWS.—Paulinism as a distinctive group of ideas was a powerful factor in the Christian thought of its own day. This was due largely to the power of its originator's personality. For as soon as Paul and those who were personally inspired by him passed out of the scene, Paulinism lapsed into apparent oblivion, to be revived only with the new interest in intellectual Christianity through the controversies of the third and fourth centuries. The literature of the subapostolic age shows scarcely a trace of its influence. Yet in the New Testament itself no writing produced after Paul gave his interpretation of the gospel has escaped the impact of his thought.[1] This is true of the Epistle to the Hebrews and the Johannine writings, but in different degrees and with different results.

The Epistle to the Hebrews represents the transition from the Pauline to the final development of the gospel. Its Paulinism is so marked, so slightly modified that many have experienced no difficulty in accepting it as a work of the apostle himself. Yet its differences from Paul's strict type are also so apparent that to the scrutinizing eye its independence is indisputable. Concerning the authorship of the writing the tradition of the earliest days was unstable. And it remained so to the beginning of the modern critical era. As early as the days of Origen differences of view were rampant. That great scholar despaired of the solution of the problem. "As to who wrote the Epistle to the Hebrews God only knows," was his verdict. Through the Middle Ages and down to post-Reformation days the opinion generally prevailed that Paul was the author. And yet side by side with this view other views were propounded and ably supported, ascribing it to Barnabas, Silas, Apollos, Luke, Timothy, or other leaders in Paul's group.

Today the only clear conclusion that may be said to have been reached is that Paul did not write Hebrews. Though negative, this result of criticism commands a larger unanimity than any other in the Biblical field. The grounds for this conclusion are altogether literary and historical. The appearance or non-appearance of the supernatural element in it plays no part in the discussion. And the content of thought which is likely to serve both as premise and as conclusion in such an investigation is secondary. Beyond the negative conclusion, however, criticism has not been able to proceed. As to who wrote Hebrews the modern

[1] In what sense I Peter and the secondary Pauline Epistles lie outside of Paul's influence has already been explained.

scholar must still accept Origen's verdict.[2] But so far as the contribution of the author of Hebrews to the development of the gospel is concerned, this uncertainty of criticism is of minor significance, since in any case the dependence of the thought of the writing on Paul and its deviation along distinctive lines from typical Paulinism are both obvious.

But the correct understanding of the message of Hebrews depends further to some extent on a knowledge of the literary form and primary object of the document. On this subject, too, widely divergent views have been entertained. The question has been raised, for instance, as to whether Hebrews is an epistle or a homily. Whether it was written to be read or composed to be delivered orally. But it is clear that the answer to this question, though of deep interest to the student of its history and inner structure, is of little moment to him who seeks only for its specific message or type of thought. For, whether prepared to be preached as a sermon or to be circulated as a letter, the content of the document must needs be the same.

The same is true of the question of destination or audience (if it should prove true that it was written as a homily). The theological drift and tendency of the thought expressed would not be materially different. Whether the author was aiming to instruct Gentiles or to admonish Jews, whether he sent an epistle from Alexandria to Christians in Jerusalem or Rome or wrote from Rome to the church in Jerusalem or Alexandria, the fact remains that he is striving to relate the gospel to the Old Testament ritual and to demonstrate its finality and its eternal value by contrasting it with the transiency and unsubstantiality of the older system.

From one point of view the author of Hebrews advances and, so far as the term may be appropriate, one may say, completes the work of Paul. Paul had made it plain that the Old Testament dispensation, as one of law, had proved temporary and partial. It had had no power to effect salvation. But it had prepared the way for Christ. It had pointed to him and proved a tutor to lead men to the Teacher. But Paul had said nothing of the Old Testament dispensation as one of ritual service. He had singled out, it is true, an act of ritual significance, that of circumcision, and had made it the sign of the whole legal type of religion contrasting it with the spiritual type of religion presented in the gospel. But he had nowhere discussed the ceremonial as a system or the principles underlying its practice before the coming of Christ or its relation to the gospel now that it was preached as the only way of salvation.

In fact Paul's attitude toward the Temple and its service was undefined and easy to misunderstand. Personally, even as a Christian, he had continued to enter the Temple and to participate in its service. He

---

[2] But criticism does not permit itself to despair of advancing beyond Origen on this question. This is evident from the new efforts which are made to answer it. Among them the most noteworthy one in recent years is that which, arguing from the alleged femininity of the writing, attributes it to Priscilla (with Aquila coöperating) the well-known friend and fellow worker of Paul (Harnack, *Probabilia über die Addresse und den Verfasser des Hebraebriefs*. Zeitsch. *New Test. I. Wissensch*, 1900; J. Rendel Harris, *Sidelights on New Testament Research*, pp. 148-176).

had found some significance in the sacrificial system as a means of explaining the efficacy of Christ's death. But again, he had intimated that with the coming of the liberty of the believer in Christ, external acts of conformity to ritual lost their binding power, and might even become a hindrance and a burden upon the faith. How was one to relate the ritual to the gospel? Was the whole system a mistake from the beginning? Or was it to be perpetuated for the Jews as a national form of self-expression in religion? Was the Christian way to diverge into two paths one marked all along the way by the observance of the ritual law for the Jews and the other liturgically barren and simple for the Christians drawn from the Gentile world? And, if a third way between these two was the right one, on what principles was it to be justified? For those who accepted the Pauline interpretation of the gospel these questions were of sufficient importance to be clearly answered.

But, not only as a means of intellectual satisfaction should they be answered, but also for the practical end of holding Jewish Christians to the freedom of the gospel. The tendency had arisen among some of these to distrust the pure system of free worship. It is always easy to add to one's creed and practice, but rarely to discard in mind or conduct what has been cherished as of value. Many were timidly holding to the validity and obligation of the ritual even though they had accepted Christ as the only Savior from sin. "Having tasted the good word of God and the powers of the age to come" they were in danger of falling away (vi. 4, 5; cf. also x. 26). It was necessary to warn these as Paul had warned the Galatian Christians, that if they expected to be saved through the ritual Christ would avail them nothing.

The author of Hebrews thus came to think of religion as the right of free access to the mercy seat. In his day the danger point had shifted from the legal conception to the priestly one. The judgment bar of God had given way, as a center of interest, to the mercy seat. But the priestly conception in the Old Testament is rooted and grounded in the idea of the covenant. The ritual was valid by appointment from above. Its priesthood was divinely ordained. Its sacrifices were prescribed. The whole of it was meaningless unless God himself required it and sanctioned its observance. The covenant idea dominates the whole system. It was necessary, therefore, to show that the gospel itself must be interpreted as a covenant. As against the old dispensation, it is the new one. As against the restricted and carefully guarded access to the presence of God, the new covenant is one of free and unlimited access. As against the temporary nature of the old it is the final covenant.

2. THE NEW COVENANT.—In using the term covenant (διαθήκη) the writer has in mind more nearly what its etymology indicates than such a matter as modern conventional language has read into the word, i.e., a disposition or arrangement of relationships. The notion of agreement is carried in the covenant only to the extent that God and man constitute two parties to the perfect execution of the dispensation.

The object of any covenant is the establishment and perpetuation of right relationships. As between God and man these exist and are expressed in the terms of a service of worship. This is prescribed and centers around an altar involving a sacrifice and a priesthood. There is a sense in which the whole service (including the sacrifice and the altar) has mediatorial significance and efficacy. Those who looked to the old ritual as the means of access to God were right in construing the covenant in these terms. But the author of Hebrews aims to persuade them that in the gospel these elements were not absent. On the contrary they were there in a more real sense.

Yet the readers of the Epistle had a right to ask: Why a new covenant at all? Why not be satisfied with the old? The author realizes the force of the question and answers in effect: First by pointing to the progressiveness of God's dealings with his people. God had spoken to the fathers, through prophets in parts and portions each of which had added to what preceded (i. 1). But as they grew from the infantile stage in which they must be fed with "milk for babes," he had given them his son to feed them upon strong meat. The new covenant came in due succession to the old in the order of progress.

But what is progress? Its badge is not mere lateness in time. It is rather greater conformity to the ideal and a larger measure of efficacy. And from this point of view the new covenant was necessary because the old was imperfect and, therefore, inadequate. It was inadequate inasmuch as its altar, its sacrifice and its priesthood were all earthly and material. They were shadows (x. 1; viii. 5) and patterns (ὑποδείγματα) devised for the purpose of bringing realities into their full revelation and service. At this point the author betrays the influence of Platonism in its Alexandrian form. Material objects were, according to this philosophy, the coarse and imperfect images of spiritual realities.

In addition to their unsubstantiality as mere material objects, the elements of the old ritual were subject to waste and decay. This was clear from the fact that they needed to be repeated over and over again (x. 2). Its priesthood, too, because of the mortality of its membership was in need of being replenished. The new covenant was necessary as a spiritual way of access to God independently of all these weaknesses and wastes of the old.

Furthermore the old was from the beginning ordained to be temporary. Its weakness was not an unforeseen failure, but due to its nature as a foreordained makeshift. For it had in itself the confession of its impotency and the promise of the better that was to follow (vii. 19; viii. 9ff.). The new was then the fulfillment of the promise of the old. It was a covenant of realities over against one of mere shadows and outlines and it was designed to abide forever.

3. THE MEDIATOR OF THE NEW COVENANT.—Every covenant, according to the author, implies a mediator. The old was mediated at its very inception by Moses and by angels (Gal. iii. 19; Heb. ii. 2). In the course of its operation through the period of its predominance, it was mediated through the Levitical priesthood. It was meet that the new,

too, should have its mediatorship. As a matter of fact the mediator of the new covenant was Christ, the Son of God. As such he was superior to all mediators.

To validate this idea the author institutes comparisons between Christ and other mediators, taking up first the angels. Christ was superior to the angels. The proof of this he finds in the words addressed to him in various Psalms (i, ii). Next he shows that Christ was superior to Moses in as much as Moses was both his creature and the servant in his house (iii. 2-6). Finally, and in a more practical way, he compares the mediatorship of Christ with that of the Levitical priesthood (iv. 14; x. 18).

In this part of his argument the author first considers the Levitical priesthood as a whole and then the office of high priest in the order. And he compares the Levitical order of priests with the order obscurely alluded to in the Old Testament as "of Melchizedek." Christ he compares with the high priest of the Levitical order. In both these comparisons he finds the new covenant mediator clearly superior to the old. So far as the comparison is between the old Levitical mediatorial system and the mediator of the new covenant, he alleges that the new is superior because it is eternal. It was a priesthood after the order of Melchizedek. Concerning this order he claims that it obtains its validity independently of the grounds which the members of the Levitical order are required to produce in qualifying for their consecration. Among these conditions was chiefly the ability to trace their pedigree to Aaron. Melchizedek was recognized as a high priest without these requisitions. He was made a priest "without father or mother, without genealogy, having neither beginning of days nor end of life" (vii. 3). Christ, too, could not trace his genealogy to Aaron, being in fact of the tribe of Judah from which no one was ever called to approach the altar (vii. 13-14).

But not only was the order of Melchizedek independent of that of Aaron, but it was also of higher rank. This superiority the author claims was conceded when Abraham, the ancestor of Levi, offered tithes to Melchizedek (vii. 4f.), and by this act of homage both recognized his own subordination to the kingly priest and bound his whole posterity to the same recognition. It is implied in the argument that if Abraham, the patriarch, bowed to the mediatorial dignity of Melchizedek, the latter must surely be regarded both by reason of his antecedence and his preëminence over the patriarch as of superior authority and efficiency.

And as the order of Melchizedek was superior to that of Aaron, so the high priest of that order, Christ, as an individual far excelled any high priest of the Aaronic succession. This was true, first of all, because the high priests of the latter order could not abide for ever being subject to death. Therefore the law provided a succession of them. But Christ, being immortal, continued from generation to generation the unique high priest of his order (vii. 23, 24). But if he was the sole and unique high priest, necessarily he was himself the founder of the order of Melchizedek, whose name the order bore, although he was nothing more than a priest in it.

But the climax of the argument for the superiority of Christ as a mediator is to be found above all the comparisons instituted by the author and in the positive declarations of his relation to God himself. Almost in its opening words the document ascribes to him divine Sonship. On examination the Sonship referred to here is more than the official Messiahship. For it involves a share in the creation ("by whom also he made the worlds" i. 2 and "upholds all things by the word of his power" i. 3). But it also includes an ineffable relation as of substance and energy. The Son is "the brightness of the Father's glory and the very image of his substance" (i. 3). There is a very close approach in this characterization to the Johannine idea of the Logos, with its Philonian antecedents. At all events it indicates a clear advance in the direction of recognizing Christ as God. When, therefore, in the course of his discussion the author refers to Christ as the Son of God (iv. 14; vii. 3) it is no longer in a sense that might be shared with any other being in heaven or upon earth.

The mediator, then, of the new covenant is a being who enters into the earthly and human sphere from the eternal world. But as a true mediator he cannot remain apart from those whom he as priestly mediator must represent. His identification with men is complete. "In all things he was made like unto his brethren that he might be a merciful and faithful high priest" (ii. 17). Thus he qualified himself to sympathize with the needs, temptations and feelings of men (iv. 15). Thus, also, he qualified himself for his priestly work by enduring sufferings along with and in behalf of his brethren (ii. 10). This is called his being "perfected," i.e., put in touch with his work and with them for whom he assumed the part of mediator.

Yet though Christ's mediatorship is unique, separated from and superior to all others it is not entirely disconnected from other mediatorships. One principle underlies it and them. The orders of Melchizedek and of Aaron unite in him in their spiritual purport and efficacy. He is the reality of which they are the shadows. They are forms and expressions; he is the substance. The Levitical priesthood was constructed in the shape of a pyramid. At the base there lay a large body with lowly tasks and restricted privileges. These are the Levites. Above these there is a smaller number with higher duties and more extensive privileges. Above these stands the high priest, one at a time, with the highest duty on earth, that of bringing into the Holy of Holies the atoning blood and sprinkling it on the mercy seat, but enjoying as a compensation the largest honor and conceded the amplest privileges in the system. Yet, as the high priest was subject to death, he was succeeded by another and thus there were many high priests in the course of time. Now, over this whole system according to the author of Hebrews stood the great high priest, one from eternity to eternity, lifting the pyramid from earth to heaven and thus completing it.

4. THE SACRIFICE OF THE NEW COVENANT.—"Every high priest taken from among men is ordained for men in things pertaining to God,

that he may offer both gifts and sacrifices for sins" (v. 1). Evidently the author's conception of the functions of the high priest is broad. It is a comprehensive mediatorship that he exercises. Yet within the large complex of the mediator's functions one objective always stands clearly in view. And that is the removal of the barrier into the presence of God. This barrier was constituted by the sins of men. Though a priest may offer sacrifices and gifts in the endeavor to express the sense of acceptance of his clients and their appreciation of God's goodness, yet as long as there is sin in the hearts and lives of men his main effort must be to remove it.

In the Old Testament the high priest was required to appear once a year in the Most Holy Place, and by sprinkling the blood of a goat upon the mercy seat to "cover" the sins of the people by the innocent life ("the blood") of the victim. Thus sin was done away with; and the presence of the high priest before the mercy seat indicated that access into the presence of God had been achieved. But two drawbacks rendered this ceremonial obviously inadequate. First the people were only representatively present there. For none but the high priest enjoyed the privilege of personal presence in the Most Holy Place. Secondly the transaction lost its efficacy with the lapse of time. The blood sprinkled on the mercy seat one season was not capable of "covering" sin for more than that season. These defects must be remedied.

In the sacrifice of the new covenant they were completely remedied. That sacrifice was the life of Christ himself. Christ as high priest "entered into the holy place, having obtained eternal redemption for us" (ix. 12). His sacrifice was, first of all, one of infinite value. He made it not in the visible and earthly temple but in "the greater and more perfect tabernacle not made with hands, not of this building." He made it "in the eternal spirit." Its merit was not dependent upon the value of earthly materials or forms, but upon his own dignity and divine character. But, secondly, his sacrifice was effectual once for all. There was no need of repeating it as the annual sacrifices of the Levitical ritual were repeated. And, most significant of all, it was the ground for free access to God on the part of all who would accept his way. "That they which are called might receive the promise of eternal inheritance" (ix. 15).

Again the pyramidal construction of the Levitical ritual comes into visibility. At the base stand many sacrifices and offerings, each with significance in some petty situation. Above these lies the one annual ritual of the cleansing of the people from their sins on the great day of the atonement. But this, too, must be repeated from year to year and it becomes a succession of annual rites. Above these, as a series, stands the one perfect and eternal sacrifice of Christ himself in which he is both high priest and atoning victim. In this idea lies the pith and climax of the author's idea of salvation. It is presented for the practical purpose of inducing such adherents of the old covenant as had accepted the new to realize how much greater their privileges than those they had enjoyed under the old. The author assumes that no one who genuinely appreciates the reality of the new will wish to go back to the old.

5. FAITH, THE BASIS OF THE NEW COVENANT.—Every covenant is voluntary to the covenanting parties. The old covenant was entered into by Moses in behalf of the Israelites. But there is a vast difference between assuming the obligations and realizing the privileges of a covenant by entering into it with a full and keen sense of its excellence and merely surrendering passively without knowing what one is doing. The author of Hebrews aims to impress it upon his readers that the new covenant offers in this particular the highest and richest experience in the type of faith it presupposes for its effectuation.

This type he deploys before his readers apparently with great enthusiasm, giving both a general definition of it and a description of its power and efficacy in a notable series of illustrations. As defined by him (xi. 1) faith is a broader and more universally operative principle than in Paul's conception of it. The exigencies of the great controversy in which Paul was engaged prescribed for him the usage in which faith appears predominantly as the means of justification. To the author of Hebrews it is generically "the assurance of things hoped for, a conviction of things not seen." It underlies not only the religious life but all life. In the realm of knowledge, for instance, the constitution of the world can be realized only by faith. Science and philosophy are absolutely impossible without it. The causes of phenomena as well as their inner relations are apprehended by faith. "Through faith we understand . . . that things which are seen were not made of things which do appear" (xi. 3).

Yet though the author's notion is broad enough to include the kind of faith which functions in science and philosophy, his own interest centers about the use of faith in the spiritual sphere. All the illustrations of it he gives from that of Abel to that of the unnamed host of martyrs and heroes (xi. 32-40) bear upon the apprehension of the promises of God and the conformation of life to the realities thus apprehended. And the aim of the whole discussion is to stimulate a more complete surrender to the "author and finisher" (the leader of the procession—ἀρχηγὸν and perfecter—τελειωτήν, xii. 2). This implies (a) that Jesus is to be taken as the exemplar of the absolute self-surrender to God's will which faith means, (b) that his words be accepted as the adequate guide in life, and (c) that his sacrifice as high priest, the "eternal redemption," be accepted and appropriated as one's ground of access into the presence of God. "Having therefore, brethren, boldness to enter into the holiest by the blood of Jesus . . . let us draw near with a true heart in full assurance of faith" (x. 19-22).

The efficacy of faith depends upon God who aims to evoke it by giving his promise or offering his grace. In itself faith is not an energy, but a means of releasing or utilizing energy supplied by God. The promises of God present opportunities which can and must be put to use. The hearing of the gospel is such an opportunity. But unless it is used ("mixed with faith," iv. 2) it becomes a ground of condemnation rather than a source of good. But the fruit of faith does not always manifest itself immediately. God always fulfils his promise; but there are times when the fulfillment involves collective fruition in which case the faith of one generation may find its efficacious result in another (xi. 39, 40).

6. THE PEOPLE OF THE NEW COVENANT.—The idea of a people is in the Bible inseparable from that of a covenant. Though a people may be thought of without the suggestion of a covenant, a covenant never exists without a people. God establishes covenants with Abraham, with Moses, with David, not only for themselves as individuals but for their posterity. The fidelity of the head of the people inures to the stability of the covenant even though the people may go far in dishonoring its terms. But there is a limit beyond which no individual or small group can save the whole people from the consequences of covenant-breaking. It was so in ancient Israel (iii. 16-19).

In the new covenant Jesus as the high priest has a people in whose behalf he lives and acts (xiii. 12). In speaking of this people the author of Hebrews is more concerned to present its ideal aspects as a community of souls animated by a common loyalty and destined to a supreme blessedness than to show the mechanism of their organization as an earthly community (xii. 18-23). Accordingly he never mentions it as an institution; and only once refers to an item of organized life among Christians when he exhorts to "remember" and "obey" "them that have the rule over you" (xiii. 1-7). He also alludes to their custom of assembling themselves for the purpose of mutual exhortation, but such assemblings do not necessarily imply organization. They are conceivable and have actually existed without organization.

7. THE LIFE UNDER THE NEW COVENANT.—In perfect harmony with the imagery of the altar and the ritual the author's ideal of the life befitting the people of the new covenant begins with the notion of their consecration. This is the condition *sine qua non* of participation in the new privileges (xii. 14). The term used is the same as that rendered elsewhere "sanctification" (ἁγιασμός). But the conception is different. The root idea of both consecration and sanctification is that of conformity to God's holiness. In the case of consecration, however, this holiness is secured through devotion to God once for all. As when the gift is brought to and laid upon the altar it becomes holy, so those who give themselves to God in consecration are holy. In the case of sanctification the holiness implied is a moral attribute of character. This cannot be acquired by a single act. It is a matter of gradual approach to the ineffable ideal. Hence sanctification is a process. It could not be conceived as an indispensable condition of seeing God, for no one could attain it perfectly.

The expression of this consecration is primarily religious. It consists of steadfast adherence to a profession of loyalty to the captain of the salvation. But this is only the beginning. The life of the faithful is one of movement and growth; it begins with elementary matters (vi. 2); but it proceeds to higher matters (v. 12-13).

The Christian virtues and graces are everywhere assumed as in various degrees essential to the believer's consistent standing among his brethren. Mutual helpfulness (x. 24) and love of the brethren (xiii. 1), sympathy with the distressed (xiii. 3), freedom from avarice (xiii. 5), chastity in the marriage relation (xiii. 4) are viewed as characteristics of the man who lives under the new covenant.

The chief virtue presented is that of perseverance. The author has a definite conviction that a second repentance is impossible to those who have believed in Christ, and have fallen back (vi. 4; 7. 26); hence his chief concern is that those whom he addresses should hold fast to their adherence to the gospel (ii. 3; iii. 14; iv. 1; xii 1). Perseverance naturally requires patience which is joined with it (x. 36; xii. 1).

The goal and ideal held in view is perfection. The old covenant (law) was not able to produce perfection (ix. 9; vii. 19). The Apostle Paul presents the same thought in the idea that the law was not competent to secure justification. But what man needs is the perfecting of himself in the achievement of his ideal (vi. 1); and Jesus Christ has achieved the perfection of those who cling to him in the new covenant (x. 1; xii. 23). He is the leader and the perfecter of faith (xii. 2). Perhaps this conception, too, was framed by the stress of the need for perseverance. The view of the danger of failure to achieve the goal leads to the apprehension of salvation as an ideal of completeness. The thought is kindred to the identification of salvation with attaining the supreme good.

8. THE WORLD TO COME.—The author is conscious throughout that the acceptance or rejection of his message involves momentous issues for the future. The beliefs in eternity and in the continuity of life for individuals underlie this conviction. Death is not the end (xix. 27).

The world to come includes an order of realities already in existence, but hidden, as it were, by a veil (vi. 19). Jesus, the high priest, has entered it after completing his earthly work (as the forerunner of Christians, vi. 20). But he was also in it before his incarnation. The Alexandrian affinities of the author's thought become clearly visible in the further details of this conception. The spiritual world is the world of realities. The material is only a series of shadows (viii. 1, 5) cast by the spiritual. When the material order perishes, as it is bound to do, the spiritual will come to its full revelation; for it is imperishable (xii. 26).

Therefore the author looks forward to a time (x. 25) when the powers of the world to come would be brought to their culmination. The first event to be looked for in connection with the coming of this time is the return of Christ (x. 37). The second is the judgment (ix. 27; x. 27).

The issues of the judgment are rewards and penalties to the faithful and the faithless respectively. To the faithful shall come rest spiritual, such as they could not gain in any earthly condition (iv. 8ff.). The same blessing is portrayed under the figure of "inheriting the promises"

(vi. 12), by which is meant in this connection the fulfilment or realization of the promises. Concerning the nature of the penalty of the faithless nothing is said in clear terms. It is, however, represented as something to be dreaded and avoided by all means. "It is a fearful thing to fall into the hands of the living God" (x. 31). "Our God is a consuming fire" (xii. 29). The supreme purpose of the author is to warn men against risking themselves to the possibility of reaching this doom.

PART IV

THE JOHANNINE THEOLOGY

CHAPTER XXVI

THE JOHANNINE SCHOOL AND WRITINGS

FIVE writings given a place in the New Testament have been traditionally attributed to John. Because of their brevity two of these have elicited no extensive efforts to test the trustworthiness of the tradition. Of the other three I John presents close affinities with the Fourth Gospel. By a large number it is unhesitatingly accepted as a second writing of the same author. A few exceptional scholars deny this. The Fourth Gospel itself and the Apocalypse have evoked conflicting views. In ancient times the conflict concerned their authority and claim for a place in the New Testament. In recent years the question is as to their authorship and value as sources of knowledge for their times. The tradition regarding these five writings raises two problems for the modern student: that of their unity as a group and that of their relation to some well-known John. These questions are so thoroughly interlaced with one another that they cannot conveniently be discussed separately.

The tradition in its earliest form pointed to John, the son of Zebedee, brother of James, and one of the twelve apostles, as the author of all the writings in the group. But in this form it has always under attack proved very weak. Dionysius of Alexandria in the fourth century flatly denied and, upon grounds essentially critical, supported the denial of the apostolic authorship of the Apocalypse. He claimed that the John of that book could not be the son of Zebedee. There were, however, other Johns in the apostolic age. Papias names "John the presbyter, a disciple of the Lord." The second century leaders were not much interested in questions of literary proprietorship and do not affirm or deny the relation of these books to one or another of these Johns. Other disturbing factors in the situation are the existence in the early church of doubts, and even opposition to the apostolic authorship of the Gospel. Epiphanius and Philaster of the latter part of the fourth century attribute both the Apocalypse and the Fourth Gospel to Cerinthus, the arch-heretic of the end of the first century. Hippolytus of Rome (195-235) wrote an essay defending the Gospel and the Apocalypse,[1] which proves that their authority, and consequently their apostolic authorship were questioned. The Alogi are well known for their rejection of the common belief of their day concerning the Johannine writings.

Though from the end of the fourth century onward the tradition crystallized and remained unchallenged to the beginning of the modern critical era, as soon as attention was riveted on the problem, belief in the direct authorship of these writings by John, the son of Zebedee,

---
[1] The title of the essay is given in a list of his writings on the seat of a chair of a statue of him now in the Lateran Museum at Rome.

suffered a severe shock. The discussion entered upon a long and intricate course, which in view of the most recent developments [2] cannot as yet be said to have closed. But while much remains to be said, the horizon has cleared sufficiently to point out the general trend of the results reached and to outline the possible views for the present seeker of light on this subject.

1. THE FOURTH GOSPEL.—The long controversy brings into view the following results so far as it affects the Fourth Gospel.

(1) The traditional theory of its apostolic authorship is driven entirely to the defensive. It is no longer a question as to whether John, the son of Zebedee, wrote the book, but as to whether he may not possibly have written it. The probabilities are all against the tradition. Regarding the personal experience of John, the son of Zebedee, a rival tradition has come to light, to the effect that he was put to death by the Jews together with James his brother. This is attested in a book by Papias, now lost, but from which a quotation from Philippus Sidetes is preserved in the so-called "De Boor Fragment." To the same purport is the testimony of Georgios Hamartolos.[3] The Syriac Martyrology places the event in Jerusalem which indicates a date antecedent to 70 A.D., and at least twenty-five years earlier than the traditional date of the composition of the Gospel.

Apart from these intimations from without the work that some other than John the apostle wrote the Fourth Gospel, a number of internal considerations point to the same conclusion. First it is difficult to conceive the intellectual transformation of the Galilean fisherman into the philosophical thinker to whom the Alexandrian doctrine of the Logos should make such an appeal as to lead him to adopt it as the master key to his interpretation of Christ and his mission. Strange transformations have occurred but in order to believe in the actuality of each more positive proof is demanded by the mind than the mere assertion that it was possible. Moreover the John of the Fourth Gospel ("the disciple whom Jesus loved") appears well-connected in Jerusalem; he has the freedom of the high priest's house, is even kin to the priestly family, and goes unchallenged when Peter's presence is detected by his Galilean accent. This John is the author of the Gospel. Can he be the son of Zebedee?

(2) But if the case for the apostolic origin of the Gospel weakens under consistent and persistent investigation, the case for a second century writer's authorship entirely cut off from the apostolic circle and writing without any direct knowledge of the life of Jesus for the purpose of magnifying the supernatural element in his life has collapsed altogether. The type of criticism practiced by such men as D. F. Strauss is no longer given even the courtesy of a serious refutation.

(3) The drift of thought has accordingly been strong in the direction of some mediating view. This means the theory that around the name

---
[2] Charnwood, *According to John;* Garvie, *The Beloved Disciple;* Streeter, *The Four Gospels,* pp. 363-481; R. H. Strachan, *The Fourth Gospel; Its Significance and Environment.*

[3] Light from Harmer, *"Fragments of Papias,"* p. 518f.

THE JOHANNINE SCHOOL AND WRITINGS 225

"John" there began to cluster a peculiar tradition ultimately developing into the belief that John the apostle furnished the data to his friends and followers which constitute the contents of the Johannine writings. If this were the case the author of the Gospel would prove to be a disciple of the apostle John. It is this disciple who calls the son of Zededee "the disciple that Jesus loved." He himself remains anonymous and gives John's report of Jesus' words and experiences. But there is no evidence of any kind that John, the son of Zebedee, ever became the head of a so-called "school" or that he had any disciples who perpetuated a peculiar tradition of the work of Jesus or a peculiar interpretation of the Gospel.

(4) On the other hand there is strong evidence that the name John belonged to two members of the apostolic circle; that besides the son of Zebedee there was among the disciples of Jesus another and much younger person bearing the name; that he joined the followers of Jesus as a youth, thus never reaching the responsibility of apostleship, but establishing a claim to direct personal acquaintance with the Master. This John later removed to Ephesus and was known as "the presbyter." But concerning him Irenæus and Polycrates bishop of Ephesus, writing about one hundred years later, speak as if he were the same as the apostle. Irenæus claims Polycarp as his informant. Polycrates manifestly follows a tradition that had hardened and had been influenced by the desire of the Ephesian leaders to secure the authority of an apostle for their practice in observing Easter differently from the Roman Christians. Behind both Irenæus and Polycrates Papias furnished clearer light regarding "the presbyter" of Ephesus. His testimony tends to detach the presbyter from the apostle and to give him independent standing.

All the witnesses agree in giving the presbyter the title "the disciple of Jesus." Polycrates adds, "and who leaned upon the bosom of the Lord and became a priest wearing the priestly plate (πέταλον)—he fell asleep at Ephesus." Combining these testimonies with the other items of information secured by modern scholarship on the Johannine situation, it seems probable, on the whole, that two Johns entered into the circle of Jesus' disciples (or if we may call Mark also by his earlier name, three). Of these one was chosen to be an apostle; the other (or the other two) continued to be known as "disciples." So long as they were known by the Christian community personally no difficulty was experienced in keeping them apart. After the lapse, however, of two generations, and the absence of distinct historical records of their lives, the two who had separately served the cause of their Lord became blended into one towering figure. Meantime if we still may think of Mark as an original John, he, too, found his mission first in the company of Paul and afterwards in that of Peter.

Was then John the presbyter of Ephesus "the disciple that Jesus loved?" The phrase occurs in the New Testament only in the Fourth Gospel. It is applied to the author of the Gospel. But whether it designates the son of Zebedee is not made clear. Undoubtedly others besides the twelve were attached to Jesus, at least during the last part of his ministry. It seems natural that among these, at least occasionally, a youth of amiable and refined character should have been in the circle with which Jesus moved in Jerusalem, being himself a Jerusalemite of good social standing. It seems also natural that Jesus should be attracted to him and give occasion for the use of the phrase by which he has become known. But the question whether it is he or the son of Zebedee that must be recognized as the "beloved disciple" is of secondary importance. If there was another John in the group, and if he possessed the characteristics and had the career in Ephesus attributed to the presbyter, it becomes much easier to account for the Fourth Gospel as his work than as that of the son of Zebedee.

Upon the assumption that the presbyter is the author of the Gospel it becomes easier to understand the difference between the earlier and the later sections of the work. That there is such a difference is clear on the face of the facts. Chapters i.-xi. deal with affairs after the manner of story and the moral which may be deduced from it. They give a chain of incidents each of which is made the basis of a conversation or a discourse expounding its inner meaning. Chapters xii.-xxi. are apparently intended to give an understanding of Jesus' attitude toward his faithful followers by one who had an experience with and among the group. While the historical material given in the first section may be, and most probably is such as the author had received from others, that in the second section bears all the marks of first-hand knowledge. If now the author was a young man who entered the group of Jesus' disciples during the last weeks of his ministry, he would be giving the testimony of an eyewitness so far as that part of his story is concerned. This does not mean that his report of Jesus' words was a verbal reproduction of them, but that so far as the intimacy and comforting and reassuring content of them was concerned the report came from a heart that had felt the irresistible appeal of the Master's expression.

It is also plain that the author of the Fourth Gospel wrote with a full knowledge of the Synoptic tradition. In fact it is quite certain that he had access at least to the Gospels of Mark and of Luke, that he used them, and that he aimed to supplement and even correct them.[4] His own point of view, methods and purpose as a writer are altogether different from those of the Synoptists. First though not most important he furnishes a chronological scheme for the ministry of Jesus. Next he supplies names of persons and places left undesignated by his predecessors. Among others that of Malchus in the scene of the arrest at Gethsemane; that of the village of Martha and Mary; that of the place

[4] As to the extent of this acquaintance there is some difference of view among those who have made it a subject of special investigation. Stanton, *The Gospels as Historical Documents*, p. 214, finds he used Mark but not Matthew and Luke; Bacon, *The Fourth Gospel in Research and Debate*, pp. 366-368, reports that he used Mark and was familiar with Luke but not with Matthew; Buckley, *Introd. to the Synoptic Problem* (pp. 27-275) is unable to find traces of Matthew but is sure that the author used Mark and Luke's "non-Marcan source"; but E. F. Scott, *The Fourth Gospel, Its Theology*, p. 32ff. assumes that he used all of the three earlier Gospels, each in a different way.

THE JOHANNINE SCHOOL AND WRITINGS 227

where John baptized and the names of Philip and Andrew as those with whom Jesus took counsel before the feeding of the five thousand.

Further he corrects misconceptions. The most clear case and best known of these is that which concerns the day of the crucifixion. While the Synoptists give this as the day following the Passover, John clearly shows that it was the day of the Passover itself, a correction which is supported by every consideration brought into the discussion in recent times.

But while all these data indicate John's self-dependence as a witness and his first-hand knowledge of some of the details in Christ's ministry, the most important point of difference between him and the earlier evangelists is his desire to produce a report of Jesus' person and work which would convince men of his divine nature and mission. Of this he wishes to leave no room for doubt. His is not a plain narrative of facts in their sequence with as much fulness and detail as the scope of his work will permit; but a selective and interpretative exposition of a few salient matters. "Many other signs, therefore, did Jesus which are not written in this book. But these are written that ye might believe that Jesus is the Son of God and that believing ye might have life through his name." He writes not in order to satisfy even the natural interest of those who have already believed, but in order to create belief in those who lack it.

This attitude carries in it the implicit claim that he possesses an inner knowledge of the meaning of his data which his predecessor evangelists have not imparted. This knowledge has come to him not in a magical way, but through a lifetime of experience. As a historian he is not a mere chronicler but an expounder of meanings. His picture of Jesus differs from that of the Synoptists as a portrait may differ from a photograph. He can point to the inadequacies of the photograph even from the realistic point of view, as when he supplements and corrects it in matters of fact. But he considers it more essential that men shall have an image of the Master in which the ideal reality is seen more clearly than the realistic outwardness of exactly what he did or said.

2. THE EPISTLES.—That I John is by the same author as the Fourth Gospel is a proposition so fully attested by characteristics of style and content of thought that it has rarely been challenged. The denial of the proposition can be made only in favor of the very slightly different one that the Epistle is the work of an imitator and disciple of the evangelist. This for our purposes is not worth discussing. The Second and Third Epistles are totally devoid of theological significance. They are private documents which have outlived the interests that occasioned their production because of the larger interest aroused by the personality of their author. They enrich the knowledge of the Christian generations concerning the attitude of mind and the charm of character of the presbyter and lead to the emulation of his forbearance and Christian love.

3. THE APOCALYPSE.—More complex is the problem of the Apocalypse and of its relation to the Gospel either from the literary or

from the theological point of view. The literary connection, however, is much easier to determine as one of complete independence. From the days of Dionysius of Alexandria in the fourth century onward doubts of the identity of the authorship of the Apocalypse and of the Fourth Gospel have been entertained by careful students of the New Testament. But only since the recovery of the Jewish and Christian apocalypses has it been realized that the author and the seer of an apocalypse are generally different persons. Aside from considerations of style and historical setting, the very fact that in the Book of Revelation the seer speaks of himself in the first person as "I, John" creates a presumptive doubt of the author's having borne that name.

This position, however, reasonable as it appears, meets with the weighty opposition of R. H. Charles,[5] who takes the position that the book is the work of an author named John though not the John who wrote the Gospel or the John, the son of Zebedee. Be that as it may the question of authorship loses its cardinal place as soon as the figure of the seer emerges into view since, of the two, the seer is the more authoritative personality and his importance eclipses that of the writer. And even if seer and author be supposed to have been the same for the New Testament Revelation, it is as seer rather than as writer that the author secures attention and authoritative hearing. And all that has already been brought into view in the discussion of the authorship of the Gospel bears with equal force on that of the Apocalypse. If the Fourth Gospel is not the work of the apostle John neither is the Apocalypse. Unless, then, another John be imagined to have flourished in Asia and have written the Apocalypse in his own name as seer, the most probable hypothesis is that an anonymous author has chosen the revered figure of the aged presbyter of Ephesus, (perhaps very soon after his decease) and centered his vision about him.

Next in importance to the question of authorship is that of literary form. That the author should have chosen to embody his message in the apocalyptic form is significant because it points to a time of tribulation. Such a time for the Christians of the first century was the reign of Domitian (90-95). This agrees perfectly with the tradition that "the vision was seen under Domitian." As an apocalypse the Book of Revelation is true to type. It is couched in the form of a series of symbolic visions designed to reassure the persecuted people of God of the ultimate and speedy collapse of the persecution and of the triumph of their cause. The hosts of heaven are enlisted on their side. God is acquainted with their need and is planning to come to their relief. What they must do is to endure for a time, defying the enemy and calmly awaiting the victory which is so certain.

But while the apocalyptic type of writing was so wonderfully adapted to the need of the Christians for the time, it proved for later ages a veritable veil concealing from the eyes of possible hostile readers of the book its meaning and message. It was meant to conceal as well as to reveal. And it did keep from the oppressor what it was imparting to

[5] *The Book of Revelation,* Vol. I, p. 38; so also Streeter, *The Four Gospels,* p. 436; and Case, *The Revelation of John.*

THE JOHANNINE SCHOOL AND WRITINGS

the oppressed. But the very means by which it hid its secret from the contemporary enemy was effective in keeping the secret also from the friends and successors of future days because they, too, have lacked the key to the writing.

In another way the form of apocalypse creates a difficulty for the modern student in that it isolates the mind of its author from the group mind with which it is working. This is singularly true of the Apocalypse of John. According to the uniform tradition, it is the same mind that speaks through all the writings bearing the name of John. But upon a superficial glance the Apocalypse and the Fourth Gospel appear to be as far apart as possible. The latter is pervaded by a strain of Hellenic thinking; the former is purely Jewish in form and thought. Apocalyptism and the Alexandrian philosophy are as impossible to mix as oil and water. Is the tradition, then, to be set aside? And is the Apocalypse to be detached from the Johannine group of writings? This does not necessarily follow. Apocalyptism and the philosophical point of view are, after all, accessories and means of thought, not essentials of it. Beneath the shell of each the kernel of thought develops the group characteristics common to both. Both present Christ as a preëxistent divine person, both sum up his saving work as that of "the Lamb of God that taketh away the sin of the world"; both look upon the opposition to him as mortal alienation from God to be visited from above with eternal death. In both Jesus is identified with the Word of God (Rev. xix. 13), "and his name is called the Word of God." Though not by the same author, the Apocalypse is dominated by the same spirit as the Fourth Gospel. Its doctrinal content is apparently different because it has been cast into a different mold from that of the Gospel but its combination with the content of the Gospel is suggested by more than one feature of it and the external (traditional) grouping of the two writings in one class is but a perception of this inner harmony of them. Gospel and Apocalypse doctrinally supplement each other and their synthesis constitutes a genuine type appropriately named Johannine.

Naturally this type shows its peculiar characteristics more clearly in the Gospel and First Epistle than in the other writings. Here the Johannine thinker works with larger freedom. His object is to save the Gospel from being dissipated in the mist of a false philosophy. In order to accomplish this he grounds it in a well-reasoned system of thought which is not a mere philosophy. On the other hand it is more than unreasoning mysticism. He appeals in behalf of the Gospel as the good news of eternal life through Christ, the Son of God, to the whole man. It is an appeal to the mind, to the heart and to the conscience. To the mind it is a call to accept Christ as the Son of God on the ground of his power to work miracles; to the conscience it is an appeal to receive his word and do the will of God; to the heart it is an appeal to accept him upon his own testimony and the testimony of God the Father through the Holy Spirit which agrees with his and bears him out.

In this appeal the gospel of Christ found its last stage and complete development. John has been called a mystic. If a mystic is one who perceives upon the presentation to his cognitive powers as a whole the reality of God and his claim on himself John is a real mystic. But his mysticism is neither the result of mere emotionalism impatient of intellectual processes, nor the claim to have attained his knowledge of reality in an occult way of which he cannot give an account to outsiders. John reasons out the grounds of his faith and invites all to share it with him on the same grounds.

Religion according to John is a vital fellowship with God, rooted in a true knowledge of Him and issuing in eternal life. True religion is a gift of God through his Son Jesus Christ to all upon the condition of faith in him. "God so loved the world that he gave his own son that whosoever believeth in him should not perish but have everlasting life." "This is eternal life, that they might know thee and Jesus Christ whom thou hast sent."

Two great needs developing in the Christian community at the end of the first century evoked from the Johannine mind two expressions of the faith adapted to hold together and to promote the aggressive life of the gospel. The first was the need of a restatement of the truth as it was in Christ for the larger circle within which it had become a power for life. This broad circle was largely under the dominance of Hellenic influences. Already irresponsible leaders were undertaking to meet this need by making a synthesis of the gospel with the phantastic mythology and theosophy of Gnosticism. John aims to save it from the danger in this direction by utilizing the Alexandrian philosophy reconstructed along mystic lines.

The second need was that of persistence under persecution for nonconformity. This need was met by the author of the Apocalypse in the way which had become customary since the days of the seer of Daniel and his visions during the persecution under Antiochus Epiphanes.

The work of the Johannine writers completed the formulation of the gospel by giving it a stable outward mould. Many interpretations were to follow, but no further development in substance or form could be put forth claiming normative value. The plastic age of the gospel ended with the labors of the last apostolic leaders of Ephesus.

CHAPTER XXVII

FELLOWSHIP LACKING

It is a fundamental assumption of the Johannine system that the great need of mankind is fellowship with God. But how this need arises is not explained. Unlike Paul John does not face the question whence and how sin entered the world. It is enough for him that it exists, and that it constitutes a barrier between man and his maker. The whole problem of evil as a question of pure thought arising in human experience is treated in the conventional way of the time. An archenemy of God looms in the background as a familiar figure. He is known under the names of "the devil" (διάβολος) Jn. viii. 44; xiii. 2; I Jn. iii. 8; Rev. xii. 9) and Satan, "the ancient serpent" (Rev. xii. 9; xx. 3). The implication is that evil in all its forms is due to the activity of the devil; but the thought is rather assumed than worked out consistently with the distinctive principles of Johannine theology.

1. THE QUESTION OF SIN.—On the subject of sin the Johannine writings and the Epistle to the Hebrews have this in common, that they place it between God and man as an obstacle to their free intercourse. But whereas in Hebrews the removal of sin is uniformly consummated upon the altar, in the Johannine writings it is sometimes viewed as a work of the Spirit begetting a new life which has nothing to do with sin (I Jn. v. 18). The communion between God and man resulting from the removal of sin is in Hebrews always achieved within the sacred precincts, whereas in John's thought it comes in daily life. "Neither in this mountain nor yet at Jerusalem" is the Father worshiped exclusively.

Surprisingly little is said of sin by John in explicit language. The word itself occurs in its conventional sense both as a substantive and as a verb, but the common conception of it is little in evidence as a ruling idea in his thought. There is an apparent definition of sin as "lawlessness" (I Jn. iii. 4). But whether the author meant by "lawlessness" absence of self-regulation or subjection to the laws governing men in social relations or, finally, rebellion against the will of God as the supreme law of all life is not clear. Neither is it clear that the phrase "sin is lawlessness" is meant as a definition at all.

But though the formal treatment of the subject is not prominent, the reality of a great evil pervading all life, corrupting it to its depths and threatening it with absolute annihilation is constantly present. This evil is in its essence alienation from God. In itself alienation might be viewed as a negative something, the mere absence of an active and moving principle. As it appears in the thought of John, however, it develops into a very positive reality. It moves men to conduct which issues in incalculable distressing consequences. Every mention of sin is aimed to bring those addressed to a sense of its gravity and of its deadly effects as enmity against God.

So long as alienation from God remains in the heart of the individual he is in danger of falling under condemnation, of being subjected to bondage, of plunging into darkness, and finally of falling under the power of death. But he who is in fellowship with God cannot sin (I Jn. iii. 6, 9; v. 18). It is from this point of view, that the whole subject of evil must be looked at. Such distinctions for instance, as that between the "sin unto death" and "sins not unto death" cannot mean that evil deeds are capable of classification into great and small, into more and less offensive ones before the law, but only that their perpetrators are nearer to full communion with God or more completely alienated from him. Hence also the exaltation of the sin of unbelief (Jn. xvi. 9) into special prominence. After all, there is only one sin that includes all others; and that is the sin of unbelief.

In the Apocalypse the verb "to sin" does not occur; the noun appears three times only in two passages. Yet the idea of enmity against God, especially as it gives vent in the oppression of his people, is everywhere present. It underlies the whole plan of the book and furnishes the background of its lurid pictures of suffering as well as of its warnings of retribution for the offender. What in the Gospel and Epistles appears as blind estrangement and is present in varying forms from the most harmless and scarcely guilty one of ignorant departure from the love of the Father to others more serious becomes in Revelation a furious and desperate hostility resorting to the most violent rebellion against God's good will.

2. THE POWER OF THE WORLD.—Half way between sin as individual godlessness and organized rebellion against God, the principle of evil assumes in the Gospel and Epistles a characteristic form in the conception of the world. The essence of the conception is the principle of social solidarity. The world becomes a power because ideally it is made up by the combination of all the individual members of the human race. While the world is not deliberately organized the social nature of its components issues in a kind of coöperation that gives it a unity of movement and community of aim and spirit. Lack of organization does not mean for it absence of coördination and sameness. The world is an organism though not an organization.

But before proceeding further with the examination of the concept, it may be helpful to clear up the use of the term. The word is applied sometimes to the material universe, with its vast variety of aspects. The world is first of all the sum total of all created beings. It includes the heavens and the earth; the starry firmament above and the mountains and valleys, oceans and rivers, continents and islands, forests and prairies, deserts and fertile plains, *i.e.*, the realm of nature as a whole. Viewed in this light the world is God's handiwork. He pronounced it "very good" as it came from his hands. He gave it to the race of men to be their home and their field of labor. It is to be enjoyed by man as well as used for his self-development and self-realization. All this, though not expressed, is implicit in the usage of John (i. 10; xvii. 5; Rev. xiii. 8). The only relation such a being as the world thus defined can have to evil is to induce men to struggle against it. For the world offers itself as the prize of the contest. In itself the world cannot be evil. It was the tendency to misunderstand this that later produced asceticism and its type of ethics. The Johannine conception is as far as possible from the ascetic.

A second usage of the term world by John makes it equivalent to the race of men pure and simple. This usage is, of course, not peculiar to John but appears among all races and tribes of men. The human population of the earth integrated in thought and personified for the sake of convenience is commonly called "the world." So also a unified tendency in human society is frequently referred to as the progress or the degeneration of the world. The judgment of the world is the supposed opinion of mankind in general. In this sense of the term "the world" is said to have "wandered after the beast" (Rev. xiii. 3 ἡ γῆ "the earth"), the meaning being obviously that all mankind had done so. The world is the inhabited earth (οἰκουμένη). Satan is said to mislead (cause to wander) the whole world (Rev. xii. 9; xiii. 14). Needless to say that the usage in these expressions involves the rhetorical figure of synecdoche, the home of mankind signifying mankind itself.

It is plain that thus conceived the world cannot be viewed as evil. God does not condemn the human race as such. On the contrary the world is the subject of his infinite compassion and solicitude. "God so loved the world that he gave his only begotten Son" for its salvation from the power of death. And reverting to the usage of the term in which the world means a principle of evil one might paradoxically say that God strives to save the world from the world.

It is not, then, either as the material universe or as the human population of the earth that the world is evil, but as human society yielding itself to the control of sin. From the nature of the case under the principle of social solidarity the sin of the individual blends with that of others, gaining new power by the combination, as well as imparting new power to all that it touches. Racial sin thus makes its appearance. But the idea of the world as racial sin is in the Johannine thought a totally different matter from that in Paul's. It is not that of the sin of one individual passing to others, but the sins of many individuals mingling together into a complex which affects all of them. Since the power of sin becomes the spirit and life of the world which yields to it even as the body yields to the soul, it becomes very proper to speak of the organism thus constituted as the world.

The world is an irresistible force. It is a stream that carries on its bosom all who will abandon themselves to it. It is a pressure that restrains and also constrains each individual in the corporate whole. Like a blade of grass in a thickly sowed field each soul is hemmed in and prevented from spreading forth in every direction. The world is a tradition hardening with each successive addition in it. And yet each unit in the group is not a mere passive element in the whole, for it contributes its share to the common pressure. The vast whole has its grip on the individual; but the individual contributes its share to the strength of the grip. It is like a mighty fog that overhangs and envelops some center of industry and population; it arises as a consequence of the activities in it and at the same time it places its creators under a pall of darkness hiding the light and diminishing the life out of which it arose.

The world, then, is a tremendous force. But its power is so imperceptibly, so subtly exercised that men do not realize its evil. John's primary concern is to arouse them to its insidious danger. Therefore he earnestly and emphatically points out that it is at enmity with God. It represents precisely the principle of alienation from God, which hinders man's supreme blessedness. He who loves the world and clings to it is an enemy of God. He runs the risk of condemnation. So long as he abides in his worldly mind and relations he is in darkness, and is contrary to God who is light. And he is under sentence of death because the world itself is destined to die and disappear.

This final sentence of destruction pronounced upon the world receives special attention in a ringing exhortation (I Jn. ii. 15-17). "Love not the world, neither the things that are in the world." And in justifying his utterance the writer pleads first the incompatibility of the love of the world with the love of God, and next the fleeting nature of all that is in the world, and of the world itself. "The world passeth away." Whether the thought here is fixed (a) on the ever-changing aspect of life as a matter of experience, (b) the certainty that all earthly ambitions will be swallowed up in the end and extinguished at death, or (c) the philosophical notion of the illusory nature of material phenomena, it makes little difference. John has discovered that the world pervaded by sin has in it the seed of corruption and is, apart from the soul's allying itself with the imperishable life of God, doomed to extinction.

3. THE WORLD POWER.—By world power is meant the secular government, arrogating to itself supremacy over all things and in so doing setting aside the authority of God. The conception is characteristically apocalyptic. It is absent from the Gospel and the Epistles. But the apocalypse in its turn fails to present the idea given in the Gospel and Epistles of a world consisting of humanity under the dominion of evil and, therefore, in opposition to God. From this it is clear that the two conceptions of world and world power are only variant forms of the same underlying thought, each of them being determined in form by the characteristic point of view of the type of writing through which it is given. Since in the Gospel and Epistle human society is viewed apart from its organization into a state, the conception of the world assumes in it the appearance of a principle pervading the social body as a whole without regard to its governing headship. Since, on the other hand, in the Apocalypse humanity has been organized and headed, with or without its consent, by a government, and since that government is the active

champion of the evil in mankind, to the Apocalyptist's eye it is the imperial world power that is to be feared and opposed by the followers of Christ.

So far, then, as that government (the world power) refuses to recognize the authority of the true God and to adopt his law as its rule, it enters upon a rebellion against God.

This idea, however, is not new. It was inherited from the Maccabean age and is reproduced almost in the identical form in which it appears in the Apocalypse of Daniel. The author of Daniel put the notion in bold perspective by portraying a succession of world powers each flourishing for a time and engaging in a warfare against the God of Israel. But each of these sank to its doom in due time, and all were to be superseded in the end by the kingdom of the Son of Man (Dan. ix. 13). The Apocalyptist of the Johannine school sees in the situation of his own day the appearance of a new, and as he believed, the last of the series of the world powers in the supremacy of Rome over the world. Moreover in the growing tendency of the Cæsars of his day to claim divine honors and homage he sees an especially abhorrent outbreak of opposition to the divine rule. For the followers of Christ this opposition was not an object of dispassionate observation, but of immediate vital concern. They, as the people of God, were directly touched and disturbed by it. Of all people upon earth they were singled out and marked as its victims. Others might bow before the world power without violating their principles; but for them to recognize and yield to it would be to renounce their essential and distinctive character. For them, therefore, the existence of the government of Rome meant an uncompromising struggle.

The necessity of struggling against the evil of the world underlies both the Gospel and the Apocalypse; and in both the objective and goal is to "overcome." In the Apocalypse the idea is clearly set forth in the refrain with which each of the seven letters to the churches closes, "Unto him that overcometh" (Rev. ii. 7, 11, 17, 26; iii. 5, 12, 21). So in the Gospel and Epistle, also, the ultimate goal of salvation cannot be reached except as the world is overcome. In fact Christ himself claims that he has had to and has successfully "overcome" the world (Jn. xvi. 33). But his overcoming does not exempt his people from the struggle in which they must engage. For them the world is an object of suspicion to be guarded against and to be conquered by faith in their leader.

4. THE ANTICHRIST.—The idea of enmity against God is further embodied in the figure of a special personality whose characteristic object and desire is to undermine and destroy the kingdom of God as established, or to be established by Christ. This is Antichrist. The idea of the Antichrist is a special Johannine development of that of the archenemy of God. Such an idea of a powerful being who by his influence mars the beauty and harmony of God's works of creation existed in the latest stages of the earlier Judaism. Though not very conspicuous, traces of it are found in the earlier religious thought of

Israel.[1] From these earlier sources the conception passed into the thought of later Judaism and ultimately entered into all apocalyptic literature both Jewish and Christian. In these developments of it, however, it is generic and vague; in that of the Antichrist it becomes specific and narrow but not much more definite.

The Antichrist is the symbol of all violent opposition to Christ and his mission. To that extent the idea of an archenemy inherited from the Old Testament is narrowed down. From the fact that the Antichrist's activity is directed against Christ he derived his name. Yet his connection with all enmity against God is assumed when he is viewed not as new power but as one that is well known. "Ye have heard that Antichrist cometh" (I Jn. ii. 18; cf. also v. 28 and II Jn. vii.).

But evidently with this more definite association of the idea of the archenemy with opposition to Christ, the idea itself became sublimated into a spiritual principle. It is no longer a single person but a type. There are many Antichrists. The characteristics of the type are: apostasy, denial of the incarnation and nullification of the work of the Redeemer. "For many deceivers are gone forth into the world even they that confess not that Jesus cometh in the flesh. This is a deceiver and an antichrist" (II Jn. vii.; cf. also I Jn. ii. 22; iv. 3).

Any one, even a merely human person, may conform to the type and deserve the title by joining the Christian brotherhood and then renouncing the vows which he takes only in form and engaging in subtle forms of warfare against the faith he had professed. Such an enemy of the faith is naturally regarded as far more formidable than a mere outsider without any connection with the Church. His renunciation would tend to do more damage to the cause than the persecuting activities of a known foe.

In all of its forms, then, the principle of evil is a development of alienation from God. It may exist as mere ignorance of moral good; or it may grow into deliberate resistance of what is seen to be right; it may advance into active opposition to some known good because of its standing in the way of selfish desire; it may go further and assume the form of active hostility to everything that bears the seal of God's approval; finally it may culminate in the association of self with others in a campaign of destruction of God's works. Always it is created in isolation from God. Its beginnings are dangerous, but its mature forms are terrible. Its end is death.

[1] Gunkel, *Schöpfung u. Chaos.*

CHAPTER XXVIII

FELLOWSHIP ESTABLISHED

IN its conception of the way of salvation the Johannine type of thought is true to the gospel already dominant before it came into being. Man cannot of himself and by his own efforts come out of his alienation from God. God initiates, continues and completes the process. The idea is identical with Paul's doctrine of grace. And as in Paul's doctrine grace is manifested and wrought out through Jesus Christ, so in John's, fellowship is established by the revelation of God's love in his only begotten Son. "God so loved the world that he gave his only-begotten Son that whosoever believeth in him should not perish, but have everlasting life." The gospel is "the word of life" (I Jn. i. 1).

1. THE KNOWLEDGE OF GOD.—The first step in the establishment of fellowship with God is to secure a vital knowledge of him. One of the chief benefits conferred by Christ to the world (some would say the chief one and some even the only one) is that he reveals God in his full nature. Be that as it may the conception of knowledge as a means of salvation is of the utmost importance in the Johannine thought, whether this is due to the prevalence in the mind of the day of a strong strain of Gnostic influence or to the point of view of the Alexandrian philosophical leaders, who had taken over the Greek doctrine that knowledge enters into, and even determines ethical values, is not quite clear. It is certain, however, that the necessity of knowledge as a means of leading men to God is often emphasized by John.

The question, "What is God?" though not formally propounded receives in various parts of the Johannine writings three brief and categorical answers. To these a fourth must be added by a process of induction from a wide range of references to God's nature and works.

The first of these answers is: "God is spirit" (Jn. iv. 24). Evidently this was not meant to be a definition. The main question in the context does not concern the nature of God, but the proper place where he may be worshiped. But the question of place and manner of worship can be correctly answered only when the nature of God is truly understood. Hence Jesus' insistence that God is not a material being but spirit. As such he is free from the limitations imposed by time and space. Thus, without being a metaphysical and complete definition, the utterance brings into view a fundamental conception possessing metaphysical value. The essence of God is spirit.

The second answer to the question, "What is God?" is given in the equally brief statement: "God is light" (Jn. i. 5). This, too, is not intended to be a philosophical formula, but a source of practical illumination in order that men may know how to adjust their relations to one

Person — an individual being possessed of self-consciousness & self-determination.

another and to God. The statement is figurative. Light is viewed as an emblem of moral purity. Communion with God presupposes the common possession of moral purity by the creature which is the inherent and inalienable characteristic of God. Elsewhere in Biblical terminology this is called holiness. But since light becomes the symbol of holiness and its opposite, darkness, the symbol of sin; and because light is seen to have power to cleanse and cheer and at the same time to enrich life, God as light may be viewed as the source of all the joy as well as of the moral strength of mankind.

The third answer to the question, "What is God?" is given in the proposition: "God is love" (I Jn. iv. 8, 16). This cannot mean the reduction of the idea of God from a person to a mere emotion or affection. The framer of the proposition was not bent upon a theosophical explanation of the substance of God. He had in view the increase of the strength of love among his readers. He understood love to be an affection; and one capable of being developed in intensity and quality. He, therefore, held before them the fact that in God this emotion was to be found in such an overwhelming volume and force as to rule all of God's activity. It is his regnant attribute. And those who would derive their inspiration from him must, like him, allow themselves to be controlled completely by love. "God is love" means that the highest and purest form of love is the distinguishing characteristic of God. This throws light on the words in the Gospel (iii. 16) concerning God's love for the world as the motive for his saving work.

The fourth conception of God presents him in the terms of his fatherhood, already familiar through the teaching of Jesus as given in the Synoptic Gospels. In the Johannine writings the conception is first of all broadened. God is, in the preponderance of allusions, spoken of as the Father, whereas in the Synoptic Gospels he is in the great majority of cases the Father of some individual. When Jesus speaks of him he says, "my Father" or "your Father."

Yet from another point of view the Johannine conception is narrower and expresses a closer and more intense concern on the part of God for those who recognize him as their father. It adopts, moreover, a mystical aspect over and above the rhetorical sense of the Synoptic image. Those who believe in the Son of God become his children in a more real sense. They are "begotten of him" (Jn. i. 12; I Jn. i. 3).

2. CHRIST.—But the best answer which John has to the question, "What is God?" is given not in words either implicitly or explicitly, but in his presentation of Jesus Christ as the mediator of fellowship with the Father. "He that hath seen me hath seen the Father." In the person, in the work and in the mind of Jesus he finds the fullest and clearest revelation of the character and of the essential nature of God. The distinctive names and titles he applies to Christ clearly bring this into view. These are the Word of God and the Son of God.

(1) *The Eternal Logos.*—The core of the Logos idea is that the world is more than a mere mechanism; that there is indwelling in it a

principle which works along lines analogous to those of the human reason. Even the mechanical features of the world betray the existence of such an immanent power; for without it they would be incomprehensible. This idea was first propounded in the sixth century B.C. by Heraclitus, and revived by the Stoics as an amendment to the Platonic doctrine of ideas which assumed too wide a gap between the material and the more dynamic aspects of the universe. As thus revived the idea was promptly taken over by the Alexandrian thinkers and remained an integral part of their world view.

But in working over the doctrine of the Logos, the Stoics took advantage of the ambiguity of the Greek term, thus developing it into the twofold conception (a) of an indwelling principle and (b) an ordered expression of reality. Just as the term "word" ($\lambda \acute{o} \gamma o \varsigma$) means not only the faculty of reason, but also the power of speech, so the Logos was thought of not only as an immanent power ($\grave{\epsilon}\nu\delta\iota\acute{\alpha}\vartheta\epsilon\tau o\varsigma$) but also as a self-expression of that power ($\pi\varrho o\varphi o\varrho\iota\varkappa\grave{o}\varsigma$) in outward form.

But while the Stoics brought into view this inner twofoldness, which after all is inherent in all reason (for reason that does not tend to come into expression is powerless) they joined the doctrine to a materialistic type of philosophy and rendered it barren and hard. The Logos of the Stoic system never rose from the level of an immanent principle of order in the universe whose essence was matter ($\mathring{v}\lambda\eta$) and whose form was controlled by the life of the Logos ($\zeta\omega\grave{\eta}$) just as the body of a living being and its life are two aspects, the one outward and the other inward, of the same reality.[1]

Philo found the Logos doctrine in its Stoic form. Its essentially spiritual texture appealed to him. He accepted it as the best that Greek thought had of help to the understanding of God and of his relation to the world. But, as a Jew with the ineradicable conviction of God's transcendence, he could make nothing of it until it was cut loose from its materialistic basis. He viewed the Logos as independent and prior to the world. Only thus could he think of the Logos as the expression of God's mind and nature. The Logos was not reason immanent in nature, but the very reason of God. In the natural world it could exist only as it was imposed on it by God.

From Philo the Logos idea passed into Jewish thinking, ultimately reaching the Christian community. At Ephesus, at least, it was apparently well known. John does not find it necessary to define it or explain what he means when he uses the term. But the conception was still in its plastic stage when John saw in it an admirable medium for his reformulation of the gospel. He evidently adopted it so far as its main features were concerned. For both his doctrine and that of Philo have some features in common.

(1) Both conceptions assume the preëxistence of the Logos. (2) In both conceptions the Logos has a share in the creation of the world. (3) In both the Logos is a means of salvation, even though by salvation each may mean an entirely different matter. The common thought is that the Logos is benevolent in disposition and beneficent in operation.

[1] This gave occasion for the designation of Stoicism as hylazoism.

The effect of his presence anywhere is satisfying, wholesome, preservative and restorative.

But with these identities there are also certain radical differences between the two notions. (1) The Logos of Philo is always a transcendent reality; the Logos of John becomes incarnate. He assumes humanity, is embodied. Philo thinks of him as an ineffable form of Deity. John asserts that he became flesh. (2) Growing out of this difference arises that of personality. Philo's Logos is impersonal. He is a principle. John's Logos is given all the attributes of personality. He speaks, he acts, he holds relations with others on terms of mutual action and reaction. Philo's Logos is personalized for the sake of convenient apprehension. John's is conceived of as originally personal. (3) While Philo is totally silent regarding any Messianic functions of the Logos, John identifies the Incarnate Logos with the Messiah of prophecy.

But the Greek idea of the Logos could never have found or made a place for itself either in Jewish or Christian thought if there had not been a preparation for it in general, but aiming to fill the same need in the human heart for the understanding of God and the world. And this preparation was made in the Old Testament idea that God's speech is possessed of efficient energy. The creation came into existence as a result of God's speaking. "He spake and it was done." "And God said, Let there be light and light was." Hence phrases like those of Moses, "I showed you the word of God" (Deut. v. 5), "He hath despised the word of Jehovah" (Num. xv. 31), or those of the Psalter, "The word of Jehovah tried him" (cv. 19), "He sendeth his word and healeth them" (cvii. 20). "Thy word have I hid in my heart" (cxix. 11) conveyed the impression that something substantial and not mere thought was meant. "So shall my word be that goeth out of my mouth: it shall not return void, but it shall accomplish that which I please, and it shall prosper in the thing whereto I sent it" (Is. lv. 11). This way of thinking culminated somewhat later, probably after the days of John, certainly after those of Philo, in the hypostatization of the word under the Aramaic term *Memra*. The Word was thus conceived as a personality distinguished and yet not separate from the Godhead. The process of the transformation is visible in the Targums (Ex. xix. 12; Deut. i. 30; iv. 19; II Sam. vi. 7; I K. viii. 60; II K. xix. 28).

And just as the Word of God was attributed an independent power (and later personality) so the Wisdom of God, i.e., his perfect knowledge of reality, perfectly utilized in the creation and administration of the world, was detached from his personality and ended by being raised to a place beside him as a coadjutor and counsellor of his in all his plans and works. The personification of Wisdom is, of course, a much earlier fact than that of the Word. It appears in the canonical writings of Job and Proverbs. In a sense it constitutes the counterpart to the Greek doctrine of the Logos so far as it expresses the immanent reason, while the idea of the Word is the counterpart of the same doctrine as it expresses the revelation of the reason in outward form. Upon the whole the Logos doctrine served Philo and John better than its Hebrew parallels, because it combined the two sides of the thought (immanence and transcendence) in a single term and at the same time was well adapted to the wider diffusion of the doctrine.

But the doctrine interested John not for its philosophical value but because it furnishes a strong foundation for the fact of the incarnation. "The Logos became flesh." The immanent but personal God conceived as the rational being of the universe, constantly and consistently expressing (revealing) himself through the world's manifold aspect, came at last into real union with real humanity. To John this is the danger point in the apprehension of Christ. His divinity can be easily believed in; but his humanity is always becoming fainter and more phantastic the more it is gazed upon. He guards against its altogether fading away from view. He uses strong language against those who would explain it away as either a temporary or imaginary humanity. Such he calls antichrists (I Jn. ii. 18f.). The terminology of the Logos philosophy appears only in the prologue to the Fourth Gospel. This fact has furnished the ground for questioning the vital place of it in the thought of John. Harnack [2] denied that the connection between the theology of the Gospel and the Logos idea was more than merely a formal one. But on closer examination, in spite of the difference of the language used, the idea appears to dominate and pervade the whole conception of the person of Christ through the Gospel and First Epistle.

(2) *The Son of God.*—Between the usage of the phrase Son of God in the Synoptic Gospels and in the Fourth there is a striking difference which at first glance is likely to puzzle the historical student. In fact no other phrase in the New Testament has undergone such a radical enlargement and deepening of its meaning. Considering the similarity of purpose of the writings as historical records one would feel tempted to lessen the difference by interpreting John's usage in the light of that of the Synoptists. Since the latter mean plainly the Messiah as peculiarly related to God in his official work and position, one would incline to read in it the same sense slightly enriched when he meets it in the Gospel of John. But this mode of treating the subject is rendered impossible upon closer consideration.

First of all the doctrine of the Fatherhood of God in the Johannine thought presents a different aspect from that in the Synoptic teaching of Jesus. While in the latter the predominant emphasis is upon the relation of men in general to God and the unique relation is referred to only exceptionally (Mt. xi. 25f.), in the Fourth Gospel God is represented as the Father of believers through Jesus whereas Jesus uniformly claims a unique and unparalleled Sonship. He is "the only begotten son" (Jn. iii. 16, 18). When the Son is named without qualification, it is Jesus that is meant (Jn. v. passim; vi. 40; viii. 35, 36; xiv. 13; xvii. 1). While this usage might by a stretch be made to harmonize with the mere Messianic usage of the Synoptists it is much more natural when understood of the unique Sonship.

But a more serious objection to the merely Messianic sense develops when the phrase is compared with the other title given to Jesus, i.e., the

[2] *Ueber das Verhältniss des Prologs des Vierten Evangelium zum Ganzen Werk.*

Incarnate Logos. The Son of God is the Eternal Logos. Since Philo looks upon the Logos as the Son of God it seems that with the adoption of the Logos idea from him John must also have taken over the idea of the spiritual or essential Sonship of the Messiah. In any case all that Jesus claims for himself in his discussions with the Jewish leaders as the bread of life, the water of life, the light of the world, the truth, the way and the life, together with all that the leaders impute to him of an effort to make himself equal with God bears out the view that in calling himself the Son of God he had a different and real Sonship in mind. Thus the difference between the Synoptic portraiture of Jesus as a teacher and preacher of the kingdom of God and the Johannine as a being entering into the world from above and revealing his own divine origin and nature in a notable series of declarations ("I am" the bread of life, vi. 20f; "the light of the world," viii. 12; "the door," x. 7; "the good shepherd," x. 11; "the resurrection and the life," xi. 25; "the way, the truth and the life," xiv. 6) is made clearer in the light of the deepening and enrichment of the idea of Jesus' divine Sonship. Finally such expressions as "Before Abraham was I am" (Jn. viii. 58) and "I and the Father are one" (Jn. x. 30), together with the numerous other allusions to a transcendent and unique Sonship as in the intercessory prayer (xvii.) lose their obscurity when the phrase Son of God is understood in the full essential sense. The conclusion seems inevitable, then, that the phrase indicates divine nature coming from out of the divine sphere into the world of mankind and placing itself under all its limitations of time and space.

Great as the advance is in the meaning of Jesus' divine Sonship presented by John beyond that of the Synoptists, it was in a large measure prepared for by Paul and the author of Hebrews. Paul accepted the current conception of the Messiahship, but saw in it much more than an earthly and political sovereignty, and realized that Jesus as the Messiah had a dignity above that of mere ideal humanity. He was the preëxistent heavenly being honored by God with a place beside himself (Phil. ii. 5-9). This spiritual transcendence of the Messiah, Son of God, was confirmed and made an earthly reality by the resurrection from the dead (Rom. i. 4). In the Epistle to the Hebrews the Son of God is viewed, as by Paul, as a preëxistent heavenly being occupying toward God the relation which the radiancy or emanation of glory occupies to a luminary (Heb. i. 2). But the question what this is exactly the author treats as of no practical interest, for he does not answer it. In John's conception the relation is one in which the sameness of nature must not be confused with the impersonal relation of an emanation to the emanating substance. This was the error of the Gnostics, which he desires to correct. And, on the other hand, the distinction between Father and Son does not lead away from the strict monotheism taken over by the Gospel from its Jewish antecedents.

(3) *The Lamb of God.*—While the Gospel and Epistles lay stress on the transcendent sonship of Chirst, aiming to explain and at the same time to stabilize the thought of Christ's grace as Savior, the Apocalypse,

true to its own method and type, reverts to the more strictly Jewish conception of the Lamb of sacrifice to accomplish the same end. The conception, however, of Christ as the Lamb of God was familiar in the Johannine circle as shown by the ascription of it to the Baptist in his testimony to Jesus (Jn. i. 29, 30). On the other hand the Apocalyptic expression "the Lamb slain from the foundation of the world" (Rev. v. 6; xxii. 1) indicates the affiliation of the conception with the Johannine idea of the preëxistence of Christ and the eternal dignity and value of his saving work.

The title "Lamb of God" applied to Christ is, of course, symbolical. The question as to what exactly it symbolizes in the Christian system can be answered only on a clear understanding of what meaning was attached to the lamb in the Old Testament sacrificial system by John. The Levitical Law prescribed the offering of a lamb in the burnt offering (Lev. i. 10ff.). But the burnt offering had no special reference to sin. And John looks upon Christ as the means of the removal of sin. Very conspicuous in the old ritual was the Passover lamb. But that was a peace offering without direct bearing upon the idea of sin. The lamb is also mentioned in prophecy. In Isaiah liii. it is the emblem of the innocent, unresisting sufferer. But in this usage the sacrificial significance of it is at the minimum, if indeed there is any. On the whole the Johannine usage, though based on the Old Testament ritual and possibly prophecy, is as a whole independent and combines ideas either suggested or presented separately. Christ as the Lamb of God is the self-consecrated means of redemption from evil patiently enduring the consequences of his devotion to the work of human redemption.

3. THE HOLY SPIRIT.—In the complete presentation of God's method of establishing communion between himself and his human creatures the Johannine thought includes a special aspect of the work attributed to the Holy Spirit. The conception of the Holy Spirit in this connection is framed in the light in which Paul had already presented the subject. The Pauline idea of the intimate association of the Holy Spirit with the person of the risen Christ is carried even further by John. In fact it appears at times as if by the Holy Spirit John meant nothing else than the glorified Christ. On the other hand the distinction between the Incarnate Logos and the Holy Spirit is quite sharply drawn.

The distinctively Johannine names for the Holy Spirit are (1) The Spirit of Truth (Jn. xiv. 17; xv. 16; xvi. 13; I Jn. i. 6) and (2) The Paraclete (Jn. xiv. 17, 26; xvi. 13, 23).

(1) *The Spirit of Truth.*—The first of these indicates the emphatic manner in which the Spirit's function of revealing the truth of God had impressed itself on the Johannine mind. The Holy Spirit is the Spirit of Truth because he reveals the realities of the eternal realm, and enables men to see the solid foundations of life. Whatsoever results the knowledge of reality may have upon the mind and in the life of him who receives it are in a real way due to the activity of the Spirit who brings that knowledge. Hence the Spirit of Truth is more than a

passive means of illumination. It frees those who accept its light (Jn. viii. 32); it sanctifies them (Jn. xvii. 17).

(2) *The Paraclete.*—The term is primarily a legal one. It designates the wise adviser who is called to the aid of a litigant to strengthen him in presenting his case and assist him to win.[3] But it appears to have found admission into John's vocabulary by way of the ceremonial of worship into which it was introduced by Philo.[4] In Philo's usage it is applied to the high priest officiating as an intercessor before the altar. But if John borrowed the word from the Alexandrian leader he certainly used it with great freedom restoring to it its original context. For in the contexts in which it occurs he attributes to the Spirit the characteristic activities of an ally and coöperator in a difficult cause. The English term "Comforter" used in its strictly etymological meaning of "strengthener" is as nearly an equivalent of "Paraclete" as can be found.

The term Paraclete implies the personality of the Holy Spirit. And the implication is borne out by what the Holy Spirit is to do. This includes speaking, hearing, judging, witnessing, guiding, convincing, reminding. In view of the fact, however, that the distinction between personality in real life and figurative personification is not sharply drawn in the mind contemporary to John to assert dogmatically that the Holy Spirit was regarded a separate personage in the Johannine thought may be going further than the data warrant. The center of interest is not the philosophical point of the nature of the Holy Spirit and its essential relation to the Godhead, but that of its place and function in bringing the light of the truth to men with a view to their accepting the offer of fellowship with God through Christ.

4. THE WAY TO FELLOWSHIP WITH GOD.—Christ as the Son of God, as the Incarnate Logos and as the Lamb of God, and the Holy Spirit as the Spirit of Truth and as the Paraclete have but one objective and goal upon earth, viz., the opening of the way for men to the very heart of God. So far as this objective is attained through the obliteration of sin it is expressed in the already familiar language of the sacrificial system. It is expressed in such declarations as "The Lamb of God that taketh away the sin of the world," and "the blood of Jesus his Son cleanseth us from all sin" (I Jn. i. 7). But this is only the external and, from the Johannine point of view, the less vital aspect of the work of establishing fellowship between God and men. That it should be brought into view at a time when the Gospel was still so closely associated with its antecedents in Judaic thought seems perfectly natural and requires neither justification nor explanation of any sort. Every Jew with his mind fixed upon being fitted for the most precious privilege of enjoying the favor of God would know what it means to have his iniquities forgiven in order that he might appear in the presence of the Lord. Neither would any Gentile Christian have any difficulty in appreciating the rationale of the process.

[3] From παρὰ and καλέω —"to call to one's side"—*ad vocatus.*
[4] *Vita Mos.,* iii. 14.

But the method of approach to the divine presence through sacrifice and expiation yields in the Johannine thought to the more direct one which is secured through the knowledge of the Truth. Far more frequently and clearly is fellowship with God traced to the enlightenment of the mind which leads men to accept his love and surrender themselves to him. To know God and to realize that he is more eager to forgive sin than the sinner is to have his sin forgiven is to go far in the direction of coming into fellowship with him. If, adopting the language of the theology of historic Christendom, we call the sacrificial mode that of "objective salvation" and the method through knowledge "subjective salvation" it would be true that John is more intent on presenting salvation as subjective than as objective.

In bringing the knowledge of God which leads to fellowship Christ and the Holy Spirit coöperate. Christ in the flesh aimed chiefly to implant the germ of divine life in the hearts of his disciples. He did this by revealing to them the true nature of God through his words, but above all, through his personality. "He that hath seen me hath seen the Father." In Christ the otherwise invisible and inaccessible God had entered into the sphere of the knowable. He is the Truth. To contemplate and comprehend him is to know God. And to hold fellowship with him, to accept him as a friend, is to accept God as such. This is the object of Jesus' mission upon earth. Viewed from the viewpoint of its outcome in life he can describe it in the words, "I came that they may have life and that they may have it abundantly" (Jn. x. 10).

But this is also the object of the mission of the Holy Spirit. While the Holy Spirit is in the world always, even during the period of the earthly life of Christ, his preëminent work is done so completely after the completion of Christ's career in the flesh that Christ can put his coming in the future, i.e., after his own departure. The Comforter will not come if he (Christ) go not away (Jn. xvi. 7). So thoroughly is the mission of the Comforter identified with that of Jesus himself that from one point of view the Comforter is merely a representative and vicegerent of Christ the glorified. Yet, in the nature of the case, the work of the Holy Spirit is also an extension and expansion of that of Christ. Not only will the Comforter bring to remembrance the things which Christ taught (Jn. xiv. 26), but he will reveal the many things which in his own day Christ himself could not reveal (Jn. xvi. 12). So far as there is a difference between the work of Christ and that of the Spirit it is that the Spirit reveals the inward nature of Christ more and more fully as men are able to understand it, and brings to its consummation the fellowship they have with the Father through him. In the light of this identity of purpose between Christ and the Holy Spirit all references to the ecstatic manifestations of the latter recede into the background and finally disappear from view. On the other hand the indwelling and dynamic presence of God in the believer comes into prominence.

CHAPTER XXIX

THE LIFE OF FELLOWSHIP

1. FAITH.—It is of the essence of the gospel that God's love flows freely toward men seeking them irrespective of their merits, but that it can become a real good in their lives only upon condition of its being accepted. In the terminology of the Johannine school this is expressed in the words, "whosoever believeth in him shall not perish but have eternal life," and "this is life eternal that they should know the only true God." Accordingly the new and normal relationship with God, which is established by Christ as Savior and the Holy Spirit, begins with the act of believing on the part of man. And faith is the pivotal point in the life of fellowship.

But just what is the Johannine idea of faith? In the Fourth Gospel the word faith is never used although the verbal form "to believe" occurs some ninety times. In the First Epistle the substantive occurs once and the verb nine times. In the Apocalypse the verb never appears and the noun only four times, in two of which the meaning shades off into that of creed or confession.

The significance of these data is not very easily seen. This is due partly to the difference between the Gospel and the Apocalypse in the matter of authorship and design. But it is also due to the point of view of the author of the Gospel and Epistle. Leaving the Apocalypse out of consideration as contributing nothing essential to the subject, the faith of Johannine theology is the act of believing. Specifically applied to the Gospel this means the acceptance of Jesus as the Son of God. Automatically, as it were, such acceptance is followed by the springing up in the heart of the believer of a new life. Just how an intellectual assent to the proposition that Jesus is the Christ begets this life is nowhere clearly set forth, but left to the Christian to work out. The assumption, however, that it does, removes the notion of believing from the realm of mere intellectual activity into that of a movement of the whole inner personality toward the object of faith.

Some light is thrown on this more vital aspect of faith by its frequent association with knowledge. (Jn. vi. 69; x. 38; xvii. 8; I Jn. iv. 16). Faith is more than passive recognition of reality in a sphere unrelated to the interest of the believer. It is conviction of truth of the utmost practical value. Such a view of faith is easily traceable back to the Old Testament conception of knowledge as the broad equivalent of an intimate relationship involving devotion. "The knowledge of Yahweh" is religion (Ps. xxv. 14; Is. xi. 2) and ignorance is irreligion (Hos. iv. 1; I Sam. ii. 12). To know God means to reverence him and obey his will.

It must be further taken into account that in speaking of "believing" as the condition of eternal life John is specifically thinking of believing that Jesus Christ is the Son of God. The stupendous importance of such an article of faith places it at once in a class by itself and apart from all mere intellectual beliefs. On one side in order to achieve such a belief, one must exercise a deeper part of his nature than his reasoning faculty. He must know what God is in order that he may be able to see whether the claim of Jesus to be the Son of God is true. Only by exercising a sense by which divinity is discerned can one be assured that he is perceiving divinity in the Son of God. It is true that John appeals to all sorts of grounds to validate the proposition, Jesus is the Son of God. He speaks of miracles ("signs," "works"), of the testimony of Moses and of John the Baptist. But oftener he claims that by a direct perception of his personal qualities, and an immediate intuition of the divinity of his words one must realize his divine Sonship and accept it. A belief born out of such antecedents cannot be imagined as barren, or as a matter of mere intellect.

But having achieved a belief of such radical significance as that Jesus is the Son of God one cannot resist the momentum of it. Without effort or conscious acquiescence the force of it must impel him to new lines of internal and external activity. Thus the paradox of believing a proposition and finding one's self the seat of a new and infinitely powerful life, finds its explanation. The Johannine conception of faith is then at its core a conception of a vital force issuing in an endless development.

2. THE NEW BIRTH.—"Whosoever believeth that Jesus is the Christ is begotten of God" (I Jn. v. 1). In these words the beginning of the new life of fellowship is described. The description is not incidental but consistently carried through. In the Gospel the new birth is made the special topic of the conversation between Jesus and Nicodemus (iii. 3-8). The aspects of the thought which are brought into view are its mysterious origin and nature; its necessity in the new order of the world to which every faithful Jew looked forward eagerly; its spiritual issues as contrasted with the merely fleshly (physical) characteristics of the bodily life and its supernatural cause (the Spirit). This whole conversation, however, was anticipated in the very introduction to the Gospel (i. 13) where as if summing up his philosophy of the Christian religion the author condenses his idea into the proposition that through the Incarnate Word God had given the right to become the children of God by believing in the Word made flesh, adding that such "were born not of blood nor of the will of the flesh, nor of the will of man, but of God."

But for the fullest characterization of the issues of the new birth we must go to the First Epistle. Here the new birth is said to bring men into a life where they do not and cannot sin (iii. 9; v. 18); that "they overcome the world" (v. 4); that they are actuated by love because God is love (iv. 7); that they do righteousness (iii. 9); and that they keep themselves and the evil one toucheth them not (v. 18).

3. ETERNAL LIFE.—Not only is the change wrought in man by the acceptance of Jesus as the Son of God compared to a new birth but the whole sequel is consistently portrayed as a new life. So prominent is the idea in the Johannine type of thinking that it practically occupies the central place in it. What the kingdom of God is in the Synoptic report of the gospel preached by Jesus and what the grace of God is in the Pauline system, that the idea of eternal life is in the thought of John. If kingdom of God and grace of God were (as they are not) mutually exclusive conceptions, one would be justified in saying that, according to John, Jesus' chief work was not to proclaim the kingdom of God— for he refers to it only on two occasions through the whole course of his ministry, and that not in public discourses, but in private, conversations (with Nicodemus and with Pilate)—but to impart to those who will believe in him the gift of eternal life. Eternal life is, to use a modern phrase, the highest good (*summum bonum*).

What then is eternal life? First of all and most obviously it is a form of life. Indeed the frequent omission of the adjective when very clearly the supreme blessing of eternal life is referred to shows that in the Johannine mind eternal life is the highest kind of life, compared to which other kinds may be regarded as not true to type. It is life by way of preëminence. Jesus "came that they may have life." "In him was life." Since, however, either as eternal life or as life in the ideal the supreme blessing attainable by men is conceived in the form of the reality which is commonly termed life, the approach to the Johannine conception must be made through the familiar but very elusive idea of life.

The distinction between the principle of vitality on the one hand and life as a product on the other was unknown to the ancients. In the antecedents upon which the Johannine thought is based life is viewed (1) by the Jews as a unitary though complex output of energies and (2) by the Greeks, as a system of energies not always working in harmony with one another. While the Hebrew view represented life as a gift of God to be enjoyed in its highest development in fellowship with himself, the Hellenic found an inner contradiction and conflict in it as between the lower or animal nature and the higher or rational one. To the Hebrew life was perfect only as man harmonized his mind with the righteous will of God and gave him whole-hearted allegiance. To the Greek it reached its ideal when the reason triumphed over the brute impulses and held complete sway over the whole course of conduct and directed it into the molds of wisdom and beauty.

The Johannine mind fell heir to both these conceptions, but on taking them over transformed and vitalized and fused them into an idea of great power and unique conformity to reality in the spiritual realm.

From the Hebrew branch of its parentage the idea of life derives the notion of its unity and integrity. Life, no matter out of how numerous and diverse strands constituted, cannot be conceived as anything but a unity. John found it impossible to separate its constituent elements and single out that which gave distinctiveness to the peculiar aspect of it which was predominant in his mind. There is only one kind of real life so far as he is able to present it. True life derives from God. "In him was life." Jesus is "the life." Yet it is unthinkable that he did not see how life takes up into itself all sorts of activities and weaves them into an organism or how it integrates and leads to coöperate the apparently diverse and divergent members of the organism. The life that he has in mind includes purely physical functions, but it also includes mental impulses and movements, assigning functions and tasks to each, yet transcending them all.

From the Hellenic side of its history the Johannine idea of life derives the notion of inner antithesis through which the superior asserts itself over the inferior and overcomes. In the Greek conception the rational nature was viewed as in conflict with the lower and physical. But life in its lowest form is an overcoming energy. The living being is distinguished from the non-living by the fact that it overcomes the subvital energies of chemical affinity, cohesion and gravity and directs them to accomplish results which are impossible where vitality does not exist. Thus on the higher level, the rational, and above the rational the ethical, and again above the ethical the Godward, struggle against, overcome and direct all the activities of the lower orders to results unforeseen and unattainable in their own spheres.

As an overcoming principle life tends to multiply itself. Life begets life. In the process of self-promotion life results in fruit. The fruit of the living being is a stage in the reproduction and multiplication of the fruit-bearer. Thus life in its spiritual form bears fruit. It issues from its primal source, the Life of God through Christ the Vine; it develops in the branches and it culminates in fruit (Jn. xv. 1ff.). The fruit of life is more life. How important this side of the conception of life is to the general completeness of the Johannine notion of it is evident from the manner in which the living organism is represented as trained and subjected to suffering (pruning) in order that life may have in it its real fulfillment.

This then is life: A principle which integrates and organizes a unified living being; a principle that overcomes lower elements and energizes and directs them; a principle that tends to continue the expansion of itself through its fruit. And this is what John attributes to the Eternal Logos, the Son of God, as the object of his earthly mission.

But John sees the supreme good in the form of "eternal" life. Just how does the qualifying adjective specialize the idea? In the Old Testament the terms eternity and eternal (*olam*) stand for permanent duration and durability. But the cause for permanent stability is freedom from the weaknesses of the order of time and space. It is because the eternal is founded upon the unchanging conditions of the sphere in which God has his being that it abides. "Eternal" means "everlasting." So in the first appearance of the combination "life eternal" (*hayye olam*, Dan. xii. 2) the phrase clearly refers to the future and endless existence of the righteous after the resurrection.

From the Old Testament, the idea passed into the New as usual through the mediation of the LXX, where it appeared in the form of αἰώνιος. Meanwhile the apocalyptic type of thinking had developed its doctrine of the "ages" (αἰῶνες). And the term eternal (αἰώνιος) was naturally affected by the emergence within it of an accessory connotation suggestive of the future age in which all conditions would be perfect. Eternal thus came to mean not only permanent in duration, but also future, belonging to the age to come. In this sense it appears in the usage of the Synoptists and also of Paul. Eternal life is to be realized in the Messianic age (Mt. xix. 26; xxv. 46; Rom. ii. 7; Tit. i. 2).

The first difference between the Synoptic and the Johannine usage of the phrase eternal life is that in the latter it no longer represents a future but a present blessing. "He that heareth my word, and believeth him that sent me *hath* eternal life" (Jn. v. 24). "He that believeth *hath* eternal life" (Jn. vi. 47). "He that eateth my flesh and drinketh my blood *hath* eternal life; and I will raise him at the last day" (Jn. vi. 54). "He that hath the Son *hath* the life" (I Jn. v. 12). These expressions can mean either that eternal life is an undeveloped power lying germinal in the soul awaiting the dawn of the age to spring up and enter upon its active course, or that it is already an active principle operating unobserved in the inner sphere. Of these two alternatives the whole tenor of the Johannine thought harmonizes with the second. Eternal life is the life of God in the human soul beginning at the very moment when the soul undergoes the new birth by the acceptance of Christ.

Yet though a present and immediately active principle, eternal life is not inappropriately called everlasting. Since its vitality is drawn not from some source which may be exhausted but from the imperishable ground of all things; and since its continuance depends not upon the shifting and changing conditions of the material world, but upon the permanent foundations of the real world, eternal life is a future, never-ending blessing. It may not be confused with immortality, for immortality is a quality or capacity of the soul leading to its survival after death, while eternal life is a positive principle allying it with the life of God himself.

The second difference between the Johannine conception of eternal life and its antecedents is that it definitely fixes the essence and content of it in the relation of fellowship established by Christ between the believing soul and God. "This is life eternal, that they should know thee the only true God, and him whom thou didst send, even Jesus Christ" (Jn. xvii. 3). This has been called a definition of eternal life. While it is not and was never meant to be a definition, it presents the reality with sufficient explicitness and fulness to stand out as the classical expression of the essence of John's thought. In the Synoptic reports of Jesus' mind and in Paul's teaching eternal life is referred to not with special regard to the manner of its generation or its nature after coming to existence. It is assumed to be life in communion with God, but life as lived among men upon earth. In this characterization of it as rooted in and arising out of the knowledge of God through Jesus Christ the preëminently spiritual character of it comes clearly into sight.

Whether John in this expression identifies eternal life with the knowledge of God or makes the knowledge of God a condition and means of securing it has been a question much discussed by the commentators

THE LIFE OF FELLOWSHIP

and critics.[1] What has already been said on the content of the conception of knowledge in the Johannine usage (1) deprives this question of its significance. Knowledge is neither the essence of eternal life nor its mere condition. It is rather the dynamic creative force which brings it into being. For the knowledge to which John refers is not mere cognition of existing reality, but that along with the appreciation of its value and the appropriation of it into one's own spiritual being. To know is to cherish and assimilate. As in the relation of husband and wife to know is to enter into the relation which brings new life into being.

Eternal life not only issues out of the knowledge of God thus conceived, but it also reflects back upon that knowledge, enlarges and enriches it and renders it an inalienable factor in its possessor's experience. This means that the knowledge which is eternal life issues in fellowship. It breaks down all barriers between God and the believer. It opens up the channels through which the divine life may freely flow. It brings into view community of interests, establishes mutual intercourse and unified movement. In a word it means that eternal life is the life of mutual love and confidence of God and man in perfect fellowship with one another. In the light of this understanding of eternal life it is no longer a mystery that the kingdom-of-God idea disappears when the idea of eternal life has dawned. It becomes unnecessary since what it was aimed to do by presenting God's will as sovereignly imperative is accomplished by the inner harmony established in fellowship through mutual confidence and love.

4. THE LAW OF LOVE.—Just as the principle of evil availing itself of the associative power of human nature masses itself in the world, so the principle of fellowship with God utilizing the same associative power welds together those in whom it has pervaded and integrated into a new organism by the power of love it begets in them. Love to God cannot be realized in a world of creatures bearing the image of God without leading to love toward men. "He that loveth not his brother whom he hath seen cannot love God whom he hath not seen" (I Jn. iv. 20). "If we say that we have fellowship with him and walk in the darkness, we lie and do not speak the truth: but if we walk in the light, we have fellowship with one another" (I Jn. i. 6, 7).

(1) *The Brotherhood.*—The first field in which love finds its object is that of fellow-believers in the Son of God. The term "love" in this application of it becomes synonymous with the other expression "brotherly kindness" (φιλαδελφία). In this sense it is used in the exhortations of the Epistles (I Jn. i. 10, 14; iv. 7, 12, etc.; II Jn. 5; II Jn. 1) as well as in the affectionate admonitions of Jesus to his followers as reported in the Fourth Gospel (Jn. xiii. 34; xv. 12, 17). The commandment of love is called a "new commandment" because it

[1] B. Weiss (*Johan. Lehrbegr.*, pp. 10, 11 & *Bibl. Theol.*, p. 614) believes in the identification of knowledge and life. Westcott, *Epistles of John*, pp. 214-218, agrees that "the definition is of the essence of eternal life." Wendt, *Teaching of Jesus*, I, p. 244 and Beyschlag, *Neutestliche Theologie*, I, 263, 264, hold that knowledge is only a condition or means of life.

252   THE PLASTIC AGE OF THE GOSPEL

defines conduct in a way formerly unknown and first exemplified by Jesus in his own life, "As *I* have loved you." But Jesus holding himself before his followers as the ideal is simply a manifestation of God himself. The divine love is characterized (1) by initiative. Man's love to God is responsive not initiative. "We love him because he first loved us" (I Jn. iv. 10f.). So should the new love of the Christian be. (2) The divine love is love to the undeserving. It asks for no merit on the part of its object. So should the new love in the Christian be. (3) The divine love is self-sacrificing love. It costs to love as God does. But the Christian should be willing to pay the price.

But though the love begins with the brethren, it does not end with them. The line between the inner circle and the outer one is not sharply drawn. God loved the whole world of mankind. Every man in the broader sense is recognized as a brother. The Good Shepherd has one flock to which he is known (Jn. x. 11), but he has "other sheep" who are not known to the members of this particular flock (cf. also Jn. xi. 52). He loves these, too, and they recognize his voice. These he must bring into the fold of his flock that they may all be one flock (Jn. x. 16). The law of love has no eye for sharp distinctions between the "other sheep" and those which are known to belong to the fold.

(2) *The Church.*—Again though the inner circle of believers in Christ is clearly before the mind in the Johannine writings, there is no trace of an organized or institutional brotherhood in them. The word "church" does not occur in the Gospel and first two Epistles. The sacraments of baptism and the Lord's Supper are evidently forms in mind; but it is the inner values rather than external forms that arouse interest. Baptism, for instance, lurks in the background in such utterances as John ii. 5 and xiii. 10; but only as early Christian usage, as discovered elsewhere, illumines the words can such an institution as Christian baptism be discerned in the words. Similarly the Lord's Supper is probably at the basis of the figurative language of John vi.; but so little does the sacrament concern the author that where the other evangelists record the institution of the Supper he makes mention only of the washing of the disciples' feet with its lessons of humility and service.

The literary form and the point of view of the Apocalypse require that the corporate nature of the Christian brotherhood should be placed more prominently in view. The body of the faithful is set over against a mighty organization—the Roman imperial world power. Yet the conception of a church is only implicit. The word "church" occurs in the first section of the book. It occurs in the plural as the name of the communities of believers to whom special messages are delivered. Each of these communities ("churches") has its "angel." But just what is meant by the "angel," and whether he is an officer in the organization or an invisible guardian or a mere symbol of the peculiar character of the local community is a debatable question.

The Christian community as a whole is engaged in a struggle for the preservation of its life. The struggle is to end in the complete victory of the Church and the overthrow of the world power. The symbolism used in the presentation of this thought is manifold and covers a great number of details; but it reveals nothing regarding the author's ideals of the principles of organization or the institutions of the church.

5. JOHANNINE ESCHATOLOGY.—The dominant spirit of John's thinking did not furnish an atmosphere favorable for the luxuriance of an elaborate eschatology. It was too much engrossed with the present power of the love of God. The victory was already won. "This is the victory that hath overcome the world" (I Jn. v. 4). The supreme good (eternal life) was a reality available in the age that now is, not one forcibly to be introduced into the world with the breaking forth of the new age. It is true that for every believer as well as for the Christian community there is a warfare to be fought and a victory to be won. But so far as salvation is a work it has been achieved. In the light of the emphasis laid on this inwardness, spirituality and present immanence of the supreme good eschatological ideas naturally recede into the background.

Yet John never looked upon the ideas concerning the future as either misleading or inconsistent with his point of view. He certainly did not believe, as Paul did, concerning the Judaistic insistence on the observance of the law, that belief in the importance of the apocalyptic eschatology was incompatible with the spirituality of the Gospel. He waged no warfare against it, but on the contrary allowed it to remain in the shadow where it is traceable both in the Gospel and Epistles, and far more conspicuously in the Apocalypse. But everywhere the apocalyptic eschatology is transformed by the new spiritual tone peculiar to John. A glance at the eschatological ideas as affected by the genius of the Johannine mind will clearly show this spiritualization.

It is scarcely necessary to point out, however, that this could not be true of the picturesque and symbolical representations of the Apocalypse. In the nature of the case the literary form of that work was bound to veil the true essence and nature of its author's thought as a disciple of John. His portraitures must be interpreted in the light of the plainer forms given in the other Johannine writings.

(1) *The Parousia.*—In its older form the idea of the parousia is unequivocally the equivalent of a second coming of Jesus in bodily form. In but three references to the event in the Gospel or Epistle is such equivalence conceivable. Two of these occur in the Epistle (I Jn. ii. 28; iii. 25). But in both of them the term used directly implies manifestation. "If he shall be manifested,"—as if he were already present but not visible. The third reference is in the well-known conversation with Peter after the resurrection of Jesus, on the shore of Lake Tiberias when Peter seeing the beloved disciple near asked Jesus, "And what shall this man do?" Jesus saith unto him, "If I will that he tarry till I come, what is that to thee?" (Jn. xxi. 22.) The question left unanswered in this word spoken to Peter by way of admonition is what sort of coming did Jesus have in mind? The answer to this question must be sought in the more direct references to his coming in his communings with the disciples.

In such references the chief point of interest is the thought of the centrality of his person, first among those who had received him, and then through them in the world. Jesus' presence in a Christianized world is the essence of the Johannine thought on the parousia. This might be and was in the apostolic generation conceived as realized in the vision of his bodily return. But it might be more dynamically realized through his spiritual return. The promise of the Paraclete (Jn. xiv. 16; xv. 26; xvi. 7) suggests this form of return. One of the comforting assurances which Jesus gives to his bewildered disciples on the eve of his departure from them in death is: "I come again" (Jn. xiv. 3). In the same discourse in which he uttered these words he incorporates the sending of the Comforter. Many have identified the two promises. Others have seen in the promise of a return the anticipation of the resurrection or the spiritual coming at Pentecost; still others, the apocalyptic coming. A fourth class give the words a comprehensive significance. The last two views are exegetically inadmissible. The safest inference from the whole context is that in John's interpretation of Jesus' mind the Master was chiefly interested in his presence with his followers in power. This at least is what the words of xiv. 23 would indicate.

(2) *"The Last Day."*—Closely linked with the second coming of Christ in the Johannine thought is the expectation of the end of the world. By the term world, however, is not meant the material universe ($\varkappa \acute{o} \sigma \mu o \varsigma$) but the existing order ($\alpha \grave{\iota} \grave{\omega} \nu$, dispensation, "age"). The transition from the world as it exists to that which will succeed it, from the present age to the coming age is in the Apocalypse depicted as a complex involving a succession of stages. To which of these the phrases "last hour" (I Jn. ii. 18) and "last day" (Jn. vi. 34, 39, 40) apply is not clear, if indeed, the thought of the two Johannine writers coalesces at this point. Between the two ages the Apocalyptist further places a period of relief from distress consisting in the temporary cessation of all evil due to the imprisonment of God's archenemy. The term "millennium" has been applied to this period from the number of years during which it was to last. The language in which the conception is clothed (Rev. xx.) is highly symbolical and it is very questionable whether in the intention of the author [2] there is any more than the assurance to the faithful followers of Jesus that they will have adequate compensation in the future for the distresses of the present age.

(3) *The Resurrection.*—The distinctive addition to the thought common to all the New Testament types concerning the resurrection is in the Johannine writings that Christ himself accomplishes it for his followers. This idea was, of course, essentially present in Paul's view of the resurrection of Christ as the "first fruits" and guarantee of the resurrection of believers. By John it is lifted into the thought of deliberate personal work of Christ's. "I will raise him up" (vi. 39, 40, 44; cf. also v. 21). The question of the manner of the resurrection which plays such an important part in Paul's discussion falls into the

---

[2] This is the only reference either in the New Testament or in the Old to any time definitely fixed as a period of utopian conditions, a fact which renders the interpretation of the phraseology exceedingly difficult.

background. The resurrection is so thoroughly inwoven with the life which Christ imparts that as he identifies himself with the life he can also say, "I am the resurrection" (Jn. xi. 25).

When this relation of Jesus to the resurrection is clearly understood, the two apparently divergent lines of allusion to the subject are harmonized as expressions of one underlying idea. These ideas are (a) that resurrection is the bodily return from the grave, illustrated in the case of Lazarus and of Jesus himself, and (b) the spiritual quickening which reduces death itself into an event of only incidental and subordinate significance in life. This latter view is clearly set forth in the words, "Verily, verily, I say unto you, he that heareth my words, cometh not unto judgment, but hath passed out of death into life" (Jn. v. 22, 23).

The allusions to the resurrection in the Apocalypse are in essence of the same import as those in the Gospel. Of course they are cast in the apocalyptic molds of the current eschatology of the day. This includes a conception of two resurrections (Rev. xx. 5, 6). The first of these has for its object the rewarding of the martyred faithful. It lifts them up to seats of honor. For they are to reign with Christ in the millennium. The second resurrection is to occur after the millennium in order that the rest of mankind may be subjected to judgment, and the unrighteous may suffer the condemnation and penalty they deserve. Then comes the "second death" (Rev. ii. 5; xx. 6, 14; xxi. 8).

(4) *The Judgment.*—From the beginning of its appearance in Jewish thought the resurrection was inextricably associated with that of the judgment, and a due distribution of rewards and punishments to the unrighteous, and righteous. In the Johannine system the idea undergoes a broadening similar to that of other conceptions. The underlying foundation of it is that of a public exposition of the distinction between those who stand for God's law and those who are against it.

(a) This distinction is made manifest by the light of the truth that those who accept or reject the truth are, therefore, automatically made the objects of judgment. Since Jesus is the light, his coming into the world is in itself a means of judgment (Jn. ix. 39; iii. 19).

(b) Judgment goes on in the world also as a moral process inherent in the nature of things (Jn. v. 27; xxii. 31). In this sense of the term, Jesus detaches himself from judgment, "I judge no man" (Jn. viii. 15; xii. 47; iii. 17). Yet this world process in which the very conduct of men tests them is related to him; for it is an inevitable accompaniment of redemption (cf. also Rev. xviii. 10).

(c) Judgment is finally associated with the end of the world. The "last day" with the change of perspective and the altered relationships it will bring about, will usher a judgment of its own (Jn. xii. 47, 48; Rev. xi. 18; xx. 12, 13). This is the judgment that is associated with the second coming (presence) of Christ (I Jn. ii. 28; iv. 17).

BIBLIOGRAPHY

GENERAL
ADENEY, W. F., *Theology of the New Testament*, 1894.
STEVENS, G. B., *Theology of the New Testament*, 1899.
BEYSCHLAG, W., *New Testament Theology*, (two vols.), 1895.
FEINE, P., *Theologie d. Neuen Testamentes*, 1910.
WERNLE, *The Beginnings of Christianity* (two vols.), 1904.
EAKIN, F., *Getting Acquainted with the New Testament*, 1927.
BACON, B. W., *The Apostolic Message*, 1925.

CHAPTER I
BRIGGS, C. A., *The Study of Holy Scripture*, 1899, pp. 569-606.
WREDE, W., *Ueber d. Aufgabe u. Methode der So-gennanten Neutestlichen Theologie*, 1897.

CHAPTER II
Original Sources: Old Testament Apocrypha. Apocalyptic writings. Works of Josephus and Philo. Hermetic literature.
Old and New: GARDNER, F., *The Old and the New Testaments in Their Mutual Relations*, 1885.
TOY, C. H., *Judaism and Christianity*, 1890.
MONTEFIORE, C. G., *The Old Testament and After*, 1923.
BOUSSET, W., *Die Religion d. Judentums im Neutestlichen Zeitalter*, 1906.
  Background: LAKE, KIRSOPP and JACKSON, J. FOAKES, *The Beginnings of Christianity, Vol. I; The Jewish, Gentile and Christian Background*, 1920.
SCHECHTER, *Some Aspects of Rabbinic Theology*, 1923.
FAIRWEATHER, *Jesus and the Greeks*, 1925.
ANGUS, S., *The Environment of Early Christianity*, 1915; *The Mystery Religions and Christianity*, 1925.

CHAPTER III
BLAKISTON, *John the Baptist and His Relation to Jesus*, 1912.

CHAPTER IV
The Gospels: PULLAN, LEIGHTON, *The Gospels*. 1912.
STREETER, B. H., *The Four Gospels*, 1925.
The Synoptic Problem: HOLDSWORTH, *Gospel Origins*, 1913.
BURKITT, C. F., *Earliest Sources for the Life of Christ* (2d ed.), 1922 (also Streeter as above).

CHAPTER V
Lives: ANDREWS, S. J., 1884.
HOLTZMANN, O. (trans.), 1904.
SMITH, D., *The Days of His Flesh*, 1905.
BOUSSET, W. (trans.), 1906.
SANDAY, W., *Outlines of the Life of Christ* (2d ed.), 1906.
Place in Historicity (Personality); GLOVER. T. R., *The Jesus of History*, 1916.
SIMKOVITCH, V. G., *Toward the Understanding of Jesus*.
Forms of Teachings: DALMAN, G. H., *The Words of Jesus* (trans.), 1892.
BURNEY, C. F., *The Poetry of Our Lord*, 1925.

CHAPTER VI
BRUCE, A. B., *The Kingdom of God*, 1891.
ROBERTSON, ARCHIBALD, *Regnum Dei*, 1901 (Bampton Lectures)

BIBLIOGRAPHY

CHAPTER VII
SHAW, J. M., *The Fatherhood of God in the New Testament*, 1925.
FAIRBAIRN, *Christ in Modern Theology* (p. 440ff.), Comprehensive discussion.
CANDLISH, R. S., *The Fatherhood of God*, 1864.
CRAWFORD, T. J., *The Fatherhood of God*, 1866.
LIDGETT, J. S., *The Fatherhood of God in Christian Truth and Life*, 1902.

CHAPTER VIII
FAIRBAIRN, *Studies in the Life of Christ*.
WENDT, H. H., *Teaching of Jesus* (trans.), 1892, Vol. II, pp. 48-114; 218-262.
DRUMMOND, R. J., *Apostolic Teaching and Christ's Teaching*, 1900, chs. VII, IX.

CHAPTER IX
MATHEWS, SHAILER, *The Messianic Hope in the New Testament*, 1907.
DOUGALL and EMMET, *The Lord of Thought*, 1922.
VOS, G., *The Self-disclosure of Jesus*, 1926.

CHAPTER X
BRUCE, A. B., *The Training of the Twelve*, 1889.
HORT, F. J. A., *The Christian Ecclesia*, 1897.
LINDSAY, TH., *The Church and the Ministry in the Early Centuries*.

CHAPTER XI
SCOTT, E. F., *The Ethical Teaching of Jesus*, 1924.
MATHEWS, SHAILER, *The Social Teaching of Jesus*, 1897.
PEABODY, F. G., *Jesus Christ and the Social Question*, 1901.

CHAPTER XII
HOGG, A. G., *Christ's Message of the Kingdom*, 1910.
SCOTT, E. F., *The Kingdom and the Messiah*, 1916.
LECKIE, J. H., *The World to Come and Final Destiny*, 1918.

CHAPTER XIII
Introduction—Acts: RACKHAM, R. B., *Westminster Commentary*, 1901.
BARTLETT, J. VERNON, *The New Century Bible*, 1901.
James: Commentaries in Oesterley, *Expositor's Greek Testament*.
ROPES, International Critical Commentary (also LAKE, KIRSOPP and JACKSON, J. FOAKES, *Beginnings of Christianity*.)
I and II Peter and Jude: Commentaries in *Expositor's Greek Testament*.
HUNT, *I Peter*.
STRACHAN, R. D., *II Peter*.
SMITH, DAVID, *Jude*.
BIGG, International Critical Commentary.

CHAPTER XIV
SCOTT, E. F., *Beginnings of the Church*, 1914.

CHAPTER XV
See Chapter X, also SWETE, H. B., *The Holy Spirit in the New Testament*, 1909.
VON HÜGEL, F., *Eternal Life*, 1912.

CHAPTER XVI
SCHMIDT, W. G., *Der Lehrgehalt des Jacobusbriefes*, 1869.
PATRICK, W., *James the Lord's Brother*, 1906.
MAYOR, J. B., *Epistle of St. James*, 1892 (Introd.).
KNOWLING, R. J., *Epistle of St. James* (Westminster Commentary), 1904.
CULLEN. *The Teaching of James*.

CHAPTER XVII

WEISS, B., *Der Petrinische Lehrbegriff,* 1855.
DALE, R. W., *Atonement* (pp. 97-148).
BRUSTON, C., *La descente du Christ aux enfers d'apres les apôtres et d'apres l'église,* 1897.
SCHWEITZER, H. *Hinabfahren zur Hölle als Mythus,* etc., 1869.
ELERT, W., *Die Religiosität d. Petrus,* 1911.

CHAPTER XVIII

CONYBEARE, W. J. and HOWSON, J. S., *The Life and Epistles of St. Paul,* 1889.
SABATIER, A., *The Apostle Paul* (trans.), 1891.
WEINEL, H., *St. Paul and His Work* (trans.), 1906.
SMITH, DAVID, *The Life and Letters of St. Paul.*
GLOVER, T. R., *Paul of Tarsus,* 1925.
FLETCHER, R. J., *A Study of the Conversion of St. Paul,* 1910.
ST. JOHN THACKERAY, H., *The Relation of St. Paul to Contemporary Jewish Thought,* 1900.
FEINE, P., *Paul as a Theologian* (trans.), 1906.
MONTEFIORE, C. G., *Judaism and St. Paul,* 1914.
SCHWEITZER, A., *St. Paul and his Interpreters,* 1912.
STRACHAN, R. H., *The Individuality of St. Paul,* 1916.
BULCOCK, H., *The Passing and the Permanent in St. Paul,* 1926.

CHAPTER XIX

PFLEIDERER, O., *Paulinism* (trans.), 1891.
STEVENS, G. B., *The Pauline Theology,* 1892.
BRUCE, A. B., *St. Paul's Conception of Christianity,* 1896.
RAMSAY, SIR WM. M., *The Teaching of Paul in Terms of the Present Day,* 1913.
MORGAN, W., *The Religion and Theology of Paul,* 1917.

CHAPTER XX

DICKSON, W. P., *St. Paul's Use of the Terms Flesh and Spirit,* 1883.
FEINE, P., *Das Gesetzesfreie Evangelium d. Paulus, nach seinem Werdegang beanstaltet,* 1890.
SOMERVILLE, D., *St. Paul's Conception of Christ,* 1897.
KNOWLING, R. J., *Testimony of St. Paul to Christ,* 1905.

CHAPTER XXI

GLACE, J., *Das Heilige Geist in der Heilsverkündigung d. Paulus,* 1888.
DEISSMANN, A., *Die neutestamentliche Formel "in Christo Jesu,"* 1892; *The Religion of Jesus and the Faith of Paul,* 1923.

CHAPTER XXII

CHADWICK, W. E., *Social Teaching of St. Paul,* 1906.
ALEXANDER, A., *Ethics of St. Paul,* 1910.
MCGREGOR, W. M., *Christian Freedom,* 1924.

CHAPTER XXIII

LAMBERT, J. C., *The Sacraments in the New Testament,* Lecture IX, 1903 (cf. also STRACHAN, R. H., *Individuality of Paul,* and BULCOCK, H., *The Passing and the Permanent in St Paul*).

CHAPTER XXIV

KABISCH, R., *Die Eschatologie d. Paulus in ihren Zusammenhang mit d. Gesammt begriff d. Paulinismus,* 1893.
KENNEDY, H. A. A., *St. Paul's Conception of the Last Things,* 1904.

CHAPTER XXV

JÜLICHER, A., *Introduction to the New Testament* (trans.), 1904.
NAIRNE, A., *The Epistle of the Priesthood*, 1913.
MILLIGAN, G., *Theology of the Epistle to the Hebrews*, 1899.
DAVIDSON, A. B., *The Epistle to the Hebrews*, 1882.
BRUCE, A. B., *The Epistle to the Hebrews, The First Apology for Christianity*, 1899.
MÉNÉGOZ, E., *La theologie de l'épitre aux Hébreux*, 1894.

CHAPTER XXVI

The Fourth Gospel: HOLTZMANN, O., *Das Johannesevangelium untersucht u. erklärt*, 1887
BACON, B. W., *The Fourth Gospel in Research and Debate*, 1910.
SANDAY, W., *The Criticism of the Fourth Gospel*, 1905.
GARVIE, A. E., *The Beloved Disciple*, 1922.
SCOTT, E. F., *The Fourth Gospel; Its Purpose and Theology*, 1906.
STRACHAN, R. H., *The Fourth Gospel; Its Significance and Environment*, 1917.
The Epistles: FINDLAY, C. G., *Fellowship in the Life Eternal*.
The Apocalypse: SWETE, H. B., *The Apocalypse of St John*, 1917.
General: SCHMIEDEL. P., *The Johannine Writings* (trans.), 1908.

CHAPTERS XXVII, XXVIII, XIX

KOHLER, H., *Von der Welt zum Himmelreich*, 1892.
LÜTGERT, W., *Die Johanneische Christologie*, 1899.
STEVENS, G. B., *Johannine Theology*, 1894.
LOWRIE, W., *The Doctrine of St. John*, 1899.
LAW, R., *The Tests of Life*, 1909.
WATSON, H. A., *The Mysticism of St. John's Gospel*, 1916.
MUIRHEAD, L. A., *The Message of the Fourth Gospel*, 1925.

INDEX

Acts of the Apostles, Book of 111ff.
Adam, First and Second, 178.
Adapa, Legend of, 164 n.
Aeon—age, 24.
Alexander the Great, 16.
Alexandrian thought, 16.
Alford, 113 n.
Allegorism, 16, 169.
Am haaretz, 90.
Amyraut, 4.
Antichrist, 235f.
Apocalypse, 223ff.
Apocalyptic Literature, 67.
Apocalyptism, 15, 229; Jesus and the Apocalyptic viewpoint, 99ff.
Apostle of Jesus, 77.
Aratus, 152.
Aristotle, 152.
Augustine on Synopt. Gospels, 30, 42.

Bacon, B. W., 37 n., 40 n., 113 n., 226 n.
Baikie, J., 200 n.
Bain, 113 n.
Baldensperger, 44.
Baptism, administered by John, 23; in earliest Church, 130f.; Paul's view, 197ff.
Baptist, John the, 18ff.
Barnabas, Epistle of, 7.
Barnasha, 68 (see also, Son of Man).
Baruch, Apocalypse of, 204 n.
Bauer, Bruno, 30, 150.
Baur, C. F., 150.
Beyschlag, 4, 46 n., 52 n., 74 n., 113 n., 250 n.
Biblical Theology, its nature and method, 4-6.
"Binding and loosing," 82.
Bleek, 74.
Body, as "flesh," 162; "spiritual," 204, 205.
Bousset, 76 n., 84 n.
Briggs, C. A., 84.
Bruce, A. B., 24 n.
Buckley, 226 n.
Buschind, 30.

Caesar or God, 96.
Case, S. J., 36 n.
Casuistry, 192ff.
Charles, R. H., 228.
Charnwood, 224 n.

Christ, in his own Gospel, 71; in Ep. of James, 133; in Peter's thought, 140; in Paul's view, 171ff.; death of, in Paul's view, 174ff.; and ethical values, 188; in John's view, 238ff.
Church, 74ff. Jesus's intention to establish, 75; Peter's relation to, 78; Paul's conception, 194ff.; membership in, 72; task of, 80f.; Early Apostolic, 129.
Cleanthes, 152.
Clement of Rome, First Epistle of, 7.
Cocceius, 3.
Comforter (*see* Paraclete).
Conybeare, 36 n.
Covenant, 72, 73, 211ff.
Covering (*see Kopher*).
Cross (*see* Death of Christ).
Cumont, 154.

Dale, A. W., 52 n.
Day of Yahweh, 16.
Death, of Christ, 73; Paul's idea of, 164.
Deissmann, 149, 152 n., 184.
Deutero-Paulinism, 50, 114, 200.
Development, Idea of, in historical study, 10, 11.
Devil, 231.
Dibelius, 161 n.
Dionysius of Alexandria, 228.
"Disciple, Whom Jesus Loved," 224.
Dispersion, Egyptian, 17.
Dods, M., 113 n.
Doellinger, 93 n.
Drews, A., 36.

Eichhorn, 30, 150.
Election, 171.
Enoch, Ethiopic, 67 n.
Epimenides, 152.
Erasmus, 149.
Essenes, 15.
Eternal life, 247.
Euripides, 152.
Evanson, 30.
Everling, 161 n.
Ewald, 30.

Faith, Jesus on, 60f.; in Paul's view, 183; in the Ep. to Hebrews, 216; in Johannine writings, 246.

261

INDEX

Family, Paul's view, 190.
Fatherhood, of God, 49ff.; in O. T., 50; as applied to Jesus, 52; different senses of phrase, 54.
Feather, 24 n.
Fellowship, 231ff.
Filial life, Jesus on, 62f.
Flesh, 163.
Forgiveness, Jesus on, 61; Fourth Gospel, author of, 224ff.
Friedländer, 93 n.

Gabler, J. P., 4.
Gall, A. von, 135 n.
Gardner, Percy, 83 n.
Garvie, 224 n.
Gentiles, 157.
Georgios Hamartolos, 224.
Gfrörer, 30.
Gieseler, 31.
Gifts, of tongues ("glossolaly"), 127; of healing, 182ff.
Gilbert, G. H., 52 n.
Glory, 135.
Glover, T. R., 151.
Gnosticism, 173.
God, Idea of in the O. T., 10; as affected by Jesus words, 50ff.; John's view, 237.
Gospel, defin. in N. T., 8.
Gospels, formation, 33; relations to one another, 27ff.; Synoptic Problem, 29; Fourth, 224ff.
Grace, 170.
Gray, G. B., 135 n.
Griesbach, 30.
Gunkel, 236 n.

Haggada, 13.
Halasha, 13.
Harnack, A., 45, 113 n., 210 n.
Harris, J. Rendel, 144, 210 n.
Hausrath, 30, 113 n.
Hebrews, Ep., 209ff.
Heitmuller, 198 n.
Hellenism, origin and diffusion, 16.
Herodians, 15, 37.
Hermas, *the Pastor*, 7.
Hillel, 155.
Hippolytus, of Rome, 223.
Historical method, 500.
Holiness of God, 11.
Holtzmann, H. J., 4, 30, 74, 206 n.
Holy Spirit, 125ff.; in Paul's view, 185; in John's view, 243.
Hort, J. A., 78.

"Interim Ethics," 101.
Irenaeus, 225.

Jackson, Foakes, 13 n., 66 n.

James, Epistle of, 113ff.
Jesus, Authority, 39; Methods of teaching, 36ff., 40ff.; Originality, 37; Self consciousness of, 44f., 68; Ethical ideal of, 91; Social teaching of, 93.
Johannine School, writings, 223ff.
John, Epistles, 227.
John, Son of Zebedee, 224.
John the Presbyter, 224.
Josephus, 14, 15 n.
Judaism, Earlier, and Later, 13.
Jude, Ep., 117.
Judgment, Jesus' portraiture of, 106; Paul's doctrine, 205ff.
Jülicher, 83 n., 113 n.
Junius, 149.
Justification, 179.

Kalthoff, 36.
Kennedy, J. A. A., 149 n., 154.
Kingdom of God, conception of, 45ff.; data in; Jesus' teaching, 46; development of conception, 46ff.
Kopher, 72.
Kurios (Κύριος), 133.

Lake, Kirsopp, 13 n., 66 n.
Lamb of God, 242.
"Last Day," "last hour," 254.
Law, in Paul's view, 165ff.
Law, Royal, 135.
Levitical priesthood, 213ff.
Lietzmann, 65.
Life, 247.
Lightfoot, 82.
Logia, 31.
Logos, 238ff.
Loman, 150.
Lord's Prayer, 51, 63f., 73, 83ff.
Lord's Supper, 199.
Loss, the Lost, 59.
Love, 251.

Machen, J. G., 172 n.
Mackintosh, H. R., 163 n.
Man, Jesus on nature of, 55ff.; on immortality of, 57ff.
"Man of Sin," 202.
Marcion, attitude towards the Old Testament, 10.
Mark, Gospel, Original Mark, 31, 32.
Marriage, Jesus, teaching on, 93ff.
Mathews, Sh., 171 n.
Mayor, J. B., 113 n.
McGiffert, 83 n.
M'Neile, 149 n., 152 n.
Mediator, in Hebrews, 213ff.
Melchizedek, 213ff.
Menander, 152.
Messiah, terms used, 66; Jesus con-

sciousness as, 68; Jesus' idea of, 69; work of, 71ff.; the Messiah in the earliest preaching by his disciples, 119ff.
Messianism, Christianity, 123.
Meyer, 30.
Millennium, 255.
Mishna, 95.
Moffat, J., 114 n.
Moulton, J. H., 113.
"Mystery of lawlessness," 202.
Mystery religions, 154.
Mystical relation of believer to Christ, 184.
Mythical theories, of Gospel history, 35f.
Mysticism of Paul, 184; of John, 230, 237ff.

Neander, 113 n.
New Testament, relation to the Old, 10.
New Testament Theology, objections answered, 6-8; relation to Old Testament theology, 10-12.
Noack, 30.

Old Testament, Jesus' attitude towards, 10; Paul's use of, 168ff.
Origen, 210.
Oxyrhynchus Papyri, 33 n.

Papias, 31, 32, 225; Fragments of, 224.
Parables, 41.
Paraclete, 244.
Parousia, 101, 195f., 146; Paul's view, 201; John's view, 253.
Pascal, 149.
Paul Epistles of, 149ff.; life and education, 151ff.; conversion, 155; idea of religion, 159.
Peter, 1 Ep., 114ff.; 2 Ep., 115ff.
Pharisees, attitude towards tradition, 14; Party, 115; Ethics of, 90.
Philippus Sidetes, 224.
Philo, promoter of Hellenism, 16, 240, 244.
Pierson, 150.
Pirkê Abhoth, 40, 88.
Placaeus, 4.
Plato, 152.
Polycrates, 225.
Prayer, Jesus on, 63.
Preëxistence, 141, 173.
Promise, its relation to gospel, 167.
Property (*see* Wealth, Wealthy).
Propitiation, 177.
Proto-Luke, 32 n.
Providence, 62, 63.
Pythagoras, 16.

"Q" Source, 31ff.

Qahal, 75, 129.

Ramsay, Sir Wm., 152 n.
Ransom, Jesus' conception of, 72.
Reconciliation, 175.
Redemption, 174ff.
Regeneration, in John's view, 247; in Paul's view, 185.
Religion, Paul's idea, 159; John's idea, 231; and Ethics in Paul, 187.
Renan, 113 n.
Repentance, Jesus on, 60.
Resurrection of believers, Paul's doctrine, 203; John's view, 254 n.
Resurrection of Jesus, in first preaching of the Gospel, 120; in Paul's view, 175, 178; in Peter's thought, 42.
Reuss, 30.
Rich (*see* Wealth, Wealthy).
Righteousness, old and new, 86f.; of God, 92; in Paul's view, 160.
Ritschl, 30, 74 n.
Robertson, J. M., 36.

Sabbath, 92.
Sacraments, 83; Paul's conception, 197ff.
Sacrifice under the New Covenant, 214.
Sadducees, attitude towards tradition, 14; party of, 15.
Salmon, 31.
Salvation, Jesus on, 60; in Peter's thought, 142.
Sanctification, 186.
Schenkel, 30.
Schleiermacher, 9, 31.
Schmidt, N., 65.
Schultz, H., 50 n.
Schürer, 45 n.
Schweitzer, A., 102 n.
Scott, E. F., 113 n., 129 n., 150 n., 226 n.
Scripture, in Paul's view, 167ff.
Sin, Jesus on, 58f.; In Ep. of James, 136; in Paul's view, 161ff.; Johannine definition, 231.
Slavery, Paul's view of, 190.
Smith, D., 149 n., 152 n.
Smith, W. B., 36.
Son of David, 66, 68.
Son of God, 66, 69, Jesus' idea of, 69ff.; John's view, 241.
Son of Man, 66ff.
Soter, Savior-god, 36.
"Spirit of Truth," 243.
"Spirits in prison," 144.
Stanley, 113 n.
Stanton, 226 n.
Stapfer, 44 n.
State, Jesus' view of, 96; in Paul's view, 189.
Steck, R., 150.
Stevens, G. B., 46 n., 52 n.

Storr, 30.
Strachan, R. H., 224 n.
Strauss, D. F., 35, 224.
Streeter, B. F., 32 n., 224 n., 228 n.
Synagogue, 37.
Synoptic problem, 29ff.

Tarsus, 152.
Taylor, C., 88 n.
Teacher, teaching, 36.
Teichmann, 206 n.
Thiersch, 30.
"Thorn in the flesh," 152.
Thorburn, 36 n.
Titius, 74 n.
Tongues, Gift of, 127f.
Tradition, 13.
Turretin, 3.

Van Maanen, 150.
Vogel, 30.
Volkmar, 30.
Volz, 125 n., 206 n.
Von Soden, 113 n.

Wardle, 164 n.
Wealth, The Wealthy, Jesus' view of, 96f.; in Ep. of James, 137; Paul's view, 191.
Weiss, B., 4, 30, 46, 113 n., 250 n.
Weiss, J., 102 n.
Weisse, 74 n.
Wellhausen, 65.
Wendt, 41, 52 n., 250 n.
Westcott, B. F., 31, 250 n.
Wilke, 30.
Wisdom of Solomon, 163 n.
Witsius, 3.
Works and faith in Ep. of James, 136; as related to Paul, 137.
World, 232.
Wright, A., 31.

Xenophon, 180.

Zacchaeus, 97.
Zahn, 113 n.
Zealots, 15 n., 37, 189.
Zeller, 113 n., 48.